DIVERSITY,
OPPRESSION,
<small>AND</small> CHANGE

Also Available from Lyceum Books, Inc.

ADVISORY EDITORS: Thomas M. Meenaghan, *New York University*

Diversity in Family Constellations
Krishna Guadelupe and Debra L. Welkley

Lesbian and Gay Couples
Ski Hunter

Social Work with HIV and AIDS
edited by Diana Rowan

Advocacy Practice for Social Justice, 2E
Richard Hoefer

Disability, 2E
Romel Mackelprang and Richard Salsgiver

Cross-Cultural Practice: Social Work with Diverse Populations, 2E
Karen Harper-Dorton and Jim Lantz

Critical Multicultural Social Work
Jose Sisneros, Catherine Stakeman, Mildred C. Joyner,
and Cathyrne L. Schmitz

Social Work in a Sustainable World
Nancy Mary

*Human Behavior for Social Work Practice: A Developmental-Ecological
Framework,* 2E
Wendy L. Haight and Edward H. Taylor

CULTURALLY GROUNDED
SOCIAL WORK

DIVERSITY, OPPRESSION, AND CHANGE

Flavio Francisco Marsiglia
Stephen Kulis

Arizona State University

LYCEUM
BOOKS, INC.

Chicago, Illinois

© Lyceum Books, Inc., 2009

Published by
LYCEUM BOOKS, INC.
5758 S. Blackstone Ave.
Chicago, Illinois 60637
773 + 643–1903 (Fax)
773 + 643–1902 (Phone)
lyceum@lyceumbooks.com
http://www.lyceumbooks.com

11   10   9   13   14   15   16

ISBN 978–0-925065–73–5

Library of Congress Cataloging-in-Publication Data

  Marsiglia, Flavio Francisco.
    Diversity, oppression, and change : culturally grounded social work / Flavio Francisco Marsiglia & Stephen Kulis.
     p.   cm.
  Includes bibliographical references and index.
  ISBN 978–0-925065–73–5
    1. Social service and race relations.   2. Social work with minorities.   3. Social work with indigenous peoples.   I. Kulis, Stephen Stanley, 1953–   II. Title.
  HV41.M282   2008
  361.3—dc22

                                              2007042993

*This book is dedicated
to the memory of our mothers,
Lucia and Dottie,
who taught us so much
about cultural diversity and resiliency.*

Contents

PART I
Cultural Diversity and Social Work

PART III
Cultural Identities

PART IV
The Profession of Social Work Grounded in Culture

Figures, Tables, and Notes from the Field

Figures

Tables

Notes from the Field

About the Authors

FLAVIO FRANCISCO MARSIGLIA (PhD, Case Western Reserve University; MSW, Universidad de la República, Uruguay) is the Distinguished Foundation Professor of Cultural Diversity and Health in the School of Social Work at Arizona State University. He is the lead instructor of the Diversity and Oppression course sequence in the BSW and MSW programs, as well as the director and principal investigator of the Southwest Interdisciplinary Research Center, which is a Center of Excellence funded by the National Center on Minority Health and Health Disparities at the National Institutes of Health. He has conducted research on culturally grounded interventions in connection with a variety of topics such as substance abuse prevention, HIV/AIDS prevention, and culturally specific social and health services. He has published more than fifty peer-reviewed articles and has presented at numerous national and international research conferences. Professor Marsiglia has received many awards and recognitions, including the 2006 National Award of Excellence in Mentorship from the National Hispanic Science Network on Drug Abuse.

STEPHEN KULIS (PhD, MA, Columbia University) is Cowden Distinguished Professor of Social and Family Dynamics at Arizona State University, and an affiliated faculty member in the School of Social Work, the School of Justice and Social Inquiry, and the Women and Gender Studies program. He is the director of research at the Southwest Interdisciplinary Research Center, which is a Center of Excellence funded by the National Center on Minority Health and Health Disparities at the National Institutes of Health. His research has focused on cultural processes in health disparities, such as the role of gender and ethnic identity in youth drug use and prevention interventions, cultural adaptation of prevention programs for ethnic minority youths, contextual neighborhood and school-level influences on individual-level risk and protective behaviors, gender and racial inequities in professions, and the organizational sources of ethnic and gender discrimination. His articles have been published in such periodicals as *Prevention Science, Journal of Cultural Diversity and Ethnic Minority Psychology, Children & Schools,* and *Sociological Focus.*

Preface

This book is the result of a concerted effort to advance the theoretical and applied underpinnings of a culturally grounded approach to social work practice. It explores cultural diversity and its relationship to oppression and transformative action in the context of social work education at both the undergraduate and graduate levels. This book was born in part out of the need for a text that explicitly addresses the dynamic intersectionalities among identities based on race or ethnicity, gender, sexual orientation, social class, religion, and ability status. The culturally grounded perspective presented here aims at making accessible culturally specific ways of helping that are not generally part of mainstream social work practice methods. In these pages, the social worker is seen as a learner and as an advocate capable of integrating community assets as the foundation for any intervention.

Most social work programs infuse cultural diversity content throughout their courses, and many require students to take courses that specifically examine cultural diversity, oppression, and race and ethnicity. We have participated in the design of diversity-specific courses and currently teach a course entitled Diversity and Oppression in the Social Work Context. This book emerged out of these teaching experiences, the burgeoning literature on the subject, findings from our own culturally grounded professional practice and research, and the shared perspectives gained from dialogue with students, community members, and colleagues. The book attempts to improve social work practice by breaking through the compartmentalized methods that are currently used to teach social work practice.

Because many readers are members or allies of cultural minorities who often travel across real or imaginary cultural boundaries, these materials are presented not out of a postcolonial need to explain identity groups to the uninformed but rather as a means of viewing cultural diversity as a strength within current social work practice. We have purposely avoided the laundry-list approach of reviewing one by one all cultural groups and identities. That method runs the risk of omitting, underemphasizing, or overemphasizing certain groups. Instead, we stress concepts that can be applied in a variety of social contexts and with different cultural communities while at the same time reviewing core cultural norms of selected groups as illustrations or examples of those concepts.

For some time in social work circles and allied professions, culturally grounded social work practice has been understood as a form of practice deliberately embedded in the culture of the client. Over time, this approach has emerged as an indigenous alternative response to Eurocentric approaches to social work that rely on an implicit Westernized belief that there can and should be a mainstream, standardized, and culturally neutral form of practice and that focus on the materialistic and individual aspects of human beings (Schiele, 1997). Culturally grounded social work is firmly rooted in the rich soil of culture. This book facilitates a process of gaining awareness about the nutrients present in that fertile ground and suggests attitudes and behaviors for culturally grounded social work practice.

Although the point of departure and key focus of this book is ethnicity and race, throughout the text there is an infusion of content on gender, sexual orientation, ability status, and social class. A main purpose is to advance the concept of *intersectionality,* that is, the belief that humans form identities that are culturally multidimensional and beautifully complex. For example, at an intake interview, a social worker may form initial impressions of a client as a middle-class African American heterosexual woman but learn that the client sees herself as an Afro-Caribbean lesbian. The client's personal struggles may be related to pressure she feels to define herself according to society's rigid classifications of race, gender, and sexual orientation. By listening to her stories, the social worker starts to understand who the client is and honestly question, revise, or dismiss any preconceived ideas or labels she imposed on her.

This book is as much about social workers as it is about their clients, but the clients are the center of the inquiry. It is the social worker rather than the client who is presented as the "other," not to induce guilt but as an exercise in awareness. This personal awareness will enable social workers to overcome obstacles that may arise when there are differences between the social worker and the client. Social workers may not share the norms and values of their clients. But they are ethically mandated to avoid imposing their own values on individuals and communities and are called upon to work with all oppressed and vulnerable populations by utilizing the strengths of the clients or communities to foster positive change.

Regardless of one's cultural roots, as products or members of academe, all practitioners are subject to the acculturative effects of higher education. This influence can lead to the adoption of white-, heterosexual-, male-, middle class–oriented attitudes that can set up boundaries that become obstacles between practitioners, their communities of origin, and the clients they serve. This book provides social workers with an understanding of the complex intersectionalities of cultural and other group identities through the introduction of culturally grounded social work practice, which will enable social workers to work effectively in collaboration with individuals and communities from different cultural backgrounds.

Throughout the text, the reader is asked the existential question "Who am I?" Answering this question entails an ongoing examination of perceptions of self vis-à-vis one's clients. Through this journey, social workers are invited to ask themselves how they are perceived by the individuals, families, groups, and communities with whom they work. Whom, and what, do they represent through their professional interactions? Issues of race, ethnicity, social class, gender, sexual orientation, and ability status—both their own status and those of their clients—are key factors that influence how they answer these questions. This self-awareness helps workers maintain their honesty and professional competency.

This text invites readers to see themselves as agents of change in partnership with individuals, groups, and communities. In order to help readers embrace such a role completely and competently, the text delves into the history and contemporary experiences of selected communities. Oppression and inequality are addressed as the essential context in which culturally grounded social work practice takes place. Social work is presented as a means to help clients move toward liberation in the manner advocated by the Brazilian philosopher Paulo Freire—that is, by recognizing both the roots of their oppression and their collective and individual resources for social action and lasting change.

Culture is approached as a means of individual strength and as a source of identity that nurtures humans on their individual and collective journeys. Culture is a lens through which people understand their lives, needs, and possibilities, and as a framework through which they construct their dreams and gain the support necessary to make them a reality. Culture is not a barrier to be overcome, bypassed, altered, or finessed by the social worker; instead, culture is a needed resource to be tapped by the professional in order to achieve effective social work practice.

The word "culture" is commonly associated with tangible objects, such as an impressionist painting or a classical opera, artifacts that are considered high culture, or *American Idol*, an example of low culture. This book, however, views culture in a more expansive way, as a very dynamic and collective process. Culture inspires and connects people. It is spoken and unspoken; it is often maintained and preserved through symbols and symbolism. It needs boundaries to survive and to be identifiable. The boundaries are dynamic and constantly shifting, always producing new sets of insiders and outsiders. Culture requires interpretation and a context for those interpretations; it needs a community in order to exist and transform itself. Culture is so pervasive that it is a constant factor in the social worker–client relationship.

In these postmodern times, culture must be approached as a multidimensional and multilayered phenomenon—as the sum of many levels of meaning. An individual's culture is the result of the intersection of factors such as ethnicity, gender, sexual orientation, ability status, acculturation status, immigration status, religion, and social class. Cultures also have a history and carry a narrative about their origins and how they came to be what they are today. For that reason, it is important to examine the oppression of cultural minority groups from historical and sociological perspectives. An outsider seeking basic information about an individual's cultural background may perceive intersectionality as a confusing web of meanings that do not always align. The outsider may ask: "What are you?" The question presumes that there is a simple unidimensional label that fits the person's identity, but intersectionality requires a different type of question: "Who are you?" This question goes beyond old labels and honors the ways in which people explain and make sense of their lives, identity, and intersectionality. Every individual is a complex collection of identities that draw from many different types of heritages and from membership in different social groups, and the individual plays a role in how these identities are brought together. The pronoun "who" is a reminder that individuals are not objects and that it is through culture that they become fully human.

This book provides a framework that presents cultural identities as a process whereby individuals integrate their contextual experiences within their communities of origin and communities of choice. Social work practice is presented as having a liberating role when it operates in partnership with oppressed cultural communities. The book's overarching theme is the importance of the recognition of these multiple layers of meaning and the ever-changing nature of culture. It rejects static definitions of culture based on labels and outsiders' perspectives of "what" the other is. Instead, it proposes a narrative approach where the social worker learns how to listen and comes to understand step-by-step "who" the client is.

Traditional ways of labeling or describing a person's culture, such as referring to an individual's race, ethnicity, gender, sexual orientation, or social class, are reflections or products of a social structure that produces privilege and oppression. At the same time, race, ethnicity, gender, sexual orientation, and social class are sources of identity, peoplehood, and support. The social work profession is called through these pages to embrace the "who" paradigm and, in partnership with communities, overcome the "what" paradigm that deters change and perpetuates oppression. Labels can be a source of oppression, while the embrace of identities carries the promise of liberation.

Information about selected communities and identity groups is presented as part of a framework for examining attitudes toward *difference*, and to suggest culturally specific professional attitudes and behaviors. The text provides both theoretical foundations and specific approaches for a humanistic social work practice that recognizes the strengths and resiliency inherent in the cultures of individuals, groups, and communities.

The overall aims of this book are (1) to provide a foundation for culturally grounded social work practice, (2) to explain how the intersectionality of social factors affects the client, (3) to foster an understanding of how the intersectionality of factors affects the social worker, (4) to strengthen critical thinking skills in analyzing oneself, other individuals, community, and society, and (5) to provide readers with the knowledge and skills needed to move beyond cultural awareness into social action.

The content of this book is organized into four main areas: an introduction to the culturally grounded approach, a review of the key theories on which the approach rests, an exploration of key identity factors, and an application of the culturally grounded approach to the social work profession.

Examples and illustrations of key concepts are presented throughout the text. The purpose of these case studies is to promote critical thinking and integration of knowledge. These case studies can be used to conduct small-group class exercises or for individual reflection. This is a possible discussion guide:

1. Summarize the content. What does it say?
2. Share your reactions, both intellectual (e.g., vis-à-vis new or old knowledge, confusion, stimulation) and emotional (e.g., anger, sadness, happiness, validation), to the material.
3. Universalize the content. What are the broad implications of this content for society?
4. Personalize the content. What are the applications and implications for you as an individual and as a professional?
5. Discuss the social work practice, policy, and research implications.

We encourage readers to integrate the content of this book by asking themselves throughout, "How do the concepts and issues presented here apply to the communities I am working with?" Further, we encourage you to use your own personal experiences and the narratives you collect from your work with diverse communities as the compass that guides your efforts to become a culturally grounded practitioner. We wish you a fruitful journey.

Acknowledgments

We would like to acknowledge the students and community partners of Arizona State University; our ongoing dialogue with them has informed and motivated us in writing this book. We thank our publisher David Follmer for his kindness and support throughout this process. Many colleagues and graduate assistants have also provided ongoing support. We especially wish to thank our dedicated graduate students: Monica Parsai for her thorough library research support in the initial stages; David Becerra, Myriam Hillin, Jennifer Jacobson, Julieann Nagoshi, and Veronica Peña for research assistance on particular chapters; and Jason Castillo and Kathryn Shahan for their assistance with case studies. Our colleagues Evelyn Hawkins, Robert Leighninger, Ben Robinson, Ellie Yepez, and Paz Zorita gave generously of their time to provide us with very thoughtful feedback. A special thank you goes to Julia Angelica and Sonia Fulop for their careful assistance in editing the manuscript.

Part I

Cultural Diversity and Social Work

1

Culture

CULTURE AND CULTURAL DIFFERENCES HAVE HISTORICALLY HAD A MAJOR influence on the development of modern nations. As ideas about cultural diversity are broadening in scope, social work as a profession is asking itself anew how culture affects the way people think and behave. Through their practice, social workers recognize culture as a source of strength for individuals and communities, and at the same time they often identify differences in culture that can create cultural boundaries, leading to discrimination, isolation, and a lack of access to resources for ethnic minority clients. These cultural differences may also create a barrier between the social worker and the client. If the social work professional does not acknowledge the differences in class and culture between the social worker and the client, then she or he will not be able to work effectively with the client. Social workers need to develop cultural competency not only to understand how culture affects the client, but also to move beyond simple cultural labels and develop a sense of the cultural identity of the client. This chapter provides social work students with an understanding of culture, how it affects individual behavior, and how social workers can acknowledge cultural differences and acquire the skills necessary to work with members of different cultural backgrounds.

When asked to describe their culture, social work students offer an array of revealing responses. They are likely to mention personal qualities or personality characteristics, such as distinctive ways of communicating and expressing emotion (e.g., "We are comfortable with loud disagreements," "We all hug a lot"). Some refer to their professional culture and shared social work values, such as the value they place on helping others. Still others connect culture to family but cast it in terms of the roles they play as daughters, sons, or parents (e.g., "We are always there for each other"). Other students are puzzled by the question and wonder if they belong to a distinctive culture at all. The students who respond by explicitly connecting their own culture to race, ethnicity, gender, social class, or sexual orientation tend to come from groups that are not always considered part of the mainstream culture. For example, students are more likely to describe their culture as Japanese American, Jewish, African American, or gay than as upper-middle class, heterosexual, or white. As the class discussion progresses, it often becomes clear that some students feel uncomfortable identifying any cultural differences that set them apart from others, as if such differences need to be deemphasized because they are irrelevant to the professional role of the social worker or are obstacles to understanding one another.

The discomfort and avoidance surrounding the topic of culture have many sources: lack of the right vocabulary, a fear of creating distance, or reluctance to acknowledge the cultural differences and power differentials that exist between social workers and their clients. Although some aspects of culture may be difficult to identify, or individuals may feel uncomfortable sharing them, conversations about culture are necessary rehearsals for negotiating the cultural differences between the social worker and the client that are an essential part of social work practice.

Recognizing the influence of culture is a necessary first step. Culture and cultural differences are elusive topics in part because culture is both an outcome and a process that arises from the meaningful interaction of people. Culture is often defined as a group's distinctive way of life as reflected in its language, values, and norms of behavior. Although cultural background influences the way people think and act, many take these cultural influences for granted and often are unaware of their profound impact on their lives and the lives of others. Members of cultural minorities, however, do not have the privilege of forgetting about their cultural background. Their minority status is always present, affecting their daily thoughts, conversations, and interactions, and often reminding them that they are viewed and treated as "different."

Still, culture is much more than a way of distinguishing groups according to their differences. Culture is not only a distinctive set of prescriptions about how to act and what to expect in the world. It also is a source of strength and inspiration that helps people cope with the daily stressors they face. When social workers welcome culture into the client-worker relationship, they allow for the utilization of the full range of resources that their clients bring with them and a more accurate interpretation of behavior.

Culture often needs to be interpreted and understood in its social context because behaviors become meaningful in a community when they are repeated and encoded and eventually take on symbolic value. Codes are the identifiable categories of behaviors or practices repeated over time. These codes become the backbone of culture. Once certain behaviors and their corresponding norms and values become familiar to a cultural group, its members develop expectations about what practices are appropriate in given situations. Some of these expectations can become resources and strengths that nurture, protect, and inspire individuals and community members toward social participation and well-being. Although those codes or behaviors are easily recognizable among members of a cultural group (insiders), they can easily go unrecognized by members of another cultural group (outsiders). Social workers' cultural awareness guides them as they navigate the uncharted waters of unfamiliar cultures and helps them recognize and decipher cultural codes and maintain a high level of professional competence and effectiveness.

Culture provides the filters through which women and men look at their lives and the lives of those in their social environments. Through culture, people find connections and solidarity as they view and interpret the world around them (Takaki, 1993). Cultures are identifiable constellations of shared ideas and values, a guide to how people should think and behave in their community. Culture allows people to share their interpretations of the past as well as the future. These shared ideas and beliefs change over time and are connected to a particular geographic place and a particular time in history. Culture is dynamic and it is constantly evolving in its social and political context. In addition, not all members of a cultural group respond in the same way to their common culture: individuals vary in their level of adherence to the collective norms and often may have their own unique interpretations of the cultural worlds they inhabit. It is therefore important for social workers to understand the value of culture and its influence on individuals, but it is also important for social workers to be aware of these potential individual differences within a cultural group so they do not perpetuate cultural or group stereotypes.

CULTURAL IDENTITY AND CULTURAL BOUNDARIES

Cultural identity refers to the set of values held by a community and its corresponding worldview. The two combine to form a referential framework that in turn influences both the relationship among individuals within that society and their collective sense of identity. Although a community has a shared cultural identity, individuals within that community have unique expressions of that collective identity. Social class, race, ethnicity, religion, and language make important contributions to an individual's cultural identity. Cultural identity is present in the institutions, the habits and traditions, and the knowledge that define any society. Virtually all societies have more than one culture, each marked by its own language or languages, diet, manners, and other characteristics. The coexistence of multiple cultures creates a system of social stratification, where differences of social class, power, and prestige can emerge among groups. Those differences are enforced through boundaries that groups develop and enforce over time. Through boundaries, people learn what is permissible and what is not permissible. Individual cultural identities are shaped and are affected by those boundaries. For example, some identity choices may be encouraged, while others may not be available to members of a group. Some members may have access to—and be expected to pursue or take advantage of—certain resources such as higher education, while such resources are not perceived as available to others.

In contemporary society, most people find themselves crossing cultural boundaries on a regular basis in their daily lives. Some may say that interacting with people who look, speak, dress, or think in ways that are different from what is perceived as the norm is a form of daily cultural boundary crossing. Most cultural groups are constantly exposed to a great variety of outside cultural influences, resulting in a constant cultural transaction where individuals adopt aspects of other cultures. Although culture is dynamic and changing, the mixture of cultural influences does not result in a simple blend where all cultures add equally to an evolving recipe. For those who are outside what is considered the cultural mainstream, cultural change occurs through a variety of processes that can involve assimilation, acculturation, and enculturation.

ASSIMILATION

Assimilation is the process of letting go of one's culture of origin while incorporating norms and behaviors of the majority or dominant culture. The unidirectional nature of this process cannot be solely explained by numbers or the relative size of the cultural groups. A dominant culture can be a numerical minority but have the most power and the ability to enforce its supremacy over a larger cultural group. For example, in some cities in the Southwest, Latino students are in the numerical majority, but it is forbidden by law to teach in Spanish. Many Latino students are forced in elementary school to speak in English instead of the language of their ancestors and later find that in high school they need to enroll in Spanish classes to fulfill the foreign language requirement. Assimilation describes a unidirectional process shaped by power differentials and assumptions about difference that are often illogical or simply false.

Assimilation involves activities by which a minority group abandons the unique features of its culture of origin and adapts to the values of the dominant culture. Often the dominant group accepts some limited aspects of the minority group's cultural or social life, and both groups become integrated into a common social structure. Assimilation can be both cultural and structural. Cultural assimilation occurs when two or more groups develop a common culture that is based on the dominant group's culture, in which minor aspects of the minority group culture are incorporated. Structural assimilation occurs when two or more groups participate in the same social institutions, organizations, and interpersonal networks—for example, through intermarriage, workplace integration, and overlapping friendships (friendships between members of majority and minority ethnic and racial groups that require the members of minority groups to adjust to the norms and behaviors of the friend representing the dominant group)—and when they hold equal positions in these social structures (Farley, 2000). The barriers to cultural and structural integration may include the prejudice and discrimination that differences in phenotype (racial or ethnic appearance), language, and surnames may breed.

ACCULTURATION AND ENCULTURATION

Because culture is a dynamic process, culture of origin is just one ingredient in the formation of cultural identity. The acculturation process allows individuals to integrate elements of other cultures as they develop their new identities. Acculturation is a form of cultural synthesis that takes place when the original norms, values, and behaviors are mixed and changed by new influences. The process is influenced by differences in social class, power, and prestige. Although minority cultures generally experience stronger pressure to change than mainstream cultures, the majority culture often voluntarily absorbs desired aspects of the minority culture. Thus acculturation is not a unidirectional process but is instead multidirectional and multidimensional. White middle-class teenagers may incorporate the dress and mode of speech of their Mexican American or African American classmates. They have a choice to do it or not to do it, while their minority classmates may feel that they need to speak and dress like their white classmates in order to advance academically and professionally.

Acculturation is the process of adapting to a non-native culture that occurs when individuals from different cultures come into contact with each other. Acculturation occurs in two distinct dimensions. Behavioral acculturation relates to the adoption of external aspects of the dominant culture, such as language and social skills that allow the individual to fit in. Psychological acculturation relates to an individual's degree of concordance with the ideologies of the dominant culture or its way of thinking and seeing the world (cosmology). These two forms of acculturation run along parallel paths but do not necessarily occur at the same pace (Marino, Minas, & Stuart, 2000).

Acculturation models were developed during the first half of the twentieth century to explain the experiences of different groups of European migrants who entered the United States in successive waves and initially faced much discrimination and had to make difficult adjustments. These groups generally became accepted and assimilated into U.S. educational, economic, political, and social institutions within three generations, during which time there was widespread intermarriage across ethnic group lines. These original assimilationist models proposed a linear and progressive process of acculturation into the mainstream culture, which are being challenged as less applicable to today's immigrants. Among the key differences between the early twentieth-century European immigrants and many twenty-first century immigrants from Latin America, the Caribbean, Asia, and Africa is the intensity and duration of the experience of discrimination and the greater ease of maintaining contact with the culture of origin fostered by cheaper and more convenient communication and transportation options. A century ago, first-generation European immigrants faced opposition from native-born Americans who questioned their loyalties and feared they would compete for the same jobs. Today, however, the second and third generations of immigrant families are often confronted by these obstacles. The self-identification of the children, grandchildren, and even great-grandchildren of Mexican immigrants as just as Mexican as American may be a reflection of discrimination and a reaction to their perception of unequal treatment and less-than-full acceptance by mainstream U.S. culture, rather than unwillingness to acculturate.

For instance, a large-scale study of Latino children in Florida and California found that even though the subjects were born in the United States, 25 percent chose to identify themselves with a unhyphenated Latino nationality group, for example, as "Mexican" rather than "Mexican-American" (Portes & McLeod, 1996). Waters (1994), in her study of second-generation West Indian and Haitian American adolescents in New York City, found three types of identities: a black American identity, a hyphenated ethnic or national origin identity (e.g., "Jamaican-American"), and an immigrant identity. The different identities reflected the youths' different perceptions of the impact of race on their social and economic opportunities in the United States. The youths who identified with a black American identity tended to experience more racial discrimination than those who identified with a West Indian identity.

The cultural adaptation of the children of immigrants is often described as problematic or troubled. Andall (2002) speaks of a second-generation "decline," a second-generation "revolt," and a second-generation "attitude." Second-generation decline describes unwillingness among children of immigrants to accept low-paying and low-status jobs that leave them stranded outside the mainstream economy. Second-generation revolt refers to the rejection of elements of mainstream culture and its opportunities for social mobility, such as the value of education as the pathway to success, by the children of immigrants. Second-generation attitude refers to the greater assertiveness of the children of immigrants compared to their parents and the resulting intergenerational conflicts. The heightened awareness of children of immigrants of their status as both insiders and outsiders shapes the way they construct and navigate their hyphenated identities, as well as the paths that they pursue in their social, economic, and political lives.

One classic typology describes four possible outcomes for those undergoing the acculturation process: assimilation, which replaces the culture of origin with the host culture; integration of elements of the culture of origin with those of the host culture; separation through the strict maintenance of the culture of origin; and marginalization through a rejection of both the host and origin cultures (Berry, Kim, Power, Young, & Bujaki, 1989). More recent research has recognized that members of groups with great cultural differences are not well accepted by the host society. They have limited opportunities to choose among these different pathways of acculturation. Many feel pressure to either assimilate or become marginalized socially and economically (Berry, 1997). The experience of male Caribbean immigrants exemplifies this situation. The pressure to replace the more polarized attitudes and behaviors regarding gender roles of Caribbean culture with a more gender-neutral and egalitarian perspective can heighten acculturation stress and contributes to their relationship problems, addictive behavior, and mental illness (Kosberg, 2002). When working with clients of different cultures, social workers use culturally competent assessment methods to understand the level of the client's acculturation. Such an assessment helps workers uncover possible acculturation stress and identify how the ethnic community may be a source of strength and assistance to cope with stress.

Enculturation is the process of connecting back to the culture of origin or to a renewed version of it. Rather than simply maintaining the elements of a culture of origin, enculturation involves recapturing that culture by learning about it, identifying with it, and reinforcing its basic norms and values. For researchers and practitioners who work with ethnic minority communities, the concept of enculturation redirects attention toward the strengths of minority cultures and their inherent cultural resiliencies. Through enculturation, individuals can become anchored in their cultures of origin by practicing aspects of the traditional culture and by identifying with that culture (Zimmerman, Ramirez-Valles, Washienko, Walter, & Dyer, 1996). When enculturation is taken into account, ethnic minorities' cultural strengths can be reinforced, cultural heritages can be reclaimed, and a renewed sense of community belongingness can be achieved (Zimmerman et al., 1996).

Enculturation is especially relevant to Native Americans, African Americans, and Chicanos because of the many historical efforts there have been to destroy and disconnect them from their original cultures, and to force them to assimilate into the white mainstream without fully accepting them. The rites of passage developed by African American communities around the nation that aim at connecting youths to ancestral African rituals as a source of resiliency are a form of enculturation. Urban Native American communities and some tribal communities have promoted enculturation through traditional community-based support systems for their members. Prevention interventions sometimes use an enculturation approach to connect to culture of origin as a ritualistic or cultural source of resiliency. The Chicano movement has used enculturation as a means to reconnect with the Native American cultural aspects of Chicano precolonial identity.

Assimilation, acculturation, and enculturation tend to stress culture over other factors in the formation of cultural identity. Cultural identity and cultural processes are often shaped by ideas about race and the existence of racial groups.

RACE

The United States is a very race-conscious society, and racial lines of demarcation still influence people's access to social and economic opportunities, as well as how individuals interact with one another in everyday life. The fact that racism has persisted in the United States is remarkable in light of the codification of laws requiring equal treatment regardless of race. The persistence of racial distinctions in social life is also remarkable given the fact that race, as a biological concept, has not survived the test of scientific scrutiny. Humans cannot be categorized reliably based on phenotypical characteristics, such as those aspects of physical appearance like skin color, hair texture, and bone structure that are often thought to be markers of one's racial background. This is a discredited idea that is a vestige of nineteenth-century phrenology, the study of the human skull based on the belief that mental faculties and personality could be determined from its shape (Blakey, 1999).

Advancements in DNA analysis have allowed scientists to trace historical patterns of migration across the globe through genetic similarities and differences among people living in different regions of the world. Even as these efforts uncover evidence of distinctive genetic markers among those who can be traced to common ancestors, this research has added to the evidence that pure races have never existed because humans cannot reliably be distinguished genetically from one another along racial lines. Indeed, genetic research has shown that humans who are labeled as belonging to distinct racial groups are, in fact, virtually indistinguishable genetically. This inability to find systematic genetic or biological variations that can reliably classify individuals by race has led researchers to conclude that the concept of race has no basis in genetics or biology. Rather, externally observable differences like skin color and facial features are influenced by evolutionary natural selection. For example, degree of skin pigmentation is explained as an adaptation to strong or weak sunlight. However, individuals who have similar skin color as a result of such adaptation may be genetically very different, while individuals who do not have similar skin color because of different selective forces may be genetically quite similar (Bamshad & Olson, 2003). Nonetheless, racial categorizations continue to influence people's perception of differences among individuals in skin color, hair texture, eye shape, height, and other physical characteristics. Yet because these differences are matters of perception, not genetics, the meaning assigned to these differences varies across societies and even within societies. In the United States there is a growing consensus among anthropologists and historians that approaching race as a biological phenomenon is inaccurate (see Smedley & Smedley, 2005).

There is some consensus that race should be viewed as a socially constructed idea rather than as a biological fact. That is, race has taken on such importance because of the cultural and social meanings that people learn to attach to it. These meanings develop through a social and historical process of "racial formation," in which racial categories are created, altered, and sometimes discarded (Omi & Winant, 1998). The prime purpose of racial formation is to establish a hierarchy and target certain groups for discrimination. People are taught to believe that there are racial groups with distinctive characteristics, and that some races are innately superior or inferior to others, thereby justifying the dominance of one over the other. The history of slavery in the United States epitomizes such dominance. Even Abraham Lincoln, the president who issued the Emancipation Proclamation, echoed the prejudicial sentiments of his time in the years just before he assumed the presidency:

> I will say that I am not, nor ever have been in favor of bringing about in any way the social and political equality of the white and black races, [applause]—that I am not nor ever have been in favor of making voters or jurors of negroes, nor of qualifying them to hold office, nor to intermarry with white people, and I will say in addition to this that there is a *physical difference* between the white and black races which I believe will forever forbid the two races living together on terms of social and political equality. And inasmuch as they cannot so live, while they do remain together, *there must be the position of superior and inferior.* I as much as any other man am in favor of having the superior position assigned to the white race. (Angle, 1991, p. 235, emphasis added)

Racism—the subordination of any person or group because of some physically distinctive characteristic—has been a central element in the foundation of the United States and its economic, political, social, and cultural development (Feagin, Johnson, & Rush, 2000). Although science has provided sufficient evidence to demonstrate that humans share a common biological and genetic heritage across racial lines, the social experience of race needs to be recognized and integrated into a culturally grounded approach to social work. Because the client's perception of the race of the social worker can influence the dynamics of the working relationship, it is necessary for the social worker to understand how race is experienced by clients, as well as negative preconceptions the clients may have toward the social worker. Such awareness helps workers foster collaboration and achieve positive outcomes.

ETHNICITY AND RACE

Despite the constantly evolving notions of what race is, what it signifies, and how prominent it is in the lives of communities, the enduring legacy of racism is one reason that race and racial identity cannot be ignored in efforts to understand cultural diversity. This book approaches race as one of several important dimensions of culture, with which it often overlaps. In the United States, as in other race-conscious societies, it is difficult to ignore the belief that race exists. As helping professionals, social workers walk the fine line of recognizing and acknowledging the impact of racism while avoiding reducing the human experience to narrow racial terms.

Ethnicity is another construct that can be applied to the human experience of cultural distinctiveness, and one where the boundary lines separating people into groups sometimes—but not always—run parallel with racial differences. By arguing in the 1970s for the use of the ethnically based phrase "African American" instead of the racially based term "black," the Reverend Jesse Jackson advanced this argument and shifted attention from reductionist phenotypical characteristics to cultural traits that unify and empower a community.

In addition, ethnicity and race intersect with other key social characteristics, such as gender, sexual orientation, ability status, social class, acculturation, and immigration status. For example, any assessment of a client who is a Haitian immigrant and works as a doctor in a clinic for refugees and immigrants must recognize that her higher social class and other educational advantages will allow her to navigate acculturation obstacles more efficiently and effectively than her patients are able to. Because of her physical appearance, she may experience racial discrimination in ways that mirror the experiences of African Americans whose families have lived in the United States for many generations, but her cultural upbringing in Haiti provides her with a distinctive ethnic identity and a different cultural heritage. Recognizing this intersectionality helps prevent simplistic generalizations and allows for an examination of within-group as well as between-group differences. If appropriately tapped, culture as a multilayered and intersecting phenomenon can be a source of resiliency, motivation, and inspiration for individuals and communities.

ETHNICITY AND CULTURAL IDENTITY FORMATION

Max Weber (1928/1968), in his pioneering work on ethnic groups in Germany and the United States, used the phrases *ethnische Gruppen* (ethnic group) and *ethnische Gemeinschaften* (ethnic communities) to describe ethnicity as a collective phenomenon. The collective dimension of ethnicity affects not only how people see themselves as members of an ethnic group but also how they are seen by others. As a result, ethnic identity requires each person to behave in ethnically consistent ways so others can identify her or him with an ethnic group. In a sense, for an individual to have an ethnic identity, it is just as important for others to identify the individual as a member of an ethnic group as it is for the individual to identify personally with that ethnic group.

Minority ethnic groups are differentiated from the dominant group through cultural differences based on their language, religion, attitudes toward marriage and parenting, dress, and the foods they eat. An individual cannot choose to be a member of an ethnic group without having any tangible connection to that group. Someone may follow the prescribed dress code, eat the same foods, and listen to the same music but not be recognized by the members of the group as one of them. In other words, one does not automatically gain membership in the ethnic group by mimicking ethnic customs; in fact, such actions can be seen as irreverent, even offensive. For example, crossover singers like the white rapper Eminem have been criticized as inauthentic wannabes who appropriate a culture and musical genre that is not theirs. This view represents a bipolar model of cultural identification in which ethnic group membership boundaries are sharply drawn and not readily crossed. A less discrete, more flowing multidimensional model allows for the possibility that human beings can identify simultaneously with more than one culture, and identification with any culture can have positive implications for an individual's personal health and social well-being.

Just as an ethnic identity cannot be chosen at will, neither can it be lived in isolation. Ethnic identity requires a connection to a community and a set of shared norms and behaviors. It is with others that members of cultural minorities assess their chances of changing conditions of oppression. In addition, it is with others that culture is defined, learned, celebrated, and preserved.

Anthropologists speak of ethnicity as an identity that is embraced under certain conditions. That is, people do not choose any ethnicity but do have a choice to learn about, accept, identify, and acknowledge their ethnicity. Acquiring an ethnic identity involves an individual act of affirmation of that identity and the adoption of various values and behaviors within a restricted range of possibilities (Dominguez, 1986). For example, research with Asian American children shows how preadolescents assess their choices based on anticipated outcomes (Tse, 1999). Embracing an Asian American identity or not embracing it brings a set of rewards or negative consequences, and the choices children make reflect the social context in which they live. A Japanese American student attending a school that is predominantly European American may choose not to accentuate her ethnic identity or her parents' culture of origin due to the lack of acceptance of diversity or fear of rejection and discrimination. At other times, children may not be aware that their ethnicity is perceived as being different from that of the majority, particularly if they live in ethnically homogenous neighborhood enclaves. However, once they start school, they may go through a stage of ambivalence, confusion, and perhaps vacillation before they identify with, reject, or selectively adopt elements of their ethnic heritage. An Asian American student may encounter racism at school, something not under her or his control. Racism, although an external force, may have a negative impact on the student's well-being and functioning as well as on her or his identity development.

There is an ongoing debate about how parents should prepare their children as they enter potentially racist environments. One point of view is that it is better not to predispose children to the idea that they will be victims of racism. Another view is that the negative effects of racism can be mitigated when parents have such conversations with their children and teach them coping strategies (Brooks & Hampton, 2005).

Being connected to one's ethnicity or race does mean that one must be cut off from the larger society and its opportunities for social and economic advancement. Nonetheless, society often conveys the message that to achieve social and economic advancement, individuals must discard their ethnicity. Such a choice results in a form of cultural deprivation. The ideal situation is to keep what is of value in one's ethnic identity—what inspires and moves the individual—while at the same time being able to benefit socially and economically from the full range of opportunities that are available in the larger society.

SOCIAL WORK AND CULTURAL DIVERSITY

Social workers play an important role in helping communities maintain the balance between social advancement and cultural preservation. Achieving this balance is the goal of culturally grounded social work. Ideally, the social worker enters the community's world in dialogue with the community members and aware of any preconceived ideas she or he has about what the client needs or who the client is or is not. Because cultural identity formation is a subjective and evolving process that involves personal choice, as well as a personal journey within the boundaries and recognition of the community, it is the task of the social worker to confirm the client's ethnicity, gender, religion, ability status, nationality, or sexual orientation, as two individuals with very similar backgrounds and appearances may identify themselves differently.

People often have a tendency to make ethnicity, gender, ability status, and sexual orientation fixed and sometimes mutually exclusive characteristics—the client *is* Latino or the client *is* gay—instead of understanding how ethnic and cultural differences intersect. It is at the intersection of identities that the social worker engages with the client (Tsang, 2001).

Listening to the client's narratives allows social workers to move beyond labels and assess the client's true cultural identity. Through these stories, they learn *who* the client is instead of *what* the client is. The client becomes a subject, not an object of the work, playing the lead character in the story, not a supporting role. In other words, a narrative approach facilitates a culturally grounded approach to practice, which in turn provides the opportunity for empowerment.

Historically, the social work profession has been committed to working with different ethnic and racial communities and has defined its purpose as working with the oppressed. The preamble to the Code of Ethics of the National Association of Social Workers (1999) calls on social workers to be "sensitive to cultural and ethnic diversity and strive to end discrimination, oppression, poverty, and other forms of social injustice" (p. 9). As a result, social work has directed considerable attention toward issues of social reform and civil rights. Thousands of practitioners join the profession primarily because of social work's abiding concern about values germane to human rights, welfare rights, equality, and the prevention of discrimination and oppression (Reamer, 2006). Because cultural minorities are overrepresented among oppressed populations, a culturally grounded approach to practice is both natural and necessary. A culturally specific approach, however, can easily be critiqued as an exercise in divisiveness. These issues are hotly debated by social work and its allied professions.

Culturally grounded social work emerged in response to the awareness of the need for social work practice to take root in the culture of the client. Social work and its allied disciplines have developed two pathways toward a more culturally grounded approach. The first pathway stresses cultural sensitivity, and the other focuses on cultural competency. The cultural sensitivity stance calls attention to the diversity among clients and communities, focusing on the cultural gap that exists between the service delivery system and the clients it serves. Simply increasing awareness of cultural diversity, however, may or may not result in the delivery of culturally relevant services. One can be aware of or sensitive to existing differences but still be unable or unwilling to reach out effectively to specific constituencies (Gutierrez, Ortega, & Yeakley, 2000).

The cultural competency stance moves the profession a step closer to the goal of culturally grounded service delivery by emphasizing the knowledge, values, and skills needed for workers to make services culturally relevant, thereby increasing their effectiveness. In addition, this approach calls on social workers to understand the dynamics of oppression and to promote social justice. To engage in authentic culturally grounded practice, members of the helping professions develop both cultural sensitivity and cultural competency.

As figure 1.1 illustrates, the progression from unawareness to culturally grounded practice is not unidirectional. Rather, the steps illustrate the possibility that one can take steps back to a lower level of awareness and competency at any time. This is not a progressive and linear process; instead the journey into culturally grounded social work can be curvilinear and can take us back and forth until we reach the desired stage of awareness and culturally competent practice. When

Figure 1.1   The Culturally Grounded Practice Continuum

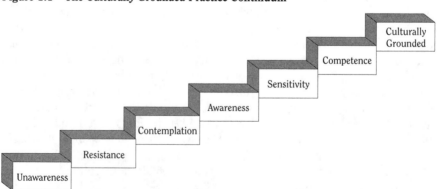

dealing with clients from various cultures, a practitioner can be operating simultaneously at different stages of the continuum.

For example, a European American practitioner who is very well versed in working with Mexican American clients might be located at the culturally grounded stage. She is able to use her clients' culture as a resource and develop immediate empathy. However, she may be at the stage of unawareness when working with Filipino clients; for example, she may have no knowledge of the norms regarding gay identity within Filipino culture, which are more flexible than those within Mexican culture. She may assume that because of their common colonial experience with Spain, she can transfer her knowledge and experience working with Mexican Americans to her work with Filipino families without modifying her approach. As a result, her lack of knowledge and awareness of Filipino culture could make her ineffectual as she proposes a family intervention that she has found effective with Mexican families when one of the children reveals he is gay.

The cultural competence stance has been challenged by claims that it is unrealistic (Dean, 2001). Critics argue that due to its very nature as a socially constructed phenomenon, culture is a moving target because, like the language that reflects it, it is an ever-evolving, emergent phenomenon. At the same time, those outside the culture produce stereotypes and biases that are very difficult to change. This point of view proposes the acceptance of the lack of competence in cross-cultural matters as an inevitable fixture of social work practice. Although this analysis provides important insights, accepting the status quo is too fatalistic a response because it does not lead to change. A more useful approach is one that promotes an ongoing process of developing cultural competency and awareness of the strengths of different cultures.

CULTURALLY GROUNDED KNOWLEDGE, ATTITUDES, AND BEHAVIORS IN SOCIAL WORK

Culturally grounded social work is realized through the acquisition of specific *knowledge*, the development of a set of *attitudes*, and the mastery and practice of certain *behaviors* (KAB). The KAB approach was originally developed and tested in the public health field and is commonly used in research related to health issues as a model for promoting the client's involvement in health outcomes (e.g., Tyler & Lichtenstein, 1997). This approach can be expanded to include the practitioner. In the culturally grounded approach, KAB is examined not only in terms of the client's willingness and ability to change but also the practitioner's ability to learn and change along with the client. A culturally grounded approach to social work practice requires that practitioners identify both their strengths and shortcomings as they integrate the different stages of the culturally grounded continuum.

In developing and strengthening these KAB dimensions, social workers use their own personal life stories as a starting point. As might be expected, social workers from backgrounds similar to their clients' do appear to have certain advantages. Among other things, they can more easily decode and interpret cultural messages than workers from other cultures. Indeed, some researchers have argued that a cultural match between providers and clients is the only way to achieve cultural competence, while other social work researchers have labeled such a stance a form of cultural chauvinism (e.g., Taylor-Brown, Garcia, & Kingson, 2001). Without doubt, given the scant evidence that cultural matching produces better and more lasting results, segregating service delivery systems seems too extreme a response to the need for cultural competency. There is certainly evidence that social service providers working with culturally similar clients do not always have an adequate understanding of their clients (Ridley & Lingle, 1996). Viewed from the perspective of the complexities of intersecting identities, this finding is not surprising: although practitioners and clients may have had similar experiences due to their gender or ethnicity, it is less likely that their lives overlap in their experience of social class.

Nonetheless, skillful social workers from different backgrounds can indeed learn how to competently decode and respond to culturally specific messages and behaviors. It is the culturally grounded *attitudes* of service providers—not simply their cultural background—that yield higher levels of client service satisfaction (Walker, 2001). The personal biography or demographic profile of a worker is no guarantee of cultural competence. An individual is not born culturally competent; rather, an individual becomes culturally competent by acquiring the necessary awareness, knowledge, and relevant skills, and developing a welcoming and affirming attitude.

The philosophy underlying a culturally grounded approach places the cultural identity of the client or consumer at the center of the social work intervention. Cultural identity that is not connected to the misuse of power or the perpetuation of privilege or oppression can be a source of resiliency. Indeed, according to the Afrocentric perspective—a perspective that places African ideas and cosmology at the center of any analysis of African and African American cultures and behaviors (Asante, 2000)—cultural identity can be viewed as a source of identity, inspiration, and pride that can be used to overcome challenges and difficulties. The culturally grounded approach values what minority cultures have to offer and incorporates the culture's natural ways of helping into the helping process. Note from the field 1.1 provides an example of how a practitioner checked her ethnocentrism. She did not utilize very specialized skills, just some common sense and cultural awareness. She knew that in some Native American cultures, direct questioning is not the norm, and that it might make some Native American clients uncomfortable. Practitioners can be more effective in developing rapport with clients by using icebreakers before asking direct questions. Quick reactions and faulty first impressions are common. When the client's communication is slower than expected, before labeling or clinically diagnosing the client, the practitioner may need to ask not only why the client is not communicating as expected, but also why the practitioner expected a different type of interaction in the first place.

PRIVILEGE AND EMPATHY

Privilege is the unearned advantages of special group membership. A social worker from a developed country working for a year in a war- and poverty-stricken developing country is privileged compared to the refugee families on her caseload. When social work professionals are working across social, economic, and cultural boundaries, their worldviews, beliefs, and values strongly influence the type of relationship and comfort level they experience with their clients, as well as their ability to empathize (Kurland & Salmon, 1999). If unchecked, the social worker's privilege can be a barrier to empathy and an obstacle to culturally grounded practice. Privilege makes professionals assume—consciously or unconsciously— certain things about their clients. For example, the practitioner may assume that the client has what she or he has, such as a car or a comfortable home, or that the client was able to eat a hot breakfast before coming to the session. It is important to be aware of one's privilege and the client's lack of privilege in order to build rapport and accurately assess and interpret the client's behaviors.

In 1990, Peggy McIntosh published the now-classic "White Privilege: Unpacking the Invisible Knapsack," in which she documented some of the daily effects of privilege that she experienced and generally took for granted as a white middle-class person in the United States. The checklist (which is available online) can be edited and updated in many ways to accommodate the experiences of different cultural groups, but the original checklist remains provocative and insightful. The checklist focuses on what the author does not need to do or think about. In other words, it is a catalog of situations in which white Americans experience the absence of discomfort, barriers, and oppression. Oppressed clients are aware of their social workers' privilege due to the practitioners' race, ethnicity, higher economic, professional, and educational status, and their differential power. A client learns quickly that the practitioner often controls the resources that the client needs. If left unaddressed, this perceived privilege can become an obstacle to effective communication and rapport building, as clients may assume that the professionals cannot understand what they are going through due to their lack of experience with certain oppressive situations. Social workers, including those from minority groups, may be in denial about the privileges they enjoy that their clients do not. Self-awareness about privilege increases social workers' effectiveness and, in the end, enhances their professional and personal growth. Ignoring privilege or minimizing its impact on the client-worker relationship may compromise rapport and trust, leading to ineffective practice.

NOTE FROM THE FIELD 1.1
The Long Bus Ride to School

Joe, an eleven-year-old Apache student, is referred to Christine, the school social worker, because he is not participating in class. Mr. Andrews, his teacher, is concerned about Joe's poor performance and suspects he may be depressed.

Scenario A
Christine attempts to engage Joe in conversation without success. She asks Joe questions that touch on his relationships with his parents, siblings, and friends. Joe feels uncomfortable talking to Christine, an authority figure and someone he doesn't know. He looks withdrawn and distant and gives short and vague or evasive answers, sometimes falling into long silences. Christine also starts to feel uncomfortable and decides to refer Joe to a mental health clinic for an assessment. The session lasts five minutes.

Scenario B
Christine attempts to engage Joe in conversation without success. She realizes that her direct questions will not help her establish rapport with Joe but instead are becoming an obstacle. After a few minutes, she suggests that they play a game. Joe is rather reticent at first but very quickly becomes involved in the game. He is having a good time and soon starts to talk about the fact that he lives far away from school. He gets up very early and often has to run out without eating breakfast. He is often hungry and sleepy until lunchtime. He does not eat breakfast at school because the county bus gets in a bit too late for him to make it before they close the cafeteria. Christine arranges to enroll Joe in the school's breakfast program and makes sure his food will be kept warm until his arrival. A week later, Mr. Andrews reports that Joe's class participation has improved significantly since his visit with the social worker.

HIGHER EDUCATION AND THE RISK OF CLASSISM

Higher education is a great cultural equalizer, as it provides very effective means for social mobility. Often, one is not possible without the other. Although the need for multiculturalism and inclusion has been extensively demonstrated, higher education and its structures are not yet sufficiently inclusive and representative in terms of cultural diversity. Social work as a profession has done better than many other disciplines in recruiting and retaining a diverse workforce. However, higher numbers of women and ethnic minorities joining the profession do not automatically translate into higher levels of cultural competence.

Higher education can also act as a cultural homogenizer, prompting students and faculty to conform to majority culture norms and behaviors regardless of their ethnic and social class backgrounds. The professional credentials imparted to them by higher education can make graduates operate from an implicitly classist standpoint. Consciously or unconsciously, they can adopt the perspective that because they have a college degree, they now know more about social problems and their solutions than the poor and oppressed people who experience them.

Classism provides justification for the oppression of the poor and the working poor by those who control the economic and social resources of society. Classism is based on the belief that working-class people and poor people in general are inarticulate, lack education, and need the leadership and guidance of the educated classes. Social work practice can be classist, as it may recognize only one source of valid knowledge—the knowledge generated in institutions of higher learning, which typically exclude the poor and the oppressed and their accumulated knowledge and wisdom.

To keep their classism in check, practitioners can use cultural experts and alternative sources of knowledge and conduct participatory action research (see chapter 14) with communities. Social work research can be an important source of new knowledge that can bridge the gap between communities and higher education. Schools of social work can take advantage of their affiliation with universities and their close partnerships with communities to produce the best science in partnership with the communities they serve. As a profession, social work has the unique advantage of living in both worlds and can serve as a link between them to produce the best possible applied social science. Culturally competent social workers recognize that regardless of their social class and cultural background, their training can give them a middle-class and Eurocentric perspective on life. Higher education has an acculturative effect that, if left unaddressed, can create cultural distance and mistrust between practitioners and clients. An individual can be born into privilege or access privilege through social mobility. Note from the field 1.2 illustrates how a social work intern was perceived as distant from or alien to her clients' world when she shared important information from her graduate student perspective yet did not effectively reach her audience. She assumed that the idea of sisterhood would immediately connect her with the group members and that they would freely share their experiences. In reality, their loyalty to their families and the academic framework Cindy used were real barriers to group discussion. Cindy shared some demographic characteristics with the group members, but in fact her presentation made her an outsider. She was lacking a link, a connection; the content and goals of the group session were not grounded in the culture and worldview of the group members.

Connecting with clients and reaching the desired level of effectiveness are

---

NOTE FROM THE FIELD 1.2
Starting out on the Wrong Foot

Cindy, a twenty-three-year-old Mexican American MSW student, is doing her internship at a women's shelter. One of her roles is to co-facilitate the young women's support group. The group members are all Mexican American, and close to her age. She starts the session by giving a mini-lecture on gender roles and the negative consequences of machismo (the traditional male gender role) in Latino cultures. The second part of her presentation centers on the implications of feminism and women's rights for Latinas. She invites the group members to share their opinions on the subject. No one speaks; two group members get up and go to the restroom, and another asks permission to go to the nurse's office. Cindy asks the remaining women to share examples of machismo in their families, starting with their fathers. No one speaks. The session ends quickly.

---

often achieved through partnerships and coalitions. When social workers become aware of the distance between them and their clients, they can work with others who are culturally close to the target population and who can help them bridge psychological or cultural distance. Note from the field 1.3 illustrates how a youth outreach worker developed a partnership that allowed him to reach out to a community and use outreach strategies with which he was already familiar with a cultural group he had not worked with before. Some commonly used strategies work across groups; some do not. Often, it is not simply a matter of choosing the right strategy. In James's case, the chance of success was higher from the start because his efforts were co-sponsored by the Office of the Cambodian Liaison, which was well regarded in the community. This is an example of coalition building as well as the language and cultural adaptation of outreach strategies.

Awareness of one's privilege, status as an outsider, or lack of understanding of a particular culture can lead practitioners to develop a sense of discomfort, which in turn may lead them to avoid certain individuals and communities. In such cases, self-reflection can help practitioners assess for privilege and ethnocentrism and, in partnership with others, develop effective strategies to reach out to the target community. The notion of intersectionality helps workers identify shared sources of identity with the clients and bridge distance while developing effective rapport. For example, a Native Hawaiian grandfather is referred to a twenty-five-year-old African American social worker who has no previous experience working with Native Hawaiian clients. As an icebreaker, the worker shares a story about his own grandfather, which allows them to begin to develop a sense

NOTE FROM THE FIELD 1.3

Reaching out to Cambodian Youths

James is a youth outreach worker at an HIV/AIDS services agency. He is African American and English monolingual. One of the goals of his agency is to increase its outreach among local Cambodian American youths. His first strategy is to create posters in English and Cambodian inviting young men and women to come to the agency for an ice cream social and to initiate a conversation about safe sex. James collaborates with Sovann, the liaison representative from the Office of the Cambodian Liaison, which is highly regarded in the Cambodian community, and together they design and post announcements at stores located in the neighborhood where many Cambodian families live. The evening of the planned workshop, he is introduced to the large audience by Sovann, who has also agreed to interpret James's remarks for a large number of Cambodian monolingual parents at a later event.

of connection and comfort. These feelings serve as the foundation for the development of effective interventions.

At times, workers' values, communication styles, and expectations are different from the clients' because the workers come from different worlds and have different worldviews. For example, if a client does not come on time to an appointment, the social worker cannot automatically assume that it is due to resistance. Instead, it would be appropriate to inquire about transportation. Does the client own a car in working condition or have the money for gas or bus fare? It is only natural to think that clients have access to the basic resources most people possess and take for granted. The social worker's privilege—that is, her or his higher status and relative wealth—may lead her or him to overlook important aspects of the client's life. More importantly, even though the more privileged are often not consciously aware of their higher status, the less privileged can quickly identify a difference in social class.

Cultural background often intersects with socioeconomic status in interesting ways. For example, some clients may feel uncomfortable informing the social worker that they do not have money for the bus fare. They may feel that sharing such information makes them lose face or is an assault to their personal dignity. An unchecked sense of privilege may become a barrier to understanding such behavior. That is why cultural awareness is a key component in the repertoire of all culturally grounded social workers regardless of their ethnicity, gender, or social class.

RECOGNIZING AND CROSSING BOUNDARIES

Social workers move beyond the demographic or identity characteristics of their clients when applying the profession's standards of cultural competency. Most social workers interact with people from more than one culture every day; therefore, they honor difference as a first step toward adopting a culturally grounded paradigm. The recognition of cultural differences ensures that, in any intervention, different worldviews are recognized and cultural boundaries are taken into consideration in their practice.

Differences in worldviews occur as a result of the individualistic views of the world that are encouraged by many postindustrial cultures and the more collectivistic view of the world that is common among traditional cultures. These divergent cosmologies can present challenges to effective social work practice because the most commonly used interventions may operate at the individual level, whereas the client's natural support systems operate mostly at the collective level. Cultural boundaries act as imaginary lines that establish comfort zones for members of different cultures and can become no-crossing zones for outsiders. Cultural minority groups, as a result of their lack of power, need to establish boundaries between themselves and the majority culture and other minority groups with more power. The dominant culture, in turn, has the power to enforce its boundaries on minority groups and overlook cultural differences.

Boundaries help groups preserve inequality by protecting the cultural capital (the social and material fruits of privilege) of the dominant group, thereby safeguarding its dominance (Schwalbe, Godwin, Holden, Schrock, Thompson, & Wolkomir, 2000). Social workers and the institutions they represent are often confronted by these boundaries and have the choice of perpetuating or overcoming them in partnership with their clients. Practitioners who come from the majority culture often lack experience with the conditions faced on a daily basis by the members of the oppressed group. Such lack of experience and awareness often prevents representatives of the dominant culture from developing the appropriate attitude and language for effective communication.

Because cultural boundaries are a constant feature in the daily life of practitioners, recognizing and honoring boundaries and finding effective ways to cross them is a lifelong journey. Particularly important is the fact that in certain social settings, boundaries make social workers the outsiders as they work with families, groups, and communities. Research has demonstrated that outsiders are not very tolerant of or open to certain practices and beliefs held by minority cultures. However, the outsider's tolerance level significantly increases when minority practices are similar to the practices of majority cultures (Shaw & Wainryb, 1999). Therefore, tolerance appears to be correlated with comfort level. In other words, the more a given cultural practice deviates from what is familiar to members of the dominant culture, the less tolerant they become. A practitioner using a culturally grounded approach addresses these issues by assessing indigenous helping practices and recognizing their inherent value and benefits to the well-being of community members.

Through their engagement in dialogue with a community, social workers learn the rituals necessary to cross the boundaries that separate them from their clients. For example, practitioners working with Latino clients must understand that the figurative traditional *casa* ("house" or "home") of the Latino family is like a circular temple with thick walls. Inside the walls, there is a courtyard surrounding the *casa*. Inside the *casa*, wonderful things happen, and many stories are shared around an altar called the dining room table. There is, however, only one gate into the courtyard. The social worker is often on the outside knocking on that gate, and the gate may not open easily. The social worker's role is to learn the right ritual to unlock the gate and gain entrance into the courtyard and eventually into the *casa*. Once they have learned the rituals, social workers are welcomed into the courtyard, and later into the *casa* as if they are family. If the time is not invested in learning and practicing the appropriate rituals, communication with the family will only happen through a closed gate and a thick wall, which inevitably leads to misunderstandings. Admittedly, such cultural rituals are sometimes straightforward and driven by common sense and basic courtesy. For example, while working with Latino families, social workers may be expected to ask about the children first, remember the names of the children, and remember to use honorifics (e.g., Mrs. or Señora) until invited to use first names. However, at other times, rituals can be much more complicated to decipher, and learning them may require much time, patience, and a willingness to be taught.

Ignoring the boundaries that result from cultural and social class differences or pretending they do not exist only detracts from efforts to develop rapport and empathize with clients. Boundaries must be crossed not only when a client is of a different ethnicity, race, or social class but also when she or he is differently abled or when there are issues regarding immigration status. Social workers are more effective border crossers when they are aware and when they know who they are and who they are not. Awareness of difference fosters honesty. Social workers often face situations where they are reminded of their own privilege and the boundaries to connecting honestly with a particular client, group, family, or community that it may create. A quick assessment may give the worker only an outsider's view, and a lack of client engagement may lead to misunderstandings. A rushed assessment and the lack of knowledge of cultural rituals may give the worker only a distant and impersonal view from outside the courtyard walls. On the other hand, spending an additional session to develop rapport will certainly lead to a more effective assessment and a more effective intervention plan that incorporates family assets.

In a cultural sense, boundary crossing requires practice and patience, but most importantly, it requires honest dialogue. Note from the field 1.4 illustrates

NOTE FROM THE FIELD 1.4
Same-Sex Love and Immigration

Alison works at the Refugee and Immigrant Families Services Center. When two professional-looking young men enter her office, she thinks they are in the wrong place. Most of her clients are families with children. One of the young men, Tom, is an American citizen; the other, Paulo, is Brazilian. They have lived together as a committed couple for five years. However, Paulo's student visa is expiring soon, and the couple's relationship is not legally recognized by the U.S. Citizenship and Immigration Service (formerly the Immigration and Naturalization Service) as a factor in whether he qualifies as a permanent resident. They have explored many alternatives, and they are running out of time. Alison realizes that she has never worked with a gay couple before. She starts by recognizing that fact and, together with Paulo and Tom, reviews their short-term and long-term strategies, as well as the community and legal resources available to help them.

a case of heterosexual privilege in which the worker is unaware of the unique disadvantages that gay and lesbian couples face because their relationships are usually not legally recognized. The social worker in this example has never before encountered two people who love each other and are not able to live together in the same country. She suddenly recognizes that she has worked exclusively within the realm of heterosexual love. Meeting this gay couple challenges her to see beyond heterosexual privilege and consider the experiences of many other couples. The case of Tom and Paolo illustrates how the privilege status that U.S.-born citizens take for granted does not automatically extend to documented and undocumented immigrants.

Language can be another cultural boundary that workers and their clients must cross. Being able to communicate using the spoken word is often taken for granted except within the hearing-impaired community. In the fields of social work, counseling, and psychology, talking is a fundamental tool for practice. Clients whose first language is not English may be the target of harassment and rejection, which may lead them to feign a level of comprehension they do not possess. Consciously tuning in to such experiences can be of great value to the worker when she or he is entering a new social and cultural environment.

Working across social and cultural boundaries can be very rewarding, and at the same time it can be challenging. Therefore, it is understandable and even predictable that social workers may feel unprepared or uncomfortable working with certain cultural groups. In these cases, it is important to identify and closely examine the sources of those feelings, and to look for ways in which to grow professionally and personally to meet the clients' needs. It is a journey that never ends, but one that needs to start right away.

In summary, being a culturally grounded practitioner means moving beyond awareness by acquiring new knowledge and developing new attitudes and behaviors. In other words, culturally grounded social work requires transformative practice or action. Change does not happen in big increments but is the result of small steps that are carefully assessed from a client-centered perspective. This process, termed *praxis* by Paulo Freire (1970), can be explained as learning by doing. Praxis leads to personal and professional growth and takes place in dialogue with colleagues and clients. In other words, it is a collective process incorporating the following components:

1. Being aware of a need or issue
2. Identifying a practical step to start addressing it
3. Taking a first small step
4. Assessing the outcome and the process with others
5. Celebrating the progress made and identifying the next step

These five action steps can be applied at field units, in social service agencies, or even with a group of social work classmates. Regardless of the setting, praxis requires awareness, the ability to engage in dialogue with others, and the courage to engage in transformative action as well as reflect on those actions. Culturally grounded social work integrates praxis as a natural component of practice.

Key Concepts

Culture an identifiable grouping of shared values, traditions, norms, and customs that guide how people think and behave in a community

Cultural codes the identifiable categories of behaviors or practices repeated over time

Assimilation unidirectional process of letting go of the culture of origin while incorporating fundamental aspects of the majority culture

Acculturation the behavioral and psychological process of adjusting to a non-native culture when two or more cultures come into contact with each other

Enculturation the process of connecting back to the culture of origin or to a renewed version of it

Cultural sensitivity understanding the diversity among clients and communities, and focusing on the cultural gap that exists between the service delivery system and the clients it serves

Cultural competency possession of the knowledge, values, and skills necessary to make services culturally relevant, thereby increasing their effectiveness

Culturally grounded social work practice the combination and utilization of cultural sensitivity and cultural competency in social work practice

Praxis learning by doing, a continuous action-reflection-action process

2

Cultural Diversity, Oppression, and Action: A Culturally Grounded Paradigm

THE OPPRESSION OF NON-MAJORITY GROUPS HAS OCCURRED THROUGH-out the history of the United States. Because the United States is a highly race-conscious society, members of racial and ethnic minorities experience prejudice and discrimination and are often underserved or poorly served by multiple systems. Becoming familiar with the strengths of minority communities allows social workers to partner more effectively with their clients and use those assets to achieve common goals and change oppressive conditions. This chapter provides information on the effects of oppression on members of different cultural groups and how social workers can use a culturally grounded approach to support oppressed communities as they empower themselves and achieve positive social change.

Cultural diversity is not an easy concept to define in part because there is no consensus about which groups should be considered to be contributing diversity to a community or society. For instance, does someone need to belong to a recognizable minority group to be considered a member of a minority cultural community? The use of the term "minority" is controversial as well, in both its accuracy and its implications for power relations. The ethnic diversity of the United States is increasing such that whites of European ancestry will soon be in the numerical minority (Lopez, 2005). Moreover, applying the term "minority" to a group can perpetuate the unequal power structure by implying that the group is the exception and out of the mainstream. However, should each cultural group that differs in some way from the mainstream be viewed as a cultural minority? One could argue that definitions of cultural diversity need to be broad enough to accommodate the wide variations and intersecting identities of those within the majority culture.

Because of the lack of consensus, there is a risk of approaching cultural diversity from an overly narrow or an overly broad perspective. For example, by stressing cultural diversity as opposed to racial or ethnic diversity in a more specific sense, society runs the risk of overlooking crucial issues related to inequality and unequal treatment of ethnic and racial minority groups. On the other hand, if diversity is approached as being based exclusively on traditional racial and ethnic paradigms, there is a risk of excluding many of the expressions of social and cultural diversity that are present in contemporary society. When defined too broadly, cultural diversity can be seen as a superficial pluralistic celebration of variety that overlooks the oppression of cultural minority groups and its consequences. The danger here is that the idea of cultural diversity is reduced to a potpourri of different ethnic group festivals and weekend parades or is watered down to describe groups that share some cultural characteristic or taste, like body piercers or Grateful Dead fans. Such an approach can be seen as throwing the net too widely and grouping too many different people with varied experiences into the cultural minority category. On the other hand, defining cultural minorities exclusively based on racial and ethnic differences may exclude other truly oppressed or disenfranchised groups such as Appalachians or gays and lesbians.

Different approaches to cultural diversity have real consequences for members of minority groups as they influence policy, equity, and access to services and benefits. When difference is defined broadly to encompass every imaginable factor that distinguishes people from one another, there is a risk of diluting key differences, overlooking their societal implications, and overemphasizing less critical factors. For example, Americans of Irish, Polish, and Italian heritage can maintain different elements of their cultural origins through the intergenerational transmission of many cultural practices, such as the use of the ancestral language and traditional foods, celebrations, and ceremonies. Historically, these European American groups have experienced different degrees of prejudice and discrimination, but they are no longer seen as minority groups due to their successful integration and assimilation into the white middle class.

The various sources of cultural identity may also differ in the degree to which they are on display and easily identifiable in social settings. An African American heterosexual professional whom we will call Ralph illustrated this point with the comment "I cannot hang my blackness in the closet." Ralph's concern is that racial oppression and oppression based on sexual orientation are experienced differently, and regarding both racial and sexual orientation groups as cultural minorities can disguise the difference. Ralph recognizes the oppression that the gay community has encountered and continues to encounter but does not feel comfortable equating that experience with the relentless social stress most African American men and women experience in their daily lives. Ralph explains that his race is always apparent when he interacts with others. In contrast, white gay men and white lesbians who do not make their sexual orientation known may be assumed to be from the majority culture. Most African Americans and many Latinos, Native Americans, and Asian Americans seldom experience the default presumption that they are part of the mainstream. How they look, dress, and speak and even their job titles and promotions are often scrutinized. A good criterion to use in identifying these differences is the intensity and frequency with which individuals are targeted for prejudice and discrimination. The more respites an individual can take from prejudice and discrimination, the more privileged she or he is.

Cultural diversity can be viewed as both a source of oppression and a springboard for liberation. The cultural orientation and the oppression or power-based paradigms have significantly increased society's awareness of the experiences of members of different cultural groups.

THE CULTURAL ORIENTATION PARADIGM

The cultural orientation paradigm is based on the premise that cultural differences exist and that becoming familiar with those differences is the solution to any intergroup misunderstandings. Problems emerge when different sets of cultural rules and norms regarding appropriate behavior get in the way of effective communication. In other words, communication is assumed not to be working because either people do not possess sufficient information about a group's norms and expectations or they operate from an ethnocentric point of view and see their perceptions and behaviors as the natural or right ones.

The cultural orientation paradigm views a lack of cultural knowledge as the source of misunderstanding, embarrassment, and anger that occur when others are perceived as acting in ways that are disrespectful, rude, or offensive. The barriers created between majority and minority groups by ethnocentric superiority and privilege often lead to the development of prejudice against groups of people or cultures that are perceived as being different. This prejudice results from the difference between the behavior of the minority group and the cultural rules and norms imposed and regulated by the majority or mainstream cultural group and thus is believed to be the consequence of misunderstanding or lack of affinity, not necessarily a form of intentional mistreatment, discrimination, or oppression.

The cultural orientation paradigm assumes that prejudice disappears once everyone understands that the problems are merely a misunderstanding. According to this framework, the solution to these problems is relatively simple: (1) become aware of the different sets of norms governing various cultural, ethnic, and racial groups; (2) set aside ethnocentric ideas; and then (3) learn each other's cultural rules and standards. These steps provide those participating in cross-cultural interactions with the tools to interpret each other's behavior correctly (Naylor, 1997). From a cultural orientation perspective, knowing each other's rules and standards is the key to eliminating misunderstanding, embarrassment, and anger, as well as to establishing clear communication in the interaction.

In recent years, so-called diversity training has become part of corporate America's lexicon. Cultural diversity training seminars aimed at improving communication between people of different cultural backgrounds are frequently offered in settings traditionally recognized as bastions of white male dominance, such as corporations, universities, and government institutions. These seminars are based on the cultural orientation paradigm, which tends to assume that cultural rules exist at an intellectual level that is easily accessible to both those who live by those rules and outsiders. Diversity training often requires representatives of minority groups to share their experiences and help with this process. In a classroom, for example, the only African American student may be asked to speak for all African Americans and explain to the class what it is like to be black in America. Note from the field 2.1 illustrates how the burden of improving communications and making cultural adjustments can be placed on an ethnic minority organization. The practices carried out by the foundation in this example are perceived by the community-based agency as expressions of cultural colonialism rather than cultural diversity. At the end of the process, not only are the agency's board members tired, frustrated, and angry, but they are unable to access badly needed resources. This example illustrates how cultural knowledge is an asset, whereas cultural ignorance is a shortcoming or deficit. The majority culture and its institutions often do not see the knowledge and expertise of minority communities as a resource or strength. On the contrary, different approaches to acquiring knowledge, expertise, and management and leadership are frequently seen as deficits to be fixed by the imposition of "neutral" or "mainstream" knowledge. For example, knowledge transmitted by way of oral tradition often is not accepted by academics as true or scientific knowledge. In reality, ethnic-specific nongovernmental organizations often have alternative ways of running a board of directors that can be as effective as more traditional white middle-class approaches to governance. If the foundation's program officer in note from the field 2.1 had been truly concerned with helping the agency build its capacity, she would have hired a consultant who was knowledgeable about Latino agencies, not an uninitiated consultant in need of training.

Overall, the cultural orientation paradigm runs the risk of not accounting for social and historical oppression. In other words, the experience of difference is not put into its social, historical, and political context. It does not account for the experiences of those labeled as different and fails to acknowledge the historical roots of existing differences. For example, someone could study cultural diversity from a naïve perspective and admire cultural products without considering the living conditions of those who created them. In contrast, as note from the field 2.2 illustrates, adopting a culturally grounded approach can counteract such cultural ignorance. Concerns such as those raised in note from the field 2.2 can surface in many settings of social work practice. In this case the appropriate community expert was invited to provide guidance in order to lead the integration of culturally specific rituals and helping techniques. Non-Native practitioners who attempt to lead traditional rituals such as talking circles or sweats outside their cultural

NOTE FROM THE FIELD 2.1
We Told You So

A charitable foundation has decided not to fund a grant proposal submitted by a local Latino agency because the agency does not have what it deems a "good" board of directors and strategic plan. The foundation's program officer decides to hire a consultant to help the agency recruit new board members, improve its organizational structure, and engage in a long-range strategic plan. The ultimate goal is for the agency to become more competitive and make itself more attractive to potential funding sources. The consultant is not Latino and has to be educated by the board members about the community's cultural norms and values, as well as the agency's history and culture. After three months and after several long meetings and interviews, the consultant feels very good about the cultural training he has received from the agency. During this time, the consultant has been well paid for his learning, while the agency representatives have not been compensated for the training they have provided. At the end of the training, the board members decide not to apply again to the foundation. They feel frustrated, have a sense that they have been used by the consultant, and are tired of having to explain themselves to the foundation. The foundation has never in its long history given a grant to a Latino agency, and it now views the failure of its strategy to improve the agency as evidence of the agency's problematic operations.

context can engage in a form of cultural colonialism. However, a non-Native practitioner such as Debbie can partner or collaborate with the appropriate community shaman or holy man or woman. Attempts to integrate culturally specific approaches are commendable, but there is a time and a place to do so. Culture and its products are never content or context free. Rather, as practitioners become exposed to other cultures, their interactions, presence, and privilege become part of the cultural diversity experience and the potential for oppression or liberation.

THE OPPRESSION OR POWER-BASED PARADIGM

The oppression or power-based paradigm sees difference as a political phenomenon with power as its central factor. This perspective recognizes that the experience of oppression shapes people's lives. Historically, race has been the most visible and dramatic source of difference, inequality, and oppression in the United States. Indeed, not only was "the problem of the color line" (Du Bois, 1903/1969)

NOTE FROM THE FIELD 2.2
An Integrated Healing System

Debbie is a medical social worker at the health center of a Native American reservation. The clinic is staffed by two physicians, four nurses, and one social worker. The entire professional staff is non-Native, while the great majority of the patients are Native. Debbie learns from some of the elders in a group she facilitates that they would like traditional healing approaches to be integrated with the work being conducted by the staff. The elders invite Mr. Thomas—the shaman in the community—to a group session at the clinic. Debbie realizes that Mr. Thomas has been a patient at the clinic for many years but no one in the professional team has known about his role in the community. In response to an invitation he receives from the clinic director, Mr. Thomas visits with the professional team. After brief introductions, Mr. Thomas suggests that a room that once served as the cafeteria be used as a place where family members can gather to pray and conduct healing ceremonies. The elders have volunteered to participate in decorating the old cafeteria with the help of some of their grandchildren, and Mr. Thomas agrees to lead prayers at the community room with families from remote areas of the reservation who accompany relatives for doctor's visits. Debbie suggests that they explore the possibility of designing a dual referral system. She explains that Mr. Thomas meets many people in need of medical care as he visits community members throughout the reservation, while she as well as the clinic's doctors and nurses often encounter patients who need more than medical care. They conclude the meeting by deciding that the old cafeteria will be transformed into a community room, and Mr. Thomas agrees to attend the next staff meeting in order to brainstorm ideas for the dual referral system.

---

the quintessential problem of the twentieth century, but some have argued that the color line and racism continue to be a major social issue in the twenty-first century (Feagin, 2000). Although the United States is often hailed as a diverse society, it has struggled with oppression and inequality in its past and present, and in ways that are both evident and subtle. The oppression paradigm recognizes these forces and offers a critique of current tendencies to make diversity a broad concept that obscures the centrality of race and ethnicity in the social construction of difference.

Cultural diversity does not exist in a vacuum but is part of a social and political context in which individuals may experience prejudice and discrimination as a result of their cultural minority status. The oppression paradigm approaches cultural diversity as an issue of politics and justice and recognizes differences as a resource in an increasingly global economy. For example, the sociologist Orlando Patterson (2003) has argued that when addressing issues of diversity, we should emphasize ethnic and racial categorization instead of using all-encompassing cultural diversity categories. He recommends that affirmative action should be targeted to avoid an overly broad and all-inclusive cultural diversity approach and remain faithful to its original goal of racial integration in all areas of public and private life.

A counterargument to Patterson's thought-provoking stance is that American society has radically changed since affirmative action was originally instituted nearly four decades ago (Girves, Zepeda, & Gwathmey, 2005). While the original race-based focus of affirmative action continues to be needed today, there are other cultural diversity factors that need to be addressed at the same time. An alternative example of the social construction of difference is the belief that men provide the social norm to which women should adjust. Although it is important from an oppression perspective to recognize that not all minority identities encounter the same kind or amount of oppression, there is a need for a broader representation of gender identities around the cultural diversity table. This breadth is especially important in dealing with dichotomies like white/black, male/female, heterosexual/homosexual, and normal/other, which, by placing those viewed as "other" in inferior positions, lead to their experience of oppression. It is for this reason that identifying oppressive conditions and working with the oppressed toward change have historically been priorities for social work. The social construction of difference can be likened to an orchard with many types of fruit trees, where the fruitful branches of different cultures become interconnected. The soil in which the trees are planted is the social and cultural context. The irrigation system does not reach each group of trees equally, and each tree reacts to the overabundance or scarcity of water. Lack of water weakens some trees and prevents them from bearing fruit. The keeper of the orchard (society and its institutions) first attempts to correct these wrongs by identifying whole groups of trees that have been consistently deprived of the water they need to bear fruit. The keeper's second step is to guarantee that all trees have an equal opportunity to access water.

For some cultural groups, lack of water in the orchard is akin to difficult social conditions that impede advancement, such as lack of jobs, good schools, or decent housing, all of which fall under the broad definition of oppression. The cultural diversity approach recognizes oppression as a key factor in understanding and addressing inequality between groups. Leaving oppression out of the diversity equation may lead to a romantic or superficial view of difference that cannot address the real needs of individuals, groups, and communities.

OPPRESSION

Paulo Freire (1970) defined oppression as human beings' perverse tendency to deprive others of freedom and happiness. In a capitalist society, oppression often manifests itself as the deprivation among certain groups of needed material resources. Some scholars, however, have argued that the opposite of poverty is not wealth but power, so the main issue in the broader social analysis of poverty is not merely economics but empowerment (Steidlmeier, 1993). For example, because empowerment is the primary issue underlying female poverty, micro approaches to dealing with the problem have produced only limited improvements. The well-publicized "micro loans" program developed in Bangladesh provides women with very small loans to establish home- and village-based businesses that make and sell textiles, crafts, and agricultural products. Micro loans have encountered some criticism because in some instances they provide funding but do not address the other resources that women in developing countries need to overcome their oppression. Critics recommend that to adequately address the problem and produce lasting changes, issues of patriarchy, abuse, and discrimination against women and macro-level reforms need to be considered (Rice, 2001).

For oppression to exist, two basic ingredients are needed: a group that is being oppressed and an oppressor who benefits from such oppression. In the process of oppression, the oppressors externalize their fears by projecting them onto those people who most seem to fit the category of the "other" (Moraga, 2004). The oppressed are perceived as socially and morally deficient or as a pathology afflicting an otherwise healthy society (Freire, 1994). The Jewish holocaust—an extreme example of oppression—was preceded by a two-year extermination program of about 50,000 mostly non-Jewish psychiatric patients, who were granted a "mercy death" under the National Socialist "euthanasia program" (Szasz, 1970, p. 314). Hitler also contemplated adopting health regulations under which physically ill people, especially those with diseased hearts and lungs, would no longer be allowed to reproduce or circulate freely in public. Such oppression has been described as the experience of "being caged in: all avenues, in every direction, are blocked or booby trapped" (Frye, 2003, p. 49). The ultimate outcome of oppression, as was amply demonstrated in Nazi Germany, is the dehumanization of both the oppressed and the oppressor.

Although the Nazi regime is an extreme example of oppression, the tendency of seemingly ordinary people in positions of power to act in barbarous ways toward subordinates has been well documented in social psychology experiments. For example, the classic mock prison experiment at Stanford University in which students were assigned at random to prisoner and guard roles had to be halted prematurely when guards began to treat their prisoners in an increasingly dehumanizing and violent manner (Zimbardo, 1971). Revelations that U.S. military guards subjected Iraqi detainees to sexual degradation and torture at the Abu Ghraib prison in Baghdad provide a more recent reminder that people are more likely to treat others in an inhumane fashion (and enjoy doing so), and that this behavior is more likely to be tolerated by others, when those being subjected to such treatment are those labeled the despised "other."

The placement of groups into the category of "other," however, is relative. Some oppressed groups may have more power than another group and may become that group's oppressor. For example, in schools with many immigrant students, those who already speak English fluently may ridicule more recent immigrants who do not. This can occur as a result of *deculturalization,* or denial of one's culture or identity, and can threaten the healthy development of the individual and the community (Fisher & Sonn, 2003). This sometimes happens when oppressed individuals fall into what Freire (1994) calls internalized oppression or a state of self-hate. At the personal level, internalized oppression can be experienced as stress, guilt, stigma, and shame. Note from the field 2.3 provides an example of a gay man who has suffered the consequences of homophobia and has internalized that oppression. Art appears to have internalized the homophobia he encountered while growing up and still perceives. He tries to enforce a form of strict behavioral heterosexism on himself and others, a form of constant role-playing. He pretends to be heterosexual in his most meaningful relationships and is looking for a same-sex partner who is willing to do the same. He is appropriat-

NOTE FROM THE FIELD 2.3
Why Can't I Find Mr. Right?

Art is a twenty-nine-year-old gay man who comes to a counseling session to discuss his difficulties finding the right partner. He has not dated since he graduated from college seven years ago. He states that all the available men he meets at social gatherings and clubs are "very out" or "too flamboyant" for him. He does not like to go out with men who might be recognized as gay or who are active in gay organizations. He is looking for a "straight-acting" and "straight-looking" partner like himself. Art believes that his parents, siblings, and coworkers do not know he is gay, and he would like to keep it that way. He states, "It is none of their business; they don't tell me who they go to bed with." He has tried online personal ads and dating services without success. He feels lonely and is concerned about turning thirty and not having a partner. He expresses repeatedly his frustration about not being able to find Mr. Right. He is having problems sleeping and often feels irritable.

ing attitudes and behaviors that oppress him and in turn uses them to avoid getting close to other gay men.

Internalized oppression can be also experienced by members of ethnic or racial minority groups. An individual who experiences racism and internalizes such oppression can in turn discriminate against other people based on their ethnic background. For example, Dolores, a Puerto Rican homemaker, does not like to send her children to a Puerto Rican dentist whose office is around the corner from her apartment building and instead drives them to see Dr. Cook, a European American dentist. She says that Anglo dentists are better than Puerto Rican dentists. She has internalized the prejudice she has experienced as a Puerto Rican woman. Instead of challenging the stereotype, she internalizes the message and perpetuates it.

What role can a social worker play in these cases? Helping the client understand why this way of thinking is important to her or him is a necessary first step. Internalized oppression and deculturalization can have negative effects on the person experiencing them. Internalized oppression can result in the rejection of oneself as well as the rejection of others. For Art, not accepting himself and trying to fit the heterosexual mold every hour of the day are very stressful, as evidenced by his irritability and trouble sleeping. His lack of self-acceptance can create distance between himself and those who love him. Moreover, how can an intimate gay relationship be formed when the identity that brings together the two men is denied, rejected, or repressed?

ACTION AS LIBERATION

The groups and individuals who experience the widespread negative effects of oppression can use different mechanisms to resist oppression. Freire (1970) argued that an oppressed individual cannot liberate her- or himself in isolation. Oppressed individuals can only liberate themselves with others, as a group or as a community. Oppressed individuals, groups, and communities can reach empowerment through a collective process of freeing themselves from the conditions that dehumanize them. This process of liberation must occur for both those who are deprived of opportunities to advance socially and those obstructing that advancement. In his seminal book *Pedagogy of the Oppressed*, Freire proposed education as the path to permanent liberation: first individuals must become aware (conscious) of their own oppression and then through praxis (which encompasses self-determination, creativity, and rationality) change that state of oppression. For instance, the gay liberation movement could only become a significant social force when individuals who had historically been isolated as a result of their sexual orientation came together. They formed communities where they could experience a sense of belonging and interact without the threat of persecution and discrimination and then went on to organize to change attitudes and policies.

Social work as a field has a historical commitment to supporting communities in their move toward liberation. However, as social work becomes more professionalized and depends more on state and private funding, its allegiance to the oppressed may become less clear. Social workers are called on to be vigilant about their allegiance and commitment to the poor and the oppressed. Social workers practice in partnership with people who have been silenced and isolated, helping them regain a voice in the decisions that affect their lives. However, some social work theorists have argued that change will not occur until social workers are able to connect the problems of clients who are members of oppressed groups to the roots of their oppression (Vodde & Gallant, 2002).

Liberating social work practice uses policy challenge as a tool for liberation. Social workers are called on to move beyond social service delivery and be involved at the macro level in the design and funding of social services for the poor and oppressed. Engaging only in micro-level practice limits the profession's ability to effect systemic change. On the other hand, ignoring micro-level practice would neglect the individual and family needs of communities. A culturally grounded approach to social work aims at achieving a balance between the micro and macro levels of practice in partnership with oppressed communities.

CHALLENGES TO ACTION: STEREOTYPES, PREJUDICE, AND DISCRIMINATION

Stereotypes

Change and the creation of a more just society can be challenged by oppressive policies, which are often based on stereotypes. Stereotypes are beliefs that individuals hold about members of a group based on generalizations about the characteristics of all members of that group. Although it is common to think that only bigoted people use stereotypes, the truth is that everyone uses them, often without knowing it. Humans have the need to belong to a group, and the tendency to see the members of their group as individuals, and the members of out-groups as undifferentiated. Thus, stereotypes emerge from in-group/out-group dynamics. Group identification can exaggerate the social distance between members of different groups and affect individuals' perceptions of others as well as their psychological well-being (Sharlin & Moin, 2001).

Once individuals are exposed to the societal stereotypes attached to a particular group, they tend to perceive individual members of that group according to those generalizations, focusing on the parts of the stereotype that they can make fit the person and deemphasizing aspects of the person that do not fit the stereotype. They see themselves and those like them as unique and as individual personalities, while seeing members of the stereotyped out-group as undifferentiated from each other—as if they share all the same traits (Hilton & von Hippel, 1996). The insider-outsider divide makes one's own group behavior and beliefs seem natural, normal, appropriate, or morally correct, while the other group's behaviors are viewed as unusual, unnatural, peculiar, deviant, or even immoral. Stereotypes often attach negative traits to members of the out-group. Once they are learned, they become part of society's cosmology and permeate most social interactions.

Besides being overly simplistic and often highly exaggerated, ethnic and gender stereotypes are usually learned secondhand—through a process of labeling and social learning—in our interactions with agents of socialization like family and school. Negative racial and ethnic stereotypes held by teachers and students have been shown to disrupt the academic functioning of African American and Latino students, both by leading ethnic minority students to question the value of academic achievement and by undermining their academic self-confidence (Ogbu, 1992). This is a reciprocal process: low academic achievement among some ethnic minority students has been linked to stereotypes (Crocker & Knight, 2005), and stereotypes feed prejudice and provide an explanation or rationale for students' low achievement and the schools' failure to address it.

Exaggerated stereotypes have long been used in television commercials and print ads to get attention, increase recall, and foster identification with products and services. One of the most effective methods is to portray the stereotype humorously, which not only uses entertainment to hold the viewer's attention but also softens the message by seeming to suggest that the stereotype is not meant to be taken seriously. Stereotypes in advertising abound, and it might be said that they make fun of all groups—even white heterosexual males. Straight white men are sometimes portrayed as obsessed with sports and inept at household tasks. To get by in life, they need the forbearance and common sense of their more knowledgeable and skillful spouses and children.

Stereotypes of African Americans have come a long way from the subservient Aunt Jemima and Uncle Ben. In contemporary commercials, media watchers have noted the emergence of a new stereotype: the heavy black woman who is verbally assertive, impatient with annoyances, and controlling—even someone who is aggressive or physically intimidating in interactions with family members and strangers (Givens & Monahan, 2005). Although the African American women in these commercials are presented humorously, critics contend that the stereotypes reflect the views of their white creators on Madison Avenue, and that people laugh at the stereotypes for different reasons (Creedon & Cramer, 2006). White viewers may laugh at the outrageousness of the portrayal, in part because they know that their own cultural group is not like that. African Americans may also laugh because they can identify with aspects of the portrayal. Although openly negative racial stereotypes are rare in today's advertising, the question remains how much these subtle messages continue to influence how cultural minority groups are perceived.

Prejudice

Prejudice is an irrational and unsubstantiated negative feeling toward members of different cultural groups, such as racial and ethnic groups, women, gays and lesbians, people with disabilities, and certain religious groups, that generates stereotypes about those groups.

According to contemporary theories of prejudice, people are reluctant to voice prejudicial attitudes unless they can do so in ways so that their views or criticisms cannot be attributed to race, thereby keeping intact the perception that they are fair and unprejudiced. For example, an undocumented Mexican immigrant in the United States has by definition engaged in illegal activity and may therefore face discrimination that is justified as being "anti-crime" rather than "anti-Mexican" (Magana & Short, 2002). However, ethnic prejudice that surrounds the issue of illegal immigration is illustrated by the round-up campaigns conducted by agents of the former Immigration and Naturalization Service, now known as the U.S. Citizenship and Immigration Service, that often target "Mexican-looking" permanent residents and American citizens. Ethnic profiling has been identified as one of the main explanations for the overrepresentation of ethnic minorities among drivers stopped by traffic police around the nation (Birzer & Birzer, 2006).

Scapegoating and projection are two processes that lead to prejudice. Scapegoating occurs when a group or individual blames others for a problem for which they are not responsible. The group or individual takes out feelings of frustration on someone other than the true source of the frustration; this someone is often a member of the out-group. Those looking for a scapegoat believe that they are society's victims and as such are being abused, whereas the scapegoat is usually incapable of offering resistance to such accusations. The most likely targets of scapegoating are people with no power, such as immigrants who have not been naturalized and cannot vote (Magana & Short, 2002).

Projection is a process through which people minimize or deny undesirable characteristics that they possess by exaggerating the same characteristics in someone from the out-group. In general, individuals have a tendency to emphasize the positive when describing themselves and those close to them. The differentiation hypothesis assumes that people look for differences between themselves and others and then balance their need for uniqueness and similarities by projecting positively onto the in-group and negatively onto the out-group (Clement & Krueger, 2002). Projection is an attempt to secure one's identity by excluding, avoiding, or eliminating the other. The deficiencies of the individual or group doing the projecting do not have to be acknowledged because these deficiencies are transferred to members of an out-group; thus projection is used to perpetuate racism, sexism, homophobia, and other prejudices.

Social work can help reduce racial and ethnic prejudice through its involvement in policy change at the macro level and through different strategies at the micro level, including persuasive communication, education, intergroup contact, simulation and experiential exercises, and therapy (Farley, 2000). Persuasive communication is a direct attempt to influence beliefs and behaviors. Through education, social workers can disseminate information to break down incorrect stereotypes. Intergroup contact shows people that the stereotypes they hold about outgroups are unfounded. Simulation and experiential exercises allow members of the majority group to experience discrimination and the feelings associated with it. Therapy is recommended only when prejudice is rooted in deep personality needs, in other words, when prejudice consumes the thoughts and emotions of an individual.

Discrimination

Discrimination is the unequal treatment of individuals based on their group membership rather than their individual qualities. Discrimination is not an individual behavior that occurs in isolation, but the expression of a system of social relations and beliefs. Discrimination involves actions by a dominant group that are harmful to the members of the subordinate group.

Discriminatory actions can vary in severity from minor to more serious forms that carry greater injury and involve exclusion from the economic, social, and political realms of society. Discrimination can range from the use of derogatory labels and pejorative ethnic references to the denial of access to housing, health, education, and justice and the use of violence against individuals or groups. An overt act of hatred perpetrated by one person toward another person due to the latter's group membership is individual discrimination. Institutional discrimination is less overt and occurs when institutions are organized in a manner that allows some privileged people to maintain an advantage over others based on group membership. Employers may rely on racist and ethnic stereotypes about the work aptitude and motivation of ethnic minorities to deny them jobs or promotions without fully considering their individual merits and qualifications. Institutional discrimination can also be an inherent part of organizational structures, such as the elaborate personnel systems and complex hierarchies of job titles that keep women from advancing in the workplace and from being fairly compensated for their work (Bielby & Baron, 1984).

Group distinctiveness is sometimes achieved when the opportunities of groups and their members are protected in ways that exclude outsiders. For example, before laws were passed to outlaw this practice, there were social and recreational clubs in the United States that did not permit African Americans and Jews to join. People who belonged to these clubs often saw this as a symbol of the clubs' respectability and social prominence, and their membership thus ensured their own respectability and social prominence.

A Culturally Grounded Paradigm

A culturally grounded approach to social work practice calls for the acquired knowledge of the roots of stereotypes, prejudice, and discrimination to be applied in context. The social worker must assess the context, or environment, for prejudice and discrimination and develop an action plan accordingly. A practitioner using a culturally grounded approach addresses oppressive conditions effectively by moving beyond the levels of practice debate and recognizing the importance of micro-, mezzo-, and macropractice as multilayered and interconnected approaches to empowerment. Inherent in this framework are several important tenets for praxis. First, the choice of intervention type is not determined by the worker's level of comfort but instead by what feels most natural to clients from their cultural perspective and what will yield the best outcomes while using the fewest resources. Therefore, the choice of any practice intervention is driven by concerns about good fit and effectiveness. Second, interventions are chosen because the change they produce is sustainable once the social worker is no longer engaged with the individual, family, group, or community. Interventions that feel strange or uncomfortable to clients will most likely not survive the test of time and will not be conducive to empowerment. Third, interventions are selected according to evidence-based research, and their implementation is closely evaluated for applicability, fidelity, and effectiveness. Formal research and innovation by the social worker facilitate the constant retooling needed for practice in an ever-changing society.

The culturally grounded approach views clients as experts and partners of theorists and helping professionals. Their joint efforts facilitate effective and ethical social work practice and result in the highest levels of client satisfaction. Note from the field 2.4 illustrates the need for practitioners to assess their own behavior and its impact on their clients, and how a lack of cultural attunement may be interpreted as prejudice. Arlene reached out to a cultural expert for help and was able to develop a culturally grounded explanation for the behavior she noticed among some of her clients. In supervision and through other confirmatory sources, she can test the explanation she received from Ms. Martinez and implement the appropriate corrective action.

Cultural misunderstandings and actual discriminatory practices affect the client's access to quality services. The ongoing delivery of equitable and effective services is at the core of continuous professional self-assessment, which examines attitudes and behaviors in addition to awareness. This process requires a constant examination of the professional and personal self and perceptions of and interac-

---

NOTE FROM THE FIELD 2.4
Don't You Like My Kids?

Arlene is in the first semester of her social work practicum. She has been assigned to a prenatal clinic and enjoys working with the mothers and children the nurses and doctors refer to her. Her role is to conduct psychosocial assessments of new patients and assess for assets and possible barriers to compliance with the regime of prenatal and postpartum visits. She has noticed that some of the Mexican mothers appear to be a bit distant with her. She decides to ask one of her clients, Ms. Martinez, about her perception. Ms. Martinez explains that some of the mothers are concerned by the fact that Arlene never touches their children, even when greeting them, which they interpret as meaning that their children are not worthy of warmth and affection or that Arlene thinks they are dirty. Ms. Martinez explains that some of the mothers expect her to touch their children's heads as if in a *bendición* (blessing).

---

tions with clients. This form of professional praxis greatly benefits from group and individual professional supervision and from ongoing dialogue with clients.

Key Concepts

Oppression the denial of an individual or group of people's freedom, happiness, and access to resources by another

Deculturalization the denial of one's culture or identity resulting from the internalization of oppression

Stereotypes the beliefs that individuals hold about members of a group based on overgeneralizations about the characteristics of all members of that group

Prejudice the irrational sense of dislike that individuals or groups experience toward members of different cultural groups

Scapegoating blaming and taking out feelings of frustration on someone other than the true source of one's frustration

Projection the process through which people minimize or deny undesirable characteristics that they possess by exaggerating the same characteristics in someone from a different cultural group

Discrimination the unequal treatment of individuals based on their membership in a particular cultural group, rather than on their individual qualities

3

The Intersectionality of Race and Ethnicity with Other Factors

INDIVIDUAL IDENTITY DEVELOPS BASED ON NUMEROUS WAYS IN WHICH people differ, such as along the lines of gender, race, ethnicity, sexual orientation, religion, ability status, and social class. The way in which these factors are weighted and how they intersect in a person's life may create disadvantages or privileges for her or him. It is important for social work professionals to understand that an individual's identity cannot be easily defined by just one factor. In most cases, a variety of factors contribute to an individual's sense of identity. This chapter provides general information on intersectionality and its effects on individuals in society and how social workers can use this knowledge to work effectively with members of various cultural groups.

INTERSECTIONALITY

The term "intersectionality" refers to the multidimensionality and complexity of the human cultural experience and describes the place where multiple identities come together, or intersect. Individuals hold positions within multiple systems of inequality based on race, ethnicity, gender, social class, sexual orientation, age, and ability status, and particular sets of identities carry important social implications. For example, issues of race and gender oppression cut across social class lines. Women experience sexism—stereotyping, male dominance, and discrimination—regardless of their education and abilities and how well they are paid for their work, while men from racial minority groups retain privileges afforded to them in a sexist society. Such intersections of race and gender lead to a variety of experiences and opportunities for different individuals, producing outcomes that may reflect an accumulation of social advantages or disadvantages. Collins (1998) described the intersection of race, gender, and social class as constituting a "matrix of domination." Within this matrix, individuals may experience disadvantage or privilege as a result of their combination of identities. Ethnic minority women may face "double jeopardy" due to the combined disadvantages of their gender and their ethnic background and may be relegated to the most devalued occupations and jobs. Ethnic minority and poor immigrant women make up the vast majority of household domestic workers, who rank as the lowest-paid occupational group in the United States. In contrast, white women are much more likely to attain white-collar positions and typically are the middle- or upper-class employers of these women (Hondagneu-Sotelo, 2001).

Increasing recognition of the intersectionality of identities has prompted extensive research on its social implications. The existence of multiple systems of inequality suggests that the social world cannot be easily divided into oppressors and the oppressed. For example, white males, who exemplify privilege in U.S. society, are quite diverse as a group, with their own within-group variations in terms of privilege. Substantial numbers of white males live out their lives in the working class, suffering economic exploitation and bearing greater occupational risks to their health than white men in higher social classes. White gay men and those with disabilities are often denied the full range of benefits that white heterosexual and able male privilege brings to other men.

Research on intersectionality has demonstrated that different systems of inequality are interconnected (Anderson & Collins, 2004). For example, African American lesbians face "triple jeopardy" because they simultaneously occupy disadvantaged positions in social hierarchies based on gender, race, and sexual orientation. Despite the identities they share with other oppressed groups like white lesbians and heterosexual African American women, African American lesbians have struggled to gain visibility and influence within the feminist, gay, and black liberation movements (Diamond & Savin-Williams, 2000). All too often these groups strive for liberation in isolation or at cross-purposes from one another and without recognizing areas where they may enjoy privilege that other groups do not. Moreover, conflict and dissension among oppressed groups can be instigated by the majority groups in power, which diverts attention from the underlying systems of privilege.

In the history of the United States, a succession of immigrant ethnic groups have been blamed for the economic ills plaguing the U.S.-born working class and become the targets of officially sanctioned discrimination. During an economic depression in 1893, strong opposition emerged against the admittance of immigrants from Italy, and Italians were suddenly regarded as paupers. Similarly, Chinese immigrants, who were originally welcomed as "honest," "peaceful," and "industrious," came to be perceived as "dangerous," "vicious," and "deceitful" when jobs became scarce and the Chinese started to seek work in mines and factories and on farms (Levin & Levin, 1982). During the late nineteenth century, when cotton prices declined in the South, there was an increase in the number of lynchings of African Americans (Behrens, Uggen, & Manza, 2003). More recently, in the 1980s, an anti-immigrant movement in California was renewed and consolidated during an economic slowdown. Disempowered Mexican immigrants working predominantly in minimum-wage jobs that few U.S.-born individuals would accept were viewed by some as responsible for the economic ills of the entire state of California.

The social implications of intersectionality, like the systems of inequality they are based on, are constantly changing. The civil rights and women's movements have produced important changes in racial and gender relations, but these successes have also helped to alter the issues in contention. The history of affirmative action is a case in point. Established in the late 1960s and early 1970s to take steps beyond the elimination of open discrimination, affirmative action actively promoted racial and gender equity in employment, government contracting, and educational access. In recent years, societal debates and legal action concerning affirmative action have been focused on the use of race and ethnicity in the criteria for admission to colleges and universities. The ensuing controversies have revealed a growing awareness of multiple systems of inequality, particularly the intersections of race, ethnicity, and social class.

Arguments against affirmative action have frequently centered on its alleged failure to provide protection and assistance to those most in need and the alleged harm inflicted on others through "reverse discrimination." Some critics of affirmative action have portrayed its beneficiaries as mostly ethnic minorities from middle- and upper-class families who do not need help as much as lower-class African Americans and Latinos or equally needy low-income whites. Debate over differences in levels of need and the application of affirmative action to ethnic minority groups, such as the exclusion of Asian Americans from affirmative action and the higher educational achievement of Afro-Caribbean students than of African American students, has also arisen. This issue highlights the significant within-group diversity that exists within large racial categories. Note from the field 3.1 provides an example of multiethnic and multiracial identities. Manuel's story highlights the complexity of intersecting identities and illustrates how discrete ethnic and racial categories may not apply to some individuals.

SOCIAL CLASS

Societies throughout history have been organized into social classes. Although there are differences among societies in the degree of opportunity for upward mobility, such social stratification is ubiquitous. Even societies that undergo bloody revolutions to effect a rapid change in social structure often merely substitute one social class system for another. For example, under the official egalitarian ideology of Communist countries like the former Soviet Union, China, and Cuba, de facto social classes existed, allowing the small elite to enjoy privileges derived from their membership in the ruling party or close association with its members rather than from inheritance.

Class is a powerful force in U.S. society, although it is not always as well

> ## NOTE FROM THE FIELD 3.1
> ### Who Is Manuel?
>
> When asked about his race, Manuel Silva self-identifies as a black man and honors his African ancestry, but culturally he also recognizes his Puerto Rican–Latino background, his Roman Catholic faith, and his Taino (indigenous) roots. Manuel's identity and social experiences emerge from the intersection of all those identities. Depending on his environment, he may stress a certain identity more than others. On the U.S. mainland, Manuel is often defined racially by others based on his physical appearance rather than his multiple cultural roots. Others' definitions of who he is often overlook Manuel's intersectionalities and multiple sources of identity. When Manuel applies for a job with the city government, he asks his social worker which race/ethnicity category he should mark on the application form. The form allows for only one choice under race/ethnicity. Because he would like to recognize all his cultural heritages, he is thinking about choosing "other."

recognized as many other forms of oppression and discrimination. Dividing lines between social classes in the United States are fluid, somewhat flexible, and often hidden. Rather than a rigid class hierarchy, the U.S. social class system is rooted in a triad of interconnected socioeconomic differences in income, education, and occupational status. Income, education, and the prestige of one's occupation determine an individual's position in the social hierarchy (and its associated privileges or disadvantages) and have wide-ranging implications for cultural identities, as differences in income, education, and occupational status are systematically associated with gender, race, ethnicity, ability status, and other cultural identities.

People do not choose their social class. Members of the poor and working classes are limited by the opportunities afforded or denied by capitalism and its controlling profit motive. Political elites, the mass media, and the education system frequently promote the idea that U.S. society is a meritocracy, where rewards are allocated based on individual merit alone. However, the uneven playing field of social class gives crucial advantages to those from privileged backgrounds. Our education system is, in fact, a prime example of class-based inequities. School districts, and even the schools within them, vary enormously in terms of the adequacy of building facilities and equipment, teacher preparation and pay, class sizes, range of academic offerings, and quality of instruction. School financing through local property taxes and the residential segregation of the poor ensure that families from higher social classes are able to transfer their wealth directly into better schools for their children. These children also benefit from cultural capital, such as their parents' better educational preparation, high educational aspirations, knowledge of educational options and purchasing power, and more extensive social networks that help them locate the "best" schools. Meanwhile, families from poor neighborhoods struggle to afford even basic education, and their modest incomes and property values limit the taxable resources that are available to support local public schools.

Overall, social class governs many of the life chances that determine opportunities for a long life and decent quality of living. The impact of social class on life chances was exemplified quite literally in 1912 when the *Titanic* sank. Only 25 percent of the third-class passengers survived, but 60 percent of the first-class passengers were rescued. Most of the passengers in first class were American or British, while most of the third-class passengers who perished were emigrating from Europe to the United States (Hanley, Turner, Bellera, & Telsch, 2003).

In the United States today, there is a persisting gap between the upper and lower classes' access to a college education. Statistics from the National Student Loan Program comparing families in the top income quartile to those in the bottom quartile (that is, the quarter of the population earning the most versus the quarter earning the least) show that whereas around 90 percent of children from the most affluent families attend college, barely half of those from the least affluent families do so, and this gap shows signs of widening rather than closing (Price, 2004). Students from families in the top income quartile are seven times more likely to complete a college degree than those from families at the bottom income quartile. Moreover, contrary to the ethos of the meritocracy, a student's socioeconomic background has been found to be a more important factor in whether she or he attends college than the student's educational ability (Berliner, 2006). Although it is a common perception that the United States is a classless society, recent trends in the income distribution suggest that wealth and influence are becoming more concentrated in the hands of a small elite. Economic analyses have demonstrated that the top 1 percent of income earners in 2003 reaped over a third of all of the nation's total gains in income that year, and they accounted for over half of those gains in 2004. On the other hand, the average person in the remaining 99 percent of the population had earnings gains of only 1.5 percent in 2004 (Aron-Dine & Shapiro, 2006; Piketty & Saez, 2003). The belief that well-educated people are making major advances socioeconomically (a characteristic of a meritocracy) is also challenged by the data. For example, U.S. census data show that real incomes for college graduates—adjusted for inflation—actually fell in 2004 (Baum & Payea, 2005).

These sharp socioeconomic differences are powerful evidence of the importance of social class in the perpetuation of inequalities in the United States. For many cultural groups whose opportunities for social and economic mobility have historically been blocked or thwarted, problems of socioeconomic inequality remain an acute challenge to their well-being.

GENDER

The United States as a society was profoundly shaped by eighteenth-century European American men who resisted or gave little thought to empowering others. Women continue to be a group that struggles to gain a place at the table of equality. Although they constitute a slight numerical majority, women remain a sociological minority in the United States, as they do in most other societies. Indeed, gender equality has yet to be achieved in many important ways. For instance, women are paid less than men for doing the same jobs. Women who are the head of their households are more likely to live below poverty levels, and they are still primarily responsible for child care even when they have a partner and are employed full-time (McKernan & Ratcliffe, 2005).

Many women dwell on the periphery of society, on the lower rungs of social and institutional hierarchies, and in positions where they face oppression. This oppression is maintained in part by cultural norms that specify appropriate roles for men and women. Men are socialized to be family providers and leaders and are provided relatively clear guidelines about how to combine occupational and family roles, while women receive mixed messages about these same roles. Male roles are associated with highly valued characteristics like authority, strength, and decisiveness, while women's roles emphasize nurturance and caring, which are judged as having lesser value (O'Brien, Peyton, Mistry, Hruda, Jacobs, Caldera, et al., 2000).

The persisting gender gap in wages makes it difficult for many women to manage financially as heads of households. This gender wage gap is perpetuated by employers' beliefs that women need to devote more of their energy to child care and family demands than men do; as a result, employers often do not consider women viable candidates for certain leadership positions. This perception thus decreases women's chances of securing the jobs with the most responsibility, authority, and remuneration. Among some minority ethnic and religious groups, education for women is still considered inappropriate, a waste of precious family resources best reserved for males. In many contemporary societies, women remain financially dependent on men because social taboos prevent them from accessing education and employment outside the home.

In societies like the United States, where women are highly involved in the labor force, they generally are relegated to less lucrative occupations and professions. As organizational management emerged as a distinct professional field in the early twentieth century, many of its defining characteristics were imbued with a masculine ethic. Men established their privileged status by describing rationality and reason, a tough-minded approach to problems, and the analytic capability to abstract and plan (all of which were viewed as male characteristics) and the ability to set aside distinctly "feminine" personal, sentimental, and emotional considerations as the essential traits of the effective manager (Kanter, 1977).

Some feminists argue that the traditional Western family, with its authoritarian adult male rule, is the training ground that initially conditions individuals to accept group oppression as the natural order (Hooks, 1984). Patriarchy has taken different shapes in different cultural subgroups and social classes but has mostly survived, if not been strengthened, over time.

One source of the power of systems of gender privilege and inequality is the idea that gender divides people in a fundamental and innate way into two clearly distinct groups. Although this idea is still largely taken for granted, there is growing evidence and recognition that gender is not a dichotomous characteristic. This fact is amply demonstrated by the existence of a transgender community, which, although traditionally grouped with gays, lesbians, and bisexuals, does not constitute a sexual orientation group but rather a gender group. Although definitions are evolving, the term "transgender" is used increasingly to refer to a spectrum of gender identities that include pre- and post-operative transsexuals (those who have gone through or will undergo sexual reassignment), a large group of transvestites and cross-dressers, and a growing population of people who identify as intersex or as not fitting any traditional notions of gender.

SEXUAL ORIENTATION

The privilege accorded to a heterosexual orientation is based on a belief system that views heterosexuality as superior and more natural than homosexuality or bisexuality. Heterosexism is a form of discrimination that reinforces systems that place non-heterosexuals in marginalized social and political positions. Heterosexism is a means of exerting social control through intimidation and exclusion. It is a way for heterosexuals to retain social positions that are widely agreed to be superior to those held by lesbians, gay men, bisexuals, and other queers. Heterosexual privilege is based on the unexamined assumption that heterosexuality is the norm and all other sexual orientations are deviations from it. Heterosexuals do not have to make public their sexual identify or come out. In contrast, gays, lesbians, bisexuals, and transgender people are part of a minority group. As a result, they are sometimes the target of homophobia (irrational fear of and aversion to sexual minorities), which is often expressed through discrimination and violence. Although the repression experienced by sexual minorities makes it difficult to obtain representative samples of them, studies of hate crimes and violent victimization suggest that a very large percentage of the gay, lesbian, bisexual, and transgender (GLBT) community is victimized by assault, vandalism, and theft. Unlike most violent crime in general, most of the crime prompted by homophobia is perpetrated by strangers rather than acquaintances (Herek, Cogan, & Gillis, 2002).

In addition, members of the GLBT community experience many legal disadvantages. In the United States, as in many other countries, they still have not been awarded equal rights in the areas of immigration, adoption, marriage, and inheritance. In old age, they face unequal treatment under Social Security (e.g., no rights to share a partner's benefits), housing discrimination, and discriminatory practices in health care and long-term care. For example, if a gay man is hospitalized, the hospital may bar his partner from visiting because he is not considered a family member. Moreover, same-sex partners may not make legally binding decisions about treatment or care for their partners when their partners are unable to. There are no federal protections for same-sex couples, and levels of protection vary greatly from state to state and municipality to municipality.

Historically, policies and laws have been used more often to oppress sexual minorities than to protect them. For example, in 1951 the U.S. Civil Service Commission, in a document entitled *Employment of Homosexuals and Other Sex Perverts in Government*, forbade the employment of homosexuals in government. One year later, the McCarran Act's categorization of homosexuality as a psychopathic personality barred them from entering the United States. The act also allowed for the deportation of alien (non-citizen) homosexuals, even those who had been living in the country for several years. Throughout most of the twentieth century, many forms of homosexual sexual behavior were explicitly outlawed in state constitutions, usually in the form of anti-sodomy laws. It was not until 1974 that the American Psychiatric Association removed homosexuality from its list of pathological diagnoses, and not until the U.S. Supreme Court's 2003 ruling in *Lawrence & Garner v. State of Texas* that remaining statutes outlawing specifically anti-homosexual conduct were ruled unconstitutional.

These government statutes were generally a rejection of male homosexuality. The process of gay liberation has also often emphasized a male gay culture while silencing or deemphasizing lesbian feminism and many other forms of gay life and identity. It is not surprising, then, that much of what social work knows about the GLBT community is based on white, middle-class male homosexuality and homosexual communities.

Oppression based on sexual orientation can intersect in complex ways with many other identities. Social workers may be unprepared if called upon to work with clients who do not fit the stereotype of the white, well-off gay man. An occupationally successful lesbian client may be entangled in a relationship with a physically abusive female partner. An African American man might be referred for the stressful and health-threatening consequences of the double life that he leads as a heterosexual married man who has anonymous sex with other men. A working-class lesbian mother may be struggling to avoid losing custody of her children to an ex-husband who says her sexual orientation makes her an unfit parent. In each of these examples, in order to intervene in a culturally competent manner, the social worker must recognize the different ways in which the client expresses her or his sexual orientation.

RELIGION

Religion can be an important source of identity and an instrument for positive social change, but at the same time, it has been used throughout history to justify social inequities and promote discrimination against individuals and communities. For example, passages of the Bible equate blackness with punishment by God—"The punishment of my people is worse than the penalty of Sodom / . . . Her crowned princes were once purer than snow, whiter than milk; / . . . But their faces turned blacker than soot, and no one knew them in the street" (Lamentations 4:7, 8). As early as the first century CE, Christian warnings about Satan such as the Epistle of Saint Barnabas drew on the same imagery: "The Way of the Black One is crooked and full of cursing, for it is the way of death eternal with punishment, and in it are the things that destroy their soul: idolatry, forwardness, arrogance of power, hypocrisy, double-heartedness, adultery, murder, robbery, pride, transgressions, fraud, malice, self-sufficiency, enchantments magic, covetousness" (qtd. in Owens, 1976).

Because religion provides the core beliefs that lay the foundation for its group members' shared perceptions of social reality, religion can play an important role in a person's identity. Not only are religious organizations important in the lives of many, but even those who do not claim religious beliefs feel the influence of religious values on social life and politics. Religious texts need to be interpreted and it is often in the interpretation that biased people are able to insert their prejudice. Christian texts, for example, are often used by some fringe groups to justify racism, anti-Semitism, sexism, and homophobia. For example, according to Christian interpretations, the city of Sodom was destroyed on the grounds of homosexuality.

Sometimes religion serves as a unifier of people and an agent of social control, while at other times it contributes to social conflict. The French sociologist Emile Durkheim (1912/1965) argued that the function of religion is to preserve social order by discouraging deviant behavior and giving moral authority to the established social system. Karl Marx (1843/1970) had originally adopted a more critical view of religion as a form of "false consciousness" that helps the ruling class perpetuate its domination by encouraging the poor and struggling to bear their suffering in the hope that they will be rewarded in the afterlife. Religion often plays a central role in defining political divisions, the distribution of power, and social inequalities. In medieval Europe, the Roman Catholic Church promoted the idea that kings ruled by divine right, thereby sustaining the feudal system. Similarly, throughout Indian history, Hinduism helped preserve the hereditary caste system that restricted certain groups to particular occupations and social circles and institutionalized segregation and oppression. Even though the caste system was legally abolished in the 1960s, it had become so entrenched over the 2,000 years of its history that it still pervades most social transactions today.

The Spanish conquest of Mexico, as in the rest of Latin America, utilized both the sword and the cross. Following their military successes, the colonizers instituted a systematic campaign to eradicate indigenous religious belief systems and replace them with Christianity. Christianity was used to justify the exploitation and oppression of the Native populations. The suffering endured by the original inhabitants of Mesoamerica was viewed by their conquerors as a form of redemption and salvation. In the United States, enslaved Africans and Native Americans were also forced to adopt Christianity. More recently, China's Falon Gong movement, a loosely organized group promoting spiritual development that meets in public places to practice its rituals, has become the target of repressive actions, including harassment and the imprisonment of the movement's leaders, by the Chinese government.

Religion, whether expressed through violence, activism, or pacifism, can be employed as a force for political and social change. The Protestant majority and the Roman Catholic minority in Northern Ireland have been in conflict for several centuries. In the decades since 1968, outbreaks of sectarian violence between those groups have claimed over 3,000 lives. When armed conflict in the disintegrating former Yugoslavia broke out in the 1990s, the most violent rifts were along the religious lines that separated Croatian Catholic, Serbian Orthodox, and Bosnian Muslim ethnic communities, resulting in systematic "ethnic cleansing" and the loss of tens of thousands of lives. Conflict in the Middle East provides almost daily examples of how religious differences can be used to ignite simmering political and economic grievances into waves of violence and retribution. In Sudan, the ongoing genocide of animists and Christians by Muslims in Darfur has had prominent religious undertones.

Despite the use of religion to incite and justify acts of violence, religion can also be a vehicle for positive social change through nonviolence. Religious leaders united at the Southern Christian Leadership Conference to launch and sustain the U.S. civil rights movement of the 1950s and 1960s, providing moral authority to their drive to end racial segregation and discrimination. In the 1970s, a liberation theology movement in Latin America developed both the religious ideas and the social organization needed to focus attention on redressing massive economic inequities within society.

In the United States, religion has been used to promote social change, defend the status quo, justify inequities, and agitate for their redress. Among Westernized democracies, the United States stands out as an unusually religious nation. Over 90 percent of the population says they believe in God, the majority claim to belong to a religious denomination and report that religion is very important in their lives, and nearly half say they attend weekly religious services (Wald & Calhoun-Brown, 2006). Stances on controversial issues like legalized abortion, gay and lesbian marriage, and the death penalty vary not only across religions but also within religions. Many religious organizations sponsor their own social service networks, and social workers may encounter conflicts between the profession's code of ethics and the policies of their employers.

ABILITY STATUS

The stigma attached to mental illness and physical disability frequently results in discrimination, and sometimes oppression, against the people who bear those labels. Since the early twentieth century, researchers have argued that individuals who are labeled mentally ill are often those who simply do not conform to the prevailing cultural definition of normality (Koh, 2006). Because normality is culturally defined, people labeled mentally ill in one culture may be able to function well in another. A respected mystic, visionary, or healer with extraordinary powers in a traditional society may be considered psychotic in many postindustrial societies. Society's views of mental illness reflect a social construction of the notion of mental illness rather than the reality and can result in feelings of distrust, embarrassment, and fear for others when they are around people who carry the burden of a diagnosis of mental illness. This is important in social work, as the mistaken and hurtful views and beliefs perpetuated by society's construction of mental illness affect many clients and their relatives. As part of the assessment of the social context, social workers can serve clients by investigating the role that cultural beliefs play in shaping community responses to mental illness. The negative attitudes held by much of society toward mental illness and the stigmatization of mentally ill individuals have eased significantly since the 1990s, but the desire that many people have to maintain their distance from people who have been diagnosed with a mental illness persists, particularly in ethnic minority communities (Link, Phelan, Bresnaham, Stueve, & Pescosolido, 1999). This stigmatization makes many people in need of psychological help reluctant to seek that help for fear that they will be labeled mentally ill.

Such responses to the label of mental illness parallel society's attitudes toward the concept of disability; disability, like mental illness, is in many ways often a matter of perception, not just a physical or bodily state. Many of the problems of the mentally ill and physically disabled arise primarily from an ideology of ableism that discriminates against and stigmatizes them. A key factor in society's treatment of people with physical disabilities is the process of social labeling, by which the disability becomes their defining or "master" status. The stigma imposed by society on people with disabilities erects social obstacles for them that may be more difficult to manage than the disability itself. People may respond to this stigma by treating people with disabilities like helpless and dependent children in need of guidance, avoiding or condescending to them, reacting to them with fear, or being reluctant to view them as having an equal claim to society's resources. More than a decade and a half after passage of the Americans with Disabilities Act in 1990, people with disabilities are at higher risk than the nondisabled of being unemployed, living on very low incomes, lacking health insurance, and being unsatisfied with life (Centers for Disease Control and Prevention, 2007). Despite the perception that they are a small minority consisting mostly of the elderly, one in five Americans—nearly 50 million people—is disabled, and 72 percent of these are under sixty-four years of age (U.S. Census Bureau, 2002). Ethnic minorities are disproportionally represented among the disabled as a result of motor vehicle–related injuries and the HIV pandemic, in part as a result of a lack of awareness of and access to services (McKenna, Michaud, Murray, & Marks, 2005).

INTERSECTIONALITIES: JEWS AND ARABS

This review of the key factors of gender, ethnicity, religion, social class, sexual orientation, and ability status provides the foundation for the rest of this book. Intersectionality will be presented as the unifying concept that allows for an integration of these factors into the lives of real people living in real social and historical contexts. The intersectionality of cultural identities is a very dynamic phenomenon and reflects changes in time and place; it is, in other words, contextual. But the full significance and meaning of intersectionality cannot be limited to a short list of its possible axes. For example, age and ageism, immigration and acculturation status, and place of residence (urban or rural) are critical factors to consider in social work practice. Jews and Arabs provide interesting examples of the complexity of intersectionality.

There is disagreement as to whether Judaism is a religion, an ethnicity, or both. Many Jews who are not religious think of themselves as being part of an ethnic group or a culture that is connected to their Jewish heritage. Social workers may encounter clients who are culturally Jewish but self-identify as secular (not religious) or clients who were not born Jewish, and thus cannot be considered ethnically Jewish, but converted and are very observant. According to those who believe that Judaism is a religion, not an ethnicity, most American and European Jews can be divided into two ethnic groups: Ashkenazi Jews, whose ancestry can be traced to central or eastern Europe, and Sephardic Jews, descendants of Jews who were expelled from Spain and Portugal in 1492 during the Spanish Inquisition. However, there are other sects of Judaism that do not fall into these categories, such as the Bene Israel of India and the Jews of Ethiopia, often called Falasha. Many of the Bene Israel and the Falasha now live in Israel.

Although the great majority of American Jews are Ashkenazi, the original twenty-three Jews who landed in New Amsterdam (New York) in 1654 were Sephardim who first immigrated to Recife, Brazil, but left when the Portuguese recaptured Brazil from the Dutch (Karp, 1976). There are families in New Mexico and in other areas of the Southwest that trace their ancestry to the crypto-Jews, Jews who were forced to convert to Christianity during the Spanish Inquisition but secretly continued to practice the Jewish faith. Although these families do not consider themselves Jewish, many of them continue to practice aspects of the Jewish faith that their families kept alive and passed on from one generation to the next.

There are several aspects of Judaism with which practitioners working with Jewish clients must be aware. Ashkenazi Judaism consists of religious branches or movements (e.g., Orthodox, Conservative, Reform) with corresponding sets of norms and beliefs and their own synagogues. For example, gender roles and the level of equality between women and men can vary greatly across Jewish communities. These and other variables such as migration history, level of assimilation, intermarriage, post-traumatic stress related to anti-Jewish prejudice and discrimination, and the family's history related to the Holocaust need to be considered.

Arabs and Arab Americans are also very diverse groups. To be an Arab is to be a member of an ethnic group, but many people think of Arab culture as synonymous with Islam. Although most Arabs are Muslim, many Arabs are Christian, and some belong to religions other than Islam or Christianity (for example, some Arabs are Jewish) or do not belong to any religion. For example, in the United States there are about six million Arabs, about one-third of whom are Muslim (Dwairy, 2006). On the other hand, millions of the world's Muslims, including those in Indonesia, the nation with the largest Muslim population in the world, are not Arabs. There are many Muslims who do not speak Arabic as their vernacular language; however, all Muslims read the Qur'an and conduct Islam's five daily prayers in Arabic.

The tragic attacks against the World Trade Center and Pentagon on September 11, 2001, exacerbated anti-Muslim and anti-Arab sentiments and fostered distrust toward Muslim communities across the nation. Many social service agencies serving these communities are attempting to convey the message that their agencies are safety zones and that they are committed to providing high-quality culturally relevant services. Muslim clients may not self-identify to the social worker as Muslim for fear of being rejected or judged (Dwairy, 2006). Because of the centrality of the faith in many Muslim families, religious affiliation is a core identity that can be integrated effectively into the biopsychosocial-spiritual assessment.

Key Concepts

Intersectionality the meeting point of multiple identities such as race, ethnicity, gender, social class, sexual orientation, age, and ability status

Double jeopardy the compounding of disadvantages based on the intersection of two individual characteristics, such as ethnicity and gender

Affirmative action legal regulations that promote racial and gender equality in employment, government contracting, and educational access

Meritocracy a system in which rewards are allocated based on individual merit alone

Part II

Theories and Perspectives on Oppression

4

Evolutionary and Structural Functionalist Theories

THEORIES ARE THE LENSES THROUGH WHICH SOCIAL SCIENTISTS EXAMine, evaluate, organize, and interpret social phenomena. Theories are often used to justify privileges for some members of society and the oppression of others. Theories are also used to explain the causes of inequality and oppression within society. This chapter reviews various theories that have been used over time to explain how different cultures interact when they come in contact, to justify oppression, or to explain injustice.

This chapter embarks on a theoretical exploration of diversity in its social and cultural context by approaching cultural diversity in relation to the social and political forces that shape it, with an emphasis on oppression and inequality. This overview of theories will act as a foundation for the following chapters, which will introduce more applied theories connected to the culturally grounded approach to social work.

This review sorts through traditional theories to identify the elements most relevant to the culturally grounded approach. This exercise is necessary because without an understanding of these theoretical perspectives, we would be unable to practice within the realm of science and would be unable to conduct professional practice. Theory provides the compass for social work practice and research with different cultural communities. Some perspectives discussed in the next pages may already be familiar to readers, but they will be reviewed with an emphasis on diversity, inequality, and oppression. Some theories have blind spots regarding diversity, while others will help readers understand how cultural differences can be recognized and addressed as assets in social work practice. Because most of the theories presented here are interrelated, some will be given more emphasis than others. Our review of each theory will be guided by three questions: How are cultural diversity and its role in the life of the community recognized? What are the root causes of social inequality and oppression, and how is the system of inequality perpetuated? And what are the theory's implications for social work practice and research?

The perspectives are grouped into families of theories according to the commonalities they share. These groupings do not necessarily follow traditional theoretical frameworks because they integrate classical theories and meta-theories with more applied social work theories. The first set of perspectives, the evolutionary and conflict theories, provides a macro perspective that has at its core ideas about sources of oppression and inequality. The second set of perspectives, structural functionalist theories, recognizes inequality and offers various explanations for it, often with an emphasis on the achievement of balance and stability at the expense of conflict and change. Chapter 5 will review the inclusiveness, constructivist, and postmodern theories, which are concerned with intergroup relations and look at diversity from a micro and subjective perspective, respectively.

EVOLUTIONARY AND CONFLICT THEORIES: EXAGGERATING AND MINIMIZING DIFFERENCE AND INEQUALITY

As stated earlier in the text, it is generally accepted by anthropologists that ideas about racial groups are socially constructed rather than biologically given. Much effort, however, has gone into theorizing about the existence of race as a real and scientific phenomenon. Such conjecture is often a thinly disguised means of justifying the privilege of some members of society and the oppression of others. Social Darwinism is a good example of an evolutionary theory.

Social Darwinism

Social Darwinism is based on the premise that Darwin's theory of the evolution of biological traits by natural selection can be applied to societies or groups within a society. Although Darwin never intended for his research on animals and plants to be applied to the study of differences between humans, social Darwinism became popular in the latter part of the nineteenth century and maintained its popularity until the end of World War II. Its main tenets are used today by xenophobic fringe groups (such as anti-immigrant groups) and xenophobic politicians. According to social Darwinists, success in life occurs because of an individual's biological superiority over others. Social Darwinists argue that since humans are a product of nature, and conflict and struggle are the law of nature, the strongest humans take the top prizes (e.g., in employment, housing, health care, and education) (Montagu, 1957). Social Darwinists believe that evolution rewards people who are strong, intelligent, and attractive (based on an ethnocentric idea of beauty) and have a good work ethic, and that it punishes those lacking these characteristics. This theory supports the categorization of people based on their racial and ethnic backgrounds. According to this theory, some people are destined by their ethnic and racial heritage to succeed, while those who are unsuccessful are simply destined to fail. Social Darwinism provided its proponents in Victorian England and elsewhere with a convenient academic justification for colonialism, slavery, genocide, and other forms of exploitation and oppression.

The legacy of social Darwinism has continued to hold sway through the twentieth and twenty-first centuries. For example, in South Africa, the laws of apartheid were inspired in part by social Darwinist ideas. Although apartheid was abolished in the early 1990s, its legacy continues to affect the opportunities for economic and social advancement of millions of black and mixed-race South Africans. Apartheid (meaning "separate") was a system of legislation in South Africa that enshrined political, economic, and social rule by a white numerical minority and the oppression of its black numerical majority. Under apartheid, whites in South Africa were considered the best race. This product of colonialism and racism was based partly on social Darwinian ideology. Although apartheid rule ended in 1994, its legacy of officially imposed poverty and discrimination continues to be felt by black and mixed-race South Africans today. The New National Party, the South African party that designed and enforced apartheid, was dissolved only in 2004. At that time, nine out of every ten acres of commercial farmland remained in the hands of 50,000 white farmers, while most of the forty million nonwhites remained landless (Louw, 2004).

The ideology behind social Darwinism contradicts all the basic principles of the social work profession; however, it is important to understand its tenets because they are based on ideas about difference that promote oppression and may still be held by some individuals and communities. It provides the ideological roots of many contemporary policies and practices that dehumanize others by defining them as different, inherently inferior, and less deserving. Sometimes social policies and social services are inadvertently influenced by social Darwinist ideas about different individuals' and communities' abilities and potential for change. For example, a social service agency may want to enforce a family planning policy that calls for any woman labeled mentally incompetent to be sterilized. Some aspects of social Darwinism have survived through seemingly benign theories, such as Murray Bowen's family theory and the theory of the culture of poverty, both of which argue that people from certain backgrounds are prone to dysfunction due to their learned heritage (Gurman & Fraenkel, 2002; Lewis, 1966; Sidanius & Pratto, 1999).

Marxist and Neo-Marxist Theories

Marxist and neo-Marxist theorists focus on social inequality, often deemphasizing racial, ethnic, and gender differences. Marxist thought proposes that social class, rather than other social variables like ethnicity, race, and gender, is the key factor explaining social inequality. Marxist theory explains that the accumulation of wealth by one social class results in the deprivation of wealth among the other class. The central belief is that the distribution of economic resources shapes social life, values, beliefs, culture, and other aspects of society. The main theoretical contribution of Marxism is the idea that people in similar economic positions share interests and become grouped together, while divergent interests between classes result in class struggle. That is one of the reasons why Marxist theories are also known as conflict theories. Groups in power may echo social Darwinist ideas, for example, by claiming that they are smarter, harder working, more entrepreneurial, or better strategic decision makers than those who are excluded from power. The groups in power develop their own explanations to justify their monopoly of power and the exclusion and oppression of other groups. Marxist theory dismisses the relevance and importance of cultural differences while stressing the importance of class differences.

Communist party rule in China and Cuba provides two examples of the political applications of Marxist theory. After the 1949 Communist revolution in China, the state promoted the identity of all citizens as workers, which supported the goal of equality between men and women. However, the Communist government also used its power to repress many ethnic minority groups and downplay their possession of separate linguistic and cultural identities. In Cuba, citizens of African ancestry benefited from the 1959 revolution, attaining equal status with non-blacks for the first time, as well as increased access to employment, health care, and education. The Communist regimes in both China and Cuba have worked to minimize the role of racism and ethnocentrism in the distribution of resources and citizens' access to social opportunities. Nevertheless, they, like the former Soviet regime, have been unable to prevent racial and ethnic social identities from persisting as a major source of identity and as an important variable in the people's social and political lives.

Marxism continues to be considered a viable theory and ideology by groups in some developing societies, especially those experiencing dramatic levels of inequality in the distribution of resources and political power and those seeking to organize for radical social and political transformation. Recent examples include Nepal, where Marxist rebels instigated revolts against direct rule by the country's king, and Chiapas in southern Mexico, where Marxist-inspired organizers have mobilized disenfranchised peasants to protect their lands from exploitation by multinational mining and agricultural interests. At the same time, as economically developed societies have moved from an industrial to a postindustrial and now to a globalization phase, traditional Marxist thought has been revisited and adapted to contemporary society by theorists known as neo-Marxists.

Some neo-Marxists believe that cultural factors play an independent role in maintaining inequalities, while others argue that ethnic identities that persist for a very long time after immigration or annexation are the result of discrimination and social rejection rather than an effort to preserve something of cultural value (Steinberg, 1981). The choice of maintaining or embracing an ethnic identity is thus seen as a way of coping with the experience of rejection by the majority culture. Therefore, in prejudiced environments, cultural segregation becomes a form of survival for ethnic minorities while at the same time reflecting their forced exclusion from society.

Neo-Marxist thought is evolving as it strives to integrate cultural variables with social class as key factors in explaining inequality. For example, some neo-Marxist theorists have argued that if people have contact across ethnic and cultural lines, they will relate differently and as a result, prejudice will decrease, which will open up opportunities for social advancement (McCollom, 1996). Some aspects of this theory can be used in the construction of a culturally grounded approach. The socialist principle of working to achieve equal access to resources for all segments of society, an outgrowth of Marxist analysis, has influenced social work in different ways. First, it has led social work to define social problems as having social and structural rather than individual causes. The social work profession views individual relationships as the product of social relations in a capitalist society. In fact, social work came into existence partly in order to identify and address social inequalities, especially those resulting from social class differences. Although Marxist theory does not recognize ethnic culture as central to the human experience, its emphasis on inequality can be helpful for understanding oppression and change.

World Systems Theory

World systems theory is connected to neo-Marxist thought and focuses on economic and social differences at a global level. According to world systems theory, the current world capitalist system is organized into a center, or core, in which the wealthy countries monopolize the production of research and technology, and a periphery, in which poor countries that provide raw materials, cheap labor, and transportation to the core are located (Wallerstein, 1974). This view is no different from the traditional colonial structure for which the terms "metropolis" (the center) and "colonies" (the periphery) were used (Ashcroft, Griffiths, & Tiffin, 2000). In both cases, the center benefits from the exploitation and suffering of the periphery. This is the reason the antiglobalization movement often uses the term "neocolonialism" in its critique of the economic world system.

This thesis is taken a step further by the world systems theorists' claims that capitalism inevitably leads to world integration and interdependency, thereby producing a system in which the core dominates the periphery. Globalization creates an integrated economic and financial system that, some have argued, influences not only the economic life of societies but their educational and cultural systems as well. Starbucks, McDonalds, and Pizza Hut can be found in cities all over the world and have become emblematic of how economic globalization is affecting local tastes and customs.

Guided by classic economic rationalism and liberalism, economic globalization determines the value of individuals solely according to their contribution to the economy. Globalization has influenced social policy in the United States and other countries under U.S. economic and political influence with the consequence that market forces are allowed to structure social relations. In response, millions of citizens across the world have demonstrated against the institutions and policies of corporate globalization. While corporate globalists see globalization as spreading democracy and generating vibrant market economies, world systems theory and many citizen movements are concerned by what they see as the power to govern shifting to corporations and slipping away from people and communities. Critics charge that globalization replaces democracies of people with democracies of money, that is, political, economic, and social policies that are dictated by the flow of economic capital. Traditional self-organizing local markets are destroyed by globalization and replaced by centrally planned corporate economies. World systems theorists also contend that the actual beneficiaries of globalization have become all too obvious: top corporate executives of the largest global companies make salaries five hundred times those of bottom-level production workers, and that gap is increasing annually. As for claims that globalization aids the global poor, world systems theorists argue that the gap between the wealthy and the poor within and among countries of the world is getting steadily larger (International Forum on Globalization, 2002).

Influenced by economic rationalism, many social workers must deliver services in an environment that seems to exacerbate inequalities and does little to advance social justice. The following questions remain unanswered: Who is benefiting from globalization and who is not? Is the role of social work to facilitate the incorporation of individuals and communities into the market economy? Are there a social and economic core and a corresponding periphery within the United States? If so, are ethnic minorities and women overrepresented in the periphery?

STRUCTURAL FUNCTIONALIST THEORIES: MANAGING CONFLICT, INTEGRATION, AND SOCIAL STABILITY

Structural Functionalism

Structural functionalism has its roots in the mid-nineteenth-century works of Auguste Comte, often called the father of sociology, as well as the works of others who compared societies to living organisms, social classes and castes to bodily tissues, cities and communities to the body's organs, and families to biological cells. Comte understood all these components as forming a functional interconnected social body. Twentieth-century theorists used these concepts to develop structural functionalism, which emphasizes the importance of social consensus in maintaining social balance and identifies some aspects of society as dysfunctional because they threaten to disrupt social stability. Within this framework, social differentiation, rather than social conflict and struggle, is seen as the key to the evolution of social systems. Differences based on gender, ethnicity, and social class are seen largely outside their political context.

Specifically, social stratification is viewed as a desirable and necessary stage of development in the evolution of complex industrial societies, with social inequalities serving larger societal needs. For example, Emile Durkheim (1933/2004) explained the social forces that assign people to different occupations—the primary basis for contemporary social class systems—as part of a larger social system that creates a rational division of labor in society. Talcott Parsons (1961) described gender roles as complementary and operating in tandem, allowing homemakers to accomplish important family and societal goals like child socialization, and breadwinners to concentrate on maximizing families' chances of upward social mobility.

Structural functionalism came under strong attack in the 1960s for its inability to explain social change, inequality, conflict, and the power of the wealthy. Feminist scholars criticized functionalist thought as a justification for male privilege that largely ignores women's contributions to society. Feminists have also criticized functionalist theory because it implicitly accepts a system of inequality within the male-dominated structure of the family. According to feminist critics, this system of inequality is often a cause of abuse and domestic violence, especially when men view the struggles of women to expand their options as a threat to male control. These power dynamics presume that women's central role and responsibility are as wives and mothers, which take precedence over their personal needs, goals, and rights. In the same vein, by focusing on shared values and the role of core societal institutions, functionalist theorists tended to treat ethnic minorities as outsiders or the "other," while placing white heterosexual males in a privileged position at the center (Farley, 2000). Far less of their effort went into understanding minority cultures than into explaining how minority cultures were different from the dominant culture.

Structural functionalism continues to influence social thought and policies in contemporary society. In fact, it could be argued that social work can be used as a tool for maintaining the equilibrium of society and attempting to remedy what is labeled dysfunctional or unbalanced before it disturbs the social equilibrium. Such an approach has important consequences for the way social workers relate to clients who come from different cultures. Therefore, some aspects of the concepts of social cohesion, balance, and stability will be useful to the culturally grounded approach, but these concepts must be integrated with the recognition of the importance of cultural diversity, equality, and empowerment. Several theories that are rooted in the structural functionalist perspective explore specific ways that this perspective has been used to understand how different cultural groups relate to society as a whole.

Assimilation Theory

Assimilation is a strategy for achieving the societal balance to which functionalists aspired by ultimately eliminating difference. The United States was transformed into a great world economy in part because of the benefits society reaped from the oppression of ethnic minority groups born out of slavery, colonialism, and annexation. As the country accumulated wealth and inequality persisted, assimilation was looked upon as a means to complete the absorption of various cultural groups into American mainstream society with the least disruption to the nation's social and economic fabric.

In the early twentieth century, Park (1930) defined social assimilation as "the process or processes by which peoples of diverse racial origins and different cultural heritages, occupying a common territory, achieve a cultural solidarity sufficient at least to sustain a national existence" (p. 281). Assimilation is often associated with a complete abandonment of the culture of origin and an unconditional embrace of the host culture. Park, however, used terms suggesting a mixture, like "amalgamation" and "fusion," interchangeably with "assimilation" and did not view assimilation as a complete and unconditional surrender of all aspects of the culture of origin. In later years other sociologists such as Milton Gordon (1964) further contributed to the development of classical assimilation theory by separating the process of acculturation from what he called "structural assimilation." Structural assimilation resulted from primary group relationships between members of the ethnic minority group and members of the majority group, for example, through intermarriage. Acculturation, which was perceived to be inevitable and a first step leading to structural assimilation, was defined as the minority group's adoption of the cultural patterns of the host society (Gordon, 1964). In other words, immigrants must acculturate in order to acquire a common cultural code for interaction with the majority culture.

Although Gordon and other assimilation theorists have been cited as proponents of what has been referred to as Anglo-conformity (Paxton & Mughan, 2006), assimilation continues to be an important theoretical concept in the consideration of contemporary society. Social workers have been traditionally described as agents of assimilation. If assimilation is a one-way train, the natural question that emerges is: Where is the train going? For most of the twentieth century, the dominant or mainstream U.S. culture—a culture based on values and norms representing white European middle-class males—was the assumed destination. However, being of European ancestry has not always been enough to facilitate assimilation: early Irish, Polish, and Italian immigrants, most of whom were Roman Catholic, were not originally welcomed by mainstream culture. For example, Ignatiev (1995) argues that the Irish were originally identified not with the WASP rulers of the nation but rather with free blacks, with whom they shared many economic and social conditions, but that over time they gained economic and social acceptance, and eventually these groups also "became white."

The implicit message of classic or "straight-line" assimilation theory—which has roots in structural functionalism and posits that the absorption of immigrant cultures into the mainstream is inevitable—is that non-mainstream cultures are maladaptive, deficient, or not as good as mainstream culture. Therefore, to advance socially and economically, people who come from non-mainstream cultures need to detach themselves from their cultures of origin and fully embrace mainstream culture. This paradigm, however, fails to account for the rejection and active suppression of certain groups by mainstream culture that have taken place throughout history as these groups have been forced to assimilate.

Since its formulation, scholars have continued to examine and reformulate the assimilation theory and its application to the study of the assimilation experiences of contemporary non-European ethnic groups. Some contemporary researchers have proposed that immigrants do acculturate into other minority groups (Alba & Hee, 1997). Others have provided alternative models; for example, Rumbaut and Portes (2001) have proposed the theory of segmented assimilation, which describes three possible paths for immigrants to America: (1) assimilation and upward mobility by immigrants who possess plentiful human capital; (2) downward assimilation by immigrants with limited resources, which confines them to poor neighborhoods, where they join a permanent lower class; and (3) selective acculturation, or biculturalism, where some aspects of the host culture are adopted and some aspects of the culture of origin are preserved. Researchers have identified numerous barriers to assimilation. In addition to a lack of human capital in the form of education and job skills, commonly cited barriers to assimilation include prejudices and discrimination based on ethnic or racial appearance, native languages other than English, and religion. The closer the group is to the norm established by the dominant mainstream culture in these three areas, the easier the path to assimilation is (Golash-Boza, 2006).

Critics of the belief that assimilation is a desirable societal goal not only argue that the cost of assimilation outweighs the benefits but also question the assumption that assimilation is inevitable and advantageous (Johnson, 1997). They point out that members of a community suffer psychological harm and serious socioeconomic setbacks when their traditions are not honored or are disrupted through forced assimilation into another pattern of life. In general, when individuals share a common social identification, the sense of group belonging contributes to the development of a positive self-concept. However, when an individual is a member of a devalued social group—especially when that group is unable to assimilate into the mainstream—her or his personal identity and emotional adjustment suffer (Crocker & Major, 1989).

Language can create various types of barriers to assimilation. Mainstream social institutions such as schools are used today as tools of assimilation, just as they were at the beginning of the twentieth century. The recent success of English-only movements and the suppression of native languages in the name of assimilation in some areas of the country show that individuals and institutions still approve of forced assimilation. By blocking access to bilingual education, mainstream society tells members of language minority groups that they need to let go of a central pillar of their cultural identity. The policies that perpetuate this message can be a great source of stress for those who are affected, who are pushed toward assimilation and at the same time not fully welcomed by society. One of the main purposes of the forced placement of Native American children in boarding schools was the imposition of English and the decimation of Native languages. During and following the Great Depression of the 1930s, the U.S. government forced a million Mexican and Mexican American individuals to migrate to Mexico. They are known as the *repatriados,* or "the repatriated." Some of these families eventually returned to the United States and encouraged their children not to speak Spanish because language had served as a way for the government to identify them for forced repatriation. The institution of slavery forbade enslaved people from speaking their ancestral African languages and seriously weakened their connection to their cultures and religions of origin (Begard, 2007).

Meanwhile, the low priority given to mastery of languages other than English has become a major liability for the United States (Welch, Welch, & Piekkari, 2005). The lack of Arabic-speaking staff in the military, the CIA, and the State Department has been well documented as a liability in the Iraqi conflict as well as in anti-terrorist efforts in general. Closer to the domestic front, in social services the need for bilingual social workers and agency staff is greater than ever (Ferguson, Lavalette, & Whitmore, 2005).

Internalized oppression and stigma often influence identity choices made by members of devalued groups, which in turn has a detrimental effect on their emotional well-being. Despite these risks, assimilation continues to be strongly supported by different private and public institutions.

The concept of straight-line assimilation is not part of the culturally grounded approach, but assimilation and its related concepts provide important insights into the lives of immigrant groups.

The Melting Pot

According to the melting pot theory, ethnic and racial groups develop relationships in successive stages that ultimately lead to cultural and social fusion, or "amalgamation" (Newman, 1973). Past generations of immigrants in America, it is argued, became successful by shedding their historical identities and adopting the ways of their new country, which allowed them to achieve social mobility. As a metaphor for the process through which homogenous societies develop, the melting pot describes how the combination of different identities meld into a single identity. Just as when cooks mix ingredients in a pot, each identity (or ingredient) loses it distinctiveness, yielding a uniform composite identity in which the original ingredients can no longer be identified.

In the United States, the melting pot is often associated with the idea of the "model minority" (Choi & Lahey, 2006). Many consider Asian immigrants a model minority group in the United States due to the widespread belief that all Asian immigrants came to America with little or nothing and through hard study and work become successful and assimilated into mainstream culture despite the initial disadvantages and discrimination they faced. However, this view fails to account for the fact that different people's experiences of integration vary widely—even when those people belong to the same ethnic or racial group. For example, some Asian immigrant subgroups tend to be highly educated at the time of migration; thus, they get a completely different start in life in the United States than other minorities. And while many people imagine that most Asian immigrants came to the United States as boat people escaping the ravages of war and Communism, this image only describes Southeast Asians, who actually have one of the slowest social mobility rates of all Asian immigrant groups (Akresh, 2006). And although many people of Asian ancestry achieve high levels of social mobility in the United States, Asian Americans still bump into the glass ceiling, receive lower pay even with the same qualifications, and have high poverty rates (Sakamoto & Woo, 2007).

The melting pot approach underestimates the unidirectional forces at work as members of minority cultures are pressured to "melt" into mainstream culture. One of the shortcomings of the metaphor of the melting pot is that it assumes that all people—immigrant groups and those who were born in the United States—are playing on a level playing field. However, in a capitalist society like the United States, economic resources are related to political power, and oppressed communities tend to have less economic power and as a consequence less political and cultural power. Therefore, the melting pot theory is applicable to the culturally grounded approach only in terms of its recognition of acculturation and assimilation as two different processes rather than as a basis for understanding differences between ethnic groups.

Structural Role Theory

While the melting pot theory argues that there are forces encouraging social equilibrium at a macro level as the cultures of different ethnic groups merge and are amalgamated, structural role theory addresses the production of social cohesion at a more micro level. Structural role theory views interactions among individuals as governed by the role expectations associated with the positions or statuses that they occupy in social structures play. Each of these positions has corresponding roles that shape its individual identity and guide how the individual occupying the position acts. Some positions—like gender, ethnicity, and national origin—are *ascribed* to individuals, often at birth, and are beyond the individual's control. Others—like occupational and marital status—are *achieved* statuses, which reflect the social opportunities that are open to them. Each position an individual holds has an associated role; therefore, one person can have many roles, each with particular behavioral expectations.

Although many theorists, including George Mead, Robert Park, Georg Simmel, Ralph Linton, and Robert Merton, have contributed to role theory, no single theorist can be considered its author, and there are important differences among theorists in how roles are conceived. Social roles can be viewed as more or less rigid and are guided by social norms that are clear, ambiguous, or shifting, depending on the social context. At one extreme, roles are like parts in a play for which every word and move of the actor is scripted. At the other extreme, roles are like the positions in an improvised game in which individuals are free to adjust their tactics in response to the moves of other players.

As a key status, or position, in social life, gender roles provide an excellent example of the various ways in which social roles are adopted and enacted. Gender socialization begins early as girls and boys are encouraged to act in different ways, play with different toys, and perform different chores around the house (like washing dishes rather than cutting the grass) and sends a powerful early message about the gendered division of labor in the family. Parents have been shown to communicate different expectations about academic performance and appropriate academic interests to their female and male children (Probert, 2005). Gender role development is the lifelong process of acquiring the attitudes and developing behaviors that are culturally defined as appropriate for members of one's sex; the beliefs that one acquires regarding how appropriate various attitudes and behaviors are to one's sex are reinforced in school, at work, and through language and the media (Constantinople, 2005). Although female and male roles are not universal even across the most traditional societies, as different cultures shape gender roles in distinctive ways, similar patterns of gender socialization have been noted around the world (Harkness & Super, 1996).

In most societies, women are socialized into submissive roles and taught not to question the privilege of their male counterparts. Gender roles in patriarchal societies tend to perpetuate these roles. From the perspective of role theory, it is not because they are female that women adopt certain roles; rather, they do so because the societies in which they live prescribe their behavior (role).

Recognizing the multiplicity of roles individuals play and the complexity of the behavioral expectations attached to each role, role theory has identified the problems of role strain and role conflict. Role strain is the stress that occurs when contradictory expectations are attached to the same role, while role conflict causes distress when two or more different roles place incompatible expectations on an individual. Many applications of role theory in social work practice and research grew out of the concepts of role strain and role conflict. One example of role strain is the situation commonly faced by low-income single mothers who turn to state assistance programs like TANF (Temporary Assistance to Needy Families) to help provide for their children's needs. Program eligibility requirements often force mothers receiving aid from TANF to leave their children in day care to attend job training or mandated job placements, which in turn may earn them criticism as poor or neglectful mothers. In their roles as mothers, they face the strain of being expected to care for their children around the clock while also being full-time breadwinners, but with inadequate outside support to do both well. Role strain may also occur within families when family members become unhappy with the conflicting demands of their assigned gender roles, as when, contrary to the expectations of her traditional parents, a young woman does not see herself as a future wife and mother (Hepworth, Rooney, & Larsen, 2002). Role conflict also causes distress from incompatible role expectations, but those expectations come from different roles, such as when an adult child's obligations to care for an elderly parent conflict with her or his job responsibilities.

Role theory is helpful for identifying contradictions and tensions that emerge from rigid gender roles, the multiplicity of statuses that all individuals occupy, the complex ways that roles may be combined or the ways in which roles intersect, and the many conflicting role expectations individuals face in their daily lives. However, role theory, like structural functionalist theory, falls short in specifying how roles come to be established and which expectations prevail when there are conflicting norms or a clash of cultures. Nor does it address role inequalities from a moral or judicial standpoint. Role theory fails to recognize culture as a force that shapes people's roles and expectations. However, an awareness of the conflicts that emerge in the lives of clients as a result of the multiple roles they play is crucial to competent social work practice. One's opportunities and choices are often influenced by expectations and boundaries set by one's culture. Identifying those boundaries and learning how to negotiate them is an important aspect of many social work interventions.

Human Capital Theory

Human capital theory focuses on the type and amount of knowledge and experience that individuals acquire through education and job training and bring to the labor market (Becker, 1975). Differences in human capital are produced by variations in the level, type, and quality of educational credentials, job training, and work experience that people have. Therefore, the income that individuals earn is a direct result of the choices available to them regarding the amount and kind of education they receive—as well as their training, work experience, and job commitment in the workplace—and how well these choices mesh with the needs of the labor market. This theory attributes the gender wage gap to the fact that women make different choices—different human capital investments—than men do about schooling and job preparation in anticipation of demands they will face as spouses and mothers. As a result, women accumulate less work experience and become overrepresented in occupations that require less education and training, as well as those that allow for more flexible work schedules and career interruptions. Furthermore, if a woman leaves the labor force to become involved in child bearing and child rearing, her level of human capital deteriorates due to non-use, and her accumulated skills could become obsolete (Gray, Stone, & Stockard, 2006).

All the tenets of human capital have been fiercely contested, and the evidence puts most of its principles in doubt. Studies of educational and occupational choices have shown that human capital factors account for only a small portion of the gender gap in pay and promotions, that female-dominated occupations do not carry lower penalties for career interruptions, and that men are actually more likely than women to have flexible work schedules (England, Kilbourne, Farkas, & Dou, 1988; Menéndez, Benach, Muntaner, Amable, & O'Campo, 2007). In addition, the theory overlooks the impact of men's unequal sharing of child-raising responsibilities with their partners, which could significantly decrease women's human capital. Moreover, economic imbalance can be due to demographic differences such as women choosing to have children on their own without a male partner. Such imbalances even exist in industrialized nations with long traditions of gender equality. For example, even though Scandinavian societies have enacted proactive work-life balance policies supporting the role of fathers among heterosexual couples with young children, Scandinavian men are still much less likely to take paternity leave than women are to take maternity leave (Aybars, 2007).

Overall, it is the roles that societies assign to different groups that influence the manner in which resources are allocated, making more or fewer opportunities available to its members. For these differences to be addressed, a redefinition of roles is needed at the personal level, and systemic changes are needed at the policy level. Such redefinition requires a reexamination of how society defines human capital. Existing patriarchal norms, for example, place no human capital value on raising children or being a homemaker. The care of children and others is devalued, not only at home but also at work. Studies of the gender wage gap suggest that jobs that require nurturing skills, and in which women are heavily represented, such as nursing, social work, child care, and elementary school teaching, carry a steep net wage penalty, even when human capital differences are adjusted for. The salaries paid for these jobs do not adequately reflect the accumulated educational skills and work experience of those who perform them (England, Herbert, Kilbourne, Reid, & Megdal, 1994).

Studies have shown the extent to which differences in education, training, and job experience account for ethnic, racial, and gender differences in occupational and economic attainment. However, they also reveal the extent of other sources of these inequalities, such as prejudice and discrimination. Studies of human capital have highlighted the fact that certain assumptions regarding such ethnic, racial, and gender differences—such as the idea that women select more flexible and low-paying jobs—are unfounded and lack economic viability. Human capital approaches add an economic dimension to the overarching culturally grounded theoretical approach.

Human capital theory and the other theories reviewed in this chapter serve as the roots or the foundation for some of the theories presented in the following chapters. The theories presented in this chapter have influenced the thinking of powerful groups in society and are an expression of worldviews that influence contemporary political, economic, and social science analyses about cultural diversity, oppression, and social change.

Key Concepts

Social Darwinism the premise that Darwin's theory of evolution of biological traits by natural selection can be applied to human beings

Apartheid a system of legislation in South Africa that guaranteed political, economic, and social rule to a white numerical minority and institutionalized the oppression of the black numerical majority

Marxist theory a theory whose major tenet is that class conflict is created because the accumulation of wealth by one social class depends upon and results in the deprivation of wealth among a lower social class

World systems theory the theory that wealthy countries (the core) monopolize the production of research and technology, while poor countries located in the periphery provide raw materials, cheap labor, and transportation to the core

Structural functionalism the theory that social stratification is a necessary and even desirable stage of development in the evolution of a complex industrial society that supports the system of interdependent and complementary social roles and structures

Melting pot the theory that different ethnic and racial groups in a society develop relationships in successive stages that ultimately lead to cultural and social fusion in which the cultures of origin can no longer be recognized

Structural role theory the theory that interactions among individuals are governed by role expectations associated with the multiple positions or statuses they occupy in a social structure

Human capital theory the theory that individuals acquire knowledge and experience through education and job training that later can be brought to the job market

5

Theoretical Perspectives on Diversity

AS THE UNITED STATES BECOMES A MORE DIVERSE NATION, IT IS IMPORtant for social work practitioners to understand how interactions between people and cultures affect behavior. While chapter 4 provided a review of selected classical perspectives on difference and oppression, chapter 5 focuses on theoretical perspectives on cultural diversity and intergroup relations. These perspectives are smaller in scope and have been developed to different degrees; however, they all recognize and appreciate the differences that exist among and between cultures and share a focus on inclusiveness, at least implicitly.

PERSPECTIVES ON INCLUSIVENESS: RECOGNIZING AND PROMOTING DIVERSITY

Contact Theory

Gordon Allport's contact theory questioned the viability of functionalism as a means of understanding intergroup relations and the origins of prejudice. According to Allport (1954), "prejudice is an antipathy based upon a faulty and inflexible generalization. . . . It may be directed toward a group as a whole, or toward an individual because he is a member of that group" (p. 9). Prejudice can be expressed through interpersonal discrimination that exists on a continuum ranging from what Allport calls "antilocution" (remarks made against—but not directly to—a person, group, or community), avoidance, exclusion, and physical attack to extermination. Prejudiced attitudes and behaviors are an expression of the social distance and antipathy that exist between people. Therefore, prejudice is an expression of people's unfamiliarity with each other and the inhumanity they carry within from an early age. Studies of children's playground behaviors have confirmed that prejudice is socially learned as children segregate themselves by ethnicity, race, and gender after a certain age. The evidence shows that by age four, children prefer playmates who engage in activities that are gender typical and that between the ages of three and five, children develop biases in favor of their own ethnic or racial groups (Alexander & Hines, 1994; Kowalski, 2003).

The contact theory of intergroup relations does not propose that individuals and groups can reduce their prejudice and get along with each other simply by sharing a common space. On the contrary, this perspective proposes that prejudice can be reduced only if certain necessary conditions are in place:

1. There must be sustained contact between people who are different from one another.
2. Individuals interacting with each other must be of equal status.
3. Individuals need to be working toward common goals.
4. There must be sufficient resources to prevent competition for these resources.
5. There must be institutional support to implement the other four conditions. (Cook, 1988)

These conditions are often difficult to achieve because of power and resource differentials between dominant and minority groups. For example, based in part on an application of contact theory, school busing was court ordered to integrate schools racially in many cities around the nation because residential and school segregation along social class and ethnic lines presented major barriers to meaningful social contact. As a response to the racial segregation of neighborhoods, children from one neighborhood were bused to a school in a neighborhood in another part of the city so that children of different ethnic and racial backgrounds could learn in the same classrooms and play together on the same playgrounds. In response, many families with the most resources took their children out of the public schools or moved to areas without busing, which resulted in schools consisting predominantly of ethnic minority children (Caldas, Bankston, & Cain, 2007). As a result, this seemingly simple solution to segregation actually increased segregation in some school districts.

One difficulty in applying contact theory is that it assumes that people want to spend time with people they perceive to be different from themselves. In reality, individuals generally follow a principle of homophily; that is, they prefer to develop social bonds with people who look and act like themselves (Lazarsfeld & Merton, 1954; McPherson, Smith-Lovin, & Cook, 2001). For example, such de facto segregation is all too common in the cafeterias of the nations' high schools as students share their unplanned time with classmates they perceive to be like themselves (Davis, 2007).

The positive impact of contact between different groups has been well documented, but the logistics of achieving contact remain unclear. For example, further theory development could address how to make voluntary social contact possible and conducive to people's acceptance of differences and the production of lasting social harmony. Nonetheless, contact theory, particularly its principles and the conditions it sees as necessary for reducing prejudice and segregation, contributes important insights to the culturally grounded approach.

Cosmopolitanism

The concept and theory of cosmopolitanism has a long history dating back to the Sophists and the Stoics (Baubôck, 2002). This discussion will concentrate on the work of Feher (1994), as it is based more directly in an application of cosmopolitanism in the United States. However, Vertovec and Cohen (2002) provide a very good additional reference for those interested in further theoretical and contextual considerations. Cosmopolitanism (from *cosmo polis*, a cosmos within a city) constitutes a notable expansion of contact theory, and it is relevant to cultural diversity within the context of globalization. Cosmopolitanism challenges individuals to come closer to the "other" and takes a step beyond contact theory by suggesting curiosity about difference and the "other" and encourages proximity to and interaction with those who are different (Feher, 1994).

From the cosmopolitan perspective, differences are not meant to define a strictly separate territory, nor should they be reduced to an insignificant variation on a theme. Rather, differences are understood as a source of attraction. A cosmopolitan paradigm is an invitation for mutual transformation through dynamic engagement with those who are different, not just polite or intellectual respect for others or a general affirmation of all humanity (Feher, 1994). It recognizes that there are different ways of thinking that create meaning and that all the resulting interpretations of reality are valid and worth knowing. Cosmopolitanism is the antithesis of totalitarian thinking, ignorance, provincialism, and prejudice.

"Cosmopolitan" was the word frequently used by the mainstream media to characterize life in Sarajevo before the onset of the war in Bosnia-Herzegovina that led to its separation from the former Yugoslavia during the 1990s (Skrbis, Kendall, & Woodward, 2004). Before the war, the city's different ethnic and religious groups enjoyed sustained contact with each other, similar status, sufficient resources, and government support. Partly as a result of its cosmopolitan character, the city of Sarajevo became a powerful symbol of unity across cultural boundaries during a cruel national war fought along bitter ethnic and religious divides (Tazi, 2007). Its experience of devastating conflict, loss of human life, and physical destruction does not negate the cosmopolitan vision but rather cautions against idealism in favor of realistic alertness to negative manifestations of differences and prejudice. In the United States, the word "cosmopolitan" has been used to describe the alliance between the African American and Jewish American communities exemplified by some aspects of the civil rights movement (Feher, 1994; Sundquist, 2005).

Prewar Sarajevo and the African American–Jewish alliance are a strong testimony that different groups can coexist in harmony and develop effective coalitions across cultural boundaries even within insular social and historical contexts. In both cases, the ability of different communities to be cosmopolitan has been challenged, creating tension within the communities themselves and also within institutions. There are parallel issues to consider within the social work profession. Are social workers cosmopolitan? Are they comfortable with the unfamiliar? Do they enjoy learning about different cultures, values, and lifestyles? Are they aware of cultural boundaries and willing to learn the rituals necessary to cross those boundaries effectively? Curiosity, not as a casual tourist but as an interested and caring person, is a valuable trait in the culturally grounded approach. Indeed, cosmopolitanism in general is a vital component in the development of the theoretical approach to culturally grounded social work, but its treatment of prejudice could be further advanced. Certain questions remain to be addressed. What are the limits of tolerance? How can democratic societies defend and nurture tolerance and prevent prejudice and discrimination?

Naturally, of the many things that happen in a city—good, bad, and neutral—not all are admirable, but many need to be tolerated. When tolerance is not part of the equation, extremism and intolerance emerge, as is evidenced in the contemporary culture wars that reflect sharp ideological divides between liberal and conservative groups over issues like evolution, gay marriage, and women's reproductive rights.

Pluralism and Multiculturalism

The pluralist perspective maintains that people should be able to advance socially and economically without having to sacrifice their values and cultural heritage unwillingly. Pluralism emerged in part because of the lack of success of the so-called melting pot (Brammer, 2004). Pluralism provided the salad bowl metaphor as an alternative to the melting pot (Pope, 1995). Each vegetable (cultural group) preserves its unique taste and texture (cultural identity), while the dressing provides unity and contributes a common flavor (national identity) to the salad (the nation or the community).

Thus, pluralism is an alternative to assimilation that entails respect among different cultural groups and encourages the retention of each group's cultural values as they incorporate the values of the host or majority culture. Different groups' cultural traits and expressions have persisted mostly because of the advocacy for cultural pluralism by ethnic, religious, and racial minorities. Cultural pluralism leads to a policy of multiculturalism, in which different cultures are encouraged to share their knowledge, experiences, and creative expressions.

Canada has followed a multicultural approach in recognizing its bilingual and bicultural (English/French) historical national identities, recognizing the rights and cultural distinctiveness of the First Nations communities, and welcoming large numbers of immigrants from many different countries, though not without difficulties and controversies (Winter, 2007). The province of Quebec, for example, has advocated and gained through its Quiet Revolution recognition as a "distinct society" with its unique language and culture (see Dickinson & Young, 2003).

Spain is another country where each autonomous region has its own distinct language and culture while maintaining a connection to the Spanish state. These two countries, like many others, have within their geographic and political boundaries a variety of cultures and identities that sometimes are labeled nations within a state. These countries can be located at the progressive end of the multicultural continuum. In the United States, some sectors of society, such as the English-only and anti-immigrant movements, have grown preoccupied by what they perceive to be the negative consequences of "radical" multiculturalism and actively advocate more homogeneity and the repression of distinctive cultural expressions.

Multiculturalism has become a main organizing concept in social work education. The influence of pluralism on social work and its affirmation of diversity are obvious in the National Association of Social Workers' cultural competence standards, which are endorsed by the Council on Social Work Education. Since 1968, the Council on Social Work Education has required accredited social work programs to reflect the diversity of a pluralist society in the composition of their faculty and student body and has mandated that the social work curriculum include content on cultural competence. Thus the principles of multiculturalism are encouraged through the representation and inclusion of multiple cultural groups in the curriculum, the student body, and the faculty. The principles encourage the development of awareness among social work academics and students of the importance of celebrating and nourishing the coexistence of multiple cultural identities within their communities.

Although the multicultural paradigm can be the basis for promoting tolerance as a means of transcending differences between people, it also constitutes an implicit critique of mainstream society. Influenced in part by critical theory, which emanated from the Frankfurt school and various French poststructuralist philosophers, multiculturalists have questioned the hegemony (the preponderant authority or influence of one group over another group or groups) of Western humanism. Multiculturalism rejects the idea that Western society is superior to other traditions. Pluralism has embraced a relativist analysis that reinterprets history by recognizing and adopting the perspectives of a broad array of social groups. With more or less success, this reinterpretation attempts to bring back, resurface, and value the contributions of different groups and traditions to the economic development of societies, knowledge, science, literature, and the arts.

Pluralism questions dogmas from structural functionalist theory about the legitimacy of systems of inequality, male dominance, and the supremacy of anything European. Nonetheless, it is notable that even though the multicultural paradigm rejects Eurocentrism, it has been developed almost exclusively from theoretical models within the European tradition. As a result, multiculturalism has been criticized for lacking a vision of how to address differences in power among different cultural groups because the very tools it uses to analyze difference are culturally specific, patriarchal, and rooted in a European and European

American perspective. Multiculturalism as a theoretical approach has some limitations in its understanding of those who have been oppressed and excluded due to the cultural and social privilege of its leading theorists. At its most extreme, this criticism views multiculturalism as perpetuating inequality by focusing attention on the heterogeneity of cultural groups but deemphasizing their differences in status and power (McKerl, 2007).

Multiculturalism is a limited perspective that may be unable to recognize its own constraints. For example, multiculturalism often fails to acknowledge that cultural symbols vary in legitimacy, authority, and power and thus risks considering all such symbols equally valid. In Western societies there is a tendency to accept Christian symbols as universal while treating symbols coming from other traditions as foreign. The constraints of multiculturalism are illustrated by controversies in contemporary democratic societies over the display of religious symbols in public life. In France, young Muslim women have been forbidden to wear the chador or traditional veils prescribed by their religious customs in public schools; however, crucifixes often hang on classroom walls and other students are allowed to wear "discreet" crosses or stars of David around their necks (Thomas, 2005). In the United States Muslim women have reported being harassed for expressing their religious and cultural identities by observing *hijab* (wearing veils) in public places (Droogsma, 2007). Do these situations reflect the failure of the multicultural paradigm to suffuse adequately into the societal consciousness? Are they evidence of a political and social backlash against multiculturalism, an attempt to set limits on its expression? Alternatively, do these situations demonstrate that, despite the growing recognition of different cultural groups in society, some are still viewed as inherently inferior? One needs to wonder if these limitations are due to multiculturalism's impotence, its failure to gain wider acceptance, or fundamental flaws in the multicultural approach.

The multicultural perspective often supports the expression and celebration of differences in the private sphere, but it fails to consider how tensions arising from these differences can be managed in the public space. President Bill Clinton's "Don't ask, don't tell" policy for gay men and lesbians in the military extends the ideal of private multiculturalism to its limits by promoting the message "You will be tolerated as long as you remain in the closet." This bare tolerance falls far short of acceptance of diversity in sexual orientation.

Multiculturalism has come under attack in some circles. The outcomes it achieves—both intended and unintended—have been questioned, and its rhetoric of tolerance has faced outright rejection. By recognizing the heterogeneity of cultural groups and the many ways in which these groups intersect, multiculturalism provides a starting point for the introduction of tolerance in democratic societies. However, the pluralist discourse that emphasizes the expression of cultural differences may not always result in the diminishment of prejudice. Therefore, if the primary purpose of multicultural efforts is to delineate and heighten boundaries and allow for the expression of a wide range of cultural differences, then it can probably be interpreted more as an antithesis of Allport's contact theory than as a perspective that complements or furthers the scope of contact theory.

Nonetheless, pluralism is an essential component of the culturally grounded approach because it assists communities in delineating boundaries and marking the lines within which minority cultures can express themselves freely. Yet sexism, racism, and homophobia continue to be barriers to pluralism. In addition, because not all cultural artifacts and cultural products are inherently good, multiculturalism can be misused to promote tolerance of oppressive behaviors such as child abuse and domestic violence. The fact that certain practices are common among members of a particular group does not mean that their consequences can be justified in the name of culture.

CONSTRUCTIVISM AND POSTMODERNISM: WORDS CREATE WORLDS

Constructivism

Constructivism—the idea that learners are able to build their own knowledge—grew out of Friedrich A. Hayek's (1963) Nobel Prize–winning treatise *The Sensory Order*, which showed that what humans believe they know about the external world is actually knowledge of themselves. Instead of seeing knowledge as existing in an objective external "real" world, social constructivism stresses that social processes generate knowledge and ideas about reality. That is, humans do not just passively receive knowledge but rather actively build knowledge as creative beings. Therefore, constructivism emphasizes that knowledge is actively constructed rather than discovered and transmitted, while social constructivism suggests that the knowledge is constructed through collaborative social interaction. In relationships with others, individuals can tell someone else about their lives. Social workers, for example, help their clients acknowledge their perceptions of self and their perceptions of their own lives as they constructed them.

Postmodernism

Postmodernism, which has been described as an alternative and collective interpretation of society, is defined as an interpretive device that questions traditional forms of knowledge construction and its dissemination (Hassan, 2003). Postmodernism does not accept the typical or normative ways of describing reality. In other words, it questions existing meta-narratives. "Meta-narrative" is a term used by postmodernists to refer to a larger story that justifies smaller stories. A meta-narrative determines which stories are "central" and acceptable to society, and which stories are "marginal" or unimportant to the understanding of society and to the way it is organized, its norms, and its practices (Foucault, 1980). The term is often seen as synonymous with "ideology" and "worldview." A meta-narrative is like a universal truth or a story about a story (Swan, 1999). Western society's acceptance of the idea that men are aggressive and women are nurturing as a fact influences the way men and women see themselves and each other. The meta-narrative that may accompany this belief is the story of the cave and how men were hunters and women were gatherers and caretakers. This story aims at providing an evolutionary rationale for a widely accepted gender stereotype. Postmodernism questions the story as well as the stereotype by not accepting the universal nature of its premise. A contemporary example of such a story is the demonization of so-called welfare mothers in the 1980s and early 1990s, which emerged as an irrational and unscientific reaction to a financial crisis but became part of the meta-narrative that resulted in the federal legislation enacting sweeping U.S. welfare reform, including the withdrawal of guarantees of assistance to mothers with dependent children and stringent work requirements for recipients.

In a now-famous 1968 speech at Johns Hopkins University, the philosopher Jacques Derrida (1982) proclaimed the end of modernism and the beginning of a postmodern era. Since then postmodernists have argued that what people call knowledge is a special kind of story, a discourse that puts together words and images in ways that seem pleasing or useful to a particular culture or to those with the most power in that culture. While modernism tends to present its fragmented view of human subjectivity as something tragic, postmodernism probes, analyzes, and celebrates fragmentation and contradictions (Kawai, 2006).

Postmodernism, however, can present some challenges for a culturally grounded approach to social work. Despite seeming to be based on the universal value of individuality and difference, it lacks a collective dimension to its understanding of the experience of ethnic minority individuals and other cultural minority communities. In many of these communities, the group—not the individual—is the primary social unit. A sense of belonging to the group and being accepted by it is a primary social goal that overrides individual needs, goals, and viewpoints. Another cultural bias that is often inherited by postmodernism is its strong reliance on the transformative power of the spoken word. Due to postmodernism's reliance on stories, the spoken word is needed to construct the personal narratives that question existing meta-narratives. Traditional cultures—for example, many Native American and Asian American communities—use various means of communication and may rely less than European-based cultures on the spoken word. Despite these limitations, postmodernism provides important insights into different perspectives on diversity in its rebuke of ethnocentrism of any kind.

Postmodernism has much in common with social work theory, as social workers are challenged to be open to different—sometimes marginal—viewpoints, to accept alternative understandings of society, and to be alert to the messages presented by meta-narratives (Howe, 2005).

Symbolic Interactionism

Postmodernism shares several key insights with an earlier theoretical approach from the first half of the twentieth century that recognized how social meaning is socially created rather than a universal given. Symbolic interactionism maintains that humans develop their social identities and formulate ideas about the social world through interactions with people and communities by using symbols like language. Following the philosopher and sociologist George Mead's insights, symbolic interactionists hold that humans act based on the meanings they attach to these symbols, images, or ideas. As they emerge through interactions between people, these meanings are modified through a subjective and interpretative process, becoming a vehicle for how people learn the values and norms of society.

Even though symbols like language facilitate the process of interacting with others, for these interactions to be effective, both parties must understand the symbols. Humans become social beings and develop a sense of self through their interactions with others. This process may involve what Charles Hooten Cooley (1918) called "the looking glass self," the notion that individuals' ideas about themselves are formed by how they imagine that other people see their behavior. The term "significant others," coined by George Mead (1934), emphasizes the role that interactions with key members of primary groups such as parents play in the development of the young self. In other words, attitudes and behaviors are shaped by others and by the perceptions the individual develops about her- or himself.

Symbolic interactionism views people as actors performing for those around them but also taking on the role of those around them. While people may sometimes imitate others to gain their approval, symbolic interaction is usually much more nuanced. It is a process of reacting to others by anticipating how they will react and imagining their point of view. This process is complex because it takes place in different social contexts involving different "audiences." Developmental issues and specific social contexts, for example, strongly influence the degree to which individuals react and how they react to outside social influences. In addition, there is disagreement among symbolic interactionists regarding the extent to which individuals improvise and actively create meanings in each interaction rather than following a predictable script as they develop a stable core self-identity.

Sandstrom, Martin, and Fine (2001) provide the following useful and succinct description of the importance of symbols in interactions between humans, which serves as an introduction to the application of symbolic interactionism in social work from a culturally grounded perspective.

◆ People are unique creatures because of their ability to use symbols.
◆ People become distinctively human through their interaction.

◆ People are conscious and self-reflexive beings, who actively shape their own behavior.

◆ People are purposeful creatures who act in and toward situations.

◆ Human society consists of people engaging in social interaction.

◆ To understand people's social acts, we need to use methods that enable us to discern the meaning they attribute to their acts. (pp. 218–219)

In the case of minority cultural groups, interactions might be heavily influenced by a core sense of identity, one of allegiance to the group and conformity to certain symbols, meanings, and group norms that may not be shared or easily transferred to the outside community. Members of an ethnic group may have their own meanings and rules about how they should act or dress in a given situation that are different from those of other groups. Thus members of ethnic groups actively define their own reality rather than passively reacting to mainstream definitions of reality.

In note from the field 5.1, two factors—age and race—create symbolic distance between Marjorie King and Claire Atkins. In addition, the worker uses a very informal approach to address an elder who is accustomed to more formal and respectful treatment from younger people. The use of a symbolic interaction perspective to evaluate this situation would probably yield alternative approaches for establishing rapport, such as acknowledging some of the differences and addressing the client in a formal manner.

In an extreme situation such as imprisonment, symbolic interaction is useful for identifying how the emotional resources of inmates are grounded individually,

---

NOTE FROM THE FIELD 5.1
R-E-S-P-E-C-T

Mrs. Marjorie King, an eighty-one-year-old African American woman, has been referred to the community mental health center by the senior center's social worker because she appears to exhibit signs of depression. She has been arriving to the senior center later than usual and does not wish to participate in any group activities. The intake at the mental health center is conducted by Claire Atkins, a thirty-two-year-old European American. The worker introduces herself as Claire and addresses Mrs. King on a first-name basis. Mrs. King says little during their meeting. Once she completes all the forms, she excuses herself and leaves. She tells the social worker at the senior center that the social worker at the mental health clinic was not respectful or professional. She did not like the way she was treated and is not willing to go back.

contextually, and culturally. For example, Greer (2002) used interactionist perspective to interpret the strategies women in prison use to develop and maintain social relationships in a very controlled and oppressive setting in which expressions of emotion are closely regulated by the prison system as well as by informal subcultures. Prison gangs provide protection and demand allegiance that often needs to be demonstrated through the adoption of symbols.

Understanding the power of symbols as expressions of culture is crucial for social workers who follow a culturally grounded approach. Symbolic interactionism emphasizes the dynamic way that interactions can socialize both parties. For example, while interacting with clients, social work practitioners are open to the subjective meanings communicated to them by their clients. Workers must learn how to take the role of the "other" and remain open to the fact that the socialization process is affecting them as well as their clients.

Symbols are rooted in culture and are expressed through behaviors. Social workers are exposed to many different symbols and codes throughout the day, sometimes without noticing them. Practitioners search for meaning and should openly ask clients for help when the meaning of certain symbols or behaviors is not clear. Symbolic interactionist approaches are sensitive to the ways individuals interpret their lives and how they make sense of them. The theory is not deterministic like Marxism or functionalism; it leaves open the range of possibilities for how any two individuals interpret and react to the same situation. Symbolic interactionism provides guideposts for social workers and cautions against generalizing behaviors based solely on the group membership (culture) of their clients. The key to understanding behavior is understanding how individuals define and organize the social situation, a process in which culture appears to play a key role.

Extensions of symbolic interactionist theory have explored in detail the question of how everyday reality is socially constructed. In other words, how is it possible that subjective meanings become objective fact? Theorists have studied the process people go through as they transform their subjective interpretations of their own experiences into something real and factual that can be seen by others, and how they challenge the assumption that the world is shared or sharable (Berger & Luckmann, 1966). The assumption interactionists make is that a different person—whether a social worker or a family member—looking at the same experience will interpret it differently. The observer's interpretations build structures of plausibility, that is, accounts of how the social world operates and consequently what can be changed. Symbolic interactionism is relevant to the development of a culturally grounded approach because—as note from the field 5.2 illustrates—it supports the principle that objectivity is elusive in the human experience. What is Sarah's role in this case? From a symbolic interactionist perspective, her question and Ann's answer reflect different perceptions of the same reality. What is the practitioner's role in situations where the client's symbology does not match the worker's?

NOTE FROM THE FIELD 5.2
Choosing to Live Outside

Sarah, an MSW student, interviews Ann, a homeless woman, as part of an assignment for one of her courses. After Ann gives her consent to participate, Sarah starts her interview by asking her, "What is it like to be a homeless woman?" Ann appears to be very upset by the question and responds, "I am not a homeless woman. I have chosen to live outside." From a symbolic interactionist perspective, how should Sarah interpret Ann's response?

Narrative Theory

Some postmodernist philosophers have argued that humans organize knowledge as novelists rather than as scientists. People think, perceive their lives, experience happiness and sadness, imagine, and make choices according to narrative structures, or the stories they have created about themselves and others around them (Sarbin, 1986). It is as storytellers that individuals get to know themselves and others, interpret their pasts, imagine their futures, make decisions, and justify their lives to themselves and to others. Individuals constantly narrate their experiences from their own point of view, assigning roles very much as a novelist or a screenwriter would. One of these roles is their own.

Narrative theory focuses on the stories that help individuals interpret and give meaning to their life experiences. Narratives also connect different generations by allowing people to link their lives with those of their ancestors. Narrative theory sees storytelling as a mode of communication that is pervasive and transcultural. Narratives are guideposts for the moral choices people make and provide organizing principles for thought and behavior. More than basic thought, narratives are a meaningful communicative tool through which individuals express themselves while creating images of the past and the present and images of their own future actions. Thus, individuals are not simply storytellers but "story dwellers," and their stories are constantly being created and modified (Fasching, 1992). People's options and choices, including those for coping with crises and challenges and those that enable them to persist in their efforts to change oppressive conditions, are embedded in stories. As a result, storytelling can be a tool of liberation.

The culturally grounded approach shares the postmodern understanding that words create worlds, or that humans construct their own reality by naming it and forming it into a story. As social workers listen to their clients' narratives, they often identify recurring patterns in the way clients portray themselves and other significant people in their lives. Narrative theory proposes that the social world cannot be treated as an objective system and the stories told are essentially subjective. From this perspective, social work practitioners must become aware and be respectful of the way in which reality is linguistically constructed by individuals, groups, and communities. The stories people tell are not just individually invented worlds that guide their day-to-day social relationships and negotiations; they are also the product of their social contexts.

People do not live in isolation, and conversely their stories are not constructed in isolation. Rather, individual stories inscribe themselves in larger narratives that create shared vocabularies (namely, life as it is perceived and interpreted by community members), delineate the structure of what was and what is (reality), and define what is possible (opportunities, followed by dreams, plans, goals, and action). These narratives define the forbidden and determine to whom prohibitions apply.

Stories are also ideological structures permeated by political and contextual realities that establish non-negotiable privileges and boundaries of freedom, and supported by meta-narratives (Gregg, 1991). Power relations are a strong external reality that individuals confront in their everyday lives. The ability to overcome obstacles and live full lives depends in great measure on an individual's interactions with master narratives—the stories that have been constructed from the point of view of dominant groups about social reality. These stories tell individuals who they are, who they are not, and what they can and cannot do or become. For example, the master narrative may tell girls in junior high that they are not as good in algebra as their male classmates. Some girls believe that message and opt out of or underperform in advanced math. These encompassing master narratives supply a ready-made template for the cultural minority individual to fit into. They furnish socializing mechanisms and justify power relations and interactions, often protecting the privilege of a few.

From colonial times, whites in what is today the United States crafted master narratives to define African Americans in ways that justified their enslavement, their denial of the full benefits of citizenship, and denigration of their culture. Master narratives were used in the twentieth century to portray all black families as dysfunctional, inevitably consigned to poverty, economically marginalized, dependent on social welfare programs, and plagued by high rates of deviant and criminal behavior and cultural decay (Williams & Peterson, 1998). Such narratives have been instrumental in halting and often reversing the progress of government poverty programs and in the dismantling of federal entitlement programs.

The culturally grounded approach shares the postmodern understanding that words create worlds, or that humans construct their own reality by naming it and forming it into a story. Narrative theory, as a direct derivative of postmodern thought, challenges social workers, educators, and other agents of socialization to support clients in their efforts to become better storytellers. A better storyteller is able to integrate resiliency into the story and to verbalize needs and paths to address those needs. Once the story is told, the client, in partnership with the worker, can examine the roles played by the different characters and the strengths and the weaknesses of her or his interpretation of the story. The social worker may perceive the influence of a powerful meta-narrative that sets limits and perpetuates oppressive relationships. Working together, the client and worker identify the strengths that have been overlooked and assess the potential for change and empowerment. The objective is to allow the client to construct a more liberating narrative that can be translated into real life, one that eventually leads to lasting change. The new narratives generated by the client allow for the emergence of new roles and a reinterpretation of stories that perpetuate oppression. In the new narratives, the assets of the client are highlighted and oppressive conditions are targeted for reflection and action. Daily life is the social context in which change will take place. The particular place and time in which narratives are constructed influence the stories that are told. Social workers may want their clients to adopt what they consider the language of aspirations and success, encouraging clients to create new stories of change and success. At times, clients say what they think is expected and satisfies the criteria established by a naive social worker. However, a situation in which the client mimics the social worker until she or he sounds like the social worker can hardly be described as an empowering or transforming process of change. Assessing progress over time based on how much the client adopts the practitioner's language, insights, point of view, and values would be the antithesis of a culturally grounded approach to practice, as it perpetuates oppressive relationships. It is through action in addition to stories (praxis) that individuals make concrete plans and plan actions toward change and create sustainable structures of plausibility.

Because most of social work practice takes place around the telling of stories, the narrative approach is central to the culturally grounded approach. Social work as a profession, in its attempts to respond to the unique needs and opportunities it faces as an applied field, has integrated many postmodernist concepts and approaches and has adopted related theories that guide social work practice and research. Narratives are a vital component of transformative social work practice.

RELEVANCE OF THEORIES TO CULTURALLY GROUNDED SOCIAL WORK

Table 5.1, which summarizes the level of fit of the different approaches reviewed, is offered as a thinking tool more than as a definitive way of organizing the theories reviewed thus far. The search for an appropriate theoretical foundation for social work is an ongoing process. Social work as a discipline has devel-

Table 5.1 Level of Fit between Theories and the Culturally Grounded Approach

Theory	Level of fit				
	None	Low	Medium	High	Very high
Social Darwinism	X				
Structural functionalism		X			
Assimilation		X			
Melting pot		X			
Marxist/neo-Marxist theory			X		
Contact theory				X	
Pluralism				X	
Cosmopolitanism				X	
Structural role theory				X	
Human capital theory				X	
Postmodernism					X
Symbolic interactionism					X
Narrative theory					X

oped approaches based on many of these theories. At the same time, it has embraced broader theoretical approaches and added its own applied flavor to them. Some of these efforts at theoretical synthesis are described in the next chapter.

Key Concepts

Principles of homophily the theory that individuals prefer to develop social bonds with people who look and act like themselves

Pluralistic perspective the belief that people should be able to advance socially and economically without having to sacrifice values and cultural heritage unwillingly

Multiculturalism the spreading of knowledge, experiences, and creative expressions of different cultures

Social constructivism the theory that individuals actively construct knowledge and ideas about reality and themselves through social processes and experiences

Postmodernism an alternative and collective interpretation of society that questions traditional forms of knowledge construction and dissemination

Symbolic interactionism interactions through which people learn the values and norms of society and learn to attach meanings to symbols, images, and ideas

Narrative theory the theory that the human experience is conveyed through stories or through storytelling and that changes in behavior and attitudes can be initiated through a rewriting of these stories

6

Social Work Perspectives: Social Context, Consciousness, and Resiliency

THIS CHAPTER PROVIDES AN OVERVIEW OF CONTEMPORARY SOCIAL WORK theories and perspectives that are based on or have been derived from the more established theories reviewed in previous chapters. These are applied theories and are commonly used to guide social work practice, research, and policy development. In their role as practitioner-researchers, social workers draw from and contribute to theory development. Through cultural grounding, they can work to operationalize notions of cultural strengths and resiliencies based on the knowledge acquired from practice within different cultural communities. Social work theory describes in applied terms how resiliency can be expressed and how change can be produced in different communities and in different social environments. The culturally grounded perspective is presented at the end of the chapter as a synthesis of many theories that help workers understand the cultural assets of clients and their role in transformation and change.

The perspectives discussed in this chapter help practitioners capitalize on the resiliency of their clients, as well as the assets of different oppressed communities, and counterbalance the so-called medical or deficiency model that is a common approach in many fields of practice. Social work and its allied fields function within environments and institutions that identify presenting problems as symptoms, and interventions as treatment, often without much regard for clients' assets or strengths. This deficiency approach tends to follow these steps:

1. Intervene when there is a problem (illness)
2. Diagnose the problem (assessment)
3. Prescribe medication to alleviate the symptoms (intervention)

The approach focuses on what is not working and runs the risk of pathologizing individuals, families, groups, and communities because they are different from the providers. These differences often lead to misunderstandings and unnecessary labeling, which can result in social services, policy, and research that perpetuate and contribute to oppression. A deficiency approach is oppressive because it inevitably exaggerates the client's shortcomings and overlooks assets. For example, phrases like "culture of poverty" and "at-risk youths" set the stage for a deficiency approach to practice with members of communities labeled in such a manner.

Practitioners can fall into the trap of assessing what the client lacks instead of trying to understand who the client is and what she or he has to offer in overcoming the presenting problem. There is also a risk of assuming that statistical descriptions of elevated risks for a social or cultural group apply equally to all its members. For example, health disparities among different groups are statistically well documented, but little is known about the members of disadvantaged communities who live healthy and productive lives against all odds. Different theoretical perspectives have—with different levels of success—been developed and tested through empirical research in an attempt to provide a more balanced approach to social work practice. The perspectives presented here were selected based on their relevance for social work practice with different cultural communities that have faced or continue to face oppression.

THE STRENGTHS, OR RESILIENCY, PERSPECTIVE

The strengths perspective, also known as the resiliency perspective, focuses on understanding the personal and social processes that help individuals maintain a positive level of functioning (i.e., productive and healthy lives) despite the environmental challenges they face. The strengths perspective is based on the belief that human beings have the inherent capacity to grow and change, even under adverse conditions.

Resiliency is the ability to cope with and bounce back from challenging and difficult experiences. For example, resilient young people can be described as having strong relationships—with their friends, family, and school personnel and classmates and within their community. Krovetz (1999) has identified a number of protective factors that are present in the families, schools, and communities of successful youths. When at least some of these protective factors are present, children develop resiliency, that is, the ability to cope with adversity. There are at least four common attributes of resilient children: they possess social competence, problem-solving skills, autonomy, and sense of purpose and future (Benard, 1991, 2002). The strengths, or resiliency, perspective proposes that these are some of the attributes that are present to some degree in most people of all ages. Whether they are strong enough to help an individual cope with adversity, however, depends on the presence of protective factors during the individual's childhood. From a culturally grounded perspective, there is a concern about how to identify and define protective factors as they may be expressed in various ways by people of different cultures.

Like individuals, families can be resilient in the way they cope with stress and respond to challenging situations (Patterson, 2002). The family resiliency perspective emphasizes family strengths and resources rather than family deficits and pathology, with particular attention to positive mental health and good functioning. The family resiliency literature provides a useful collective or systems approach to understanding resiliency and introduces a level of complexity to understanding the source of resiliency. Culture plays an important role in family resiliency. In some cultures family resiliency can be interpreted as the sum of the individual family members' resiliency, while in other cultures, family resiliency may be seen as independent from the resiliency of its individual members. In work with more collectivistic cultures, family resiliency needs to be considered an important resource in addition to individual resiliency.

Some of the criticism of resiliency theory focuses on its lack of an empirical basis. However, important culturally specific resiliency research has been conducted with children and families. For example, a longitudinal study (over a forty-year period) was conducted with seven hundred Hawaiian residents born under adverse circumstances such as chronic poverty (Werner & Smith, 1992). The sample was composed of children whose parents and grandparents had immigrated to Hawaii from Asia or Europe. Approximately two-thirds of the sample had various diagnosable conditions during childhood, while one-third had none. By the time the study participants reached their mid-thirties, almost all (including many who had experienced problems) had become positively motivated and were productive and well-adjusted adults. A distinguishing factor shared by the individuals who showed resiliency was a close long-term childhood relationship with a caring, responsible parent or other adult. Only about thirty of the original group of seven hundred individuals did not "bounce back" from the adverse circumstances in which they grew up. Interestingly, the researchers found that socioeconomic and ethnic background did not have explanatory power for the experiences of the non-resilient study participants.

Other resiliency-focused studies have used data from the National Education Longitudinal Survey to examine family influences on children's achievement, paying special attention to ethnic variables. For example, Hao and Bonstead-Bruns (1998) found lower levels of parent-child interactions among immigrant Mexican Americans than among immigrant Asian Americans. However, immigrant students from Mexico had one strong advantage: knowledge of their parents' language. Proficiency in the parental language significantly improved achievement and grades in math.

In a study with Latino youths in an urban school, the principle difference between socially and academically resilient and non-resilient students was that the resilient youths had more confidence in their cognitive abilities (Gordon, 1996). Students excelled academically because they believed that they could understand the material and information presented in class and that they could do well on homework and tests. Where did these perceptions come from? How were those positive messages conveyed to the children, and by whom? Research in the fields of child and human development, schools, and communities reveals that successful development in any human system relates directly to the quality of relationships in the system and opportunities for participation in those relationships (Benard, 1991). Three key characteristics support productive development: (1) caring relationships, (2) communication of high expectations, and (3) positive beliefs and opportunities for participation. The most important of these protective factors is a caring relationship with someone, regardless of whether that person is a parent, teacher, or community mentor (Werner & Smith, 1992).

In sum, the literature on resiliency identifies five key protective factors of families, schools, and communities: (1) supportive relationships, particularly encouragement from school personnel and other adults; (2) individual characteristics such as self-esteem, motivation, and accepting responsibility; (3) family cohesion factors such as parental support/concern and school involvement; (4) community cohesion factors, such as the availability of community youth programs (e.g., sports, clubs); and (5) school support for pro-social activities and academic success (Feinberg, Rindenour, & Greenberg, 2007) and pro-social skills training. Social work plays a key role in strengthening or restoring the social contexts and the social processes identified in this research.

Table 6.1 provides a summary of selected protective factors identified by the

Table 6.1 Psychosocial Protective Factors for Children

Characteristics of the child	Family characteristics	Social support from outside the family
Is positive, has easy temperament	Child lives at home with parents.	The child has an adult mentor outside the immediate family.
Shows autonomy and independence as a toddler	There is a secure mother-infant attachment.	The family caretaker has help.
Has high hopes and expectations for the future	Child has warm relationship with a parent.	The child has support from friends.
Has internal locus of control as a teenager	Parents practice consistent discipline.	The child receives support from a mentor at school.
Is interpersonally engaging, likable	Child perceives that parents care.	The family receives support from a religious congregation.
Has a sense of humor	There are established routines in the home.	The family receives support from the workplace.

resiliency literature on children. If a child does not have positive relationships within her or his immediate or extended family, social workers can help connect the child and the family with resources that can provide those relationships; for example, such relationships might be found through organized religion, Boys and Girls Clubs, or a community center. Although there is agreement about these factors, some concerns remain regarding their cross-cultural generalizability and how they are measured or assessed (Torres Stone & Meyler, 2007). A white middle-class American expression of parental care may be very different from a Tongan expression of parental care. The main role of the social worker working from a culturally grounded perspective is to identify with clients these strengths and resources in a culturally appropriate manner and make use of them to help clients achieve their goals (Saleebey, 2002).

In the strengths-based approach, social workers support the client's engagement in behaviors that respect the needs of other community members and promote personal gratification and a sense of accomplishment (Kisthardt, 2002). Clients transform themselves by getting in touch with their own natural resources that equip them with the power and tools to become effective agents of change. The strengths perspective follows the philosophies of contact theory, cosmopolitanism, and pluralism because it proposes that a caring community is one that affirms diversity through egalitarian relationships that give each person (or group) an opportunity to be who she or he is and contribute her or his share toward change and social advancement.

Although the bulk of research on resiliency has focused on individual response to adversity and crises, the concept can also be applied to larger social systems like families and communities, as well as to the broader social context of human behavior and development. The ecosystemic resiliency perspective suggests that protective influences (e.g., personal attributes, family strengths, culture, social policies promoting education) can be introduced into an individual's life through any relationship in any part of the ecosystem and that this positive change can have reverberating positive effects throughout the individual's ecosystem that enhance the possibility of desirable outcomes (Schwartz, Pantin, Coatsworth, & Szapocznik, 2007).

The resiliency perspective recognizes that all cultural groups have unique strengths that can be used to empower their members. When applying the strengths perspective and empowerment models, practitioners build an awareness of their own culture, are open to cultures different from their own, and become committed to a client-oriented and horizontal way of relating that suggests constant learning.

The strengths perspective recognizes culture as a source of resiliency; culture is approached as a potential protective factor against adversity. For example, the ecological risk and resiliency approach proposes to understand and integrate the cultural and contextual processes that make interventions effective, as well as the cultural circumstances under which these interventions fail to work (Bogen-schneider, 1996). This perspective assumes that effective interventions are those that focus on learning or relearning (through enculturation) the attitudes, behaviors, and strategies that foster strengths rather than those that undermine social competencies. Culture of origin plays a key role in this process, as it often provides a connection to the collective strengths and traditional helping and support systems that are rooted in and nurtured by culture. The strengths perspective occupies a central place in the culturally grounded approach, as it informs the client-worker relationship and capitalizes on the client's culture as a source of strength to be tapped.

Resiliency theory can guide practitioners as they work with families from different cultures. The following guidelines for practice are resiliency based and illustrate the connection between resiliency theory and social work practice:

- Listen to the story.
- Acknowledge the pain.
- Look for strengths.
- Ask questions about survival, support, positive times, interests, dreams, goals, and sources of pride.
- Point out strengths.
- Link strengths to the client's goals and dreams.
- Link clients to resources to achieve goals and dreams.
- Find opportunities for clients to be teachers (Benard, 2002).

Some of these guidelines are particularly relevant in work with cultural minority clients. For example, cultural pride can be a very useful counterbalance to the acculturation stress that clients may be experiencing.

PERSON-IN-ENVIRONMENT PERSPECTIVE

The person-in-environment (PIE) perspective is a social work adaptation of an ecological approach to integrating individuals, families, and communities within their unique social contexts. The influences from the different ecosystemic levels can be strengths or sometimes barriers to change and self-realization. Following a PIE perspective, social work practice aims at enhancing the psychosocial functioning of individuals and supporting them in their efforts to change the oppressive social conditions that have a negative effect on the interactions between individuals and their environments (Longres, 2000). Clients are viewed by the social worker as possessing untapped reserves of mental, physical, and emotional resources that can be drawn from to help them develop, grow, and overcome the different challenges they face as they interact in different social environments. The PIE perspective provides a broad ecological perspective that guides social workers in identifying naturally occurring support systems and resources at the disposal of the client.

The PIE perspective also provides social workers with a common classification system for communicating about challenges their clients face. It offers four dimensions for describing, classifying, and approaching possible client stressors: social-role stressors, environmental stressors, mental disorders, and physical disorders (Ashford, LeCroy, & Lortie, 2001). Each of these dimensions can appear in different communities, social environments, and contexts, which in turn provide resources that can be used to overcome or cope with the identified stressors. Culture is a key component of the environment or social context. Key concepts related to a culturally grounded approach are found in the cultural context of the client.

For example, organized religion plays a very important role as a source of cultural identity in many African American communities. The Taylors, an African American family, reside in a suburban neighborhood and face the decision of whether to drive an hour on Sundays to attend services at a historical African American church where the children's grandparents worship or attend a predominantly white church of the same denomination located only two blocks away from their home. What are the pros and cons of each decision? What are the advantages or disadvantages for the parents and children? The PIE perspective provides a much-needed emphasis on the environment or social context. Attending the grandparents' church offers the family an opportunity to strengthen their bond with family, community, and culture. On the other hand, because the Taylors' children attend school and live in a white neighborhood that is not close by, they may be seen as outsiders and may not be readily accepted by other African American children living in the neighborhood surrounding the grandparents' church. Social workers applying a PIE perspective can help families and individual clients manage the tension that can emerge between cultural maintenance and ethnic identity as they navigate other environments.

FEMINIST THEORY

Social work has been at the vanguard in the development of feminist theory and its application to professional practice. Contemporary social work methods are firmly grounded in feminist and postfeminist theory. It can be argued that feminism has existed for a long time, as women have struggled for centuries for their rights. Since the late nineteenth century, a defined set of principles has emerged and evolved into a relatively unified theoretical body of work examining the subordinate position of women and their struggles to overcome their oppression. Feminist theorists like Dorothy Smith have explored the everyday lives of women and their subordinate positions. Smith (1988), a sociologist, has attempted to interpret the structures of male domination experienced by women and to identify how women think and feel about these experiences. The study of the gendered nature of all relationships is generally at the center of most feminist theory, which aims at understanding how gender is related to social inequalities and oppression. Thus these gendered relationships are interpreted as social creations that can and should be changed.

Some branches of feminism incorporate elements of micro social theories related to constructivism and postmodernism but also look at the macro social variables affecting the lives of women. For example, neo-Marxist feminism views hierarchical social class relations as the source of coercive power and oppression, and gender oppression as a dimension of class power. According to this perspective, gender inequality emerges from the unequal economic base of society, one that first created private wealth in a class system while treating women as a form of property. The economically based devaluation of women in contemporary society can be seen in what has been called the feminization of poverty, the sharply higher risk of living in poverty that women, especially minority women, and their children face compared to men. The division of labor between the sexes also contributes to women's unequal status. Traditionally, women have carried out a variety of domestic duties that are unpaid, and they continue today to shoulder most of those tasks. In the workplace they are still hired disproportionately to occupy administrative positions (i.e., secretary, receptionist) while men retain a disproportionate share of the management ranks. By hindering women's access to institutional power, this system perpetuates gender inequality and oppression.

One theme of feminist theory that is often adopted by social work is feminism's celebration of differences. In addition, feminism is congruent with the PIE perspective, as it emphasizes social context. Feminist social work is influenced by the relational model of women's development, which emphasizes connection and mutual empathy in the development of a woman's sense of self. In this model, the client-worker relationship is egalitarian and characterized by reciprocity as an alternative to patriarchal models.

Social work as a profession is overwhelmingly female, and the majority of the people it serves are women (Stewart, 2005). It is only natural that the profession has engaged in an effort to integrate feminist thought into social work practice and research. Furthermore, a feminist perspective occupies a central place in the development of a culturally grounded approach. This perspective can be useful in assessing specific client needs. In a study of homeless women receiving treatment in a hospital, researchers found that feminist frameworks allowed social workers to approach women's needs on a personal level and within their social and political context (Boes & Van Wormer, 1997). Feminist theory places great importance on the helping relationship, in which the capacity to produce change (power) is understood to take different forms and have different implications (Cohen, 1998). Within a relational model of women's development drawn from feminist theory, change is used in social work practice to empower people and promote the client's goals. Feminism calls upon social workers to identify, acknowledge, and struggle against the macro-level forces that oppress women, including inadequate funding sources, accrediting bodies, and agency bureaucracies.

INTERSECTIONALITY THEORY

The intersectionality of gender, ethnicity, social class, and sexual orientation has become an important area of research and concern among feminists. An evolving body of theory on the intersection of race/ethnicity and gender addresses concerns that early feminist theory represented the experience and cosmology of white middle-class women. Within that framework, women's experience was made synonymous with what it was like to be a white woman. In exploring the structures of domination, women from ethnic minority groups may see their own experiences and opportunities as being very different from those of their white middle-class sisters. bell hooks (1981), among others, questioned the analysis of the oppression of women and blacks as separate and discrete phenomena. Such practice, she explains, undermines the experiences of black women because it implies that all women are white and all African Americans are male. The intersectionality perspective addresses this problem by following the premise that race is gendered and gender is "raced" and by considering the simultaneous and interacting effects of categories of difference such as race and gender (Hancock, 2007b). These explorations have led to calls for intersectionality and a form of multiracial feminism that recognizes that because of their racial and ethnic backgrounds, there are important differences in the types and levels of inequality experienced by women of color.

Contemporary Chicana and African American feminists, among others, are addressing these intersectionalities and shining some light on how women of different ethnic backgrounds experience social class, and their potentially divided loyalties. Women are often put in the unfortunate position of having to favor one identity over another: Am I a woman who happens to be African American or am I an African American who happens to be a woman? White privilege may lead feminists to overemphasize gender oppression by treating it as a discrete phenomenon separate from racial and ethnic oppression. Many feminists and other commentators have come to realize that the advances many white women have made in their professional careers were only possible because of the low-wage positions minority women assumed as their families' housekeepers, nannies, and day care providers (Baker, 2005).

Important theoretical developments have been made in understanding and addressing the unique experiences of lesbians, who may experience double (as women and lesbians) or triple jeopardy (as women, lesbians, and people of color).

African American lesbians are a group that has faced a triple dosage of silence and marginality because of homophobia within some African American communities and churches, the relative invisibility of lesbians in black feminist thought, and the fact that less attention is paid to lesbians than to gay men in studies of sexuality (James, 2001).

Intersectionality theory is an alternative to approaches that are solely gender based or race based. It recognizes the unique experiences that result from the intersection (i.e., meeting point) of gender, race, and other categories and how the coexistence of multiple oppressions affects the individual. Although the term "intersectionality" and its related contemporary body of literature has become better known since the 1980s, intersectionality theory has deeper roots. W. E. B. Du Bois, for example, has been identified as one of the forefathers of intersectionality due to his pioneering recognition of the roles of race conjoined with class, and race conjoined with gender (Hancock, 2005).

Intersectionality provides a compass for gaining a better understanding and promoting recognition of the unique experiences that emerge from the possession of multiple subordinate statuses as opposed to a dominant or master narrative (McCall, 2005). The concept of intersectionality provides a culturally grounded lens through which to look at the complex identities women and men form through their multiple experiences of race, gender, social class, sexual orientation, national origin, and other categories of difference (Hancock, 2007a). Intersectionality theory offers an alternative perspective to the one-size-fits-all approach to addressing multiple sources of discrimination and provides a counterpoint to the assumption of sameness or equivalence of social categories connected to inequalities and the mechanisms and processes that create and perpetuate them (Verloo, 2006).

Practitioners, policy makers, and researchers interested in quantifying the oppression of African American women may fall into the trap of combining the results of studies of gender focused on white women with those of studies of race focused on black men. This strategy perpetuates the view of race and gender as separate, parallel phenomena. The intersectionality approach avoids falling into this trap by adding categories and their possible equal explanatory power. It proposes an interactive, mutually constitutive relationship between identity categories in shaping the experience of oppression of women and men and their related behaviors (Hancock, 2005). Intersectionality theory aims at integrating interconnected categories from the start and avoids approaching them as discrete or separate variables. The outcome of looking at conditions from the point of view of intersectionality, or the merging of conditions—rather than viewing the conditions as separate entities—is the phenomenon to be studied. Such an approach allows for the recognition and the inclusion of intergroup diversity as well as the identification of the implications of intersectionality for policy, practice, and research.

The intersectionality perspective is also useful for examining privilege. Those who enjoy normative or nonmarginalized statuses such as whiteness, masculinity, heterosexuality, and upper-class status do not simply experience the absence of oppression but enjoy direct social and material benefits resulting from the intersection of those statuses (Bonilla-Silva, 1997). Because hierarchies of power intersect, it is likely that a person will be simultaneously advantaged by particular identities and disadvantaged by others (Steinbugler, Press, & Johnson Dias, 2006). For example, a gay Asian American man may experience privilege as a result of his gender but may be marginalized because of his race and sexual orientation. These hierarchies intersect at all levels of social life, in both social structures and social interactions (Baca Zinn & Thornton Dill, 1996). Individuals differ in terms of which identities they share with others and how their identities are expressed differently across different social contexts. Individuals who possess multiple marginalized identities have experiences that are probably different from the experiences of individuals who have a combination of marginalized and privileged identities (Hancock, 2005). For example, the income gap between lesbian and gay men working couples can be explained in part by the privilege experienced by gay men couples as two male income earners compared with the two female income earners in lesbian couples (Leppel, 2007).

The concept of structural intersectionality is useful for understanding how inequalities and their intersections are directly relevant to the experiences of real people in a given social context (Crenshaw, 1991). Structural intersectionality can explain why a Mexican American woman may not be considered for one job because she is Latina, since the norm employee is an Anglo woman, while other jobs are also unavailable to her since the jobs available to Mexican Americans are generally given to men. Structural intersectionality highlights the fact that heteronormativity (the traditional gender expectations of men and women in a given society) is also part and parcel of gender inequality, which means that the position of lesbians is very different from the position of heterosexual women. Key questions to ask in analyzing structural intersectionality are: How and when does racism amplify sexism? How and when does class exploitation reinforce homophobia? How and when does homophobia amplify racism?

Researchers have advocated the development of a battery of survey items that measure how race is gendered and how gender is "raced" across a number of gender/racial categories (Steinbugler et al., 2006). They suggest, for example, that researchers consider developing scales on Asian masculinity, white femininity, Chicana femininity, and so forth. Such a project would require resources and effort to construct and refine intersectional stereotype measures, but such investments are necessary if scholars hope to use social surveys to understand the complicated relationship between intersecting prejudices, public policy, and social work practice.

Lastly, the intersectionality paradigm can provide clients and practitioners with common ground as well as a realistic view of their social and cultural boundaries. For example, their common ground can be a shared gender identity, and ethnicity can be a border to be crossed and negotiated. On the other hand, the client and the practitioner may share the same ethnic background and gender but come from different social classes or have different sexual orientations. Intersectionality theory provides a useful framework for sorting similarities and differences and discovering the common ground needed to develop a strong therapeutic alliance.

LIBERATION PEDAGOGY

The term "social pedagogy" came into general usage in Germany in the nineteenth century when Friedrich Diesterweg used the term to argue for a social pedagogy, or educational action, to help the disadvantaged, believing that people were capable of respecting others and working for the good of the community. The linking of pedagogy to community and democracy was later adopted by Paulo Freire (1994), whose original interest was primarily in addressing the needs of the illiterate and oppressed unskilled workers of Brazil. Extending the traditional definition of pedagogy, Freire integrated elements of different perspectives such as Marxist and neo-Marxist thought, symbolic interactionism, and other constructivist and postmodern philosophies to develop liberation pedagogy, the comprehensive cultural transformation of the learner. He understood that human relations are influenced by power and wealth and that the oppressed, as a first step toward changing their conditions, need to become conscious of their oppression. For example, the working poor must become aware of the forces that prevent them from accessing the educational system as a means of ensuring the continuous supply of cheap labor before they can attempt to change it. Liberation pedagogy strives to help the oppressed take a step back from their daily existence and see how they are affected by interrelated societal factors, ultimately becoming aware of the barriers they need to overcome to change their lives and the lives of other members of their communities.

This awareness can be achieved only through challenging what Freire (1994) referred to as the "banking approach to teaching," where classrooms are organized like banks. The teacher, who has a monopoly on knowledge, stands in the front of the room, while the students are treated like empty vessels. The teacher's role is to deposit knowledge into the empty vessels. The students' positioning facing the teacher, with their backs to each other, gives students the implicit message that they have nothing to share with each other and nothing of value to contribute because the teacher possesses all the real knowledge. Such an unequal relationship gives all the power to the teacher and ensures that the students remain disempowered. Freire proposed that students should be allowed to recognize the knowledge and experience that other students bring with them to the classroom. Thus the role of the teacher is to facilitate the dialogue from which critical consciousness will emerge. Critical consciousness is attained through dialogue as part of a collective process that cannot be achieved in isolation. Awareness is possible only through the collective nature of the exchanges, the sharing of ideas and knowledge that emerges from individual and collective life experiences.

Freire's core concept of critical consciousness has been applied in social work as a means for individuals and communities to identify, examine, and act on the root causes of their oppression (Gutierrez & Lewis, 1998). This process involves a gradual and cyclical action-reflection-action chain of behaviors, or praxis. A culturally grounded approach to social work practice incorporates praxis by using the narratives of community members as the means for raising their consciousness and inspiring them to engage in transformative action by using their resources and validating what they already know to be true from their experiences. To them, poverty is not an abstract concept; they know what it is like to be poor and to lack the resources to pay the electric bill.

Although praxis was developed and tested in South America and later in Africa, it has been found to be a useful approach in the United States, Canada, and Mexico in the creation of more just social structures and more caring communities (Abram, Slosar, & Walls, 2005). Praxis advances the social justice–social diversity mission that is central to the social work profession. Freire's work occupies a central place in the culturally grounded approach because it directly addresses both oppression and action and advances the notions of critical consciousness and empowerment—both of which are critical to culturally grounded social work.

SYNTHESIS: AN ECLECTIC THEORETICAL APPROACH TO CULTURALLY GROUNDED SOCIAL WORK

The theories discussed in this chapter offer a number of valuable concepts for a culturally grounded approach to social work. The key elements of the culturally grounded approach derived from these theories can be conceptualized as three main theoretical components: honoring narratives, integrating those narratives in their appropriate social and political contexts, and developing critical consciousness. These three components are interrelated and complement each other through a web of theoretical connections and practice applications.

Narratives

Culturally grounded social work begins with stories based on the client's life, stories that honor both the individual and her or his collective experiences (shared experiences she or he had at the family, group, or community level). Because social workers may be unaware of what it is like to be a member of a particular cultural group, they may start by recognizing their own lack of knowledge and engage in dialogue with the client simply to find out what the client is experiencing and what she or he is doing about it. The way that the client tells her or his story provides important information about how she or he interprets the presenting problem and about the resources within the client's culture that are available to help her or him overcome challenges. Social workers honor the client's expertise, strengths, and abilities to cope and overcome distress. At the same time, social workers start to identify their professional helping role in partnership with the individual, family, group, or community. In this way, the client's stories become a pivotal starting point, as they provide the social worker with information about the client's culture, which checks the social worker's ethnocentric views and attitudes. Social work aims at helping clients dream of a better future. The stories clients share are based on their interpretation of their daily experiences and pave the way for change. The subjectivity of the social worker is as important as her or his objective knowledge. Strong rapport and an open mind are necessary to prevent unnecessary editing of clients' stories. The social worker avoids making any kind of biased judgment such as "That's a very unusual behavior," as such comments will only deter clients from telling the story as they perceive it. The culturally grounded social worker is more than anything else a good active listener.

Social workers play an important role as partners of cultural minority clients in their efforts to enter mainstream society and to access its benefits. Integration, however, is understood as a process through which the stories of the cultural minority client transform the dominant ideology. These stories are rooted in clients' collective memories, or the way in which the community has interpreted certain events, statuses, and choices. For example, a recent immigrant community approach to housing is to rent residences from landlords from their country of origin that are located close to relatives of friends from home, which limits their choices and can lead to lost employment and educational opportunities. Once the stories and explanations for this choice of housing emerge, the narratives can be used as springboards from which clients engage in praxis (Freire, 1994). The narrative approach creates cognitive, emotional, and behavioral links between cultural minority clients and their efforts at change and advancement (Vygotsky, 1979). The process can be summarized in three questions that can be posed to the client: What is the presenting problem? How do you feel about the situation? How can you produce change? These questions are connected, and community or culturally based explanations and community experiences help workers understand the behavior. For example, housing discrimination could be the main reason why community members do not venture outside their enclaves.

When clients perceive a connection between their cultural norms, values, and experiences and the social work intervention, they are able to make effective links among the different dimensions of their lives. These connections make it easier for them to respond favorably to the intervention and become engaged in the process. On the other hand, if the intervention feels strange or alien and the cultural link is missing, clients will feel uncomfortable and will probably stop participating fully or drop out.

Linkages are created in two ways: through the exploration of the network of clients' stories (the client's stories as well as the stories of members of the family and community, the messages of which are repeated over and over and become accepted as truth) and through the inquiry into how the dominant narrative of the majority society affects the client. As clients share their narratives, their network of stories is strengthened, expanded, and enriched. For instance, when Latino clients use words such as *casa*—meaning both house (a place) and home (an emotion)—the practitioner may discover that the word has a different connotation than non-Latino clients' use of the word "home." Latinos often feel a devotion and loyalty to *la casa* that is difficult to explain to others. This understanding can be integrated into the assessment and valued as knowledge by the social worker.

The culturally grounded approach maximizes the potential of clients' linguistic and narrative legacies as it supports their cognitive development. Narrative traditions (proverbs; stories, both fiction and nonfiction; songs; biographies) that are familiar to the client act as a cognitive bridge (the cognitive link) for the acquisition of new and unfamiliar knowledge. Through the use of accessible and familiar types of narratives, clients can venture into the unfamiliar and become committed (the emotional link) to their own change process (the behavioral link). Clients' narrative networks are further enriched and validated by the use of short stories, metaphors, and parables common to their communities of origin, stories that often provide insight into the experiences the clients are living out every day.

Narratives related by the client to the practitioner or shared in group sessions can be enriched by the examination of stereotypes about minority communities. For example, while discussing professional choices in a teen support group, Trisha says that she wants to be an electrical engineer. The other group members—male and female—make fun of her and say that her choice is not appropriate for a girl. Trisha does not respond and remains quiet. The group facilitator questions the group and helps them examine their reactions to Trisha's comment. In this process the group worker attempts to honor Trisha's narrative by providing the group with new knowledge and helping the group reexamine her wishes in light of that knowledge. For example, the group worker introduces a statistic on the percent of female electrical engineers in the nation and their ethnic breakdown; this information expands the group's perception of the realm of possibilities open to women. The incident strengthens the group members' analytical abilities. This process starts with the language or terminology used by the clients. The narratives are then enriched by the awareness or consciousness process. Note from the field 6.1 provides an illustration of how a client's concerns can be reframed in this way. In this example, the dominant narrative of society can be subjected to scrutiny through the facilitation of the social worker. For example, Jane may blame herself for not being awarded a promotion, question her motivation or her abilities, or react passively to a situation that she feels is beyond her control. The social worker must not act in a condescending or dismissive manner but must lead the conversation toward a discussion of oppression in the workplace.

A culturally grounded approach would validate Jane's experience and perspective while also suggesting alternative ways to reframe her story and understand the institutional reasons why she may have been denied the promotion. Validating the feelings of the client—even if they appear counterproductive—is the first step to developing an effective and honest cross-cultural relationship.

Social and Political Context

The culturally grounded approach is not just a celebration of diversity and multiculturalism but also a process of action and transformation. An important part of culturally grounded social work practice is its contextual approach, or the assessment of social conditions and their ability to nurture change and quality of

---

NOTE FROM THE FIELD 6.1
What's the Matter with Jane?

Jane is referred to a social worker by her doctor because he suspects she is depressed. As Jane's story unfolds, the social worker notices that Jane is focused on having been denied a promotion at work. Jane knows she was the best-qualified candidate and the only woman ever to have applied for such a high management position in her company. She tells of her middle-class background and of the support she received from her father for her educational achievement and career advancement, as well as the more mixed signals she received from her mother. Jane wonders if she should be so focused on career objectives or should perhaps redirect her energy to her parenting responsibilities. The social worker explores her depressive symptoms not in isolation but in the context of the sexism and discrimination that may exist in her company, and Jane begins to relate what she has seen and heard of the company's unfair treatment of other women. By encouraging Jane to tell her story and by placing it in its proper organizational and societal context, the social worker helps Jane reframe her difficulties and see them as much more than a personal failure, an individual inability to cope, or misplaced priorities.

life and the determination of whether or not they need to be transformed because they deprive individuals and communities of opportunities and limit their quality of life.

The contextual approach in the health care field, for example, focuses on the fundamental causes of illness as a way of balancing biological and medical conceptions of risk with those from the social and behavioral sciences (Link & Phelan, 2000). In past decades, epidemiological research has focused attention on risk factors like diet, cholesterol level, and exercise as the proximal causes of disease. Researchers have argued that greater attention needs to be paid to basic social, or contextual, conditions. For example, to craft effective interventions that improve the nation's health, individually based risk factors need to be contextualized; this involves asking probing questions about what puts people at risk. Social factors such as socioeconomic status, access to health information and health care, and social support within family and friendship networks are relevant to disease prevention and treatment because they affect the outcomes of multiple diseases, including diabetes and asthma, as well as drug abuse and HIV/AIDS, and influence whether people have the resources to remain healthy.

Many cultural minorities do not have access to culturally competent social services. Although efforts have been made to increase their availability, the political context of the nation limits availability and accessibility, particularly in certain regions. For example, in "English only" states, making language-specific social services available to clients could be more difficult than in other states where workers' need to communicate with clients in a language they comprehend is not questioned (Ortíz Hendricks, 2005).

Ethnicity and culture are important social contexts that influence socioeconomic status and shape social support. Although membership in a particular ethnic or cultural community is not itself a social risk factor (even though membership in some racial and ethnic groups may be inherent risks for stressors such as discrimination stress), it may influence an individual's access to prevention resources and effective service delivery systems. It is important for practitioners to maintain an ecosystemic perspective that attends not only to the relationship between the individual and the stressor (discrimination) but also to the context in which this relationship takes place. Conversely, culture also produces indigenous resiliencies. Considering the relational and ecosystemic contexts of clients' life stressors enhances practitioners' understanding of why some individuals live healthier lives than others.

Consciousness and Liberation

Culturally grounded interventions promoting social justice start at the cultural awareness level or with conscientization efforts. Conscientization is a process of learning to become aware of social, political, and economic conditions in order to take action against the oppressive elements present in one's social and political context (Freire, 1970). It is from this perspective that a culturally grounded approach to social work emerges as a means to resist oppression and promote social justice through praxis.

As social workers attempt to decode narratives, stories, and symbols in partnership with their clients, they become aware of the master narrative that frames those stories. That is, the narrative process is embedded in the social, political, and cultural contexts of clients' communities. In the process of understanding these narratives, a liberating cultural transformation emerges and the client is able to question larger narratives and work toward personal affirmation and liberation. Larger narratives, often produced without the input of minority communities, are connected to policies that can either facilitate social advancement or block it. When these policies block social advancement, communities' narratives can eventually lead to policy advocacy as a means to create better conditions for all.

Cultural identity and social advancement are woven into one comprehensive approach, which facilitates the cultural grounding of policies and services. If transformative processes focus only on equalizing opportunities but fail to encourage individuals to retain and nurture the aspects of their culture that make their lives worthwhile and give them meaning, cultural deprivation may result. On the other hand, if cultural maintenance is supported to the detriment of social advancement, the result may be oppression. In other words, completely assimilating into mainstream culture and taking advantage of the opportunities it provides may leave members of ethnic minority groups feeling empty inside. However, if they decide to maintain their ethnic identity by not participating at all in society, they risk not being able to access the benefits, resources, and services to which they are entitled as members of society and as taxpayers.

APPLYING A CULTURALLY GROUNDED APPROACH TO SOCIAL WORK PRACTICE

The theoretical synthesis provides guidelines for a culturally grounded approach to social work practice. The starting assumption is that the possession of relevant information about a particular ethnic group or culture alone is not enough for social workers to practice in a culturally responsive manner. The methods a social worker acquires through professional education need to be examined for cultural bias. Those methods may reflect an ethnocentric cosmology and culturally specific understandings of how people seek and give help.

Empowerment scholars have expressed concern about the belief that some practitioners have that social work methods can be viewed as culturally neutral and that with a few adaptations they can be universally applied across cultural groups (Lee, 2001). There is growing consensus, however, that social work methods are the product of their social and economic context and as such they cannot be applied in different contexts without in-depth adaptations or fundamental changes (Reamer, 2006). The universality of social work methods versus the need to adapt them to unique environments is an important and complex issue that requires careful examination.

The traditional way to describe classic social work methods is to group them according to the type, or level, of intervention—micro, mezzo, and macro. Most schools of social work embrace a generalist approach, educating social workers to function effectively in different settings by utilizing a variety of interventions. The interventions most commonly used by practicing social workers are micro, or one-on-one, interventions. Yet one-on-one helping may not be the preferred approach or most natural way of helping for members of many cultural groups. On the other hand, individuals belonging to predominantly collectivistic (as opposed to individualistic) communities may welcome the opportunity to meet alone with the social worker without their relatives' presence and scrutiny. Note from the field 6.2 provides an example of such a situation and shows that applying a culturally grounded social work generalist approach generally entails a consideration of timing—when to use different methods—more than a decision about which level to use.

SHIFTING FROM A "CULTURALLY NEUTRAL" TO A CULTURALLY GROUNDED PARADIGM

Social work methods cannot be completely culturally neutral because they are the product of certain worldviews and reflect particular social contexts. As a

---

NOTE FROM THE FIELD 6.2
Individual or Family Sessions?

Cheryl is an African American teenager who feels very close to her extended family and has an active social life. Cheryl requests a private session with the school social worker—without any members of her family present—in order to address concerns about her family relationships. Eventually, the social worker may invite the parents to join in, but initially, one-on-one sessions address Cheryl's needs and allow Cheryl and the worker to build rapport. The social worker is aware of the interdependence between Cheryl and her family but involves the parents based on the needs of the client. The family members may not be physically present at the first few sessions, but they are included because the social worker is aware that they are the client's key social support system, as families are for most school-age children and youths regardless of their ethnicity.

result, they tend to perpetuate specific cultural paradigms and reflect existing power relationships in the larger society. From a culturally grounded approach, social workers are most effective when they are wary of assimilationist tendencies that are embedded in so-called standardized interventions. These are practices that may implicitly encourage clients to let go of their cultural norms and values and adopt the majority culture's norms and values. For example, the insistence of some workers on personal autonomy in family relationships undervalues many minority clients' experiences of interdependence—for example, children living in extended family households well into adulthood, or the very close relationships that often exist between parents and children. Interdependence, which is healthy and provides a means of emotional and financial support for family members, can sometimes be mistaken for codependence. Being interconnected, basing family relationships on interdependence, supporting one's family, and being supported by family are all strengths, not weaknesses.

Imposing external values and using culturally inappropriate approaches to helping may underutilize the wealth of naturally occurring resources within communities that are already effective. Some of these natural ways of helping have been perfected over millennia (Werbner, 2005). However, a social worker who is a cultural parachuter—an individual who drops into the community without any awareness or knowledge of the community—could easily overlook, misunderstand, or underutilize such rich resources. Outsiders often make assumptions based on their previous experiences and are unaware of what the community has long been doing successfully. In contrast, workers grounded in the culture of the community naturally embrace what already works as they contribute their professional expertise and support. Another risk is that communities may lose their own abilities to help themselves and become dependent on professionalized service systems. For example, it has been demonstrated that the enormous growth of the death-and-dying field has weakened traditional ways of assisting the dying in the United States and in China (Pressman & Bonanno, 2007). Heightened cultural awareness and vigilance can help ensure that effective natural or culturally grounded approaches are supported, not just supplanted by the professionalized service delivery system. An informed and well-researched integration of both systems (the traditional and the professional) is the ideal outcome.

Culturally grounded social work avoids simplistic overgeneralizations by validating community-based narratives and integrating community-based practices into the helping process. This approach increases the effectiveness of social work interventions by recognizing existing natural helping and informal social networks as valuable resources to be tapped by professional interventions. Culturally grounded social work is a form of quality control that improves the effectiveness of the services provided to cultural minority clients. It is based on a theoretical framework that advances social justice and as such is guided by the common good. Instead of merely adapting existing models, this approach questions the assumptions behind the models and starts with the client's worldview and strengths.

Culturally grounded interventions integrate community-based perspectives and resources into services that promote equity, access, and effectiveness. Clients who find their culture reflected and recognized in the substance and the format of interventions and services are more likely to participate in and benefit from the experience. Prevention programs for youths—whether targeting substance use, unsafe sex, or suicide—have long recognized that it is important to represent the culture of the targeted youth in the prevention message in authentic ways. Programs and services for particular cultural groups need to incorporate central cultural values, styles of learning, and ways of interacting. It may be important to include examples or representations of the culture in the design of the program or service. For example, the illustrations and pictures on a program's Web page or brochure need to celebrate the heritage and the identity of the targeted youths and their subcultures. A graphic designer needs to think of this form of cultural branding not just as Vietnamese cultural branding, but as Vietnamese American youth cultural branding. This level of specificity gives the target audience a sense of connection with the characters conveying the message. However, a symbolic representation of a culture that goes beyond the culturally appropriate visual images or language may be needed. For example, youth may use certain terms that are not entirely English or Vietnamese but rather a fusion of the two. Key terms that are used in focus groups conducted with youths can add depth and specificity to the message, which can increase its effectiveness. The same can be said about social work interventions in general. Awareness of specific cultural products is essential. In addition, project design teams applying a culturally grounded approach must constantly check themselves for stereotypes that may unintentionally emerge as a result of these efforts.

Culture is best approached as the platform from which social work practice is launched. When treated as an addendum to the services planning and design process, culture becomes an afterthought rather than an integral part of the intervention. The culturally grounded approach honors and integrates culture from the start of the planning process and delivers services through social workers whose practice modalities are grounded in the culture of the clients they serve. As social workers work in partnership with cultural minority communities, cultural and social boundaries must be honored and negotiated. Members of the targeted population can be engaged through focus groups or other methods in the service design process. Such a practice ensures representation and helps the design team check for biases.

As agents of change, social workers must engage in their own transformation by scrutinizing their own narratives and heightening their own consciousness. To facilitate this exploration, social workers can be encouraged to form inquiry teams not only as a professional development and support mechanism but also as a tool for gaining personal awareness and professional retooling. Inquiry teams can function as sounding boards for workers to examine and challenge each other's knowledge, attitudes, and practices. Members of these teams can discuss their own reality frames, biases, preconceived ideas, and fears about change. In this way, the social worker begins to experience some of the same conflicts with hospitals, social service agencies, schools, and other institutions that some of their clients may experience. As a result, the institutional culture of social service agencies (the guiding values and norms that give the agency its identity) is questioned, and clients and social workers can come together to advocate changes that anchor the agency more firmly in cultural groundedness. These change processes are particularly important in agencies that are not culturally aware and have not incorporated the assets of minority clients or responded to their unique needs in a culturally competent manner.

When the culturally grounded approach is incorporated into social work practice, clients encounter social workers who are engaged in a process of inquiry about themselves and their positions in the social service delivery system. Such inquiry can correct erroneous perceptions that they may have of themselves as gatekeepers guarding resources and services from ethnic minority clients or as agents of the assimilation of ethnic minority clients.

REVISITING PRAXIS

An understanding of social and cultural identities, social representations, and shared power is crucial for constructing a social psychology of participation (Campbell & Jovchelovitch, 2000). Communities cannot, however, preserve and integrate their unique social identities, worldviews, and natural helping practices if they are not aware of them. As a result of assimilation, younger generations may have lost a connection to their cultural roots. This is why culturally grounded interventions start at the cultural awareness level, or what Freire called conscientization efforts. Although awareness as a collective phenomenon is the product of a group or community, the social worker plays a key role in facilitating its emergence and channeling its use. Individuals and communities who have been alienated from their culture can be encouraged to identify, examine, and act on the root causes of their oppression. Such critical consciousness involves a gradual and cyclical action-reflection-action chain of group behaviors, also known as praxis (Freire, 1970).

Praxis implies that clients identify issues and look for solutions. The role of the social worker is to help clients become aware of their power to act and to transform their social environment. In becoming a transforming force, clients initially decide on small action steps, then develop plans to implement them. Once the course of action is implemented, they reflect on and evaluate their accomplishments and their plans' shortcomings. In doing so, they link the outcome to the larger social phenomena that concern them and start planning the next action step. This process empowers cultural minority clients to challenge and reject the messages they receive from society that say nothing can be changed. As note from the field 6.3 illustrates, they relate personal problems to political issues by connecting their personal and group-defined issues to larger societal issues such as racism, xenophobia, sexism, and heterosexism.

Social workers cannot define for the community what social justice is or suggest the right steps to bring it about, but neither is it their role to remain neutral. Freire (1994) stated that "claiming neutrality does not constitute neutrality; quite the contrary, it helps maintain the status quo" (p. 141). Social workers become openly political as clients become political by starting to take a position on human rights and social justice and weighing conceptual, cultural, and political aspects of their lives and their communities' lives. Social workers can explore social justice issues with community members and look for solutions with them.

In this way, praxis becomes a compass not only for clients but also for social workers. It helps workers find a balance between the needs of the individual, family, group, or community, on one hand, and their worldviews and the profession's code of ethics, on the other hand. As note from the field 6.4 shows, social work methods that are grounded in the client's culture can contribute to the neutralization of the power differential and oppression exercised or perpetuated by the worker. As in Andrea's case, many clients may be experiencing oppressive

---

NOTE FROM THE FIELD 6.3
Don't Rock the Boat!

A neighborhood committee is concerned about the lack of appropriate street lighting in their neighborhood. Individually, the members of the committee have already attempted to deal with city hall, but without success. As a committee, they assess the situation, including the ways in which the city hall representatives perceive them and their neighborhood. They conclude that the fact that many of the families are recent immigrants and not yet eligible to vote in municipal elections has disempowered them, and politicians do not take them seriously. The message they have heard is "Be happy with what you have. Do not rock the boat." As they plan and implement small and larger steps to overcome their oppression, they become more ambitious dreamers and formulate larger goals such as promoting equal treatment; they realize that they are tax-paying residents regardless of their citizenship status. They begin to frame their situation as a social justice issue, not as a favor asked of those who are supposed to be serving them.

NOTE FROM THE FIELD 6.4
Immigrant Labor Rights

One of Francis's clients is Andrea, a mother of three who is pregnant with her fourth child and is very distressed. Her family immigrated to the United States four years earlier, and both she and her husband have been working for minimum wage, which makes it very hard for them to meet the family's needs. When Francis asked Andrea at intake what was troubling her, she first said that she has lost her job but did not elaborate. After Francis offered her a cup of tea, Andrea became more comfortable and began to explain that she had worked for the same company for three years. The company paid her for eight hours of work a day, but her supervisor forced her to work up to ten hours a day, and six to seven days a week. She was told that if she did not do this, they would terminate her. During those three years, she had no vacation days and no sick days, and she worked on every holiday. Some years she was allowed to go home to her children and husband at midnight on Christmas Eve. When it became obvious that she was pregnant, her supervisor started to harass her and tell crude sexual jokes. She was told that she was lazy and nobody would hire her because of her limited English proficiency. Her life at work became intolerable, and she often went home crying. Seven months into her pregnancy, exhausted and frustrated, Andrea dared to request a day off. Her boss told her, "Sure, but don't bother to come back because someone else will be doing your job." She was worried about the upcoming birth of her fourth child and the fact that the family did not have enough money to meet their basic needs, so she continued working. At the next payday, however, she was told that she was being laid off, and her paycheck was half what was due her.

As Francis explored the situation with her, Andrea mentioned that other employees suffered similar treatment. They were all immigrants who spoke very little English and did not know what resources were available to them. Francis told her about the options available to her and encouraged her to think of ways she could contribute to making changes so other people would not suffer the same treatment to which she and her coworkers had been subjected. Eventually, Andrea contacted the U.S. Labor Department and asked to speak with a Spanish-speaking employee to make her complaint, and she encouraged a couple of other former employees to do the same. The Labor Department was able to act on the complaints and made the company pay back wages on all overtime to the three ex-employees. In addition, the Labor Department is now monitoring the company's labor practices closely. Andrea's situation, while still economically challenging, is better. The former coworkers have developed a strong friendship and support system. They take turns babysitting for their children and attend evening ESL classes.

situations that are part of a larger context. Praxis helps the worker and the client integrate the presenting problem into that larger context and recognize their strengths and resources as tools for achieving lasting change.

Key Concepts

Strengths/resiliency perspective the belief that human beings have an inherent capacity to grow and change, even under adverse conditions

Praxis the transformative cyclical process of action, reflection, and action

Person-in-environment perspective a perspective that integrates the individual, family, and community within their unique social contexts

Feminist theories cultural and group theories that generally incorporate elements from micro social theories and macro social variables affecting the lives of women

Culturally grounded social work an approach to social work practice, policy, and research that incorporates culturally specific ways of helping and community-based tools promoting social change

Part III

Cultural
Identities

7

The Formation and Legacies of Racial and Ethnic Minorities

THE PREVIOUS CHAPTERS HAVE ARGUED THAT MANY SOCIAL DIFFER-ences between individuals and groups are socially constructed rather than a reflection of intrinsic biological differences and that these constructed ideas about difference are often used to justify or perpetuate oppression. Ethnic and racial distinctions, for example, are routinely taken for granted and assumed to represent fundamental differences between groups of people. Whether true or fictitious, these ideas about racial and ethnic differences have been used throughout history to categorize people. At the same time, identification with ethnic and racial groups, and the sense of belonging they foster, is often a source of pride, resistance, and resiliency. Ethnic and racial groups are a vital part of the fabric of society, and we will review some of the historical and social processes that led to the emergence of the minority status assigned to several ethnic and racial groups in the United States and explore how the minority status of several different ethnic and racial groups is rooted in a legacy of oppression and discrimination and a rich history of resistance and resiliency. Minority status will be explained in its social and historical contexts. The minority status assigned to some groups is not a natural given but the product of particular historical contexts and events (Preece, 2006). For example, being black in Nigeria does not make a person part of a racial minority group; however, being black in the United States or in Brazil makes a person part of a minority group. It is the history of slavery and its legacy of oppression in Brazil and in the United States that gave this group its minority status. The term "minority" is not used in this chapter in a numerical sense but instead is used in a sociological sense to describe the group's lesser power and status compared to other groups, particularly vis-à-vis the white majority. Likewise, when the term "majority" is used, it is not used in a numerical sense but reflects the concentration of power within that group.

COLONIALISM AND GENOCIDE: NATIVE AMERICANS

Colonialism is a system of organizing society that concentrates all the power over the local population in the hands of an invading outsider group. The process of colonization not only targets land but also aims at colonizing the minds, the emotions, the bodies, and the labor of those residing on the occupied land (Brown, 1993). The process of colonization is justified by the oppressor or dominant group's definition of the conquered group as inferior. Conversely, adopting a social Darwinist viewpoint, the dominant group views itself as superior and better equipped to rule.

Colonialism has been part of the human experience since the beginning of civilization: examples of empires that have practiced colonialism are the Roman, Portuguese, Spanish, British, and Japanese empires. Although Rome, Lisbon, Madrid, London, and Tokyo were very different colonial metropolises that reached their zenith of power and expansion at different times in history, these empires shared much in terms of goals, organizational styles, and outcomes. In all cases, the top authority of the colonial power (the Caesar, the king or queen, or the emperor) never resided on the colonized lands. The empires not only imposed their culture on the colonized populations, but they extracted raw materials from the colonies and made them buy back the manufactured goods they produced using the raw materials. The original residents of the colonized lands were viewed by their conquerors as lacking the social and intellectual capacity to govern their own affairs.

During the nineteenth and early twentieth centuries, Africa underwent an intensive process of colonization. With very few exceptions, by the beginning of World War II, Africa had become a fully colonized continent. The colonial political map of Africa shows how European powers carved out pieces of the continent and its wealth to benefit themselves. The colonial ambition of rulers such as King Leopold of Belgium has been well documented in books such as *King Leopold's Ghost* (Hochschild, 1998). The resurgence and expansion of slavery is intimately related to the colonial experience of Africa from the sixteenth to the nineteenth centuries. Slavery on such a large scale and such a high level of organization would not have been possible without colonialism as its economic and political engine. The legacy of colonialism continues to cast its shadow over Africa. For example, artificial national borders created by European powers and favoritism toward one indigenous group over another during colonial rule led to ethnic group conflict and genocide in Rwanda in the mid-1990s. Colonial administrations deliberately suppressed or stunted the development of strong educational and health institutions. Since political independence was won in the second half of the twentieth century, African nations struggled in a global economy dominated by the West, subject to rich nations' manipulation of the raw materials and commodities that are Africa's chief revenue source. Beleaguered by the demands of rapid population growth, the HIV/AIDS pandemic, interethnic strife and civil war, falling agricultural production, and poor industrial and technology capacities, even very resource-rich countries like the Congo (formerly Zaire) have seen their average incomes cut in half in recent decades.

Colonialism is closely related to the concept of internal colonialism, which was first introduced by Robert Blauner (1972) to show how African Americans faced social conditions in the United States that were similar to those faced by developing nations as a result of European colonialism, such as lack of political and economic power. Internal colonialism does not require incursions across international borders. The oppressive power relations take place within national borders, although the relationship and its end results are similar to the classic forms of colonialism. The United States followed a colonial path, subjugating African Americans, Native Americans, Native Hawaiians, Mexicans, Filipinos, and Puerto Ricans to colonialism when their land or labor became attractive economic and political targets. Internal colonialism continues to be a means for the dominant racial group to perpetuate social inequalities for its own benefit. The shadow of internal colonialism is reflected in contemporary society's perception that some groups are racially inferior as well as in the persistence of racially segregated ghettos and neighborhoods. The extreme social isolation and economic marginalization of some African American and Latino urban communities has been attributed to their lack of economic, administrative, and political control, which are typically held by white outsiders. In the 1960s, for example, young black militants interpreted their racial oppression as a form of internal colonialism and aligned themselves with developing countries and groups struggling for liberation from the legacy of colonialism in Africa (Takaki, 1993). Despite these important struggles, the legacy of internal colonialism persists, as evidenced by the fact that one in every four black men comes under the control of the criminal justice system at some point in his life, the majority for nonviolent offenses (Brown-Dean, 2007). This has very damaging consequences not only for these men but also for their families and their communities.

The concept of internal colonialism explains how racial inequality in the United States has been perpetuated over time, but it lacks explanatory power for the changing conditions of African Americans and members of other ethnic minority groups, such as the gains that have been achieved in educational and occupational opportunities and in earnings, which have increased upward mobility for some. Although the concept of internal colonialism needs to be updated to maintain its relevance in a rapidly changing world, it continues to provide important insights into the ongoing oppression of ethnic and racial communities in the United States and around the world.

Genocide is often connected to colonialism, but it can occur autonomously within nations without outside intervention. Genocide is the organized effort to eliminate an entire group of people. The United Nations (1951) defines genocide as "actions committed with intent to destroy in whole or in part a national, ethnic, racial, or religion group as such." Some argue that this definition is too narrow because it limits genocide to the killing of a group and does not consider policies of cultural, social, political, and economic destruction. It also leaves out classes and groups that are not necessarily ethnic or communal, such as gays, lesbians, and transgender groups (Melson, 1992). These groups were targeted by the Nazi party and continue to be vulnerable to the threat of genocide in many societies (Abed, 2006). Other definitions of genocide as organized state murder highlight the role of the state as a key component of modern premeditated genocide (Fein, 1979).

Genocide has devastating consequences not only for those who perish but also for those who survive. Native American scholars have argued that some contemporary ills experienced by Native American communities in the United States can be traced to their ancestors' experience of genocide. That is, the post-traumatic stress disorder experienced by survivors of genocide can be passed on to later generations, as shown by research on descendants of Holocaust survivors and Bosnian survivors of "ethnic cleansing" (Becker, McGlashan, Vojvoda, & Weine, 1999; Bower, 1996). These studies all demonstrate that the PTSD associated with survival of genocide is as much of a collective phenomenon as that associated with genocide itself. Genocide that is connected to colonialism and internal colonialism is part of the legacy of many ethnic and racial communities in the United States and other countries. For example, the legacy of colonialism and genocide affects many Vietnamese, Cambodian, and Laotian refugee communities that have settled in the United States. It is often through narratives that those legacies surface, which allows them to be honored so that the related trauma can be addressed.

The experience with both colonialism and genocide and their legacy resulted in the present minority status of the descendants of the original inhabitants of what is today the United States. Native Americans, also called American Indians and First Nations people, were for many centuries the only inhabitants of the United States centuries before the European arrival. These groups developed a variety of cultures (identities) and political organizations. When the Europeans invaded the Americas in the late 1400s, Native Americans were a numerical majority, but over time and due to colonialism and genocide they were decimated, and in addition to becoming a sociological minority (that is, they had less power than those in control), they also eventually became a numerical minority.

Genocide commenced almost immediately after the arrival of European explorers in the so-called New World, beginning in 1493 with Christopher Columbus's enslavement and mass extermination of the Taino population of the Caribbean. Within three years, 5 million Taino had perished, and a Spanish census from fifty years later records only two hundred left alive. Columbus's contemporary, the historian Father Bartolomé de las Casas (1992), reported numerous atrocities perpetrated on indigenous people, including mass hangings, the roasting of people on spits, and the hacking of children to pieces for use as dog food.

Later European colonists and subsequently the United States government resorted to various means for removing Native Americans, including the extermination of whole villages, bounties on the scalps of Natives, and bacterial warfare. In one of the first reported uses of bacterial warfare, British agents murdered more than 100,000 members of the Mingo, Delaware, Shawnee, and other Ohio River tribes by distributing blankets purposely contaminated with smallpox, an Old World disease to which the Native population of the Americas had virtually no resistance. The same measure was used against the Ottawa and Lenape tribes, and the U.S. Army successfully duplicated the practice on Plains tribal populations (Friedberg, 2000). The colonial governments offered large sums of money to whites for the scalps of Native Americans. The state of California spent approximately $1 million a year from gold rush revenue to finance campaigns whose purpose was exterminating the Native people during 1851–1852. Whites received between fifty cents and five dollars for each severed head (Chatterjee, 1998). In addition to this intentional slaughter, Native Americans were forced by whites to give up their traditional occupations, which resulted in poverty, hunger, illness, and death (Berkhofer, 1978).

The enormity of what David Stannard (1993) has called an "American holocaust" parallels the unfathomable and more recent human losses suffered during the Holocaust. The systematic murder of European Jews under the Nazi regime is estimated at around 65 percent of the prewar population, while the rate of attrition of indigenous populations in the United States is calculated at around 98 to 99 percent, meaning that only about 1 to 2 percent of the original indigenous population survived genocide (Friedberg, 2000). White attitudes to the slaughter are exemplified by an editorial by L. Frank Baum (the author of *The Wonderful Wizard of Oz*) that was printed in the *Aberdeen Saturday Pioneer*, a weekly South Dakota newspaper, in 1890: "Our only safety depends upon the total extermination of the Native Americans. Having wronged them for centuries we had better, in order to protect our civilization, follow it up by one more wrong and wipe these untamed and untamable creatures from the face of the earth. In this lies safety for our settlers and the soldiers. . . . Otherwise, we may expect future years to be as full of trouble with the redskins as those have been in the past" (qtd. in Ritter, 1997, p. 21). In addition, cultural misperceptions and stereotypes contributed to the cultural demise of Native American communities. European and European American failure to appreciate the cultures and tribal identities of the Native American nations led to a history of confusion, myths, stereotypes, and misunderstanding that has been particularly destructive to Native communities. Native Americans were viewed as savages and as scalp hunters. The Europeans' lack of appreciation for and understanding of the Native American cultures as well as other indigenous cultures in colonies such as Australia allowed them to label the Native people they encountered as less than human and to target them for elimination (Fenzsch, 2005).

Although Europeans had engaged in a nearly continuous history of warfare before coming to the Americas and continued fighting among themselves for control of the New World, in order to justify their genocide of Native people, they constructed an image of the Native Americans as fierce and savage fighters (Mihesuah, 1996). Even the U.S. Declaration of Independence refers to Native populations as "merciless Indian Savages." This helped disguise the reality that many armed conflicts with the Native communities occurred because the Europeans wanted to expropriate Indian land and enslave Indians to serve as laborers for mines and farms. More often than not, Native Americans were merely defending their territories, families, ways of life, and sovereignty from the intruders.

Through government decrees and policies, surviving Native people lost not only their lands, but also their parental rights. This practice started as early as the 1540s, when Franciscan friars took the children of the leaders of tribal communities in the Yucatan in Mexico away from their families to be educated in Franciscan schools (Pagden, 1975). In 1898, the U.S. Indian Peace Commission recommended that Native children be educated in the ways of European Americans so their cultural differences would disappear (Johnson, 1974). The mission boarding schools created in light of this recommendation, largely under the control of the Federal Bureau of Indian Affairs, took Native children from their parents, homes, and communities—often forcibly—to distant institutions (Cross, Earle, & Simmons, 2000). Forbidden to speak their own language, and given European-style clothes and Christian names, the Native American children who would become tribal leaders once they returned to their communities were systematically stripped of their cultural heritage. These boarding schools took generations of Native Americans away from their homes, and since their way of learning was different from that of European Americans (traditional Native American learning often took place through observation, listening, and hands-on activities rather than through passive lectures and readings), these children struggled in school (Becker, 1998). Torn between their own culture and the one they were supposed to embrace, Native students were often made to feel inferior, and many ultimately lost their connection to Native American culture and never became accustomed to European American ways (Larsen & Jesch, 1980). It was not until 1978 that the Indian Child Welfare Act was created to protect Native American children in need of homes from being placed in non-Native adoptive and foster homes, although today there is still a disproportionate number of out-of-home placements of Native children (Hand, 2006).

Reservations are another legacy of colonialism. As a result of treaties and forced relocation, the number of Native Americans living on reservations had reached 300,000 by 1880 and continued to grow (Thorton, 2000). Although it was not easy to leave their lands and lifestyles behind, Native Americans demonstrated their resiliency by adapting to reservation life. In Oregon, the Native Americans of Grand Ronde demonstrated creativity, flexibility, and initiative during the transition from their vast ancestral lands to the much more limited reservation by developing an agricultural life but continuing to use tribal doctors and methods of healing (Leavelle, 1998). Native Americans viewed their lives on the reservation as different from their lives "outside"; they struggled to maintain their traditions and cultural knowledge and many started to view reservations as safe places where they were able to preserve and nurture their cultural identity (Lone-Knapp, 2000).

Native American youths who attend school on reservations may develop stronger connections to their cultural heritage because they are not exposed to prejudice from the dominant culture. However, families who decide to stay on the reservation often face inequalities, as they do not have access to the resources and opportunities available in cities. The social problems those inequalities engender, such as unemployment, poverty, and alcoholism, have a negative impact on the well-being of the whole family. Urban tribal members in need often go back to their reservation of origin because the reservation is home. This can present challenges to limited reservations resources and infrastructure, as those returning for help may have multiple and acute needs. In addition, the Community Policing Consortium (2004) reports that returnees often "bring with them attitudes and values that conflict with traditional ways[,] causing disorder and crime" (p. 11).

During the 1950s, in yet another attempt to promote assimilation into the dominant culture, the Bureau of Indian Affairs coordinated efforts for relocation that would lead more than 160,000 Native Americans to leave their reservations by promising them jobs and housing in cities across the nation. Since then, the number of Native Americans leaving the reservations has continued to rise, and currently more than 60 percent live outside Native American communities and reservations (Duran, 2005).

For most of its history, the Bureau of Indian Affairs was paternalistic and authoritarian in nature, and it was regarded with justifiable suspicion by Native American communities. By the 1960s, federal policy began to shift toward a goal of self-determination, meaning that Native American nations would have the power to govern themselves and in turn preserve their culture. The core components of self-determination were the preservation of treaty rights, consultation on policy making, and economic self-sufficiency (Riggs, 2000). New approaches to furthering the Native American cause appeared in 1972, when the American Indian Movement staged the Trail of Broken Treaties, a cross-country protest that brought attention to the mistreatment of Native Americans and the drastic effects of colonization and genocide. Although nothing ever came of the movement's twenty-point paper advocating the restoration of Native governments (American Indian Movement, 1972), the Self-Determination Act of 1975 granted all tribes the right to manage services and programs formerly administered by the Bureau of Indian Affairs.

Despite the organized attempts by European colonial powers and later by the U.S. government to exterminate the original inhabitants of the land, and subsequent policies designed to destroy their cultures and forcibly assimilate them into the dominant society, the number of Native Americans has increased by at least

30 percent in each of the last four decennial censuses (Wilkins, 2006). The census for the year 2000 reported a doubling of the Native American population over the prior ten years, with over four million individuals claiming heritage as a Native American or Alaska Native. This makes them America's fastest-growing ethnic minority group (U.S. Census Bureau, 2006). Nonetheless, this group still constitutes less than 2 percent of the total U.S. population and only a minute fraction of the estimated 15 million Native people residing in the territory that is now the United States during the 1500s (Wissler, 2005).

In their struggle for survival, Native Americans have made use of a range of strategies for dealing with oppression while maintaining or renewing their connections to their cultural heritage. One way of accommodating the outside pressures involved not calling attention to themselves or to their cultural differences. Those who adapted in this way may sometimes be seen by other tribal members as not being Native American enough (Ring, 2001). Despite these strategies for survival, the dominant culture's failure to validate Native American pain has resulted in unresolved historical trauma and a myriad of social problems connected to generational post-traumatic stress and its symptoms of alcoholism, rage, depression, and anxiety (BraveHeart, 1995).

Recently, a shift from tribal or clan identity to a broader umbrella Native American identity that has variously been called a pan-Indian, pan-tribal, and pan-traditions identity has taken place. Pan-Indianism offers Native Americans the opportunity to practice Native traditions and retain or regain (through enculturation) a Native cultural identity when away from tribe of origin and even while living among a dominant culture that rejects it. Instead of clustering in neighborhood enclaves, Native Americans living in cities—who now constitute the majority of all Native Americans—tend to live in the midst of other ethnic groups (Powers, 2006). In contrast to reservation identities tied to a specific place and tribal enrollment, membership in urban Native American communities is defined by various criteria that can include Native American ancestry, cultural or tribal knowledge, and active participation in Native American community activities.

Urban Native Americans are often described as "invisible" to non–Native Americans, mainly as a result of their wide geographic dispersion (Jojola, 1999; Lobo, 1998). Urban Native American communities are also very fluid because of frequent movement back and forth between the city and reservations for educational and employment reasons as well as return visits for ceremonies and family responsibilities (Guillemin, 1975; Straus, 1998; Weibel-Orlando, 1991). As a result, not only are Native Americans frequently underserved by the health and mental health service systems, but misunderstandings and disagreements about who is eligible for social services can result in an inability to access services mandated by federal law to be available to all Native Americans through the Indian Health Service (Frith-Smith & Singleton, 2000). Some nations have been able to develop their own sources of revenue through mining, farming, fishing, industry, and gambling and are using generated revenue to improve the educational, health, and social services infrastructures of their communities. For the first time since colonization started, many individuals are meeting their basic needs and advancing economically and socially without having to let go of their cultural traditions. The use of culturally grounded social work can support a community's efforts to achieve self-determination and improve its quality of life.

SLAVERY: AFRICAN AMERICANS, EMANCIPATION, RECONSTRUCTION, JIM CROW, AND THE CIVIL RIGHTS MOVEMENT

Slavery, which many consider a tragic but distant chapter in U.S. and world history, actually continues to be a major problem in contemporary societies. It encompasses a variety of widespread human rights violations, including the traditional slave trade, the selling of children, sexual exploitation of children and women, the use of children in armed conflicts, debt bondage, and the selling of human organs (United Nations, 1991).

Slavery dehumanized both those who were enslaved as well as the enslavers who benefited from this form of oppression. Prior to the Civil War, there were approximately four million enslaved African Americans in the United States, numbering more than ten times the number of African Americans living as free men and women (Franklin & Moss, 1994). In order to justify slavery, and very much in alignment with the social Darwinist principles reviewed previously, the ruling elite established an elaborate theory of biological inferiority based on skin color to support the idea that slavery was the proper state of the "inferior" race (Blumberg, 1984). Because people who were enslaved were brought to the American colonies involuntarily, racial inequality had existed from the start (Farley, 2000). Africans who were enslaved as well as free blacks were the victims of discrimination, segregation, violence, and negative racial images that contributed to their racial degradation and poverty, which in turn reinforced prejudice (Takaki, 1993). Slavery provided economic rewards for those involved at every level of the slave trade except for those who were enslaved and their descendents. Slavery benefited slave traders, plantation owners, exporters, and merchants. These dynamics played a large role in the pervasive acceptance of a slavery system that today is universally condemned.

Unlike most of the instances of slavery around the world today, the slave trade in the Americas was part of a system of exploitation that was officially sanctioned by major societal institutions, from politics and law to education, the family, and religion. The slave system in the New World started in the sixteenth century as a way to provide free labor to European colonies in Central and South America and the Caribbean; it was spurred in part by the colonists' inability to turn many of the indigenous peoples of the Americas into readily exploitable slave labor due to cultural resistance, susceptibility to Western diseases, and genocide (Eltis, 2000).

During the seventeenth century, the first generations of Africans were brought involuntarily to what is now the United States. The first to arrive in the English colony in Jamestown, Virginia, were indentured African servants from the West Indies who were sold by a Dutch ship captain in exchange for supplies (Rawley & Behrendt, 2005). Initially, indentured Africans in British North America had a legal status somewhat comparable to that of English indentured servants, which meant that they were servants for a limited period of time, after which they were released to live a free life and given land of their own. All indentured servants at that time, both white and black, were considered personal property. Soon, however, a legal precedent for racially based discrimination was set. In a 1640 case involving the capture of three runaway indentured servants, the two white runaways were given thirty lashes and an extra four years of servitude, but the black servant was sentenced to servitude for life (Catterall, 1968). By the 1660s, it was understood in the English colonies that black slaves were property with few or no legal rights (Farley, 2000).

Upon their arrival on American soil—after a perilous ocean voyage in inhumane conditions that claimed many lives—African people who were enslaved confronted a painful period of adjustment and disorientation and then had to face illnesses, a life of hard work, and often an early death. Africans captured and forced into slavery were considered expendable, and many slaves died at the hands of their masters through beatings, lynchings, and burnings. In the New World, they lived mostly on plantations, growing cash crops such as cotton, sugar, and tobacco, in dilapidated dwellings and cramped quarters, with substandard food and clothing. Spouses, parents, and children could be separated at the slave owner's whim and sold to different masters because African slaves lacked legal sanction for their marriages. Sexual assaults of women of color by their owners and other white males were common, and because slavery was defined as a racial and hereditary condition, children born of an enslaved mother and her white owner were considered slaves and were sometimes sold by their own biological fathers for a profit (Campbell, Miers, & Miller, 2006). Interracial marriage was outlawed in 1662 throughout the English colonies.

People who were enslaved were considered objects with no legal rights and could not act in their own defense. They could be convicted by the testimony of only one white accuser (Outwin, 1996). The only right that most slaves retained was the right to profess their religious beliefs; in 1670, the colonial government of Carolina declared that religion only alters people's souls, not their civil state or rights; therefore, all people, slaves included, were free to follow their own religious beliefs. However, even that prerogative was limited. Although the open practice of their ancestral African religions was suppressed, many aspects of these religions came to be integrated in the enslaved people's expression of Christianity

(Griffith & Savage, 2006). Even before Emancipation, African Americans developed their own religious institutions. Richard Allen, a free black who was an ordained Methodist minister, founded the African Methodist Episcopal Church in Philadelphia in 1794. Organized religion became a crucial part of African American culture, providing the cohesive force that helped Africans resist slavery (Clarke, 1976).

During and in the years following the U.S. Civil War, African Americans eventually gained their freedom through the passage of several Constitutional amendments, but Emancipation did not mean equality. Segregation and discrimination continued to be practiced and were reinstated through laws that provided a legal framework for racial discrimination, exclusion, and the denial of access to economic and educational opportunities and social advancement (what are known today as Jim Crow laws) in the South, and informal practices that had much the same result in the North. In 1896, with the U.S. Supreme Court's decision in *Plessy v. Ferguson*, a doctrine of "separate but equal" helped to entrench the system of legal and social resegregation in the South. Under *Plessy*, African Americans were disenfranchised at the voting booth and relegated to second-class status in the public school, transportation, housing, health care, and economic systems.

Throughout history, violence against African Americans often has increased as they have gained more social and political power. For a century after the Civil War, African Americans were routinely victims of violence at the hands of white individuals and mobs (Watson, 2006). Lynchings were used regularly by whites to instill fear, to intimidate African Americans, and to enforce economic exploitation and residential and educational segregation. According to civil rights activists, lynching continues to be practiced in contemporary U.S. society, but under the guise of self-defense or punishment. For example, according to the Stolen Lives Project, 90 percent of unarmed civilians who are suspected of no crime and are shot or killed by police in the United States are black (Lawson, 2003).

During the 1950s and 1960s, two distinct versions of black resistance gained national visibility: one a nonviolent movement inspired by Gandhi, and the other embracing more direct confrontation as the means to produce change. Malcolm X, the leader of the latter group, disagreed with the nonviolent approach of Dr. Martin Luther King (Blumberg, 1984). Before both were assassinated in the 1960s, both Dr. King and Malcolm X worked at improving the life conditions of African Americans, but through different means. These two traditions continue to be used today to analyze current events in African American communities across the nation. To some degree, they have influenced the design and implementation of many community-based organizations where social workers are employed (Sherr, 2006).

As an outgrowth of the civil rights movements and the related passage of civil rights legislation, African Americans slowly gained political power from the dismantling of state laws that had disenfranchised them for a century, and they experienced an increase in electoral participation and coalition building. During the administration of President Bill Clinton, six African Americans served as secretaries of commerce, agriculture, energy, labor, transportation, and veterans' affairs. Unfortunately, these positions did not entail broad policy-making powers providing opportunities to change the distribution of economic and political resources. Nonetheless, these appointments did reflect an increased representation of African Americans in high government positions. The administration of President George W. Bush continued this trend to some degree by appointing African Americans to selected top posts, including two successive African American secretaries of state. These appointments have been interpreted by some as a form of tokenism rather than a reflection of true equality or representation, but they are also indications of ongoing changes in the national boundaries of political participation.

Slavery has been identified as a cultural marker that continues to influence the identity formation of African Americans today (Eyerman, 2002). Slavery left a legacy of both collective memory and collective trauma and is being reinterpreted by African American communities around the nation. As part of the reconceptualization of slavery, the postcolonial interpretation of the institution of slavery which takes into account the slaves' experiences of oppression and perspective of the institution and at the same time calls attention to the bountiful benefits that slavery produced for the slaveholders in black Atlantic America, is being questioned, and a more accurate and complete story is being developed in its place (Sweeney, 2006). This analysis aims at recognizing the resiliency and the cultural contribution of African American slaves and at the same time advocates the recognition of the enormous economic contributions they were forced to make as slaves. Slavery, for example, has been described as a key institution that allowed the United States to develop into the economic superpower that it is today (Wright, 2006). Inhumane free labor provided the basis for the accumulation of extensive sums of capital that made possible the enormous economic development of the country. A national campaign seeking reparations is underway to persuade the federal government and local governments to approve some kind of compensation for the descendents of the victims of American slavery and the century of de jure racial discrimination that succeeded it.

There is a continuing generational legacy of mistrust toward people outside the African American community as well as a style of communication that has been passed down within families. In her book *Yearning,* the African American feminist writer bell hooks (1990) tells of how her grandmother taught her grandchildren to keep their distance from white outsiders in order to be safe and to protect their "otherness." The federally funded Tuskegee experiment provides an example of the mistreatment African Americans received at the hands of outsiders, in this case the scientific establishment. This study, which began in 1932 and ended only in 1972, tricked impoverished black sharecroppers who had syphilis but were told they had "bad blood" into taking part in a "treatment plan" that, unknown to them, offered no medical care, even after penicillin became the standard treatment for syphilis. Scientists documented the men's declining health but did nothing to cure the disease, which over time can cause tumors, paralysis, blindness, insanity, and death. In addition, because the men were not told that they had syphilis, many passed the disease on to their wives and children. In 1997, President Bill Clinton offered an apology to the eight remaining survivors of the Tuskegee syphilis experiment.

Culturally grounded social workers can honor this legacy by designing and implementing interventions that take into account the African American community's history and traditions. Honoring the struggles of African Americans throughout history is a key component of culturally grounded interventions with this community.

ANNEXATION: MEXICAN AMERICANS

"The border crossed us before we ever crossed the border" is a common saying among older Mexican Americans residing in the borderlands of the Southwest that refers to the annexation of Mexican territories by the United States. Annexation occurs when a group expands its territory by taking control of an area occupied by another group through military action or when residents of the area request annexation (Farley, 2000). Although similar to colonialism in its impact on the local population, annexation occurs when the territory that is conquered is contiguous or next to the expanding territory. For example, the Anglo leaders of the Republic of Texas—then a part of Mexico—requested annexation by the United States in 1837, but the original request was refused by the federal government out of fear that Mexico would be offended. The "voluntary" annexation of Texas into the United States occurred because of agitation for independence by Anglo settlers in Texas and the subsequent war between the United States and Mexico that it triggered.

In the United States, the idea of Manifest Destiny gave rise to the annexation of vast territories and, during James Madison's presidency, the belief that the United States' mission was to spread democracy, the only fair way of government. Advocates of Manifest Destiny believed that expansion was necessary, good, obvious ("manifest"), inevitable ("destiny"), and ordained by God. Originally a political catchphrase of the nineteenth century, Manifest Destiny has served as a historical metaphor for the territorial expansion of the United States across North America toward the Pacific Ocean, which displaced both the previous colonial rulers and indigenous populations. Manifest Destiny has racist overtones, as it suggests that white European Americans should lead the expansion over territory already occupied by other peoples without any regard for them, their rights, or cultures.

Annexation may occur in peaceful or violent ways; for example, the United States' acquisition of Louisiana from France in 1803 (the Louisiana Purchase) was a peaceful annexation, in contrast to the vast territorial annexation of what is now the Southwest United States, which was accomplished through an expansionist war with Mexico in 1846. This war and its consequences have in many ways shaped the history and current status of the Mexican American community. Through forced purchase of land and armed conquest, Mexican territories originally located in the northern territories of New Spain's colonies and later the independent nation of Mexico, and the people residing in them, became part of a new country, and Mexican Americans became a subordinate ethnic group (Bacal, 1994). This experience and its consequences have shaped the history and current status of the Mexican American community.

During the centuries when the Southwest and California were under the political control of Spain and later Mexico, vast regions of the present-day states of California, Texas, Colorado, Utah, New Mexico, Nevada, and Arizona were sparsely populated by Mexican settlers. Thus when English-speaking Americans started to move into these regions in the 1800s to farm and look for gold, they were usually welcomed by the Mexican inhabitants, and mixed marriages between members of the two groups were common. During the gold rush the Anglos' efforts to displace Mexicans, Spaniards, and Native Americans intensified and the efforts toward independence intensified as a means to secure control over the resource-rich lands (Truett, 2006).

In 1846 the United States invaded Mexico and its northern territories. A final military attack on Mexico City gave the Mexican government no choice but to agree to a peace treaty, which took place at Guadalupe Hidalgo in 1848 and forced Mexico to relinquish approximately a third of its national territory to the United States (Weber, 1973). Under the Treaty of Guadalupe Hidalgo, Mexicans who remained in what became U.S. territory were nominally guaranteed all the rights of citizenship, protection of their property, and the right to maintain religious and cultural integrity, including the use of the Spanish language for all government transactions (Rosales, 2000). However, only the state of New Mexico has honored these provisions. Soon after the treaty was signed, the other territories and states began ignoring the provisions that protected the cultural, political, and economic integrity of Mexican American families and communities (Weber, 1973). A classic example of a violation of the treaty was the lack of recognition of the property titles (land grants) of Mexican families, as a result of which great extensions of land were taken away from their lawful owners. These families appealed to the courts of their new country without success, and many cases reached the Supreme Court (Soltero, 2006). As a result, even though they had been guaranteed citizenship, Mexicans in the U.S. territory became a disenfranchised minority, foreigners in their own land. At best, Mexican Americans were treated as second-class citizens; at worst, they were victims of overt discrimination (Weber, 1973). Mexican Americans were divested of their properties through legal and political ploys by Anglo farmers, who coveted the land and used claims that the new Americans were not industrious and used the land inefficiently to justify their seizure (Rosales, 1996). This process was facilitated by two conflicting legal systems: the Napoleonic Code of Spain and Mexico and the new U.S. legal system. The latter often refused to recognize the property rights established by the Napoleonic Code, including property rights for communally or collectively owned agricultural lots (*ejidos*), which U.S. law treated as land without ownership (Taylor, 1972). As a result, many families of Mexican and Spanish heritage lost their ranches and found themselves reduced to day laborers on land that was theirs. Overt discrimination, including the loss of property and status in society, forced others, many of whom had never been to old Mexico before, to cross the newly drawn border to return to a shrunken Mexico (Weber, 1973).

At times during the early and mid-twentieth century when their labor was needed, Mexicans were encouraged to cross the border to become temporary workers through the Bracero Program but were not truly welcomed. Mexicans were excluded from mainstream society and isolated by ethnic segregation. Discrimination was rampant even in schools, where children of Mexican descent were trained to become obedient workers and discouraged from pursuing white-collar careers (Rodriguez, 2005). In California and throughout the Southwest there were elementary schools for Mexican Americans only, leading to unequal educational opportunities for Mexican American children. The Mexican American community again went to the courts and in 1946 won the first significant legal case against school segregation with *Mendez v. Westminster*, which served as a springboard for the later case of *Brown v. Board of Education* (Valencia, 2005).

Over time, a Chicano identity developed in reaction to the history of oppression experienced by U.S. Mexican communities. Originally meant as an insult implying a lack of sophistication, the term "Chicano" was appropriated during the 1960s by youthful political militants to signify Mexican Americans' growing awareness of their special ethnic and cultural heritage (Rinderle, 2005). Chicanos saw themselves as an exploited and conquered people suffering from the deculturalization carried out in schools. *Chicanismo* emphasized the ideology of *La Raza* (the people), which favored collective versus individual achievement of goals. Some of the main goals of the Chicano movement were to strengthen the ethnic identity and pride of Mexican Americans and to advance a civil rights agenda aimed at ending discrimination and promoting equality in jobs, housing, and education (Chávez, 2002). Although in some communities the word "Chicano" has lost its connection to the Chicano movement and is often used as a synonym for "Mexican American," the term "Chicano" continues to signify a more defiant approach to ethnic pride and identity.

Even before the height of the Chicano movement, Mexican Americans had displayed a great deal of strength in the face of oppression. By 1933, Mexican field workers' protests against their degrading living conditions and poor wages were taking the form of strikes (Takaki, 1993). During the 1950s and 1960s, a Chicano organization called the GI Forum fought discrimination and conducted voter registration drives throughout the Southwest and California (Farley, 2000). It also focused on system reform to improve the educational attainment of Mexican Americans by challenging school segregation. It was also during the 1960s that Mexican Americans turned away from assimilation and started emphasizing a self-defense ideology that promoted the preservation of the Spanish language and Mexican American culture and heritage (Torres-Saillant, 2006).

In order to ease the shortage of workers produced by World War II, the U.S. government established the Bracero Program, which brought five million Mexican-born farmworkers to the United States between 1942 and 1964 (Borjas & Katz, 2007). The Bracero Program was abruptly discontinued, but migrant workers (both documented and undocumented) continue to be hired to work in the fields and they continue to come to the United States in great numbers. Today Mexicans account for approximately 77 percent of the total number of migrant workers and continue to endure the most oppressive working and living conditions. César Chávez was raised under such conditions and in 1962 started the National Farm Workers Association, a crusade he called *el movimiento*. Chávez used Gandhi's nonviolent methods to unionize farmworkers and improve their working conditions and overall quality of life. He dedicated his life to the struggles of migrant workers and fought for basic amenities and decent wages, as well as protection against occupational hazards like exposure to pesticide spraying. At this time, farmworkers' exploitation and misery resulted from the fact that corporate farm owners were either too far away or too indifferent to notice their workers' suffering, even when conditions were so bad that children were dying of malnutrition. Although Chávez was successful and saw changes in many areas, migrant farmworkers continue to face oppressive conditions such as lack of medical insurance and decent housing.

After more than a century of domination, exploitation, and oppression, Mexican Americans continue to be targets of stereotypes and prejudice. Mexican immigrants who have arrived recently regularly find that their choices in jobs, housing, and political participation are restricted (Gutierrez, Ortega, & Yeakley, 2000). Despite all the challenges Mexican Americans have faced as a subordinate group, their experiences with discrimination have produced an "ethnic consciousness" that in turn has helped them develop a strong ethnic identity (Bacal, 1994). In many Mexican American communities, murals are a display of community strength, providing a canvas on which to demonstrate pride in a common cultural heritage and articulate struggles against historical and current oppression (Barton & Delgado, 1998).

Mexican and Mexican American culture has been identified by some as a source of strength that has given rise to the so-called Mexican paradox: despite the fact that Mexican-born mothers (as well as other foreign-born Latina mothers) tend to have lower incomes and less access to health care and begin prenatal care later than other groups, they give birth to healthy babies at rates higher than other ethnic minority groups and non-Latino whites (Buekens, Notzon, Kotelchuck, & Wilcox, 2000). Infant mortality rates are lower for Mexican-born mothers than for whites and African Americans, and even lower than for Mexican American mothers born in the United States. Similar patterns of low infant mortality have been found for mothers from many other parts of Latin America. Immigrant Latina mothers, especially those from Mexico, appear to possess some protective factors related to pregnancy and childbirth that outweigh other risks they face. However, those advantages appear to weaken over time as Mexican mothers become more acculturated. Culturally grounded social work aims at identifying protective factors that lead to positive outcomes so that interventions that capitalize on the strength of families navigating the acculturation process can be designed and implemented.

An example of such an intervention is Keepin' It REAL, a culturally grounded intervention that utilizes the protective factors that inhere in the culture of origin to help participants retain healthy behaviors and attitudes. Keepin' It REAL is a substance abuse prevention program designed for and tested with predominantly Mexican and Mexican American middle school students in the southwest United States. It draws on the values and communication styles of Mexican American culture to teach youths strategies for resisting drugs—refuse, explain, avoid, and leave, or REAL—in ways that are appropriate for the social situations that the youths encounter in daily life. Results from the randomized trial conducted to evaluate the effectiveness of the program showed that recent Mexican immigrant students who spoke predominantly Spanish had a significantly lower drug use rate and significantly stronger anti-drug attitudes than their more acculturated Mexican and Mexican American classmates. The lower levels of acculturation found among students who still used Spanish at home and with friends appeared to offer a protective effect against alcohol and other drug use. This protective effect weakened over time as students began to use English as their primary language. Ironically, the intervention was particularly effective among the more acculturated students, mostly because they were more at risk for substance use than their less acculturated counterparts (Marsiglia, Kulis, Wagstaff, Elek, & Dran, 2005).

Despite such hopeful illustrations of the strength that comes from culture, in many parts of the country Mexican Americans are at risk of poverty and poor physical and mental health. They are overrepresented in the criminal justice system and typically have low levels of education, alarming school dropout rates, and high unemployment rates. Anti-immigrant attitudes have caused community members to be fearful of using social services (Paris, Añez, Bedregal, Andrés-Hyman, & Davidson, 2005). Therefore, culturally grounded social work with Mexicans and Mexican Americans starts with the recognition and validation of the civil and human rights of all clients.

MIGRATION, EXPLOITATION, REJECTION, AND THE MODEL MINORITY: ASIAN AMERICANS

Migration has played a central role in the formation of most major American ethnic groups, including Asian Americans. Migration has been part of the human experience for millennia. It can be defined as the movement of people from one geographic location to another; it can take place within a country or across international borders. Migration can be voluntary (e.g., migration of Europeans in the nineteenth century) or involuntary (e.g., slavery and human trafficking). Migration is a complex process entailing the need to let go of a familiar environment and adjust to an unfamiliar environment. Migration processes are very diverse because they can be triggered by different factors at the sending point and are influenced by different sets of conditions at the receiving point. For example, the migration experience of a wealthy English-speaking family from Hong Kong relocating to Vancouver, Canada, is very different from the experience of a Sudanese refugee family from Darfur relocating to Minneapolis, Minnesota. These differences are often captured by terms used to describe migrants such as "immigrant," "undocumented immigrant," "refugee," "asylum seeker," "permanent resident," and "naturalized citizen" that are imposed from the outside to describe different journeys in legal but not necessarily psychosocial terms.

In 1882, the United States passed a law that banned Asians from immigrating to the country. Although ethnic prejudice might have played a role in such an exclusionary policy, economic competition between whites and Asian Americans was more likely the major cause (Farley, 2000). Asians had been coming to the United States in debt as a result of the large amounts of money they had to pay to immigrate and were willing to work for lower wages than whites. Thus negative stereotypes of Chinese and Japanese immigrants stemmed primarily from their roles as laborers and their impact on the job market, allegedly one that drove down wages for native-born workers. The term "coolie labor" (denoting undignified work) dates from this period. The perception that Asian immigrants were taking jobs away from whites or lowering their wages created tension and fed the xenophobia of working-class whites who felt threatened by the influx of Asian immigrants. In some areas with larger Asian communities, intergroup tensions resulted in widespread violence against Asian immigrants (Anbinder, 2006).

In addition, prejudice was fueled by myths that racial mixing through intermarriage between whites and minorities resulted in the contamination of white racial purity and was therefore dangerous (Kenney, 2002). In 1880, California and other states and territories passed anti-miscegenation laws (the first of which had been passed in the colony of Maryland in 1661 but applied only to marriages between blacks and whites) prohibiting marriages between whites and individuals of other races; this was the first such law to outlaw marriages between whites and Asians (Takaki, 1998). These laws not only served to maintain group boundaries and the power and privilege of the dominant group but created other problems owing to exclusionary laws that made it difficult for Chinese immigrants' wives to migrate to the United States and resulted in serious gender imbalances within the Chinese community in America (Lee & Fernandez, 1998; McKeown, 1999).

Another devastating aspect of the so-called yellow peril was the widespread fear that Chinese and Japanese immigrants were loyal only to their countries of origin and, if not stopped, would take over the United States. This social hysteria reached its height after the bombing of Pearl Harbor, when much of the Japanese American population, most of whom were American born and therefore denied the fundamental civil rights guaranteed by the U.S. Constitution, was interned. The internment experience meant that Japanese Americans had to liquidate their businesses; lost their life savings, homes, and possessions; and lived with the knowledge that American democracy had failed to provide protection for all its citizens. (The belief that immigrants constitute a foreign peril has resurfaced recently in response to newcomers from Mexico and other countries in Latin America.)

Anti-Chinese laws, economic exploitation, and racial antagonism set up an effective exclusionary system that ensured that Chinese immigrants remained strangers in their adopted land (Takaki, 1998). Even today, certain Asian groups are victims of antagonism and are perceived to be foreigners regardless of their immigrant status or history. For example, a customer at a local store may express her surprise when the third-generation Asian American cashier responds to her in unaccented English. Seemingly innocent questions about their origins that imply that they do not belong (e.g., "And where are you from?") constantly remind Asian Americans whose families have lived in the United States for many generations that the majority culture sees them as outsiders. Those who are immigrants continue to experience hardships related to migration. Asians of lower socioeconomic status often face mistreatment as they attempt to immigrate to the United States and are employed by individuals and companies that exploit their precarious financial situations. During the 1990s, federal investigators found seventy-two Thai immigrants indentured illegally in Californian sweatshops—living in virtual slavery behind barbed-wire fences—while their salaries were confiscated to pay the costs of their trip to the United States (Finnigan, 1995).

Recent changes in the way Asian Americans are viewed in our society demonstrate that their status is determined not only by their behaviors and achievements but also by the dominant group's openness to and approval of them. Asian

Americans are no longer perceived to be inassimilable and exotic but are now viewed as industrious and smart. Today, Asian Americans often need to cope with the stereotype of the model minority. The image of Asian Americans as a monolithic group characterized by supportive and self-reliant family ties, high educational aspirations, and personal discipline was created by a changing racial climate rather than by the inherent characteristics of this very heterogeneous group. Attitudes started to change in the 1960s as the term "Asian American" started to be used instead of "Oriental," and Asian Americans' incomes and educational attainment began to resemble those of whites (Zhou, 2004). The model minority stereotype has been exploited by political conservatives and used by policy makers who believe that nongovernmental assistance (i.e., help provided by NGOs) is the key to helping ethnic minorities get ahead. Unfortunately, this stereotype of Asian American self-sufficiency, enterprise, and success leaves many Asians at the mercy of underfunded community assistance programs (Thrupkaew, 2002). A comprehensive review of published social work research on Chinese Americans concluded that they continue to be "essentialized," "otherized," and viewed in a negative light (Tsang, 2001). The stereotype not only promotes antagonism between ethnic minority groups but also overlooks the real needs many Asian American have and makes them vulnerable to being underserved.

THE END OF RACISM?

Since the civil rights movement and the rights legislation it triggered, public opinion polls have revealed that an increasing number of people think that racism has weakened or even disappeared from U.S. society (Bonilla-Silva, 2006). When people think of racism, many think only of public expressions of extremist racist attitudes and behaviors (like the hanging of a noose from a tree at a Louisiana high school by white students in 2006), which have become increasingly rare; they do not think about the more subtle expressions of racism and discrimination that are still prevalent in our society. There has also been a sharp increase in the number of whites who believe that racial equality exists in most arenas of public life, including access to education, jobs, and public services (Schuman, Steeh, Bobo, & Krysan, 1997). The struggle led by African Americans and their allies during the second half of the twentieth century has produced significant results. In fact, society has witnessed an important reduction in personal racism (i.e., individuals overtly espousing racist and bigoted views and subscribing to stereotypes). There is, however, ample evidence that racism and the problems it engenders have not faded away. The National Opinion Research Center's General Social Survey shows that about one in six white adults still holds the opinion that laws should prohibit marriage between whites and African Americans and that whites should have the right to keep African Americans from living in their neighborhoods (Paradies, 2006). Racially prejudiced attitudes have also been shown to be a source of the opposition of a substantial number of whites to school busing (a measure implemented to create more racially integrated schools), bilingual education, affirmative action, government assistance to ethnic minorities, and residential integration; it also influences their views of how crime should be fought (see Bobo & Fox, 2003). Institutional racism continues to be present in the workplace and politics, often in subtle, symbolic, and indirect ways that are transmitted during early childhood socialization (see Feagin, 2000). Even though institutional racism may be subtle, unintentional, nearly invisible, and virtually undetectable, it can be measured more by its impact than the intentions behind it (Keleher & Johnson, 2001). One way to see institutional racism is as a barrier within organizations that prevents ethnic minority employees from reaching higher positions in the system. Within the health care system, racism has even been found in patterns of organ donation and organ transplants. Even though African Americans are more often in need of kidney transplants, they are much less likely than whites to be referred for or receive a transplant, and they wait twice as long on waiting lists before receiving transplants (National Institutes of Health, 2006).

Despite the scientific evidence developed over the last century showing that race is a socially constructed concept, racism continues to pervade contemporary society, and socially constructed categories of race are still used to set up social hierarchies that affect millions of individuals' experiences and opportunities (Esposito & Murphy, 2000). Regardless of its roots, racism continues to limit the independence and freedom of America's racial and ethnic minorities, reduce their empowerment, and deny their dignity and inherent worth. Racism—whether conscious or unconscious, deliberate or unintentional—continues to be present in society. Racial and ethnic appearance has historically constituted an important line of demarcation in U.S. social, cultural, economic, and political life, and it continues to do so. Although judging people based on color lines seems like a remnant of the nation's repudiated past, contemporary studies show that African Americans and Latinos with darker skin tone face more challenges and disadvantages than those with a lighter complexion and more European facial features. Skin tone and facial features continue to predict objective quality-of-life indicators such as educational and occupational advancement, even after differences in educational and socioeconomic backgrounds are adjusted for (Herring, Keith, & Horton, 2004; Murguia & Telles, 1996; Telles & Murguia, 1990). Studies have also found that relatively darker skin tone has negative effects on self-esteem, perceived attractiveness, life satisfaction, and depression (Boyd-Franklin, 1991; Brown, Ward, Lightbourn, & Jackson, 1999). Rather than reflecting some inherent racial quality, these disparities arise from an individual's awareness and internalization of the dominant culture's norms and beliefs, which continue to give preference to light complexions and European features (Bond & Cash, 1992; Porter, 1991).

Border vigilante movements (e.g., the Minutemen) are contemporary forms of racism that target groups whose often imagined differences in appearance are perceived to signify much more fundamental cultural differences. For example, Mexican American families in Arizona border towns who can trace their ancestry many generations back have reported repeated incidents of harassment by the Minutemen militia (Rosas, 2006). Many members of the Minutemen and related fringe anti-immigrant organizations harass anyone around the border who "looks" Mexican.

It is important to be familiar with the history of different ethnic and racial groups, as this history can often help explain status differentials that exist among individuals and groups. Social workers can become better practitioners by becoming aware of the long struggle that members of those communities have led and of their ability to endure and overcome difficult situations, both individually and collectively. Culturally grounded social work honors those struggles and encourages practitioners to partner with ethnic and racial minority communities as they overcome oppression and work toward creating a more just society.

Key Concepts

Colonialism a system of oppression of and domination over the local population imposed by an invading outside group

Internal colonialism oppressive power that is exerted by the majority culture over minority groups within national borders

Genocide the organized effort to eliminate an entire group of people

Jim Crow laws post–Civil War laws that provided the "separate but equal" legal framework for the racial discrimination against, segregation of, and denial of political, economic, educational, and social opportunities to African Americans

Annexation the taking of an area already occupied by another group, either through military action or the invitation of residents living there

Treaty of Guadalupe Hidalgo the treaty that ended the war between the United States and Mexico and forced Mexico to cede the territories of what is now most of the states of New Mexico, Arizona, California, Colorado, Nevada, and Utah to the United States

Chicano (Chicana) a Mexican American; a term that came out of, and often continues to signify solidarity with, the Chicano movement

Migration the movement of people from one geographic location to another either within a country or across international borders

8

Gender

DIFFERENT SOCIETIES HAVE DIFFERENT GENDER ROLE EXPECTATIONS. Although children are taught that their genes decree whether they will grow into men or women, people are not born socially or culturally female or male. Like race and ethnicity, gender can be thought of as socially constructed. Cultures have different ways of teaching children how to be male or female based on shared norms and values. These agreed-upon patterns of expected behavior often reinforce a dichotomous view of gender and the relative power of men and women. The growing transgender community—a group that may include transsexuals and cross-dressers as well as certain gay and lesbian subgroups, depending upon the definition to which one subscribes—is a reminder of the oppressive nature of these restrictive gender labels, yet the influence of gender roles extends to everyone. Because gender role expectations are contextual, there are great differences concerning these expectations not only between cultural groups but also within groups. Intersectionality plays an important role in explaining some of these differences. Religion, ethnicity, and social class—among other factors—strongly influence how an individual perceives her or his identity and gender roles.

Social work professionals work with individuals of different gender identities and individuals who grew up with different gender role expectations. It is important for social workers to understand how these factors interact with other factors that influence an individual's overall identity and behavior. This chapter explores some of these issues and provides some suggestions for gender-aware social work practice.

GENDER, GENDER ROLES, AND GENDER IDENTITY

The term "gender" refers to the social and cultural patterns associated with women and men; in other words, gender defines what behaviors are expected from men and women and which behaviors are considered out of bounds. Like race, gender is not a biological category but rather a socially constructed one. In fact, one's biological sex does not have to be consistent with one's gender identity. The binary conception of gender reflects a taken-for-granted view of humans as inherently male or female by virtue of their genetic or biological makeup, despite the reality that an appreciable portion of the population has ambiguous primary or secondary sex characteristics (Fausto-Sterling, 1993).* In actuality, it is through social learning that individuals organize information in gendered terms (Bandura & Bussey, 2002). Ideas about distinctively feminine and masculine behavior have varied widely across cultures and throughout history.

Gender identity is learned at an early age and is institutionally enforced by family, religion, the media, and politics. Those individuals who internalize a gender identity incongruent with their genital configuration typically are subjected to severe sanctions because they do not enact gender in socially prescribed ways. The earliest emergence of gender identity is membership knowledge ("Are you a boy or a girl?"), whereas gender constancy (the idea that sex does not change over time) is achieved later. Studies of gender development provide considerable evidence that young children manifest gender preferences and gendered behavior before they develop an intrinsic sense of their gender identity, and that these preferences reflect social influences rather than an innate impulse to adopt a self-concept consistent with gender stereotypes (Bandura & Bussey, 2002). The problems and lack of acceptance encountered by girls who are "tomboys" and boys who are labeled "sissies" illustrate the social sources of gender identity. Sanctions against gender nonconformity start early in a child's life. By the age of three, membership knowledge sets in motion intergroup processes that prompt children to interact mainly within same-sex groups; these interactions trigger other dynamics, including preferential treatment of the gender in-group and devaluation of the out-group (Carver, Yunger, & Perry, 2003). In many cultures, including mainstream American culture, female roles are believed to encompass nurturance and emotional expression, while male roles emphasize achievement, control, and autonomy (Barbee, Cunningham, Winstead, Derlega, Grulley, Yankeelov, & Druen, 1993).

Both females and males develop a gender strategy, or a "plan of action through which a person tries to solve problems at hand, given cultural notions of gender at play" (Hochschild & Machung, 1989, p. 15). The kind of strategy that a person chooses depends on her or his learned beliefs about womanhood and manhood. Gender ideology is rooted in early experiences and is the result of internalized messages received at home from one's family. Gender is an ongoing social creation that can go through radical changes throughout the life span. Because

---

*The term "intersex" is used to refer to individuals whose sex assignment is ambiguous because they possess a mixture of male and female gonads and/or genitalia. Fausto-Sterling (1993) identifies three main types that nonetheless overlook many variations within each group: true hermaphrodites, who have both an ovary and a testis; male pseudo-hermaphrodites, who have only testes but also some female genitalia; and female pseudo-hermaphrodites, who have only ovaries but some male genitalia as well. Infants and children have often been referred for surgery to make their sex less ambiguous, but this practice is becoming increasingly controversial (Kessler, 1997).

our society views gender differences as natural, individuals rarely question the extent of these differences. In fact, males and females tend to accept such stereotypes even when their own behavior differs from them, because they learn to see their behavior as anomalous if it is not congruent with the stereotypes created by society. As society's ideas about gender identity are systematically reinforced through socialization, gender can become associated with many different attributes and qualities; for example, leadership is often confused with masculinity. Such stereotypes often have a prominent role in shaping reality: the belief that men are more assertive than women results in men occupying leadership positions more often than women. Research shows that the social construction of gender reinforces power differentials between men and women and perpetuates the oppression of women (Kanter, 1977; Kidder, 2002).

In many societies, even the forms of language that are used deny women's importance and represent men's experiences as the norm. It is often argued by traditionalists that male "generic" language (such as "businessmen," "chairman," and "mankind," or the use of "he" to mean "he or she") is gender neutral, but researchers have demonstrated that this type of language is perceived as referring predominantly to men (Wood, 1994). Thus the gender patterns of dominance and subordination that characterize sexism may be reinforced in communication. The gender power imbalance is manifested as well in conversations. Despite the stereotype that women are the talkative ones, communication researchers have shown both in experimental and real-life settings that in mixed-sex groups, men tend to initiate more conversations, monopolize conversations, and talk for the longest time (Edelsky, 1981; West & Zimmerman, 1983).

SEXISM

Sexism involves the negative evaluation of an individual or group of individuals based merely on the individual or group's membership in a particular sexual category. Sexism is the product of norms and expectations that exist in religious dogma, kinship relations, and the laws that assign women a subordinate place in society. Due to the unequal treatment of women in most societies, sexism is usually associated with the oppression of women. Both women and men, however, may be the victims of sexism. Men's organizations such as the National Organization for Changing Men and the National Congress for Men argue that the stereotypes that men are tough, unemotional, and aggressive can subject men to unfair treatment in several arenas, such as in evaluations for certain jobs, and in divorce and child custody proceedings.

Sexism is commonly defined as the subordination of a woman or group of women and the assumption of the superiority of a man or group of men based only on sex. This view of sexism attributes the oppression of women to patriarchy, which is a whole system of gender inequality that operates throughout society. Such sexism can be encountered at both an interpersonal level and an institutional level. At the interpersonal level, sexism may first be experienced within the home when children witness a gendered division of labor in the tasks performed by mothers and daughters versus fathers and sons, such as assumptions that mothers have sole responsibility for cooking, cleaning, and caring for children while husbands have ultimate authority and control over important decisions. Male chauvinist beliefs, such as the stereotype that women are less competent than men, are also expressions of sexism. Rather than regarding women as the targets of discrimination, chauvinist beliefs support the view that women actually enjoy unearned or undeserved privileges that are denied to men, such as preferential treatment in hiring practices and promotions. Such beliefs may account for the indifference or outright opposition to policies designed to improve women's status in society. Institutionalized sexism is present in all spheres of society and can be more subtle than interpersonally expressed forms of sexism. In the classroom, it exists in the form of stereotypical images in textbooks; lack of recognition of female authors, female historical figures, and women's point of view in standard curricula; teachers' tolerance for sexist remarks; and sexual harassment (Wood, 1994). At work, institutionalized sexism may be either hostile or benevolent: hostile sexism is manifested through dominant paternalism and the idea that women are inferior and unable to do the same work as men, while benevolent sexism reflects the belief that women are better suited to nurturing occupations like nursing or are in need of the protection of male mentors. In addition, many organizations have a masculine culture in place, which means that power is asymmetrically distributed between men while female employees hold lower-status jobs (Bonvillain, 2001). Institutional sexism can also manifest itself in the differential treatment of men and women that results from institutional policies. Those involved in institutional sexism do not need to be prejudiced against women or even intend to be engaging in discrimination, but the effect is the same as if there were blatant discrimination (Kammeyer, Ritzer, & Yetman, 1990).

There are many different forms of institutionalized sexism in the workplace. They encompass a wide array of ways that men benefit from occupational and organizational privileges. These benefits are built into the system so that men reap rewards denied to women without having to actively or consciously discriminate against women (Tomaskovic-Devey, 1993). These privileges become codified within workplace norms, recruitment procedures, the division of labor, and informal networks of information and decision making (Alvarez & Lutterman, 1979; Bielby & Baron, 1984; Feagin & Eckberg, 1980; Reskin & Hartmann, 1985). The norms in place at the office may pressure women to seek advancement by moving into positions in which they supervise other women in clerical jobs rather than those in which they would have to supervise men who are uncomfortable with a female boss. Women who try to ascend the organizational hierarchy face elaborate screening, not just to guarantee that they meet requirements and have the right credentials, but also to determine if they have social backgrounds and outlooks similar to those of the men already in dominant positions (Blum & Smith, 1988; Kanter, 1977). Men can control the highest organizational positions by spreading word of openings and seeking nominations of promising job candidates through informal male-dominated channels and activities, such as golf games with fellow employees. This kind of gender discrimination allows men to maintain their privileges by keeping jobs requiring the highest levels of skill and offering the greatest authority, status, and remuneration among men.

The magnitude of continuing gender discrimination is suggested by the almost complete exclusion of women from the upper reaches of the workplace pyramid, among top management (Kimmel, 2000; Roth, 2006; Thompson & Sekaquaptewa, 2002). Fewer than 10 percent of all senior executives and only 3.9 percent of the 4,341 top-paid CEOs and directors in Fortune 1000 corporations are women (Krishnan & Park, 2005). Even in professions dominated by female workers, like social work, men appear to have advantages over women in authority and pay. Although women make up an overwhelming proportion of the students who receive MSW degrees and are active social work practitioners, they are much less well represented among social work faculty, and men are still more likely than women to occupy the top rung of positions in social work programs as dean, directors, and chairs (Di Palma & Topper, 2001; McPhail, 2004). Salary studies have shown repeatedly that men in social work tend to make more money than their female counterparts; this is true among social work faculty, social workers employed outside academia, and even social workers in private practice (Gibelman & Schervish, 1995; Landers, 1992; Koeske & Krowinski, 2004; McPhail, 2004; Sowers-Hoag & Harrison, 1991). These gender gaps in salary are not explained away when gender differences in educational degrees or academic rank or differences in setting, auspices, function, experience, and geography are taken into account.

Some people believe that the gender gap in pay has been erased as women have entered the labor force over the last few decades in rates nearing those of men. In fact, although the gap has narrowed somewhat, women's pay continues to lag behind that of men doing the same type of work (Farrell, 2005). Another myth is that barriers to women's participation in politics have been breached. The reality is that women make up 51 percent of the U.S. population but hold only 12.1 percent of the seats in the U.S. 106th Congress (McGlone, Aronson, & Kobrynowicz, 2006).

Much of the workplace gender inequality in pay, authority, and opportunity for advancement persists as a result of gender segregation of occupations and jobs (Bielby & Baron, 1984, 1986; Huffman & Cohen, 2004). A large part of the gender gap in pay is due simply to the fact that so many women are concentrated in low-wage jobs that men rarely occupy and that offer fewer opportunities for advancement. Some of the lowest-paying jobs in the United States are occupied almost exclusively by women; for example, women make up over 95 percent of secretaries, receptionists, and dental hygienists (Lippa, 2005). Although the divergent occupational paths of men and women reflect gender socialization that starts in childhood and continues through the school years, it also reflects our society's evaluations of work that is done by men and women. For example, jobs within companies and agencies are structured—through a system of elaborate job titles and job ladders called an internal labor market—to segregate men and women even more acutely than might result from their preexisting differences in educational and occupational choices. In the 1980s it was established that men and women are so segregated into different jobs within firms that over 80 percent of men and women in U.S. firms would have to switch job titles to make the gender composition consistent across all jobs (Bielby & Baron, 1984, 1986). Furthermore, the gender segregation of jobs is most acute at the top of the organizational hierarchy.

Occupations in which gender composition changes over time also show traces of institutionalized sexism. For example, in its early stages, computer programming was thought to be a suitable occupation for women because it resembled the relatively low-skilled and modestly paid keypunch operations that women generally performed. Only when it was recognized as a highly valuable, marketable, and financially rewarding skill did society begin to see computer programming as a job more appropriate for men. Bakers, on the other hand, have gone from being predominantly male to female, but that transition has witnessed relative declines in wages, as baking increasingly uses semi-automated or routine methods in supermarkets. Labor market studies have also shown that women pay a salary penalty for doing nurturing work that involves caretaking (e.g., nursing, elementary school teaching, and social work), which is not highly valued by society, and that work that becomes female dominated over time loses the ability to command high status and wages (England, 1992). Similarly, even in fields once dominated by men where women have gained a stronger presence, like law and medicine, their pay still lags significantly behind that of men doing the same work (Burstein, 1994; Dixon & Seron, 1995).

Such extreme gender disparities are clearly inconsistent with the widely held view that gender equality of opportunity has been achieved. Researchers have explained this as a form of modern sexism, one that is replacing the "old-fashioned" sexism that defended traditional gender roles and the unequal treatment of women and men based on gender stereotypes about competence and intelligence. Modern sexism is characterized by a denial that women are still targets of sexism; exaggeration of the extent to which women have achieved economic, political, and social equality with men; rejection of policies that aim to help women advance in the workplace and in education; and general antagonism toward women's demands for equality (Swim, Aikin, Hall, & Hunter, 1995). People—both men and women—who hold this view perceive greater gender equality than really exists and tend to blame individual women for segregation in the workforce and in politics. Women may minimize the impact of sexism on their lives by using as their reference group women in situations similar to their own, rather than men, a strategy that may be a coping mechanism to deal with discrimination.

Women and their lower economic status are affected by sexism outside the workplace as well. For example, reforms in divorce and child custody laws are commonly thought to benefit divorced women and their children. However, research has shown that after divorce, women and their children typically suffer a serious drop in their standard of living, whereas men see an improvement even after paying alimony and child support (Hanson, McLanahan, & Thompson, 1998; McKeever & Wolfinger, 2006; McManus & DiPrete, 2001).

Although most people believe that there is widespread support for women's rights in the United States, the fact is that the Equal Rights Amendment, which was enacted by Congress in 1972 and would prohibit discrimination based on sex, was passed by only thirty-five state legislatures, three short of the required two-thirds of all the states. Sexism continues to affect women's family lives, educational and career plans, and success in the workplace and in politics. Sexist discrimination has been associated with changes in adult identity and identity crises among women and can affect women's physical and mental health (Anthis, 2002). It may be important for social workers to consider how sexism affects a female client's sense of self and help her to reexamine her identity.

THE WOMEN'S MOVEMENT AND FEMINISM

Feminism is the result of the various ways that women have struggled collectively in response to their specific forms of subordination. All versions or strands of feminism are grounded in the premise that differences in women's and men's positions in society are the result of social factors and that women's experiences, ideas, and concerns are as valuable as men's and deserve the same respect. A central feature of feminism is the differences in female access to power, a power differential that is related to class, race, ethnicity, religion, and sexual orientation (Moane, 1999). In the United States, the first wave of the women's movement started in 1848 with the efforts of Elizabeth Cady Stanton and Susan B. Anthony, among others, to gain political equality for women through suffrage during their involvement in the antislavery movement. Anthony focused on economic independence for women while Stanton explored the sexual emancipation of women (DuBois, 1999). During what is referred to as the first feminist wave, the domestic roles assigned to women were not challenged directly, but organizations such as the Women's Christian Temperance Union were formed to fight for child labor laws and female prisoners' rights (Wood, 1994). First-wave feminists were concerned with securing women's access to education and certain occupations such as clerical work (Cohn, 1985). First-wave feminists also worked to secure protections for women in the areas of marital property rights and child custody laws. These feminists were mainly responding to injustices that they themselves had experienced as middle-class women.

By 1960, a second feminist wave was underway, propelled in large part by developments within the civil rights and antiwar movements that revealed the need to address persisting inequities affecting women. Through her activism and now classic book, *The Feminine Mystique*, Betty Friedan (1963/2001) exercised a pivotal leadership role in shaping the modern feminist movement. Her description of the oppression of the "happy housewife" ignited a revolution that radically altered the consciousness and lives of women as well as the culture of society as a whole.

Several branches that emerged from this second wave of feminism have advanced different solutions to discrimination against women while promoting women's rights and identities within the spheres of reproduction, sexuality, living arrangements, and the larger culture. One branch, liberal feminism, has concentrated on reforms that would better integrate women into existing social, economic, and political institutions rather than working to change these institutions fundamentally. Organizations like NOW (the National Organization for Women) have pursued this agenda through antidiscrimination lawsuits, political lobbying, and educational campaigns to increase public awareness of issues affecting women, such as domestic violence. Radical feminism, in contrast, focuses on achieving fundamental change through the rejection of patriarchal institutions like marriage and emphasizes ways for women to support one another in resisting oppression in their personal lives. Radical feminists have explored female-centered redefinitions of the notion of family and new ways to conceptualize the division of labor at home and at work. Another branch, Marxist or socialist feminism, emphasizes the harmful role of capitalism in the lives of both women and men, and the way that sexism undermines the ability of the working class to address their economic exploitation. The different branches of feminism have increased awareness of women's issues in general and have created new ways for women to explore the roots of oppression in their personal lives, allowing them to pursue new avenues for effecting change and to enlist new allies, including pro-feminist men who support the feminist movement (Wood, 1994). Amid the successes of second-wave feminists, divisions also emerged among the different branches of feminism, and the voices of black feminists, Chicana feminists, and lesbian feminists came to the fore.

In the 1990s, amid questions about the identification of younger women with earlier feminist ideals and the co-optation and depoliticization of feminist issues, a third wave of the feminist movement emerged, one emphasizing individual rights and empowerment and focused mostly on women between the ages of fifteen and thirty. This wave emphasizes intersectionality and has sought to connect women who continue to strive for self-determination in their personal lives and local communities; raise awareness of human rights issues; and increase appreciation for the impact of race, ethnicity, religion, and class in women's lives. Despite the advances made by the three waves of feminism to date, women in the United States retain their lower status in almost all aspects of life.

According to public opinion polls, the majority of U.S. women support feminist ideas like equal pay for equal work; greater opportunities for all women regardless of race, class, or sexual orientation; and prevention of violence against women (Jennings, 2006). However, feminism is often equated erroneously with a hatred of men or estrangement from them, lesbianism, and political extremism. Some women reject feminist ideas because they hold these misconceptions and wish to avoid being associated with them, while others may think that feminism is passé or no longer necessary. In addition, it is commonly (and erroneously) assumed that all heterosexual men who support gender equality or take courses on feminism must be gay (see White, 2006). Being a gay man does not, of course, mean that one is aware or supportive of the women's movement; however, it appears that men who adopt less stereotyped gender roles, regardless of their sexual orientation, are often strong supporters of the feminist movement (Suter & Toller, 2006).

Despite all the differing perceptions of what it means, feminism offers a much-needed perspective. One important goal of feminism is to make information available to women so they can make choices. Social work plays a key role in this regard and as a profession has embraced a feminist agenda, recognizing the unique perspectives of women and their abilities to overcome oppressive conditions. Yet much of the oppression that exists goes unidentified because it constitutes part of women's daily lives—what Slattery (2004) describes as "walking with two-pound ankle weights—impediments that are overlooked until removed" (p. 67).

SEXISM AND INTERSECTIONALITIES

One of the most important contributions of third-wave feminism has been its acknowledgment that gender cannot be considered in isolation; women experience their gender status as it intersects with their social class, race, ethnicity, nationality, immigration status, religion, and sexual orientation. Women from lower socioeconomic backgrounds, for example, face compounded disadvantages in health, education, and employment due to gender and social class inequities in society. Women in Western societies tend to live longer than men but experience more chronic illness, in part because of their longevity. However, lower-class women—those with lower education, income, and occupational status—have much higher rates of morbidity and mortality than women from the middle and upper classes, and certain groups of poor women are at especially high risk (Feinstein, 1993; Marmot, 2003). Some working poor women earn too much income to qualify for Medicaid and earn too little to purchase private health insurance. Therefore, these women and their children are more likely to receive care in hospital emergency rooms (because they do not have a personal physician) and often do not seek care because they lack transportation or child care. As a result, poor women give birth to more babies with health problems, and infant mortality is higher among this population. In the United States, there is a nexus connecting gender, poverty, marital status, and infant and maternal health because single mothers and divorced mothers are more likely than married women and men to live in poverty (National Center for Health Statistics, 2006; Stewart, Dean, & Gregorich, 2007).

Feminist ideas and feminist organizations have helped to awaken our society to the plague of domestic violence, and third-wave feminists have pointed to ways that a woman's intersecting identities can elevate the risk that she will experience such violence. Intimate partner violence occurs at unacceptably high rates among all ethnic and racial groups because of gender inequities that permeate society. However, the risk of domestic violence is magnified for women whose ethnicity or race places them at an increased disadvantage. While approximately 20 percent of heterosexual couples in the U.S. general population experience intimate partner violence, African American and Latino women experience intimate partner violence at higher rates than whites do (Field & Caetano, 2005). Ethnic minority women experience multiple layers of oppression and may not report intimate partner violence in order to protect their families and their communities from stereotyping and as a result of distrust of the police (Sokoloff & Dupont, 2005).

Immigrant women often face a similar set of compounded disadvantages due to their cultural backgrounds, the isolation they experience following migration, and restrictions imposed by their immigrant status—a form of triple jeopardy. These disadvantages have been described as contributing to an epidemic of intimate partner violence among immigrant women in the United States that affects from 30 to 50 percent of women immigrants from Latin America, South Asia, and Korea (Raj & Silverman, 2002). A number of factors converge to place immigrant women at special risk of domestic violence. They and their partners often have been socialized into traditional gender roles that assign men ultimate authority and power within the relationship and within the family. There may be cultural norms that approve of or tolerate men's use of physical discipline when women stray beyond the limits of their prescribed spousal and family roles. These norms, along with rejection of marital separation and divorce, are sometimes supported both by male perpetrators and female victims, and their immigrant communities (Kulwicki & Miller, 1999; Morash, Bui, & Santiago, 2000). Some members of immigrant communities may not be aware that intimate partner violence is a criminal offense in their adopted country and, even if they are aware of this, may not accept it (Tran & Des Jardins, 2000). Immigrant women are more vulnerable to domestic violence when they are cut off from family and friendship networks of social support, which increases their dependence on male partners and the in-laws with whom they may be living (Morash et al., 2000). When subjected to violence, their options for seeking information and help can be further limited by their immigration status and insecure economic position. Documented immigrants' immigration status may be tied to their husbands', which would limit their options for obtaining legal employment. Undocumented immigrant women may justifiably fear deportation if they seek help from authorities.

Prompted by a feminist approach that explores how women may face oppression on many levels, practitioners are increasingly recognizing that it is necessary to move away from a culturally neutral approach to intimate partner violence. Social workers, who often encounter clients and families ravaged by violence at home, have begun to acknowledge the importance of racial and social class awareness in the prevention and treatment of intimate partner violence, thus confirming the need for a culturally grounded approach to social work practice (Richie, 2000).

MEN AND MASCULINITY

Robert Connell (1987) introduced the concept of hegemonic masculinity to describe the kind of masculine character that is idealized in Western cultures, an ideal that associates manhood with power and dominance, condones violence, and marginalizes many men. The notion of hegemonic masculinity recognizes the very dynamic nature of cultural ideas about gender, and the fact that gender is socially constructed in everyday life for men just as it is for women. Studies of hegemonic masculinity have emphasized the ways that economic and institutional structures affect the prevailing conception of masculinity and have recognized important variations among groups of men who adopt different forms of masculinity. The concept of hegemonic masculinity is a reminder that it is more accurate to speak of "masculinities" than of a singular "masculinity."

The concept of hegemonic masculinity operates at many levels. When applied to individual men, it describes each man's quest to accumulate and display accepted cultural symbols of manhood. Looking at differences among men based on race and ethnicity, social class, ability status, and sexual orientation, hegemonic masculinity points out that not all men have equal claims to the privileges of manhood. The concept also aims to clarify the roots of gender inequalities in society by describing an overarching cultural system that gives a privileged group of men the power to maintain dominance over all women and many other men (Connell, 1987).

In the United States and many other societies, the defining cultural image of hegemonic masculinity is of men who hold power. Their manhood has been tested in a figurative or literal field of battle—the marketplace, politics, war, or sports—in which they have demonstrated the supposedly necessary masculine traits of aggression, competitiveness, strength, toughness, and success. Their predominant position is reflected in power relations, giving them the upper hand when their interests conflict with those of women and other men. Masculinity is a critical part of the system of gender politics: men who are viewed as economically successful, racially or ethnically superior, and visibly heterosexual sit at the top of a pyramid of privileges. Masculinity is thus not defined in isolation but is constructed in relation to ideas about femininities and marginalized masculinities. In this way, hegemonic masculinity is linked to all the major stratification systems of Western societies, whether economic (rich versus poor), racial/ethnic (white versus nonwhite), religious (Christian versus non-Christian), gender (male versus female), or sexual orientation (heterosexual versus homosexual). The characteristics of hegemonic masculinity can evolve over time and differ from one culture to another, and they actually describe only a small proportion of all men. Nonetheless, all men have to confront and adapt to the hegemonic version of masculinity that governs their particular society.

The cultural ideals of masculinity that men in the United States and other postindustrial societies strive to meet have been aptly summarized by Robert Brannon (1976):

- ◆ "No Sissy Stuff": Men do not display feminine traits like vulnerability.
- ◆ "Be a Big Wheel": Men become successful by acquiring power, wealth, and status.
- ◆ "Be a Sturdy Oak": Men control their emotions, are tough and self-reliant, and never cry.
- ◆ "Give 'Em Hell": Men are aggressive and enjoy taking risks.

The social implications of these rules are wide ranging. The repudiation of "sissy stuff" doesn't simply mean that men have to avoid acting in effeminate ways; rather, men can bolster their manhood by denigrating marginalized groups that our culture places most clearly outside the hegemonic masculine realm, with women and homosexual men topping that list. Men can achieve masculinity by *not* being or appearing feminine or gay, and by expressing approval of homophobic and sexist ideas and behaviors, either implicitly or openly. The second rule effectively weakens the claims of most men to full-fledged masculinity, including those from the working class and men of color, who are less likely to be a "Big Wheel," that is, to ascend to the top ranks of organizational and political hierarchies. These groups could be seen as being consigned to pursue a form of "failed" masculinity. The last two rules pose difficult dilemmas for all the men who try to follow them. They urge men to lead a constricted emotional life and fear the intimacy that would provide them with needed social support while also encouraging them to engage in risky behaviors that threaten their mental and physical health.

Could masculinity be hazardous to men's health? The danger lies in the health risks that are associated with aggressive and risky behaviors like drug and alcohol consumption, hazardous occupations, stress-related illnesses, and reluctance to seek preventive medical care (Staples, 1995). Rates of accidental deaths (often alcohol related), vehicular accidents, suicides, and homicides for men are at least double those for women. Among those under thirty, the homicide rate is eight times higher for men than for women. Mortality rates due to disease are higher for males than females at every age, from conception on. Men are more likely than women to die from nine of the ten leading causes of death (diabetes is the exception). Men are almost twice as likely as women to die of heart failure, the number one killer, because they smoke more and engage in more Type A (competitive, impatient, ambitious, aggressive) and Type D (strong, silent, unemotional) behaviors (Heron, 2007). Approximately 356,600 men die of heart disease each year, and approximately 5.8 million men alive today have suffered a heart attack or chest pain (Barnett, Braham, Casper, Elmes, & Halverson, 2007). The role they are expected to perform as providers can lead men not to take time off for health care unless illness is critical and overt. Men are also more likely than women to be the perpetrators and victims of violent crimes (Bureau of Justice Statistics, 2007). Male bodies are expected to be tough, to endure pain and abuse, and to be under the owner's complete control at all times.

Being masculine is also increasingly associated with having a very muscular body (McCreary, Saucier, & Courtenay, 2005). The belief that bigger is better—that muscular males are taken more seriously—may account for the new male syndrome of muscle dysmorphia. This disorder is characterized by excessive exercise and consumption of proteins, great attention to diet, dissatisfaction with body image, and an almost compulsive tendency to check one's body in mirrors (Clark, 2004). Adolescent boys are at particular risk because of anxiety about their stage of physical development relative to that of their peers. The cultural expectations that contribute to their feelings of dissatisfaction and inferiority are reflected in the tremendous increase in the size of male action figures over the last three decades. The 1964 original GI Joe, converted to life size, would have been a 5'10" male with a 32" waist, 44" chest, and 12" biceps, close to average proportions for American males of that time. The more recent GI Joe Extreme dolls have the equivalent of a 30" waist, 57" chest, and 27" biceps—bodily dimensions that are far larger than those of any bodybuilder in history. It may not be surprising, then, that although about 90 percent of all teenagers treated for eating disorders are female, the occurrence of eating disorders in males appears to be increasing (Cassin & von Ranson, 2005).

Cultural ideals about masculinity can also complicate intimate relationships across gender lines. Strict adherence to the rules of masculinity may undermine men's abilities to form strong and supportive ties with significant others. Men's emotional lives may be stifled by socialization that tells them always to keep their emotions hidden under a shield of calmness, strength, and rationality. They may think that only women explore their inner emotional lives, and that for them to do so would be unmanly. They may approach dialogues with their spouses or romantic partners as another way to establish and protect their superior status, rather than as an opportunity to create rapport and connection. Researchers who observed couples therapy found that men commonly rely on emotionally skilled girlfriends, wives, or partners to help them sense what they are feeling and then name and interpret the feeling (Chodorow, 1978). Men may resist women's desires for more intimacy in committed relationships because they are taught to be independent and are ambivalent about taking emotional refuge or receiving comfort from another. Male emotional inexpressiveness may also be a way for men to maintain power in relationships with women by demonstrating that they are acting rationally (not emotionally). It also protects men from the exposure, shame, and loss of status that may result should they reveal their vulnerabilities.

MASCULINITIES AND INTERSECTIONALITIES

Several decades before the concept of hegemonic masculinity appeared in scholarly explorations of gender, the sociologist Erving Goffman (1963) captured an essential aspect of the idea: "There is only one complete unblushing male in America: a young, married, White, urban, northern, heterosexual Protestant father of college education, fully employed, of good complexion, weight and height, and a recent record in sports. . . . Any male who fails to qualify in any of these ways is likely to view himself . . . as unworthy, incomplete, and inferior" (p. 128).

Hegemonic masculinity creates whole categories of marginalized men whose membership in the masculinity club is denied or who are relegated to second class; these groups include members of racial and ethnic minorities, gay and bisexual men, the elderly, the working class and the poor, and the disabled. These out-groups are seen as feminine or nonconformist, or as "failed" masculinities. Poor and working-class men may fail to live up to expectations that they be successful providers. Yet white working-class men seldom blame more privileged upper-class white men for their plight, perhaps because they think that they deserve these privileges simply because they are men. Asian American men face stereotypes that serve to emasculate them. They are perceived as physically inferior and less attractive than men of European heritage, as well as more polite, nurturing, and exotic; better educated; and better family men. Interestingly, these stereotypical views of Asian men have been found to be held by college-age women of all ethnic and racial backgrounds—including Asian American women (Espiritu, 1996). For many other men of color, economic marginalization compounds their problems of "failed" masculinity. Among Latino and African American men, the social expectations and the ethnic/cultural requirements for men may conflict. Men are supposed to be competitive, aggressive, and successful, but in African American and Latino culture, men must also promote the survival of the group through cooperation and place the welfare of the extended family and community above individual desires for achievement.

Gender politics—the interpersonal power dynamics between the genders— have an added cultural dimension in relationships between men and women of color. African American men and women have been described as approaching relationships with non-complementary gender role expectations. Because of the legacy of racial discrimination and economic marginalization of African Americans, and the resulting emasculation of African American men, African American women often have relatively high economic power compared to their male counterparts. These women may embrace stereotypical roles of expressivity, nurturance, and warmth but reject the idea that they should be emotionally or economically dependent on men. African American men receive conflicting messages regarding their race and their gender. They may struggle with a sense of emasculation in the face of a history of racial subordination, feelings of powerlessness, and the messages they receive from society that tell them they are inferior. With fewer opportunities than white men to display a successful masculinity through dominance at work or career success, they may express their masculinity in relationships with women through sexual dominance and physical aggressiveness (Di-Piero, 2002). Similar dynamics have been described in heterosexual Latino couples and attributed to the hypermasculinity known as machismo. However, there is disagreement about the source of the conflicts introduced by machismo. Working-class Latino males may adopt domineering and patriarchal attitudes and behaviors within their families not only or even principally for cultural reasons but rather, like African American men, in reaction to their loss of economic status in mainstream U.S. society (Baca Zinn, 1982).

The myriad ways that cultural ideals about gender are translated into real people's lives suggest that men are at least as diverse as women. One can argue that the concept of hegemonic masculinity fails to capture the experience even of most white men in the middle class. Hasn't popular culture become increasingly comfortable with the ideal of the sensitive man? Perhaps, but Robert Bly (1990), a leading representative of the men's movement that seeks to liberate men from oppressive socialization, has pointed out that even the expectations society has of the sensitive man can be a burden. Because of the stereotype that men are unable to express their feelings as articulately as women can, these expectations can become a source of shame for the sensitive man, another way to manifest a "failed" masculinity. Some men's movements, called mythopoetic movements, seek ways for men to (re)discover a more primeval sense of deep masculinity allegedly lost in the face of industrial society's insistence that men be competitive. The appeal of these movements, which are popular mostly among middle-class men, has been attributed to their vague suggestion that men and women are essentially different and that men are not brutish and domineering but the actual victims of hegemonic masculinity (Schwalbe, 1998).

THE TRANSGENDER COMMUNITY

A person's identification as male or female is established very early in life and is highly resistant to change. Most people who are born with female bodies have a female gender identity, and most individuals born with male bodies have a male gender identity. Sometimes, however, there is a conflict between physical sex and gender identity. The word "transgender" describes a growing array of people whose gender identity does not fit into a simple binary system in which genitalia dictate a clear turn down one of only two identity paths. Traditionally, the transgender community has been mistakenly grouped with the gay, lesbian, and bisexual community. However, in reality, a transgender person can be heterosexual or homosexual. The word "transgender" was often used early on to distinguish between gender nonconformists and homosexuals, or between cross-dressers and surgically reassigned transsexuals (Wilchins, 2004). However, a much broader definition of transgenderism has since gained acceptance; this definition encompasses the experiences of all people who live outside normative sex and gender relationships, among them transsexuals, cross-dressers, masculinized women, butch lesbians, effeminate gay men, drag queens and drag kings, and intersexuals. According to this broad definition, the transgendered can include those who engage in same-sex relationships, have sex with both males and females, prefer clothes and adornments used by people of the opposite sex, or seek a new identity as members of the biologically opposite sex through surgery. Many members of the transgender community share the experiences and challenges of homosexual men and women because they face society's negative reactions to those who have same-sex relationships. Nevertheless, these individuals may not identify themselves as gay men or lesbians, preferring an identity focused on their sense of gender identity rather than their sexual orientation. This is also the case for many members of the transgender community who have only opposite-sex relationships.

Regardless of their sexual behavior, transgender individuals often face rejection, as indicated even by the terms used to define them: "Tellingly there is not a single word for people who don't fit gender norms that is positive, affirming, and complimentary. . . . Because all our language affords are strings of insults, it is impossible to talk about someone who is brave enough to rebel against gender stereotypes without ridiculing or humiliating them at the same time" (Wilchins, 2004, p. 38). Historically, many societies, including the United States, have considered transgenderism an aberrant form of "gender confusion."* From this perspective, transgenderism might be viewed technically as a problematic medical and mental health condition. The American Psychiatric Association and the medical profession have designated some forms of transgenderism "gender identity disorders," and some members of these groups argue that these conditions require treatment. Rather than pathologizing transgender individuals, one can consider the alternate viewpoint that Western society considers transgenderism deviant or disordered primarily because it does not conform to the dominant culture's expectations that gender and sex be congruent. Because of this strongly held belief, individuals whose gender does not match their sex have little social, organizational, or institutional space in which to live comfortably with themselves and without fear of psychological and physical assault. As a result, some transgender individuals undergo hormone therapy and sexual reassignment surgery to change their physical sex and alleviate the emotional conflict and pain they experience owing to their unmatched anatomical sex and gender identity. Other gender nonconformists who in the past felt pressured to align themselves with conventional gender expectations are coming forward in increasing numbers in a transgender rights movement to claim their right to enact a gender identity that feels authentic to them. About one in seven cases filed with the federal Equal Employment Opportunity Commission now involves men claiming harassment by other men, mostly for perceived gender nonconformity such as transgender identities (Clair, Beatty, & MacLean, 2005). These claims are challenging society's thinking about gender-based discrimination.

The emerging transgender community has found important allies among feminist, gay, and lesbian movements but has also raised some uneasy questions. Some feminists may be uncertain how to interpret the role of patriarchy in a female-to-male sex reassignment surgery or may question how much gender solidarity a male-to-female transsexual shares with other women (Stryker & Whittle,

---

*In contrast, many Native American cultures hold transgender individuals in high regard. For example, the Lakota Winkte (from *Winyanktehca,* meaning "two-souls person") is believed to possess a special spirituality and have unique abilities to fulfill community needs. The source of these special capacities is thought to be their ability to adopt the perspective and draw on the insight of both sexes. In both Zuni and Diné (Navajo) culture there are two-spirited deities who are revered for their ability to help make peace and ensure the survival of the tribe. The Europeans who first encountered two-spirited people in the Americas recoiled at what they interpreted to be simply same-sex sexual behavior and reacted with cruel brutality. During the Spanish Conquest, two-spirited people were sometimes burned to death. The societies that embraced two-spiritism were viewed as meriting enslavement under religious law because they demonstrated the irrationality and immorality of the people.

2006). In the gay and lesbian activist community, the *B* and *T* have been incorporated into the mission of most GLBT organizations. However, there continues to be discussion and dissension about how to prioritize and align the interests and special forms of discrimination that the many different types of transgender people face relative to each other and gay men, lesbians, and bisexuals. For example, should the transgender movement champion the rights of the large "silent majority" of cross-dressers (men, often heterosexual, who dress as women but do not consider sexual reassignment) who lead lives that are more conventional? Should it focus its energy on what is probably a much smaller number of transsexuals (those who have gone through sexual reassignment or are in the process of doing so)? One interesting development that has emerged from the alliances among these movements is that as gay and lesbian organizations are increasingly emphasizing that homosexuality does not dictate gender identity, the transgender movement is making the case that gender identity does not necessarily dictate sexual orientation.

As the meaning of transgenderism evolves and acceptance of transgender individuals in our society—along with the number of groups claiming an identity under that umbrella—grows, it is likely that people will increasingly identify as having a transgender identity. The number of transgender people cannot be gauged precisely and varies greatly according to different definitions. Some rough estimates place the number of transsexuals (both pre- and post-operative) alone at one in every three to five hundred people in the United States and the United Kingdom (Roughgarden, 2004). In addition, even though intersexed individuals—those whose gonads, genitalia, and hormonal development are neither unambiguously male nor female—may not adopt a transgender identity, they may account for as many as 4 percent of the population, or one in every twenty-five individuals (Fausto-Sterling, 1993).* Another group that may claim membership in the U.S. transgender community—cross-dressers—has been estimated to number in the several millions (Wilchins, 2004).

As societal and self-awareness of transgender identity grows, social workers are increasingly likely to encounter transgender clients who bring with them unique narratives and life challenges. Personal narratives and reports from therapists indicate that many, and perhaps most, transgender individuals sense some

---

*The rates of different forms of intersexuality vary greatly across different ethnic, racial, and geographic groupings. Roughgarden's (2004) review of the various studies concluded that true hermaphrodites, who have both an ovary and a testis, are rare—only one in 85,000 people worldwide. The chromosomally intersexed, individuals with chromosome configurations other than the typical XX or XY pairings, are far more common (approximately one in 1,000 people). Even more common are people who have typical sex chromosomes but other genetic variations that influence sex hormones, such as those with congenital adrenal hyperplasia or androgen insensitivity syndrome.

inconsistency between their bodies and their gender identity from an early age, well before puberty. They feel intense pressure from their parents, families, play-mates, and teachers to conform to stereotypical gender expectations. Many de-velop—at least for a time—ways to pass as normatively gendered but continue to feel that they do not really fit in; at some level they may secretly hope to outgrow their nonconforming gender identity. To the extent that their gender nonconfor-mity is on display in their behavior or personality, transgender individuals—especially effeminate boys and very masculine girls—are targets for bullying and violence. The onset of puberty is often especially traumatic for transgender teens, who may feel acute anxiety or disgust at the emerging signs of their sexualized bodies (Pauly, 1990). In navigating typical adolescent development and identity struggles, transgender youths are likely to experience especially acute uncertainty and confusion about who they are. They may be unaware of the range of transgen-der people in society and may not understand the concept of a transgender gender identity or even have words to describe it. Contacts with physicians, counselors, therapists, and social workers may represent their first encounters with the no-tion of transgenderism. Unfortunately, until recently the medical professional subscribed to a highly stigmatizing disease model of transgender identity. Some psychiatrists continue to view transgender youths and adults as suffering from a gender identity disorder or transvestite fetishism, for which they sometimes claim they can provide therapy (Winters, 2005). The persistence of these views within professional circles is a sobering reminder of the power of our society's negative stereotypes about transgender people.

Because their transgressions of gender role stereotypes are often quite evi-dent, transgender individuals are especially vulnerable to blatant social rejection, public ridicule and harassment, and physical and sexual assault. The term "trans-phobia" has been coined to describe prejudice and discrimination against trans-gender individuals. Transphobia is an emotional fear of, aversion to, or sense of revulsion toward people who express an internal gender identity that does not conform to society's expectations (Hill & Willoughby, 2005). Many hate crimes commonly categorized as anti-gay violence actually involve transgender prejudice. Brandon Teena, whose life, rape, and murder were recounted in the movie *Boys Don't Cry*, was sometimes portrayed by the media as a cross-dressing lesbian but actually had the gender expression of a male (Halberstam, 2005). The persecution and violence directed against Teena were prompted by extreme reactions to per-ceived transgressions of gender boundaries. Similarly, Barry Winchell, an army private murdered on an army base in 1999 by another soldier for allegedly being gay, was actually dating a transgender woman whom the media misidentified as a gay man (Belkin & Bateman, 2003). While public sentiment has at times been effectively mobilized to publicize and condemn anti-gay violence, as in the case of the 1998 murder of Wyoming college student Matthew Shepard, violence against transgender individuals has yet to evoke high levels of widespread public outrage.

In addition to being aware of the extreme prejudice that transgender individuals confront daily, as well as their vulnerability to harassment and violence, social workers with transgender clients need to consider how lives that do not strictly follow polarized gender roles can be made healthy and fulfilling. The ever-present possibility of rejection for a life led openly and the need to maintain a separate secret life both create stress that may lead to depression, coping through substance use, and risk of suicide. Like some gay men and lesbians, transgender people are likely to have to navigate a coming out process that begins with denial and ends with acceptance, a process that has been described as similar to grieving (Emerson & Rosenfeld, 1996).

A policy statement on transgender/gender identity issues put forward by the National Association of Social Workers states that social workers can support and empower transgender individuals in coming out; dealing with family, friends, and coworkers; and finding ways to face societal stigma (Lev & Moore, 2000). Historically, research, assessment, and treatment in social work and allied professions have tended to pathologize transvestites, transgender individuals, transsexuals, and transqueers (lesbians and gay men who openly defy gender conventions). Through courses in degree programs or continuing education, practitioners can increase their awareness of the transgender community. Acquiring knowledge about the differences between sex, gender, and sexuality will give them more familiarity with the issues concerning transgender, queer, and intersex populations. Practitioners can learn much by simply adopting the attitude that people are who they say they are, and by accepting the identity that the client presents. Considering their high risk of isolation and exposure to violence, this population may benefit greatly from information about how to become involved with transgender-friendly organizations.

Overall, gender is a multilevel system: at the individual level, it consists of identities and roles; at a mezzo level, it involves the ways in which people interact with one another and the influence of the gender composition of groups; and at the macro level, it is an influential component of cultural beliefs and societal institutions for distributing power and resources. A working understanding of the intersection of gender with race, ethnicity, sexual orientation, and social class is at the core of a culturally grounded approach to social work practice.

Key Concepts

Gender the culturally and socially constructed expectations of behaviors for male, female, and transgender individuals

Sexism the subordination and oppression of women based on the assumption of the superiority of men based solely on their biological sex

Hegemonic masculinity the type of masculinity idealized by a particular culture, for example, the stereotypical view in the West of men as domineering, unemotional, and violent

Transgender a spectrum of gender identities that include pre- and post-operative transsexuals, transvestites and cross-dressers, and a growing population of people who identify as intersex or as not fitting any traditional notions of gender

9

Sexual Orientation

TODAY, "SEXUAL ORIENTATION" IS THE WIDELY PREFERRED TERM FOR DE-scribing how people classify themselves—and others—sexually. Sexual orienta-tion involves feelings of attraction to other people, the gender categories of the objects of people's romantic as well as erotic desires, and the models of socially prescribed sexual behaviors that individuals follow. Like ethnic and gender cul-tures, sexual orientation has an effect on an individual's attitudes, values, and behaviors, as well as how that person is viewed and treated by others. It is impor-tant for social work practitioners to understand how sexual orientation can affect not only the behavior of the individual, but also how that person is treated by others, and how beliefs concerning sexual orientation can lead to prejudice, dis-crimination, and oppression.

DIFFERING VIEWS ON SEXUAL ORIENTATION

The categories used to describe different sexual orientations vary across cul-tures and across time. In the United States and other Western societies, people mostly identify as homosexual or heterosexual and divide others into the same two categories. In other cultures, people may not make such definite or clear distinctions, approaching sexuality more as a continuum than a dichotomy. For example, historians have documented the widespread practice of same-sex sex in classical Greece. The ancient Greeks celebrated love between men, and sex be-tween men was often a part of men's socialization into sexuality, just as it contin-ues to be in some contemporary Mediterranean and Latin American societies (Dode, 2004). Some, but definitely not all, of these manifestations of sexuality were rooted in what would be thought of today as romantic or erotic desire. How-ever, ancient Greek society, and the men themselves, did not categorize individu-als based on the biological sex of their sexual partners; thus same-sex sexual rela-tions among men in ancient Greece were not thought to signify a homosexual sexual identity. Foucault (1978) argued that the notion of different sexual orienta-tions emerged only in recent centuries.

This categorization—today referred to as sexual orientation—is, like most identity factors, socially constructed. Modern Western conceptions of sexual ori-entation have been shaped by political and religious ideas that enshrine heterosexuality as the preferred "default" option and deem all departures from that norm undesirable and deviant (Foucault, 1978; Kimmel, 1996; Naphy, 2006). Among Native Americans, it was once acceptable for two-spirited people to engage in same-sex sexual relations, and at times they were expected to do so; in these cultures, religious or spiritual power often was assigned to those not following the "heterosexual norm" (Wald & Calhoun-Brown, 2006). However, because of colonialism and other forms of oppression, such as the imposition of Christianity on Native peoples, many cultures that once embraced different manifestations of sexuality now condemn homosexuality (Aldrich, 2003). Nonetheless, there are signs of growing acceptance and increased understanding of homosexuality and bisexuality in many societies, including the United States.

EXPLAINING HOMOSEXUALITY: ESSENTIALISM AND CONSTRUCTIVISM

Western science and medicine have demonstrated an intense interest in explaining homosexuality that has at times bordered on obsession. Nearly a century after Freud introduced the idea that homosexuality results from disorders in the natural process of psychosexual development, researchers have still not arrived at a consensus regarding the nature of homosexuality. Although it could be argued that there is as much need for an explanation of heterosexual orientations as there is for an explanation of homosexual orientations, the origins of heterosexuality have received far less attention. The Heterosexual Questionnaire (figure 9.1) was developed to make the point that heterosexual desire and behavior tend to be regarded as a norm that does not require any explanation. In contrast, the voluminous research on the origins of homosexuality can be divided into two main types: studies emphasizing biological factors and those emphasizing social and contextual factors. A common theme in these studies, and their counterparts in both social science theory and popular thinking, is the debate regarding the role of choice in sexual orientation. Do people have a choice to be or not to be gay, lesbian, or bisexual? Similarly, do people make a choice to be heterosexual?

Various biological explanations for sexual orientation make an argument for an essentialist view of sexuality; that is, they approach sexuality as a product of fundamental biological and/or psychological drives that are hardwired within an individual, perhaps genetically. According to this view, homosexuality is the result of an unknown factor that all homosexuals share, regardless of race, ethnicity, religion, or class. The biological approach was originally concerned with the study of hormonal levels and their influence on sexual orientation. Although some studies of hormone levels in the 1970s found differences between lesbian and heterosexual women, more recent research has failed to find significant hormonal differ-

Figure 9.1 Heterosexual Questionnaire

This questionnaire is for self-avowed heterosexuals only. If you are not openly heterosexual, pass it on to a friend who is. Please try to answer the questions as candidly as possible.

1. What do you think caused your heterosexuality?
2. When and how did you first decide you were a heterosexual?
3. Is it possible your heterosexuality is just a phase you may grow out of?
4. Could it be that your heterosexuality stems from a neurotic fear of others of the same sex?
5. If you've never slept with a person of the same sex, how can you be sure you wouldn't prefer that?
6. To whom have you disclosed your heterosexual tendencies? How did they react?
7. Why do heterosexuals feel compelled to seduce others into their lifestyle?
8. Why do you insist on flaunting your heterosexuality? Can't you just be what you are and keep it quiet?
9. Would you want your children to be heterosexual, knowing the problems they'd face?
10. A disproportionate majority of child molesters are heterosexual men. Do you consider it safe to expose children to heterosexual male teachers, pediatricians, priests, or scoutmasters?
11. Even with all the societal support for marriage, the divorce rate is spiraling. Why are there so few stable relationships among heterosexuals?
12. Why do heterosexuals place so much emphasis on sex?
13. Considering the menace of overpopulation, how could the human race survive if everyone were heterosexual?
14. Could you trust a heterosexual therapist to be objective? Don't you fear she or he might be inclined to influence you in the direction of her or his own leanings?
15. Heterosexuals are notorious for assigning themselves and one another rigid stereotyped sex roles. Why must you cling to such unhealthy role-playing?
16. With the sexually segregated living conditions of military life, isn't heterosexuality incompatible with military service?
17. How can you enjoy an emotionally fulfilling experience with a person of the other sex when there are such vast differences between you? How can a man know what pleases a woman sexually or vice versa?
18. Shouldn't you ask your far-out straight cohorts, like skinheads and born-agains, to keep quiet? Wouldn't that improve your image?
19. Why are heterosexuals so promiscuous?
20. Why do you mistakenly claim that so many famous lesbian and gay people are in fact heterosexual? Is it to justify your own heterosexuality?
21. How can you hope to actualize your God-given homosexual potential if you limit yourself to exclusive, compulsive heterosexuality?
22. There seem to be very few happy heterosexuals. Techniques have been developed that might enable you to change if you really want to. After all, you never deliberately chose to be a heterosexual, did you? Have you considered aversion therapy or Heterosexuals Anonymous?

Source: Adapted from Rochlin, M. (1992). Heterosexual questionnaire. In W. Blumenfeld (Ed.), *Homophobia: How we all pay the price* (pp. 203–204). Boston: Beacon Press.

ences on multiple measures (Barinaga, 1991; Dancey, 1990; Downey, Ehrhardt, Schiffman, Dyrenfurth, & Becker, 1987).

Studies of twins in the early 1990s provided evidence for a possible biological basis for sexual orientation but failed to settle the matter. These studies typically estimated the rate of homosexual "concordance" by asking gay individuals with twin siblings if their twins were also gay. They found that the concordance rate for identical twins, which ranged from about 25 to 50 percent, was double or more that of the rates found for fraternal twins (Bailey & Pillard, 1991; Bailey, Pillard, Neale, & Agyei, 1993; Whitam, Diamond, & Martin, 1993). One study that identified twins from a registry rather than by recruiting convenience samples of gay twins through gay-oriented media, as prior studies had done, also found a higher concordance rate in identical twins than in fraternal twins, although the highest rate of concordance—for male identical twins—was only 20 percent (Bailey & Martin, 1995). Because identical twins share the same genetic makeup, while fraternal twins do not, these results point to a genetic predisposition to homosexuality. However, while some interpret these findings as showing that genes account for as much as half of the variation in sexual orientation, it can also be argued that the social environment may be 80 percent responsible for determining sexual orientation. In recent years there has been a growing emphasis on the role of genetics in the determination of an individual's sexual orientation. The media has devoted much attention to scientists' quest to identify the so-called gay gene (Burr, 1996). Despite the mixed nature of the evidence, some researchers now conceptualize sexual orientation as a polygenetic trait, one that is influenced by a number of genes (Brookey, 2002; Hyde, 2005).

On the other side of the debate are social environmental explanations like social constructivist perspectives, which argue that sexual orientation is shaped by the social environment and individual choice. For example, the psychological literature about the etiology of homosexuality once associated male homosexuality with emotionally absent or weak fathers. Darwinist economists have explained the rise of modern homosexuality in industrial societies as a product of affluence and its resultant low mortality and low fertility, which lowers social pressure to procreate. Sociologists and historians have argued that as workers moved from farms to factory jobs in the city and work life became separated from home life, men could gather more often in groups away from home, which offered opportunities for sex away from the strictures of the men's families and hometowns (Giddens, 2006). It has also been theorized that newly acquired wealth in industrialized societies allowed more people to forgo marriage and having children, which permitted greater freedom for individual sexual choices (Jandt & Hundley, 2007). This sort of argument has also been used to explain the emergence of a counterreaction in the form of the strongly enforced dichotomy between heterosexuality and homosexuality that has emerged in Western societies over the last few centuries (Foucault, 1978).

An essentialist explanation for sexual orientation supports the argument for homosexual normalcy—that homosexual orientations are expressions of naturally produced, innate, and immutable forces. Essentialists view homosexuality as a biologically driven phenomenon, rather than a choice made by the individual. At the same time, this argument could be used to support policies that would allow doctors to "prevent" homosexuality by altering biological or genetic processes. For example, if genetic screening could identify a fetus's future sexual orientation, expecting parents might decide to end pregnancies if they learned that their offspring were destined to be homosexual or try to modify the genetic base of the fetus's sexual orientation to satisfy their own desires. These and other dilemmas generated by genetic and biological research findings will continue to arise if scientists find that there is a definitive genetic basis for sexual orientation.

Research findings that provide evidence for a social or behavioral basis for homosexuality can be misused to argue for the "sexual preference" position, which maintains that homosexuality is a choice made by the individual. If homosexuality is a choice, then widespread homophobia could motivate society to implement interventions to change the sexual orientation of individuals. This position has been promoted by fringe groups that are often sponsored by religious organizations that aim at "converting" gays and lesbians to heterosexuality. Variously called conversion, reparative, and sexual reorientation therapy, these methods attempt to change gay and lesbian sexual orientations by suppressing or extinguishing same-sex desires and behaviors through the use of such techniques as behavior modification, aversion therapy, psychoanalysis, prayer, and religious counseling. These interventions have shown little evidence of lasting success (Committee on Lesbian, Gay, & Bisexual Concerns, 1999). Whereas no sound evidence shows that any so-called therapies to cure homosexuality have ever changed anyone's sexual orientation, it is clear that failed treatments like aversion therapy and even electroconvulsive shock treatment have inflicted unnecessary pain on thousands of individuals (LeVay, 1996).

Because of the prevalence of the belief that homosexuality is an abnormal condition that needs to be fixed or cured, the professional community only recently completely abandoned both its attempts to cure homosexuality and the disease model that underlies such efforts. It was not until 1998 that the American Psychoanalytic Association acknowledged its own history of homophobia and brought its official position on homosexuality in line with that of the American Psychiatric Association, which had removed homosexuality from its list of diagnosable mental disorders twenty-six years earlier. The major psychiatric and psychological professional associations in the United States have also concluded that conversion therapies targeting gays and lesbians are not only ineffective but harmful. Homosexuality cannot be cured because it is not a disease.

THE NUMBERS GAME: HOMOSEXUAL BEHAVIOR, ATTRACTION, AND IDENTITY

Alfred Kinsey's classic studies on sexuality and sexual orientation in the 1940s and 1950s were the first to muster data—rather than anecdotes—contradicting the essentialist view that sexuality is binary. Kinsey, Pomeroy, and Martin (1949) found that sexual experiences between people of the same sex varied widely in frequency and intensity, and that it was not uncommon for individuals to alternate between heterosexual and homosexual sex. Kinsey's studies made many methodological breakthroughs by asking people direct questions and requesting detailed information about their sexual behaviors at different times over the life course. The results showed that substantial proportions of men engaged in same-sex sexual behavior for at least some part of their lives, and that the sex lives of an appreciable subgroup of these could be classified as mostly or exclusively homosexual. However, Kinsey's larger contributions have been overshadowed in some ways by estimates based on his work that have been used to set the prevalence of homosexuality in the United States at 10 percent. Because Kinsey did not select random probability samples for his studies and relied on respondents' recall of past sexual behavior, which can be inaccurate, it now appears that he substantially overestimated the prevalence of homosexual behavior (Fay, Turner, Klassen, & Gagnon, 1989). His (in)famous 10 percent estimate of homosexual prevalence actually reflected the proportion of men—overwhelmingly white men—who were exclusively homosexual in their sex lives for at least a three-year period, while only 4 percent were exclusively homosexual throughout their lives. Kinsey's figures regarding the extent of homosexual behavior are much higher than those shown by more recent population surveys, which find the proportion of the population that is exclusively homosexual to be something more in the range of 1 to 5 percent, of whom there are about twice as many gay men as lesbians (Michael, Gagnon, Laumann, & Kolata, 1994). In addition, a study using a national sample of 1,511 men and 1,921 women concluded that 4.9 percent of the male respondents and 4.1 percent of the female respondents reported having engaged in sexual behavior with a person of the same sex since the age of eighteen (Laumann, Gagnon, Michael, & Michaels, 1994). This study has been identified as one of the most authoritative studies estimating the percentage of lesbians and gay men in the United States (Kurdek, 2005).

It is important to remember that Kinsey—as well as other researchers after him—investigated sexual *behaviors,* not sexual orientation specifically. Nonetheless, Kinsey's studies made important contributions by showing that homosexual behavior, desire, and identity do not always go together. That is, some sexual fantasies are never acted on, and sources of pleasure, excitement, upset, and guilt can change or remain the same over a lifetime. Moreover, sexual behaviors may or may not affect whether an individual self-identifies as heterosexual, homosexual, or bisexual. An individual can engage in same-sex sexual behavior without homosexual desire, as in prison (by volition or by force) and in strict traditional societies in which young men have no sexual access to women (Bejel, 2001; Van Wormer, 1984). The evidence indicates that an even more common behavior is hidden same-sex sexual behavior among individuals who do not self-identify as homosexual, which is reported frequently both by gay people who later come out and by youths who experiment with different types of sex before becoming exclusively heterosexual.

A more recent study of a national probability sample of U.S. adults showed that reports of homosexual behavior, desire, and identity vary according to gender, ethnicity, and age (Laumann et al., 1994). Among men, same-sex sexual behavior, same-sex attraction, and homosexual/bisexual identity were all more commonly reported by college-educated whites in their thirties than by African Americans, the less educated, and both older and very young men. The gender differences are even more striking. Same-sex sexual behavior was more commonly reported by men than by women, whether in the previous year, after age eighteen, or at any point in the life course (see figure 9.2). Much of the men's same-sex sexual experience apparently occurred at a very young age. Men were also more likely than women to report having felt sexually attracted to other men and to identify themselves as homosexual. Both men and women were far more likely to have engaged in same-sex sexual behavior than to self-identify as homosexual. The proportions of women who reported having experienced same-sex attraction and same-sex sexual behavior were very similar, while more men reported having sex with men than being attracted to them.

In the same study, the discrepancies between same-sex behavior, same-sex attraction, and homosexual identity were more pronounced for men than for women: of all the men reporting homosexual behavior, desire, or identity, only one-fourth reported all three. Nearly all those men and women who did self-identify as gay or bisexual also reported homosexual desire and homosexual behavior. Although they are only a small fraction of all the individuals who have sex with individuals of the same sex, they are clearly the group most likely to fit widely held definitions of who is considered homosexual. This core group of people who identify themselves as gay or bisexual, have same-sex sexual partners, and experience homosexual desires constitutes perhaps 3 percent of men and 1.5 percent of women in the United States. They also make up a group that is growing in size, and gaining increasing visibility and recognition within U.S. society—same-sex couples.

In 2000, for the first time in its history, the United States census provided

Figure 9.2   Prevalence of Same-Sex Sexual Behavior, Desire, and Identity among U.S. Adults

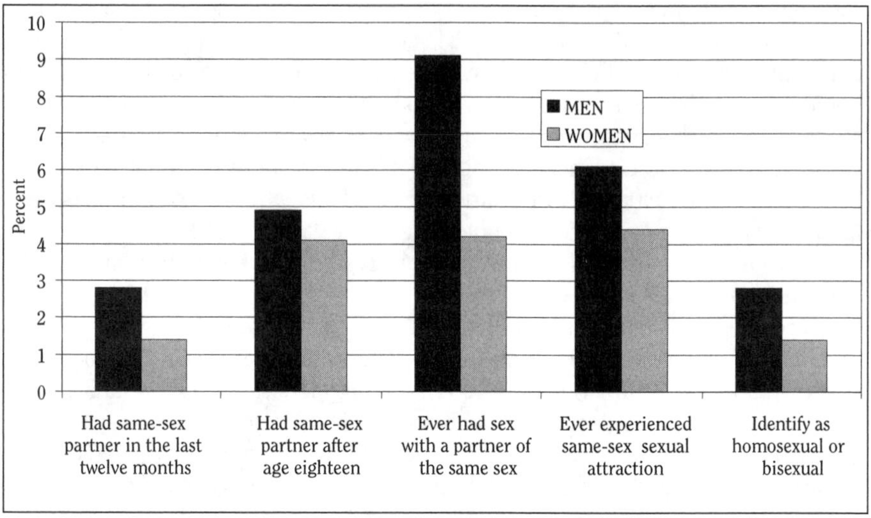

Source: Adapted from Laumann, E. O., Gagnon, J. H, Michael, J. T., & Michaels, S. (1994). *The social organization of sexuality: Sexual practices in the United States.* Chicago: University of Chicago Press.

information on gay and lesbian couples living together. The census estimated that there were about 600,000 gay and lesbian households in the United States, which accounts for .5 percent of all households (Simmons & O'Connell, 2003). These gay and lesbian households were nearly evenly divided between those with two adult male partners and those with two adult female partners. While the U.S. census estimate is probably subject to some bias due to both under- and overreporting, most analysts consider it to be, on balance, an underreport due to people's reluctance to admit to living in a household arrangement that is not universally accepted. Some estimates suggest the 2000 census undercounted households of same-sex couples by 62 percent and that the actual number of gay and lesbian households in the United States lies somewhere between 800,000 and 7 million (Smith & Gates, 2001). Notably for social workers, about 750,000 to 9 million children under eighteen years old live in these households.

The most recent national study of sexual behavior, conducted in 2002–2003, found patterns of same-sex sexual behavior among men that mirrored those found a decade earlier (Mosher, Chandra, & Jones, 2005). However, results for women differed, possibly because same-sex sexual conduct was defined more broadly for women than in earlier studies. Among adults between the ages of twenty-five and forty-four, 6.5 percent of the men reported having had anal or oral sex with a man, while 11 percent of the women reported having had some kind of sexual experience with another women. In the twelve months prior to the study, 2.9 percent of the men had had a male sexual partner, and 4.4 percent of the women had had a female partner. In addition, while only 1 percent of men reported having had both male and female partners in the previous year, about 3 percent of women did. This survey also detected a subgroup whose members identify their sexual orientation in a flexible rather than fixed way. Although the percentages of respondents who self-identified as homosexual—2.3 percent of males and 1.3 percent of females—were similar to those from the early 1990s, nearly 4 percent of both men and women described their sexual orientation as something other than heterosexual, homosexual, or bisexual. As the stigma attached to any non-heterosexual sexual expression has diminished, our categories for describing sexuality are undergoing scrutiny and expanding. Scholars who are interested in how gender and sexuality are fused into identities are beginning to recognize individuals who resist sexual identity labels. Ritch Savin-Williams (2005) describes many contemporary gay teenagers as "post-gay," meaning that they have moved beyond the developmental trajectories and identity struggles that characterized the coming out process in the latter part of the twentieth century. In the absence of the intense stigma that once surrounded homosexuality, these youths have greater freedom to feel, explore, describe, and act on their same-sex attractions without the need to conform to stereotypical homosexual identities.

In considering the increasingly diverse ways in which people think of and describe themselves as sexual beings, practitioners need to be mindful that same-sex couples and those individuals who identify themselves as gay or lesbian represent only a portion of those who may be engaging in same-sex sexual behavior or navigating complex or conflicting sexual desires. Discrepancies in reports of homosexual behavior, desire, and identity underscore the need to recognize that sexual orientation requires an understanding of oneself and the choices one perceives as being available for expressing one's sexuality. Individuals who engage in homosexual behaviors may not think of themselves as being gay, lesbian, or bisexual. They may even reject all sexual identity labels as irrelevant or too constraining. The social context and the norms and values present in the environment also have a strong influence on this kind of self-identification.

Stigma theory suggests that sexual minorities are likely to avoid disclosure of their sexual identity when they expect to be viewed unfavorably by it. It is more than a matter of social embarrassment and gossip. When sexual minorities disclose their sexual orientation, they are at appreciable risk of becoming the victims of hate crimes, which tend to be underreported and result in prolonged psychological distress (Herek et al., 2002). In certain workplaces, gays and lesbians live in constant fear of being outed and losing their jobs as a result. Because discrimination based on sexual orientation is not specifically prohibited in many states and localities, such fears are realistic and can be a constant source of stress.

INTERSECTIONALITIES: GAY MEN OF COLOR

Sexual minorities experience proportionally more negative life events than heterosexuals because they often have to cope with many stressors, such as sexism, racism, and heterosexism, simultaneously. African American gay and bisexual males, for example, face the challenges of managing a dual minority status (Crawford, Allison, Zamboni, & Soto, 2002). Facing the prospect of disapproval or condemnation, some African American gay and bisexual men feel compelled to conceal their sexual orientation in order to gain acceptance, both within the African American community and the larger society. Always aware of the possible negative reaction if they reveal their sexual orientation or behavior to their own communities, they often feel they must live a dual existence, presenting an image as exclusively heterosexual men to the outside world. These challenges confront gay and lesbian people from all ethnic communities because homophobia exists in all ethnic groups. However, there is a distinctive set of pressures faced by gay and bisexual men from African American communities. The legacy of slavery and continuing oppression of African Americans may be experienced by African American men as a form of emasculation that needs to be countered with strong expressions of heterosexual masculinity, or hypermasculinity (Crichlow, 2004). When they are associated with effeminacy, homosexual acts and identities may be seen as contributing to African American men's relative lack of power and status in society (Lemelle & Battle, 2004). Black nationalist ideology at times has promoted hypermasculinity and rejection of male homosexuality as a way to protect the African American community from racism and exploitation (Ward, 2005). Another potent force is the highly influential role of black churches in the African American community, many of which subscribe to conservative religious ideas that condemn same-sex sexual activity as sinful and unnatural (Griffin, 2000).

These converging cultural and institutional homophobic pressures present difficult choices for African Americans who are gay and bisexual and restrict their ability to live open and authentic lives. Some of them seek European American gay communities in which to explore and express their sexual identities, but they do not always find complete acceptance. Gay and lesbian African Americans have reported encountering race discrimination in gay and lesbian bars and clubs and at social gatherings (Adams & Kimmel, 1997). The lack of a sense of belonging and a sense of recognition and support from within the community of origin or the larger gay community can affect the well-being of African American gay and lesbian individuals, as well as the larger communities to which they belong.

Recently much media attention has been given to a so-called down low subculture rooted at the intersection of sexual orientation and ethnic identity. The phrase "on the down low" is used to describe African American men who have sex with other men but lead lives as heterosexuals in public. Their need to hide their attraction to men is shaped by cultural forces in their communities that contribute to internalized homophobia, the acceptance of homophobia by a lesbian or a gay man and its incorporation into her or his self-concept. Internalized homophobia has been linked to substance abuse, self-destructive behavior, and feelings of powerlessness (Renzetti, 1998). The challenge is not one of simply emerging from a figurative closet. Some of these men are torn between their true feelings and desires and cultural ideals of masculinity—their roles as procreators and responsible fathers—and the denigration of homosexuality as a perversion that belongs to white culture and has no place in African American communities. The secrecy embraced by these men may create serious health risks for them and their sexual partners—both male and female. Their closeted existence and the stigmatization of homosexuality in their communities tend to block these men's access to HIV/ AIDS-related information and services that are more widely available to white middle-class gay men. In addition, cultural attitudes sometimes discourage condom use. The down low phenomenon is suspected of contributing to the developing crisis of HIV infection among African Americans, who now make up half of all new HIV cases in the United States, and statistics place African American women among the groups with the fastest increases in rates of HIV infection (Centers for Disease Control and Prevention, 2006).

Still, the precise role of the down low phenomenon in the spread of HIV is unknown, and it is important to remember that the down low phenomenon occurs in all ethnic and racial groups, not just among African Americans (Boykin, 2005). Some women do become infected by bisexual men, but the inherent difficulty of identifying men who are on the down low means that little is known with certainty about their relative HIV risk level, tendency to engage in risky sexual behavior, and role in HIV transmission. Although there is evidence that openly gay African American men are more likely to practice safe sex than African American men on the down low (Centers for Disease Control and Prevention, 2003), it is important to avoid stereotypes and to approach the phenomenon as a public health and social issue in need of further research and effective prevention interventions (Centers for Disease Control and Prevention, 1999).

The down low phenomenon has been reported to be as common among Latino men as among African American men (Boykin, 2005). Latino men who are attracted to men must contend with similar cultural and religious pressures to deny or hide their sexual identities. They face not only the church's refusal to accept gay and bisexual identities but also beliefs in Latino cultures that men's identity is closely tied to their privilege of giving life to many children (Abalos, 2002). The concept of machismo refers to the ideal of what it means to be a man in Latino culture: that is, controlling, possessive, sexist, and domineering, as well as chivalrous and protective of kin. Its female counterpart, *marianismo,* describes the virtuous, self-sacrificing image (associated with the Virgin Mary) of Latinas, as well as a sense of powerlessness and resignation in the face of sexist oppression. Latino gays and lesbians may experience conflict between these gender roles and their sexual identities. Because machismo focuses men's behaviors on penetrative sexual practices, sex without penetration is not considered to be sex by large sectors of Latino communities (Diaz, 1997). Some Latino men may thus engage in same-sex sexual behavior without feeling that such behavior conflicts with their heterosexual identity. At the same time, cultural perceptions and internalized stereotypes about low sexual control among gays can result in unprotected sex and an increased risk of HIV infection among this population (Exner, Meyer-Bahlburg, & Ehrhardt, 1992; Ostrow, DiFrancesico, & Kalichman, 1997). Because of the shame they often feel, Latino gay men may tend not to make an effort to learn about prevention strategies and delay seeking medical help as the HIV/AIDS epidemic within their communities spreads (Ramirez-Valles, Fergus, Reisen, Poppen, & Zea, 2005).

A recurring theme in the narratives told by gay men and lesbians from ethnic minority communities is that the intersection of their ethnic identities and their sexual orientations often makes their experiences quite different from those of white gays and lesbians. Social movements advocating recognition of the rights of gays and lesbians have rapidly spread from community to community and from nation to nation. The result is that the idea of a distinctive gay identity and gay community is rapidly being adopted around the globe (Altman, 1996). The identity that is often believed to represent and be embraced by all gays and lesbians is that of a white middle-class male gay culture. For example, because the much-emphasized coming out process—which may be less common among ethnic minorities than among whites—implies both an acceptance and an assertion of one's sexual identity, for some it may create conflicts over the priorities given to their intersecting identities. For members of ethnic minority communities, asserting a gay identity can be especially stressful if it carries the risk of rejection by the ethnic group, the place in which they have found refuge from the racism or ethnocentrism of the uncomprehending or hostile mainstream.

These examples of incompatible cultural pressures on African American and Latino gay men show how historical prejudices toward gays and lesbians can be perpetuated by a culture. Sometimes these pressures are deeply rooted in polarized ideas about gender roles or a culture's historical alignment with religions that condemn homosexuality. Rather than coming out in a dramatic way to friends and family, gay men and lesbians may find acceptance by some cultures in a more tacit manner. For example, cultural notions of family may be flexible enough to include gay and lesbian members and their partners around the table while maintaining taboos against speaking of gay identities, a family version of "Don't ask, don't tell." Cultures may even lack adequate or appropriate language for describing gay life and identity. That is, members of ethnic minority cultures—both gay and lesbian individuals and their families and friends—may be reluctant to use their own culture's derogatory vocabulary for gays and lesbians but also feel uncomfortable with the language of identity preferred by the white gay and lesbian community. This kind of communication blockage leads to frustrations and misunderstandings.

Therefore, it is important for social workers working with gays and lesbians from ethnic minority communities to respect the ways that these individuals decide to handle their intersecting identities. It would be hasty to assume that those who choose to give priority to ethnic identity and community solidarity over the full disclosure of their sexual orientation are in denial of their gay or lesbian identity or are showing symptoms of emotional dysfunction. Some families may employ a dual approach to relating to a gay or lesbian child, disclosing more and showing greater acceptance or tolerance at home than in public. Although these differences in treatment may be stressful and glaringly inconsistent, what appears to be denial in front of the community and more extended family may reflect a desire to protect a lesbian or gay family member from rejection rather than a conscious attempt to oppress her or him.

HETEROSEXISM AND HOMOPHOBIA

The term "homophobia" was coined by George Weinberg in the early 1970s. Defined as both an attitude and a disease (Victoroff, 2006), homophobia is the "fear, disgust, anger, discomfort, and aversion that individuals experience in dealing with gay people" (Hudson & Ricketts, 1980, p. 358). Such prejudice against homosexuals is generally expressed more openly and is seen as more acceptable than other kinds of prejudice, such as racist attitudes (Farley, 2000).

In a society where openly gay and lesbian individuals appear on television and cross our paths every day on the street, the continued presence of homophobia may be difficult for some to grasp. Only fifty years ago, open displays of homosexuality were likely to land a person in jail. In the 1950s, gay bars were raided by police and their customers were arrested; even a group meeting of gay men was illegal under the anti-vice statutes of the time. In 1953, President Eisenhower declared "sexual perversion" (i.e., homosexuality) a national security risk. Homosexuals were prohibited from holding government jobs and were banned from licensing for a wide variety of professions (including teaching, law, and medicine). By the 1960s, Americans rated homosexuals as more harmful to the country than any other group except Communists and atheists (Lewis & Rogers, 1999).

The climate has clearly changed in dramatic ways. Today, public expression of anti-gay intolerance is more likely to be condemned than sanctioned by the media and important social institutions. When a California teen sued his high school for the right to wear a t-shirt with an anti-gay biblical quotation, the school defended its ban on such displays as fulfilling the school's legal responsibility to protect all youths from a hostile environment, a defense that was upheld in federal court in 2006. A federal judge in Idaho ruled in 2004 that Hewlett-Packard was justified in firing an employee who posted anti-gay verses from the Bible at his desk in view of other employees, citing the company's need to attract a diverse workforce. These cases show how much society has changed to extend basic rights, recognition, and protections to gays and lesbians, but also how much prejudice against them continues to be openly expressed by some segments of the population.

Although U.S. public opinion has evolved to the point where the majority no longer supports anti-gay discrimination in politics, housing, and jobs, there is still widespread opposition on moral grounds to full acceptance of homosexuality in our culture (Loftus, 2001). Nearly half of U.S. survey respondents continue to express the opinion that homosexual sex "is just plain wrong" or "disgusting" (Herek, 2002). These negative attitudes are more widely held toward gay men than toward lesbians, and such disapproval is more often voiced by heterosexual men than heterosexual women, and by individuals with less education (Garnets & Kimmel, 2003; Herek & Glunt, 1993; Loftus, 2001). Homoprejudice is rooted in the persisting view that homosexuality is abnormal, an empirically unsound view that has seriously negative consequences for gays and lesbians. Society's view of homosexuality has been influenced by dichotomies defining what is natural and unnatural and what is moral and immoral, based primarily on fundamentalist religious beliefs. Some mainstream Christian denominations, for example, continue to treat gays and lesbians as errant sinners who can remain in the church only if they refrain from the "intrinsic moral evil" of homosexual behavior. Such sentiments are conveyed in religious sayings such as "The church loves the sinner but not the sin." Some other Christian denominations (and most branches of non-Orthodox Judaism) are, however, fully welcoming and affirming communities that provide deep reservoirs of solace and social support to their gay and lesbian members.

Societal rejection of homosexuality facilitates the privileging of the members of another group—heterosexuals. Heterosexism pervades our society at all institutional levels and conveys the message that there is a hierarchy of sexuality in which heterosexuality is the ideal, and homosexuality a poor, if not unacceptable, second choice. Heterosexuals are assumed to have an automatic right to live their lives openly in all public spaces, while homosexuals are expected to live in silence and obscurity. This expectation is reflected in commonly held opinions like "I don't have a problem with gays and lesbians as long as they don't flaunt it." In practice, these opinions often mean simply that people should not be openly gay. In light of such prejudices, gay rights organizations sometimes attempt to use straight-appearing spokespeople, which has led to observations that gays have won the right to be gay *as long as they don't look or act gay* (Clarkson, 2005).

Some scholars have argued that homophobia has its roots in sexism (see Appleby, 2001) and others have asserted that homophobia is the driving force behind sexism, heterosexism, and racism (see Connell, 1990). Clearly, these claims are connected on many levels. Like other forms of oppression, homophobia is used to impose control over others through an existing or perceived power differential. Being a "real" man is often defined as the opposite of being feminine, or as not being gay or weak (Schultz, 1995). Boys are taught that exaggerated masculinity can dispel perceptions that they are unmanly or, worse, gay. One way of preventing such perceptions is to engage in sexist behavior by putting women down, attempting to exclude them from public and occupational spheres, and treating them as objects for sexual predation. In addition, exaggerated masculinity is often expressed through the perpetration of violence against members of ethnic and racial minority groups.

Gay men are thus defined as the cultural embodiment of "non-men," unmasculine "sissies," and unnatural sexual "inverts." Homosexuality represents a major detour from the path to culturally ideal masculinity and is associated with many aspects of femininity that are often viewed as inferior or undesirable. Just as women are often stereotyped as sex objects, gay men and lesbians are often perceived almost exclusively in terms of their sexuality. As was suggested in the previous chapter, homosexuals lead the cast of characters whose denigration has helped support heterosexual men's claim to a privileged place in the system of hegemonic masculinity. This may explain why heterosexual men condemn homosexual sex more strongly than heterosexual women do, and why they are often especially disapproving of sex between men. Straight men may feel threatened because they view gay men as representing sexual "inverts" whose behavior models that expected of women; they may also feel the need to distance themselves from the homosexual desires they themselves experience but fear will stigmatize them.

Unfortunately, homophobic views start forming early in life, in school. By the fourth grade, children have begun using homophobic labels such as "fag" and "queer" as insults for boys they see as not conforming to gender stereotypes (Barrie & Luria, 2004). One study in a school in New York found that 94 percent of the students surveyed reported hearing anti-gay epithets in school either "frequently" or "sometimes," and that sexual harassment was rarely confronted by school officials (Peters, 2003). Because of such harassment, the targeted students learn to internalize this homophobia, which places them at high risk for suicide, substance abuse, and sexual risk taking (Savin-Williams & Ream, 2003). Homophobia also results in violent attacks against gays (Wood, 1994). The hostility toward homosexuality that exists in our society also serves to keep a lid of secrecy on experimentation with same-sex sexual behavior, which is quite common among all youths, including those who eventually become exclusively heterosexual (Barrie & Luria, 2004). Moreover, the view that homosexuality is abnormal is perpetuated by sex education programs in schools, in which homosexual identity and behavior are either omitted or talked about in a negative manner (Sears, 2005).

Because everyone deserves to belong—to be seen as "normal"—the privileges that are granted to heterosexuals should be given to everyone. Yet lesbians and gays in many parts of the country have been denied the fundamental right to marry and bring up or adopt children. Many people believe that members of these groups are unable to raise children without causing them irreparable damage. However, studies of children raised by gay single parents and gay couples have shown that the children are no more or less likely to be gay themselves, nor do they have unusual gender identity or sexual orientation issues (Patterson & Redding, 1996). Moreover, studies using large representative samples have failed to detect any significant differences between teens living with gay parents and those living with straight parents on measures of psychological well-being, academic achievement, parent-child closeness, peer support, peer victimization, involvement in romantic relationships, initiation of sexual intercourse, substance use, and delinquency (Wainright & Patterson, 2006; Wainright, Russell, & Patterson, 2004).

GAY AND LESBIAN RIGHTS MOVEMENTS

Throughout history, gay men and lesbians have struggled to gain societal, legal, cultural, and religious acceptance, have challenged anti-gay prejudice and discrimination, and have worked to gain legal rights and protections. In the twentieth century, these efforts began to take the form of organized large-scale social movements, starting after World War II with the Homophile movement, which emphasized love as the basis for homosexuality; the gay liberation and gay and lesbian rights movements of the 1960s and 1970s; and more recent lesbian feminist, queer, and transgender movements. These movements have varied in their specific aims and tactics, but they have all pursued the ultimate goal of achieving social equality for lesbian, gay, bisexual, and transgender individuals.

The impetus for these movements has been the humiliation, discrimination, and violence that gays and lesbians suffer because of their sexual orientation. This population has historically been afforded little protection under the law and has even suffered persecution and harassment from those whose job it is to protect them. Throughout much of the early twentieth century, gay bars and clubs were typically denied liquor licenses, so that they were forced to sell liquor illegally. This made them vulnerable to sometimes violent raids by police, after which the names of their patrons were often published in community newspapers. Although the gay liberation movement was already underway in 1969, it is often dated as starting with protests that broke out that year after police raids at the Stonewall Inn in New York City's Greenwich Village, when gay, lesbian, and transgender patrons decided that they were no longer willing to tolerate police harassment.

Following Stonewall, many local gay and lesbian liberation groups, and a handful of national ones, were formed; these often adopted the word "gay" to signify both members' positive view of their non-heterosexual sexualities and their desire to transcend fixed heterosexual and homosexual dichotomies. These movements were contemporary with other movements of the 1960s and early 1970s, including the black, Chicano, and women's liberation movements, and sometimes pursued alliances with them, with limited success. They utilized some of the same ideology and tactics of these other movements; for example, the emphasis on "gay pride" was modeled on the "Black is beautiful" movement. By the mid-1970s, gay and lesbian movements had refocused on the goal of gaining recognition for gays and lesbians as a minority group and obtaining civil rights similar to those being sought by women and ethnic and racial minorities and had established the rainbow flag as the symbol of the ideal of equal rights for people of all sexual orientations.

From the beginning, gay and lesbian groups faced internal challenges that shaped their future, questions about membership, goals, and tactics and spurred the creation of separate groups. Distinctive groups promoting lesbian feminism and challenging the dominance of men in the gay liberation movement emerged in the mid-1970s; these groups focused on the logical implications of feminism for lesbians and for all women rather than focusing exclusively on rights for homosexuals. The gay rights movement was (and still is) criticized for being predominantly male, white, and middle class, and as such lacking adequate representation of ethnic minorities, women, and the working class. For example, the concept of coming out of the closet is based on a white middle-class viewpoint that emphasizes the importance of establishing an autonomous individual gay identity and often does not appeal to members of collectivistic ethnic cultures.

External challenges, most notably the arrival of AIDS in the early 1980s, led to the emergence of gay and lesbian groups employing militant activism to respond to the health crisis, such as ACT-UP and Queer Nation. Transgender movements of the 1990s presented additional challenges for gay rights groups concerning their identity and membership, because these movements refocused attention on discrimination based on gender nonconformity rather than sexual orientation. By the end of the 1990s, however, renewed efforts by gay rights groups to build alliances and promote awareness of common concerns found expression in the adoption of such acronyms as LGBT, LGBTQ, and LGBTI that are inclusive of transgender, questioning, and intersex individuals.

As organizations striving for gay and lesbian liberation have matured over the years, differences in goals and tactics have emerged. There is neither consensus on the key items on the agenda for change nor agreement on priorities and the best strategies to attain them. For example, while initiatives at the state and federal levels to both ban and legalize gay marriage have captured the political and media spotlight, the legitimization of gay marriage is not the primary objective of many gay and lesbian organizations. Indeed, some criticize the pursuit of gay marriage as an inappropriate attempt to imitate heterosexual models defining relationships and families (Josephson, 2005). Others argue that the most important objective of these legalization efforts is to gain the same rights that heterosexuals have regarding inheritance, adoption, medical decisions, Social Security, and spousal benefits, not to mimic a heterosexual (patriarchal) way of organizing the relationship of two people who love each other.

Unfortunately, there remains widespread misunderstanding about the meaning and goals of the gay liberation movement. When gays talk about gay rights, heterosexuals often hear talk about sex, not personal freedom. Furthermore, many people believe that gays and lesbians want special rights, but in fact, gay rights are an issue of individual liberty, and many GLBT rights organizations are at work today to secure for their constituencies the liberties that are protected by the U.S. Constitution.

SOCIAL WORK PRACTICE WITH GAY AND LESBIAN CLIENTS

In working with gay, lesbian, and bisexual clients, social workers must check their own attitudes toward homosexuals and the extent to which they subscribe to stereotypes or long-discarded professional models, such as those attributing homosexual orientations to psychopathology, developmental arrest, or some psychological disorder. Perhaps the most important lesson is that social workers cannot make assumptions about the sexual orientation of a client; the client deserves for the identity she or he presents to be accepted, not discounted or questioned. Intake and assessment tools can be heterosexist and as such may be biased against gay, lesbian, and bisexual clients. The assessment of family support needs also to be inclusive of gay and lesbian partnerships. Exclusive use of words such as "husband" and "wife" conveys the message that only heterosexual norms and behaviors count. In states such as Massachusetts, where gay marriage is now legal, the meaning of these words needs to be reassessed. From a culturally grounded perspective, families are defined by the role they play or by what they do for the client, not by what they look like. Families of choice often serve the needs of individuals much more effectively than families of origin. In addition, using the wrong labels can obscure the support systems or stressors that play key roles in the lives of clients.

Practitioners need to view their gay and lesbian clients as whole people, neither under- nor overestimating the role of sexual orientation in their lives. They should be alert both to overt and more subtle forms of prejudice and discrimination that the client may be experiencing at home, school, and work, even those that the client has not fully recognized; practitioners can validate that these problems are real. Practitioners should monitor any signs of internalized homophobia that may manifest as depression and low self-esteem and disempower the client; they must also consider the adverse repercussions of these negative self-perceptions on the client's emotional and sexual development. At the same time, practitioners cannot assume that all of the client's issues and problems are connected to her or his sexual orientation or identity. They need to assess the role of the client's sexuality, along with all of her or his other defining identities, including the complex family and communal identity issues faced by ethnic minority clients. It is the practitioner's responsibility to become familiar with the diverse ways that lesbian and gay individuals develop sexual and gender identities, as well as the diverse forms and special challenges of their intimate and family relationships. By recognizing the diversity that exists within this population, practitioners will not presume that a particular arrangement is best for all clients.

Key Concepts

Sexual orientation how people classify themselves and others sexually, based on feelings of attraction to other people, the gender categories of the objects of people's romantic and erotic desires, and the models of socially prescribed sexual behaviors that individuals follow

Stigma theory the idea that sexual minorities are likely to avoid disclosure of their sexual identity when they expect to be viewed or treated unfavorably as a result

Machismo the ideal of what it means to be a man in Latino culture, which views men as controlling, possessive, sexist, and domineering, as well as chivalrous and protective of kin

Marianismo the ideal of what it means to be a woman in Latino culture, which views women as virtuous and self-sacrificing and implies a sense of powerlessness and resignation in the face of sexist oppression

Homophobia fear of and aversion or hostility toward homosexuals or homosexuality that results in prejudice and discrimination

Internalized homophobia the acceptance of negative views of homosexuality that are incorporated into the self-concept of a gay or lesbian individual

Part IV

The Profession of Social Work Grounded in Culture

10
Cultural Norms and Social Work Practice

THE CULTURALLY GROUNDED PERSPECTIVE VIEWS SOCIAL WORK INTER-
ventions as products of unique cultural contexts. Interventions designed for and
tested with one community may not work with others unless there is a systematic
and comprehensive adaptation process. Lack of cultural specificity can yield ineffective interventions or, even worse, can be more harmful than beneficial. Assessing a client's culture requires that the practitioner adopt a researcher role and
approach the culture of the client as a learning tool. Sue (1998) has suggested
three components for effective culturally competent practice:

1. Hypothesis testing: the use of cultural knowledge about groups in a tentative, exploratory fashion without arriving at any definitive or premature
   conclusions about clients or their cultures (remember social context and
   intersectionality)
2. Dynamic sizing: the ability to know when to generalize certain attitudes
   and behaviors exhibited by the client to other members of the same identity group (i.e., when certain norms or behaviors are culturally based and
   may be common to others in the identity group) and when to individualize
   (i.e., when they are a function of the client's personality and there is no
   cultural explanation for such behaviors or attitudes)
3. Culturally specific expertise: the ability to work effectively with individuals
   from a particular culture and the possession of skills and abilities to develop rapport, to have a strong client-worker alliance, and to achieve the
   desired outcomes when working with members of that group (i.e., becoming a bicultural practitioner)

This chapter discusses the various factors that practitioners must consider in
order to choose an intervention that is culturally appropriate for the client and
some ways that practitioners can incorporate aspects of clients' cultures into the
helping process as Sue recommends.

INDIVIDUALISM AND COLLECTIVISM

The United States, like other Western societies, can be described as having an
individualistic orientation, meaning that the most common psychosocial unit of

operation is the individual, not the group. Individualistic societies believe that the needs of the group are satisfied when the needs of the individual are satisfied, while collectivistic societies believe that individual needs are met when the group's needs are met. These orientations can have a profound impact on how clients describe their presenting problems. Clients from collectivistic societies may tell the social worker that they are anxious because they feel powerless to help a family or community member, while clients from an individualistic society may feel anxious because they are unable to solve problems alone.

American society fosters individualism, and its citizens expect the government to defend individual rights even at the expense of the collective well-being. Progressive and conservative social policy positions share a common heritage that places great stress on the individual and the individual's rights and well-being. Individualism has been part of the ideological core of many European Americans since the inception of the nation. In contrast, indentured Europeans and African servants, enslaved Africans, colonized Native Americans, annexed residents of Mexico, Native Hawaiians, and many descendents of these groups, as well as women in general, have had less opportunity to share in these privileges. The more oppressed the group, the more its members have needed to rely on fellow members for survival. Strong community bonds have helped historically oppressed communities survive against difficult odds, and their members have relied on collective traditional helping systems. The collectivistic or communitarian approach rejects the individual-centered focus and favors the common good over individual concerns. At a global level, Jewish communities across many nations and throughout history have had to rely on their own religious and secular organizations to cope with persecution and exclusion. Many immigrant and refugee communities have developed grassroots organizations to welcome newcomers and serve their basic needs. In the United States collectivism is probably as much a part of the fabric of the nation as individualism, but it is not a prominent part of the American national myth, nor is it well represented in the laws of the nation.

Collectivistic cultures such as those of the Chinese and the Diné (Navajo) view mental and physical health as expressions of group harmony; the absence of health is regarded with shame and perceived to be the result of broken rules. These beliefs need to be taken into account by practitioners as they develop services for these populations. Research conducted with collectivistic populations has illuminated how groups' natural ways of helping are shaped by a collective orientation. For example, many Palestinians live in interdependence with others. Families are the main source of economic security and other forms of support. Palestinian nuclear families live surrounded by an extended family of fifty to five hundred people (Haj-Yahia, 1995). Because of the societal context in which Palestinian families live, individuals rely on their families to survive, and the consequences of individual misconduct are shared by everyone within the larger extended family. A study conducted with Native American women from a Montana reservation investigated a related phenomenon called communal mastery

(Hobfoll, Jackson, Hobfoll, Pierce, & Young, 2002). Communal mastery has been defined as the belief that individuals can attain their goals through their close interconnection with others (Hobfoll, Schröder, Wells, & Malek, 2002). Unlike the typical individualistic strategies of the mainstream culture, which rely on first-person statements and a sense of personal control, communal mastery relies on the individual's social attachment to others. Instead of "I" statements, individuals with high levels of communal mastery tend to use "we" statements. One of the main findings of the study was that women with high levels of communal mastery experienced less anger and depressive moods than women with low levels of communal mastery (Hobfoll, Jackson, et al., 2002). Individuals from collectivistic cultures who are separated from their communities of origin as a result of migration or other reasons can experience high levels of stress resulting from the disappearance of their support systems. Such experiences can be traumatic for families and individuals who find themselves for the first time without a natural and culturally grounded support system.

It appears that individuals from groups that practice a more collectivist approach to family and group social organization bring with them unique sources of resiliency that may manifest in different ways in different cultural groups. The culturally grounded paradigm for practice both recognizes the risk of psychosocial imbalance and stress and integrates into the professional helping process the sources of resiliency embedded in the cultural backgrounds of individuals and communities, as well as their natural helping practices. Understanding and welcoming these culturally embedded collective approaches to helping and their corresponding forms of social organization is a prerequisite to effective social work practice. There is a risk that practitioners may oversimplify or generalize the impact of collectivism on ethnic minority groups or other identity groups. A cross-national meta-analysis of dozens of studies on collectivism across the globe suggests that many developing societies that are assumed to be very collectivistic, such as those in Latin America and Asia, often use individualistic ways of seeking and giving help, while some developed societies in Europe have strong collectivistic features (Oyserman, Coon, & Kemmelmeier, 2002). Thus, while practitioners must take into account their knowledge of the client's culture, they must avoid pigeonholing clients based on that knowledge and must endeavor to learn about the community from which the client comes, as well as what kind of role the norms, values, and beliefs of the culture and the community play in the client's life.

Cultural norms are values and beliefs that influence the attitudes and behaviors of members of different cultural groups. Norms are learned from parents, teachers, peers, elders, and institutions such as organized religion and social clubs, and through traditional rituals and practices. Some norms are healthy and liberating, and some are unhealthy and oppressive. Cultural norms provide a consistent predisposition toward certain ideals, as well as a distaste for others, and prescribe standard behaviors as well as ritualistic practices. Norms are a summation of the typical activities and beliefs of a group of people. In the sense that they can be used by individuals to formulate expectations in interactions with others, cultural norms can be described as gentle stereotypes. Note from the field 10.1 illustrates the fine line between cultural norms and stereotypes. When one approaches cultural norms as all-or-nothing dichotomies, disregarding middle ground and gray areas, they risk becoming stereotypes.

Table 10.1 points to several areas where culture and cultural differences may be highly salient as the practitioner works to understand the client's worldview and identify instances where differences with the worldviews of others (including the practitioner) may lead to misunderstandings that become problematic for clients. Culture can produce distinctive expectations about how people should identify themselves, interact and communicate with others, define their families, and prioritize family, religion, and work life. Culture even influences how people learn and approach problems. Although it is useful in that it provides a general set of normative themes that can help social workers understand cultural minority clients, workers must remember that it can be harmful to generalize these norms to all "other" cultures in a broad and all encompassing manner. Such dichotomies, such as comparisons between Western and non-Western orientations or between whites and people of color, do not provide sufficient substantive information to identify culturally appropriate social work interventions. Because of the fluidity of culture, in categorizing whole groups of people in such a manner, one runs the risk of oversimplifying the cultural journeys of many individuals and communities.

NOTE FROM THE FIELD 10.1

Family Stereotypes

A group of high school students is producing an educational video for their middle school peers under the supervision of a professional video director. They were charged with the task of portraying Latino culture and its norms. The director, who is not Latino, suggests that the family in the story should have many children. Some of the students object; they perceive this to be a stereotype rather than a Latino cultural norm. The students from Latino backgrounds share stories about their parents' and grandparents' generations, among whom larger families were common, but note that their own older siblings and younger aunts and uncles who are married tend to have no more than two children. The script is rewritten to represent the modern Latino family more accurately, and a scene in which the question of the ideal family size comes up at a family birthday celebration is incorporated.

Table 10.1 Comparison of Cultural Norms and Values

Aspect of culture	Mainstream American culture	Other cultures
Greetings	Informal, handshake	Formal embrace, bow, handshake
Communication and language	Explicit, direct communication; emphasis on content (meaning found in words)	Implicit, indirect communication; emphasis on context (meaning found around words)
Dress and appearance	Dress-for-success ideal; wide range in accepted dress	Dress is seen as a sign of one's position, wealth, and prestige (religious rules may apply)
Food and eating habits	Eating as a necessity (e.g., eating fast food)	Dining as a social experience (religious rules may apply)
Time and time consciousness	Linear and exact time consciousness; value on promptness (time = money)	Elastic and relative time consciousness; time spent enjoying relationships
Relationships, family, friends	Focus on nuclear family; responsibility for self; value placed on youth; age seen as handicap	Focus on extended family; loyalty and responsibility to family; age given status and respect
Values and norms	Individual orientation; independence; preference for direct confrontation of conflict	Group orientation; conformity; preference for harmony
Beliefs and attitudes	Egalitarian; challenging of authority; individuals control their destiny; gender equity	Respect for authority, social hierarchies, and social order; individuals accept their destiny; different roles for men and women
Mental processes and learning style	Linear, logical, sequential; problem-solving focus	Lateral, holistic, simultaneous; acceptance of life's difficulties
Work habits and practices	Emphasis on task; rewards based on individual achievement; work has intrinsic value	Emphasis on relationships; rewards based on seniority, relationships; work is a necessity of life

Source: Adapted from Gardenswartz, L., & Rowe, A. (2006). *Managing diversity survival guide: A complete collection of checklists, activities, and tips.* Burr Ridge, IL: Irwin Professional.

Despite the shortcomings of such typologies and categories, practitioners can be expected to look for some descriptive information regarding cultural norms as a guide or reference for their work with different cultural communities. Workers need to have some form of "social address" (i.e., a starting point or a tentative point of departure) for locating the client's culture (Bronfenbrenner, 1986). The desire to place the client somewhere in the cultural continuum often leads workers to assign the client an ethnic or other identity label. However, because identity is a personal choice, only the client can pick the right set of labels. The worker's role is to access all the available information about cultural attributes and use it as part of the assessment process. Cultural attributes identified through assessment are reviewed as part of clients' needs and strengths and are placed within the social context of the community.

THE CULTURAL PROFILES OF SEVERAL IDENTITY GROUPS

The following review of cultural attributes and natural helping styles of selected groups is offered as an initial introduction to possible attributes that can serve as the foundation upon which culturally relevant interventions are implemented and evaluated. Because of the ever-present risk of overgeneralization, this information needs to be used with caution.

Native Americans

Native Americans' traditional holistic approaches to helping rests on a cultural belief that humans are an integral part of their environment and that their physical, emotional, spiritual, and biological dimensions cannot be separated. This cultural approach to wellness has been used by healers and other medical personnel to address the difficult living conditions experienced by members of many Native American communities. Native Americans face persistent health disparities such as high rates of diabetes, substance abuse, and infectious diseases, in addition to high rates of violence. Practices that have helped Native people overcome challenges need to be examined and integrated whenever possible into the social service delivery system with this population.

Native Americans often have social service needs that are different from those of other people in the United States, and their needs deserve special attention. Lack of transportation may be an insurmountable barrier for families living in remote areas of their reservations and far from social and health service providers. Native Americans often do not receive preventive and early care as a result of their fear of hospitals and the fear that they will become guinea pigs for experiments and research projects, as well as the knowledge that many Native Americans received poor treatment from these institutions in the past (Jones, 2006).

Although most Native Americans reside in cities, most Native American–specific social and health services are located on tribal lands. Urban Native Americans are often reluctant to seek health services in town because they feel like outsiders at doctor's offices, mental health clinics, and hospitals that do not observe Native American customs. For example, health care and social service professionals often fail to introduce themselves or do not inquire about the patient's extended family, courtesies that may be considered very important by the Native patient. Lack of cultural competence becomes an obstacle when doctors, nurses, and social workers ask direct or very personal questions, indicate that they have little time to spend with the patient, or make the Native patient wait for long periods of time in an unfamiliar environment without any personal contact.

The social and emotional challenges experienced by Native American clients can often be linked to their unresolved grief and historical trauma (Weaver, 1998). For example, Native youths who were taken away to boarding schools suffered not only the trauma of separation from their families at a very early age, but frequent abuse in these institutions. For some, the lack of healthy role models initiated a cycle of poor parenting (Morrissette, 1994). Family and multigenerational interventions can provide the support the client needs to heal.

The legacy of genocide gives Native Americans little reason to trust professionals outside the community or clan. Non-Native social workers need to use perseverance and work around client resistance in order to establish trust. In order to work effectively with Native American clients, the practitioner needs general and containment skills. General skills include communication and problem-solving skills based on a definition of the problem and arrival at a solution from a Native American perspective. Containment skills refer to the ability to listen, tolerate long periods of silence, and be patient (Weaver, 1999). As the tempo of communication is generally slower in traditional communities, more assimilated Native social workers and non-Native social workers often need to slow down their natural tempo in order to communicate effectively.

As the example in note from the field 10.2 demonstrates, social work practitioners working with Native Americans may need to assess their clients' level of traditionalism. In this case, the worker assessed the group's communication style and concluded that they would not be comfortable with verbal and direct communication about their feelings. Although it may be appropriate to relate to a nontraditional client much as one would relate to a non–Native American individual, more traditional Native clients may respond better to culturally specific interventions (Thomason, 2000). Selected elements of traditional culture can be integrated into practice with respect and care. This integration is based on the recognition that culture and rituals are connected to a spiritual dimension of clients' lives. To attempt to appropriate those traditional and sacred practices, for example, by assuming the role of a traditional healer and attempting to perform traditional rituals, would be a form of colonialism. However, the respectful integration

NOTE FROM THE FIELD 10.2
Speaking with Our Hands

Janet is a Native social worker who has been assigned to a pediatric oncology clinic operated by the American Indian Health Services, where she is to run a youth support group for cancer survivors. There are six people in the group: three boys and three girls ranging in age from nine to fourteen years old. They have been meeting for three weeks now, and the group members do not talk much. They mostly listen. Janet has tried different techniques to help them externalize their feelings about their diagnoses and the fact that their cancer is in remission. This week she proposes that they paint vases. She explains the meaning of vase painting in their cultures and shows examples to the group. Pottery makers in their communities paint vases as a way of communicating their dreams and wishes for the future. The group members like the idea, and each one portrays her or his individual experiences, feelings, and hopes for the future on her or his own vase. Once finished, they share their work and everyone comments on the others' vases and the messages they convey. Janet summarizes the comments and proposes to the group that they exhibit their vases in the waiting room of the clinic for other children and their families to see.

of culturally based knowledge, beliefs, and rituals can be conducted effectively in partnership with the recognized holy person in the community. The shaman or her or his equivalent can help introduce the traditional content in an authentic manner and let the practitioner know of boundaries that must be respected.

African Americans

African Americans constitute a very diverse cultural group, and the intersectionality of many factors such as social class and gender creates many within-group differences. There is, however, some agreement that African Americans constitute a distinct ethnocultural community whose existence is valued for its own sake (Blum, 2006). An important first task for the social worker is recognizing the importance that clients place on maintaining connections to the African American community and its many sources of identity. African Americans have developed cultural products (e.g., music, literature, and science) that have enriched their community, U.S. society, and the whole world. Those cultural gifts are the product of enormous resiliency and are often expressions of cultural norms within African American culture, such as connectedness, equality, emotional vitality, collective survival, cooperation, sharing, interdependence, reconciliation, and respect (White & Parham, 1990).

Spirituality is another important component of African American culture that has shaped family and individual relationships, fostered political mobilization, and served as a source of hope and resiliency. Congruent with African American values, spirituality supports interconnectedness with the community, the divine, and the ancestors. Organized religion (especially Christianity and Islam) has sustained and continues to sustain black identity, created institutional settings for pursuit of social and political goals, and nurtured religious values and dignity (Ferraro & Koch, 1994). Although the majority of African Americans are Christian, Islam and other traditions connected to African spirituality (e.g., Yoruba and Candomblé) play an important role in many communities around the nation. African Americans are more likely to attend religious services and pray in private than their white Christian counterparts (Taylor, Chatters, Jayakody, & Levin, 1996). Because of its cultural relevance, the infusion of spirituality into interventions with African Americans appears to be a natural integration. The use of prayer, quotes from the Bible or other holy books, and spiritual metaphors can be appropriate in certain circumstances. However, role definition and role differentiation are of concern here and must be addressed in supervision when one chooses to integrate spirituality into an intervention. There is a fine but important line between helping clients explore and draw upon salient aspects of their spirituality and providing spiritual direction. The integration of spirituality into social work practice needs to be done with caution.

African Americans also place a high value on family and children. Families vary greatly in size and structure as well as in composition. Ritual kinship, where "uncles," "aunts," and "cousins" may not be related by blood but have a commitment to the family as if they were family in a biological sense, is common in many communities. The practitioner working with African American families must honor and support their historical resiliency and ability to adapt through the use of highly effective support systems such as ritual kinship.

Trisha's story in note from the field 10.3 illustrates the cultural tradition of "informal adoption" (Boyd-Franklin, 2003). It is an example of how family is defined in some African American communities—and in many other cultures—based on its function and the benefits an individual receives from belonging to the family rather than on blood ties between individuals. Trisha's case presents an opportunity to incorporate cultural practices into the social services system. Such incorporation, however, requires changes not only by the individual worker but also to agency policy and at the legal level. The social worker can facilitate collaboration between the different parties in order to arrive at a decision that will be beneficial to all.

African American grandmothers have historically served as the primary caretakers of the children in the family. During slavery, African Americans relied on

NOTE FROM THE FIELD 10.3
Who Is Family?

Mrs. Johnson's best friend, Phyllis, died recently after a short illness. Phyllis had a three-year-old child named Trisha. Although there is no blood relationship between them, Trisha always calls Mrs. Johnson "Auntie." After the funeral, Trisha goes to Mrs. Johnson's home for a few days. A week later when her grandmother comes by to pick her up, Trisha refuses to pack her backpack and says that she wants to stay with her auntie. Her grandmother is surprised by Trisha's reaction, but after discussing the situation with Mrs. Johnson, she allows Trisha to stay for another week. Trisha hardly knows her grandmother because her mom and her grandmother stopped communicating after Trisha was born. The worker handling the case from children protective services questions the fact that Trisha is staying with a person who is not kin and starts an investigation.

extended family networks that made fewer clear distinctions between the roles of the mother and the grandmother. The tradition continues to be practiced as grandmothers take care of their own grandchildren as well as their grandchildren's children, nephews, nieces, and other non-kin members of the extended family. Intergenerational African American families with grandmothers and great-grandmothers at their helm have grown exponentially in the past decades as a result of high rates of substance abuse and an increase in the number of incarcerated African American women. After biological mothers, African American grandmothers and fathers have been identified as providing the highest quality of parenting (Simons, Chen, Simons, Brody, & Cutrona, 2006). Although these findings are encouraging in terms of the well-being of children, they raise some concerns about the well-being of the grandmothers who are doing the caregiving. The caregiver role can bring much stress to older women, especially when the mother is absent. The stress can be physical, emotional, and financial, as many grandmothers are not recognized as caregivers in the foster care system.

African Americans have developed abilities and coping mechanisms to deal with racism, and they rely on social support systems that have been perfected over generations. Therefore, one of the roles of the social worker is to help clients tap these resources and strengths as they create better conditions for the community. The social worker plays a broker role by connecting clients to services and resources outside their family and community networks. Social workers can also facilitate a balance between the natural supports existing within the community and the more formal resources and services that can ease the burden of caregivers.

A culturally grounded approach to social work practice celebrates African

American culture and its expressions of resiliency and supports individuals in their efforts to resist racism and cultural assimilation while producing lasting changes leading to the development of a more inclusive and just society. The culturally competent social worker can be effective by adopting an Afrocentric perspective, one that focuses on collectivity and on spiritual and moral development (Schiele, 1997). While working with families, for example, social workers can take into account how African American parents socialize their children to live in hostile environments in which their culture and race are not always valued. Parents may feel the need to have a family conversation or may wait until their child experiences her or his first racist incident. From a culturally grounded perspective, the professional's role is to provide a safe environment where these important decisions can be thought through and where the interests and well-being of the child and the family are paramount. Sensitive and emotionally charged topics require an environment where self-disclosure is possible and where empathy and trust prevail. To provide such an environment, social workers of all ethnic backgrounds need to examine their own beliefs, attitudes, and behaviors toward racism. Self-examination can foster increased empathy and greater cultural competence.

Mexican Americans and Other Latinos

Mexican Americans constitute the largest subgroup of a very diverse umbrella group generally called Latino or Hispanic. Latinos constitute the largest ethnic minority group in the nation and many of them are Spanish speakers, the second most commonly spoken language in the United States. Many Latinos trace their ancestry to the Southwest before the Treaty of Guadalupe Hidalgo was signed, whereas other families have come to the United States more recently. Many others have ancestors who came from one or more of the twenty-one nations in which Spanish is a principle national language. The terms "Latino" and "Hispanic" describe a diverse multiracial and multinational group of people with a connection to Spain, Latin America, and the Commonwealth of Puerto Rico.

It is important to remember that not all Latinos speak Spanish. There are hundreds of languages spoken in Latin America. Spanish and Portuguese are the two most commonly spoken European languages, but there are hundreds of Mayan languages, as well as other languages such as Nahuatl Aymara, Guaraní, Quechua, and Creole. Those who speak languages other than Spanish in many of these countries are often members of indigenous communities that predate the arrival of the Europeans and continue to face prejudice and discrimination as well as the consequences of centuries of social, educational, economic, and political inequality. When these individuals come to the United States, their lack of proficiency in both English and Spanish complicates their adjustment to U.S. society. As migration streams into the United States continue to expand and diversify, many social service agencies encounter clients from Latin America whose needs go beyond the ones presented by the traditional Spanish-speaking client.

As note from the field 10.4 illustrates, Latinos are a multiethnic and multiracial group with Amerindian, European, African, and even Asian ancestry. Many Latinos identify as *La Raza*, or "the people," the product of centuries of *mestizaje*, or the mixing of Native people of the Americas with people of Spanish and other European backgrounds as well as African and Asian ancestry. A shared Spanish colonial past and a strong connection to Roman Catholic traditions and beliefs provide a set of cultural norms that are shared by many different Latino groups. However, not all Latinos are Roman Catholic, and not all Latinos observe these norms. It is possible to discern a set of norms that appear to be a common denominator across subgroups while remaining mindful of the richness and diversity of various Latino groups.

Familismo is commonly recognized as a core Latino value. *Familismo* involves strong identification with and attachment to a nuclear and extended family,

---

NOTE FROM THE FIELD 10.4
Recognizing Latino Diversity

La Casa de la Solidaridad is a well-established Latino social services agency located in a large city in the Midwest. Casa received an urban renewal grant and has started to implement a community development plan. Twelve representatives from different community agencies, social clubs, and churches form the leadership team. The social worker assigned to staff the leadership team notices that one man who introduced himself as José Rocha did not speak at all during the first session, although the agency provides simultaneous Spanish-to-English and English-to-Spanish translation services. During the coffee break, the social worker introduces herself and learns that Mr. Rocha comes from the state of Oaxaca in Mexico and does not feel comfortable speaking English or Spanish in public. His first language is Huautla Mazatec, one of the many Mayan languages spoken in southern Mexico and in Guatemala. At the beginning of the next meeting, the social worker speaks with the elected chair of the group, Mario Guttmann, an Argentinean American of German ancestry who speaks fluent German, English, and Spanish. Mr. Guttmann thanks the social worker for the information and suggests that Mr. Rocha's organization find a substitute for him who is fluent in Spanish and/or English. Another board member calls a vote and the motion does not pass. The board members propose that they look for alternatives that will facilitate Mr. Rocha's full participation, such as finding an additional interpreter who is fluent in Huautla Mazatec.

and an obligation to provide both material and emotional support to one's family (Marin & Marin, 1991). *Familismo* exerts influence on Latinos regardless of the length of time they have lived in the United States. *Familismo* involves rituals such as gathering on Sundays for meals, going to church together, celebrating the *quinceañera* (a girl's debut as a woman on her fifteenth birthday), and participating in making decisions that affect the family. *Familismo* is associated with protective factors like interdependence, cohesiveness, cooperation, pride, and respect among family members (Comas-Diaz, 1997). It is also a protective factor against alcohol abuse and delinquency in Latino adolescents (Frauenglass, Routh, Pantin, & Mason, 1997). An important aspect of *familismo* is *compadrazgo* (godparenting), in which the *compadres* (godparents) are considered something akin to co-parents and help raise the child, providing a culturally based form of social security and child welfare in the event that the biological parents are absent or unable to provide for the child's needs.

Other Latino cultural norms that have implications for social work practice include *personalismo* and *simpatia*. *Personalismo* is the valuing of interpersonal relationships (being friendly) while *simpatia* is a word used to describe the cultural expectation that individuals avoid conflict and act in a good-natured and pleasant way toward others regardless. A social worker who shows respect for Latino clients and treats them in a friendly manner while recognizing the family hierarchy will be judged to have *personalismo* and the client will be more likely to become engaged in the helping process and return for future sessions.

Cultural values and norms often influence the communication style of traditional Latino clients. For example, clients may avoid saying no to the social worker because "no" is perceived to be a rude word. Clients may not be in agreement with practitioners but will express their disagreement without saying no out of respect for the authority of the worker. In such clients, agreement is expressed more enthusiastically and the clinician can tell that the client is engaged from her or his body language. The client's behavior following the session may not be consistent with the social worker's understanding of the discussion, but the client may see no contradiction. Body language indicating anxiety, silence, and other expressions of discomfort need to be noted and recorded. In mainstream non-Latino U.S. culture, direct communication tends to be the norm. One person directly asks a question, and the other directly answers. In Latino cultures, as in most traditional cultures, direct communication with direct questioning can be viewed as impolite. Latino clients prefer not to address sensitive or personal matters right away. Instead, traditional clients feel more comfortable when they are allowed to arrive at the topic at hand in a more roundabout way and address the topic in their own time.

Latino children are often taught not to say yes in some situations or to delay giving an affirmative answer for as long as possible. If someone offers something that an individual wants or needs, it is considered polite to say, "No, thank you," and wait for the offer to be repeated a second or third time before accepting. Note from the field 10.5 provides an illustration of the misunderstandings that can result from such differences in communication styles. When Graciela initially declined the offer of lemonade, Mrs. Williams probably thought she meant it. In clinical situations, similar misunderstandings can occur. For example, Latino clients may be very uncomfortable answering certain questions but will not say anything about it. If asked directly, they will not let the worker know that they are uncomfortable. They may feel that they should respect the authority of the worker—"She knows, she is the professional; who am I to tell her that the information she wants is too private?" This kind of misunderstanding, however, can lead clients to drop out of treatment if they do not feel respected by the practitioner. Body language can be an indication of such discomfort, and these cues need to be assessed continuously in order to foster the strongest therapeutic alliance possible. The verbalization of dissatisfaction with services or a practitioner's approach is rare, especially among less acculturated Latinos. Ignoring this style of communication can undermine the development of a strong therapeutic alliance (Paris, Añez, Bedregal, Andrés-Hyman, & Davidson, 2005).

NOTE FROM THE FIELD 10.5
"No, Thank You"

Graciela is a fourteen-year-old seventh grader with a very active social life within the boundaries of her own neighborhood. She has not had many opportunities to interact with youths and families from different ethnic backgrounds. This summer she is participating in her school's Family-to-Family exchange program and she will be spending a week with a family in another town and of a different ethnicity. The Williamses have a daughter her age named Tracy, who will go back with Graciela to her home once the week is over and complete the exchange. Graciela is dropped off at the home of her host family by her father, who leaves promptly after meeting the Williamses. It is a very hot day and Graciela is invited to sit with the family on the front porch. Mrs. Williams brings a tray with a large pitcher of lemonade and glasses for everyone. When offered a glass of lemonade, Graciela responds, "No, thank you." Nobody asks Graciela again if she would like to have a glass. Graciela was behaving as would be expected in her family. Her mother always says, "When you are visiting another family and you are offered refreshments, you first say no and only accept the second time around. It is not polite to accept right away." Graciela is very thirsty but remains quiet, waiting for Mrs. Williams to ask her again, but she never does.

Immigrant and refugee Latino families often experience unique mental health needs. Many women and children are forced by their economic, political, or family situations to immigrate to the United States, and as a result, they may feel angry, detached from their natural support systems, and isolated. Couples may experience marital problems due to the disruptions and adjustments precipitated by the migration process. Regardless of whether migration is forced or voluntary, recent immigrants often experience feelings of loss, grief, homesickness, and sadness (Van Ecke, 2005).

Although the Latino norm of relying on family provides great support to immigrants and refugees, it may also allow them to delay seeking social services; this explains in part the underutilization of services by Latinos. The costs and burdens of immigration can place tremendous strains on immigrant families and the kin they rely on for much of the assistance they need. Networks of mutual assistance can break down when both the newcomers and those who have came before them are poor and needy, sometimes leading to sharp conflicts and even fallings-out that make them even more dependent on help from social services (Menjivar, 2000).

A major challenge in social work practice is the shortage of bilingual and bicultural practitioners. Even when Latinos master English, they may prefer to use Spanish to communicate their feelings. They may use English effectively in the transactions of daily living (i.e., when speaking from the head) but feel that English is an unnatural means for conveying emotion (i.e., when speaking from the heart).

As Antonio's case in note from the field 10.6 demonstrates, being culturally grounded may require the practitioner to go beyond language to attempt a cultural connection. It is often critical for practitioners to master another language when working intensively with a community that has many members whose English is limited. However, being culturally competent with Latinos, as with many other ethnic groups, goes beyond language proficiency and requires a comprehensive bicultural approach to practice.

Asian Americans

Despite great differences among ethnic groups, people of different national origins described as Asian American appear to share some common cultural values. Some of these commonalities can be traced to Buddhism and Confucian philosophies. There are six cultural values that are shared to some degree by different Asian American groups: collectivism, conformity to cultural norms, emotional self-control, and family recognition through achievement, filial piety, and humility (Kim, Atkinson, & Yang, 1999).

Collectivism refers to a tendency among community members to think about the group first, and a strong sense of allegiance to the group. Achievements are

> ## NOTE FROM THE FIELD 10.6
> ### Saying *Adios*
>
> Antonio is an engineering student at a large university in California. His mother suddenly passed away in Mexico six months ago. Although he was able to attend the funeral, he feels that he was not able to say goodbye to her properly. He feels depressed and starts to see a social worker at student health services. The death of Antonio's mother immediately surfaces as the presenting problem. After four sessions during which they talk about her death, it becomes clear that Antonio needs to say goodbye to his mother in a more meaningful and culturally significant way. The social worker is Japanese American and only speaks a few words of Spanish. Despite his limited Spanish-language skills, he suggests that Antonio use the session to express to his mother all the things he did not have a chance to say to her. Antonio tries in English but cannot do it because he never spoke to his mother in English. The worker suggests that he conduct the conversation in Spanish and requests permission to tape it. Antonio is able to say what he needed to say, and the session becomes a turning point in his grieving process. Later they listen to the tape and discuss its cultural meaning and personal significance. In some regards, the social worker gave up his power by switching to a language he did not understand to serve the needs of the client.

not attained individually, but as a group. Family or group needs take precedence over individual needs. Community members have well-defined social roles and expectations, and a sense of communal responsibility and respect for authority (Dhooper, 2003).

Conformity to norms is inculcated in Asian American families, like many other traditional cultural groups, under a principle of interdependence. The social work practice of encouraging clients to explore their personal goals and desires, with the ultimate objective that clients will develop into independently functioning individuals, contradicts some Asian philosophies according to which parents' wishes are expected to influence children's decisions regarding friends, spouses, housing arrangements, and residential locations, even during adulthood (Brammer, 2004). As family members go through the acculturation process, intergenerational disagreements may emerge, but not in the form of direct or open conflict. Interpreting behavior within the appropriate family and cultural context requires a proactive approach to decoding communication patterns and may require some triangulation. If the social worker gathers information from different members of the family through different channels, such as individual, family, and couples' sessions, and carefully compares the information gathered about the same event, phenomenon, or topic, contradictions can be identified, interpreted, and addressed.

Cultural differences in communication style may be misinterpreted as resistance by social workers who received a Western-style education. For example, discussing personal and family problems outside the family is considered taboo in some Asian American communities, which may prevent their members from seeking outside help (Dhooper, 2003). However, when clients of Asian heritage do seek help, they often view the practitioner as a healer and leader who will provide direction. Therefore, the practitioner needs to make the role of the social worker clear to the client and help her or him set realistic expectations (Brammer, 2004). The fact that many recent immigrant families are unfamiliar with the social service system and with Western theories of health and illness may prevent them from seeking assistance or lead them to misunderstand the purpose of the intervention. Often, respectfully integrating traditional values and practices into the intervention can increase service utilization rates and services quality (Dhooper & Tran, 1998).

Asian Americans are sometimes described as possessing great self-control and restraint regarding emotional expression. Expressions of extreme happiness or sadness may not be demonstrated but the lack of expressivity does not mean that clients are not feeling these emotions at a very deep level (Browne & Broderick, 1994). Being stoic and enduring suffering in silence are important expressions of self-control. Clients' body language and verbal communication may be disorienting for uninitiated social workers. For example, in many Asian cultures, there is an implicit understanding of parental love and as such, it is felt that there is no need to express it verbally. Some parent-child bonding assessment scales would not be appropriate for clients from Asian backgrounds, as the scales may ask pointed questions such as "How often do you tell your child you love him or her?"

Some Asian American views and practices with respect to illness and health that are considered appropriate by the native culture may be seen as questionable in the United States. For example, a patient who takes a stoic approach to pain and believes that suffering is an inevitable part of life may share very little information with a physician or hospital social workers. Some Asian worldviews consider sadness a healthy or ultimately positive experience that helps people move along the path to a more enlightened life, rather than a sign of depressive symptoms that may indicate pathology (Krause, Rosser, Khiani, & Lotay, 1990). On the other hand, displaying emotion is considered pathological or shameful (Cheung, 1993). Social workers can play a role as cultural mediators in facilitating the best possible utilization of the care systems available for patients.

Family recognition through achievement (e.g., academic achievement or professional success) is related to the idea of honoring the family through one's actions. Families also work together to achieve economic and social advancement. This approach can be a source of conflict, as there still tend to be different expectations for women and for men. For example, many Asian women in the United States work along with their husbands in family-owned businesses but are expected to remain subservient. This expectation can lead to marital conflict and sometimes abuse. Family harmony is also at risk when immigrant children become more receptive to ideas of individualism and independence than their parents are and wish them to be (Dhooper, 1991).

Filial piety is veneration and respect for one's elders. Age is equated with wisdom. Older family members are expected to offer advice, and younger people are expected to seek advice from their older relatives. Filial piety also implies taking care of older relatives as their health declines rather than placing them in nursing homes.

Humility relates to collectivistic values that frown upon any behavior that calls attention to oneself or one's personal achievements. Being humble implies deflecting attention from oneself even when one is being praised for achievements or for possessing a commendable attribute or qualification. In mainstream American corporate culture, many forms of performance reviews are based on self-appraisals in which employees are expected to "blow their own horn." Such a practice would be unthinkable for a traditional Asian American employee. Similarly, clients from Asian backgrounds may have difficulty with the notion that one can enhance one's own self-esteem by focusing on one's positive qualities and achievements.

There are a number of factors that can weaken individuals' and communities' observance of these six cultural values. For example, acculturation is believed to weaken the centrality of traditional cultural values in the lives of second- and third-generation immigrants. This process appears to be slower for Asian Americans than for other immigrant groups, as they appear to retain a strong connection to traditional norms and values longer (often up to three generations). However, Asian Americans do appear to undergo behavior changes (behavioral acculturation) at a fast rate (Kim et al., 1999). The pace at which value acculturation and behavioral acculturation occurs may be an expression of biculturalism, which allows young people to maintain two separate sets of values, one at home, and the other outside the home.

A study conducted by Kim, Yang, Atkinson, Wolfe, and Hong (2001) with American college students of Chinese, Japanese, Korean, and Filipino ancestry found that participants assigned similar meaning to the six value dimensions but their levels of adherence to them varied by national origin. For example, Filipino Americans indicated lower levels of adherence to the practice of emotional self-control than the other three Asian American groups. The legacy of the Spanish and American colonization of the Philippines may account for this difference. Japanese Americans reported the strongest adherence to traditional values, although as a group they were farthest removed from the immigration experience. These findings reinforce the cautionary note about avoiding generalizations when one is identifying similarities across subgroups. Southeast Asian communities, for example, present some unique needs.

Because many Southeast Asian clients are members of refugee families, social workers with working knowledge of the symptoms of post-traumatic stress can provide invaluable support. Members of these communities suffer the stresses associated with migration and acculturation, which often result in depression and anxiety problems. Having become used to relying on a large informal social system (family, friends, and community) in their countries of origin, immigrants who have lost that system can spend much time and energy dealing with economic survival, racism, cultural conflicts, and isolation. A successful intervention with members of this group, as with any group, needs to be congruent with the client's belief system.

Social workers and their Asian American clients can benefit from an exploration of the client's new life in comparison with the old life and the transition and adaptation processes. The person-in-environment perspective can be most beneficial in work with Asian American refugees and other recent immigrants, as it considers all levels (interpersonal, intrapersonal, organizational, community, and policy) of adjustment and well-being. In work with older generations, a narrative approach can be very useful for validating lost status and happiness as a step toward creating new narratives centered around hope and the future.

GENDER AND SEXUAL ORIENTATION

Social work is a predominantly female profession. Not only are most social work professionals and students female, but historically, most of the people receiving social services have been female (Shaw & Shaw, 1997; Hudson, 2006). The predominance of female clients occurs for many reasons. Not only are men less familiar with social services and available interventions, but they are also more apprehensive than women about seeking help (Kosberg, 2002). The underutilization of services by men raises the question of whether there may be a normative gendered approach to social service delivery that is unintentionally alienating men. For example, some of the female-centered social work literature shines a negative light on heterosexual men as abusers and absent fathers. These perceptions can create an unwelcoming environment for the male client.

Men are often referred to programs and services that have been developed for and evaluated with predominantly female clients by predominantly female social workers. For example, agencies with a family focus tend to have a difficult time engaging fathers in family sessions. It would be easy to conclude that fathers are not interested, are not committed, or simply do not want to participate. However, an alternative analysis may suggest that men experience great discomfort in the agency, in the treatment modality, and in their interactions with almost exclusively female social workers and other agency personnel.

One could argue that there is also a need for a sexual orientation match between clients and workers. Such a match is probably not necessary or feasible most of the time. More important is a high degree of awareness and competence. For example, when working with a lesbian client who has just broken up with her partner, a heterosexual social worker may feel the need to make her sexual orientation explicit. Is such self-disclosure an attempt to avoid transference or is the social worker just trying to be honest with her client? Here are three statements a practitioner might make in such a situation:

1. "I am straight, but I believe I can understand what you are going through. However, I may need your help sometimes in order to understand your feelings. I am here to help."
2. "I have a husband and three kids. I want to make it clear that I am not a lesbian and that I do not really understand lesbian love."
3. "Transitions like the one you are going through are really difficult. I know just how you must feel. I was dumped by my boyfriend two weeks ago, but I am seeing someone else already."

Each of these responses uses self-disclosure differently. In the first statement, the worker is trying her best to be honest, to share something about herself in order to establish trust and empathy. This statement may not be considered ideal, but it is certainly affirming of the client-worker relationship. The second statement discloses personal information but only out of fear or homophobia. The social worker stresses who she is and who she is not in order to establish a boundary. This statement clearly reflects a lower level of awareness. Instead of self-disclosing to assist with the process, she self-discloses to avoid having to cross the boundary of sexual orientation and in order to remain in her biased comfort zone. The third statement shows how, in an attempt to create immediate rapport, the worker makes explicit her heterosexual status, vents about her own experience, and makes light of the client's distress by drawing an inappropriate parallel between their personal experiences, all without much regard for the client. Most definitely, this use of self-disclosure is inappropriate: the worker shares personal information without connecting it to the client. Self-disclosure can be a professionally responsible strategy, but only if it helps the client move on or become more engaged.

Practitioners become more competent in their work with lesbian and gay clients when they ask themselves and their staff how to incorporate the experience of gay, lesbian, and bisexual clients into their protocols and into the overall culture of their agencies. For example, social workers and clients can make decisions together about whether to chart information about the client's sexual orientation.

Their partners and children should be considered emergency contacts and have the right to receive information and make health decisions about the client.

Working with the gay, lesbian, or bisexual client is not the only way in which social work practitioners can help reduce the stressors that result from prejudice and harassment. School social workers are in a position to help both teachers and students overcome homophobia, and prevent the school bullying that often takes a tragic toll on gender-nonconforming youth. Often, school is the social context in which the young GLBT student most needs an intervention to make it a welcoming place. Several national school programs such as the Gay, Lesbian and Straight Education Network, which has chapters at schools all around the nation, offer support to students and their teachers. For parents, PFLAG (Parents, Families and Friends of Lesbians and Gays) is also a very good resource.

Sexual orientation may present the same challenges reviewed under the prior discussions of ethnicity and gender, raising again the question of whether it is necessary for the social worker to have the same sexual orientation as the client. In fact, gay and lesbian practitioners can be of help to heterosexual clients and vice versa, just as heterosexual practitioners can be effective allies to their gay and lesbian colleagues and clients. Nonetheless, displaying certain symbols and becoming familiar with the experiences specific to gays and lesbians make that alliance more real and advance professional competence. The rainbow flag, for example, has been adopted by the gay movement as a symbol of pride and identity. It is common to see stickers of a rainbow flag displayed at social workers' offices. The rainbow flag indicates that the office is a welcoming place regardless of the sexual orientation of the worker.

ETHICS AND CULTURE: CULTURAL VALUES AND PRACTICES ARE NOT ALL INHERENTLY GOOD

It has been argued throughout this book that social workers need to be aware of different cultures and their histories in order to identify the right interventions for clients and increase their professional competence. Historically, social work has proceeded along two paths, one focusing on helping individuals adapt to society—the approach of the Charity Organization Society—and the other focusing on changing society, for example, through social reform efforts, in order to help the individual. These two approaches can be seen as parallel paths for promoting the welfare of the most vulnerable sectors of society, but they may also come into conflict or introduce tensions.

People who come from more traditional cultures may find that some of their traditional practices are in conflict with the practices or expectations of mainstream society. Parents in the United States, for example, are advised to use methods such as time out and grounding to discipline their children, but some parents may come from cultures where spanking and other harsh methods of punishment are the disciplinary norm. If investigated by child protective services, these families face the possibility of becoming the object of certain corrective actions that can carry serious consequences for the whole family. What is the role of the social worker in such cases? Child protective services in New York has reported that social workers who are themselves immigrants have a hard time with this particular cultural clash and tend to judge what others see as excessive punishment as acceptable (Dugger, 1996). On the other hand, a worker who is not familiar with the cultural background of certain parenting practices may be more likely to overreact, alienate the parents, and even harm the family by making recommendations before knowing all the facts.

It is important to remember that cultures are constantly changing and that not all culturally based attitudes and behaviors are inherently good. Most of the time, culture heals, or, as the traditional Spanish-language saying states, *La cultura cura*. There are times, however, when oppression takes place in the name of culture. Examples of oppressive behaviors that have cultural roots are many. In recent years, there has been growing press coverage of female circumcision—various forms of genital cutting—in Africa and among African immigrant communities in the United States, Canada, and Europe. Female circumcision, which is banned by law in the United States, is one example of a practice over which there is a sharp disagreement. The larger society, including both mainstream society and other cultural minority communities, strongly oppose such practices, because they view them as a form of genital mutilation with serious negative physical and psychological consequences for young girls. Nonetheless, because the practices are grounded in notions of ethnic culture and religion, one needs to be aware of the risk that cultural minority communities may perceive objections to female circumcision to be anti-African. Moreover, although many African women have denounced the practice of genital cutting, and some mothers have even sought asylum status for themselves and their daughters in the United States and other countries to avoid having the practice forced upon their daughters, others have demanded the right to continue with the practice and in some cases have taken their daughters to other countries to be circumcised (see Abusharaf, 2007, for a variety of women's perspectives on female circumcision). The academic consensus is against the practice and some authors have identified the practice as a contemporary example of cultural relativism (Galotti, 2007). The debate has raised important questions about who has the right to impose values on whom and how cultural relativism and the universal liberal values embraced by social work can somehow be part of a normative continuum. At the end, the debate can only be addressed from an ethical standpoint protecting the rights and well-being of the individual.

Ethical dilemmas emerge when cultural norms and practices promoted by some members of a group are in direct conflict with the code of ethics of the profession and the law of the land. The question members of many minority cultures ask is, Who has the right to determine which cultural practices are acceptable or unacceptable? The right to self-determination and to practice the traditions of one's culture appears to be limited by the law, but not all legal behaviors are ethical, and not all ethical behaviors are legal.

In such cases where cultural clashes emerge with recent immigrant families, a necessary first step is to inform and educate the community about the law and explain how the cultural practice conflicts with it. Punitive measures should be used only when there is a clear sense that the information was understood but the behavior has not changed accordingly. There will be gray areas where a behavior may not be illegal but is considered unethical. In such cases, consulting with elders or cultural experts in the community may help the worker have more of an impact and achieve the desired changes. These very difficult ethical dilemmas need to be brought up first at the agency level in supervision, and if necessary in consultation with the agency's legal counsel, and the confidentiality of the client must always be protected. The next chapter delves more deeply into the question of how to apply specific social work methods in ways that recognize, honor, and capitalize on the cultural backgrounds of clients and how to address possible value-based conflicts.

Key Concepts

Individualistic societies societies that believe that the needs of the group or society are satisfied when needs of the individual are satisfied

Collectivistic societies societies that believe that an individual's needs are met when the needs of the group or society are met

Cultural norms values and beliefs that influence the attitudes and behaviors of different cultural groups and are learned from parents, teachers, peers, elders, religion, social clubs, and traditional rituals and practices

Hypothesis testing the use of existing cultural knowledge about cultural groups in a cautious or exploratory manner without arriving at any conclusions about clients or their cultures until more information is available

Dynamic sizing the ability to know when to generalize certain attitudes and behaviors exhibited by the client to other members of the same identity group (i.e., when certain norms or behaviors are culturally based and may be common to others in the identity group) and when to individualize (i.e., when they are a function of the client's personality and there is no cultural explanation for such behaviors or attitudes)

Culturally specific expertise the skills and abilities necessary to work effectively with individuals and groups from a particular culture by developing rapport and a strong client-worker alliance and achieving the desired outcomes when working with clients from that culture

Mestizaje the mixing of Native peoples of the Americas with people of Spanish and African ancestry

Familismo the strong identification with and attachment to a nuclear or extended family and a willingly accepted obligation to provide both material and emotional support to one's family

Personalismo the valuing of interpersonal relationships

Simpatia the cultural expectation among Latinos that individuals avoid conflict and act in a good-natured and pleasant way

11

Culturally Grounded Methods of Social Work Practice

PROFESSIONAL SOCIAL WORK IS A WESTERN INVENTION, BUT OFTEN IT IS taught as if its methods of interventions are culturally neutral. Because of this oversight, not only do practitioners run the risk of implementing interventions that are ineffective due to a lack of cultural fit between the intervention and the targeted population, but they also miss opportunities to incorporate culturally grounded ways of helping. For example, agencies and providers often target language as a key aspect of cultural diversity. A child welfare agency may develop policies to place foster children in families by matching the primary language spoken by the child while deemphasizing assessments of other relevant cultural factors. Although the agency workers are following an important component of a culturally grounded approach, reliance on language-matching addresses just one dimension of a successful culturally grounded intervention. When the desired results are not attained, there is a tendency to blame the client rather than to assess the cultural relevance of the service delivery system. The assimilationist model perpetuates the myth that if clients were just a little more like the white middle class, everything would be fine. Social workers must remember that the ultimate goal of any social work intervention is to serve, not to colonize (Aponte, 1994). Workers who are culturally unaware can easily become instruments of assimilation, misinterpreting difference as deviance or as a deficiency, and failing to recognize the strengths coming from culture that keep individuals and their families healthy.

Since the inception of the profession of social work in nineteenth-century England, most social work practice and research have focused on one-on-one interventions. Such models may feel natural and comfortable to many white middle-class clients and clients from other backgrounds who are acculturated or assimilated to mainstream culture. However, this individualistic approach may feel foreign or uncomfortable to others. In addition, definitions of well-being and happiness may vary between communities, and the means and approaches to intervene in times of crisis may vary as well.

Although the profession is now practiced globally and with clients from different cultural backgrounds, the cultural relevance of this traditional intervention is limited. One-on-one interventions present challenges because the social worker often has more power than the client does. As a result, the worker may unconsciously place her- or himself at the cultural center of the relationship, forcing the client to adjust to the cultural framework and the resulting boundaries imposed by the worker. Practitioners can greatly influence their clients' lives, and practitioners' actions in one-on-one interventions can affect their clients for better or for worse. Unlike family interventions, group work, and community interventions, which are naturally conducive to horizontal relationships and client participation and empowerment, one-on-one interventions require a conscious effort to place clients and their culture at the center of the worker-consumer relationship. Thus, when practitioners engage in one-on-one interventions with clients, it is important that culture play a central role in the design and choice of the intervention. The client's culture must be approached as a possible source of strength, and the worker must take into account and incorporate the cultural and spiritual beliefs and practices of the client from the beginning, at the intake and assessment points.

So-called culturally neutral services and methods tend to disregard the unique contributions and needs of different ethnic communities. These interventions often enforce the dominant narrative and reflect a view of the world that does not recognize or celebrate the client's cultural heritage. When working with clients from different cultural backgrounds, social workers need to ask themselves not only what the right type of intervention is for the presenting problem but also what the right type of intervention is for the client. If a one-on-one intervention is the answer to both questions, practitioners who are working with members of strongly collectivistic communities must find ways to integrate this type of intervention with a more collectivistic way of helping through group or family interventions. Change does not occur in isolation; new behaviors need to be rehearsed in social contexts as similar as possible to the daily life of the client.

CULTURALLY GROUNDED SOCIAL WORK WITH INDIVIDUALS AND THEIR FAMILIES

One way of implementing the culturally grounded approach in many agency settings is through family interventions. These interventions tend to pay close attention to the practitioner's impact on family members, and vice versa, focusing not only on the needs of individuals but taking into account the whole family system. Family interventions emphasize connections between individuals and view interactions systematically and structurally, but they seldom see families as networks that extend beyond the nuclear family. Different ethnic and identity groups may view their extended family networks in ways that need close exploration and understanding. For example, traditional Chinese identity is heavily influenced by relatives, and any attempt to empower an individual of Chinese background needs to involve or at least acknowledge all of the client's family members. Because interpersonal family relationships and harmony are very important in Chinese culture, social workers can best achieve the empowerment of clients as individuals by advocating for their rights and responsibilities in the context of their family roles and social statuses. The following set of principles can guide a culturally grounded approach to working with families.

1. Practitioners and families work together in relationships based on equality and respect.
2. Family members are a vital resource.
3. Practitioners enhance families and their capacity to support the growth and development of all family members: adults of all ages, youths, and children.
4. Interventions affirm and strengthen families' cultural, racial, and linguistic identities and enhance their ability to function in a multicultural society.
5. Practitioners are embedded in their communities and contribute to the community-building process.
6. Practitioners work with families to advocate services and systems that are fair, responsive, and accountable to the families served.
7. Practitioners work with families to mobilize formal and informal resources to support family development.
8. Interventions are flexible and continually responsive to emerging family and community issues.
9. Principles of family support are modeled in all program activities, including planning, governance, and administration. (Jepson, Thomas, Markward, Kelly, Koser, & Diehl, 1997).

Recognizing the key role of family is just the first step. The next step involves the recognition that families live in densely interconnected social networks. They are part of a neighborhood, a house of worship, a tribe, a clan, and/or an identity community such as the gay, transgender, or deaf community. The connection to other institutions or informal networks is a key element to consider during the assessment and action plan phases. Ignoring these connections may lead to misinterpretations and mistaken assessments. Note from the field 11.1 illustrates the strong connections between culture, mental health, spirituality, and religion, and how these links can affect assessment and family interventions. In this example, the social work intern effectively integrated the belief systems and spiritual dimensions of the presenting problem, which resulted in an appropriate course of action for the family. She might have chosen a behavioral approach instead, one that encouraged the client to replace her disturbing thoughts about her niece's

NOTE FROM THE FIELD 11.1
Let Her Soul Rest in Peace

Leticia is a bilingual (Spanish/English) advanced practice MSW intern at an elementary school situated on the outskirts of a large city in the Southwest. For several weeks, she has been working with a Mexican family who recently immigrated to the United States. In supervision, Leticia expresses concerns about her perceived lack of progress with the Rodriguez family. The two children continue to present symptoms of depression and anxiety. Their symptoms are very similar to those shown by their mother after a niece who lived with them committed suicide six months earlier. Mother and children have recurring dreams about the dead young woman. Leticia has been encouraged by her field supervisor to address this issue directly with the mother. At their next meeting, after a few minutes, the mother shares her concern that the lack of a proper burial prevents her niece from resting in peace and moving on to the other world. No funeral mass or blessing of any kind took place because, given her understanding of the Roman Catholic Church's stance on suicide, she believed that no priest would perform the ceremony. Leticia is encouraged by her supervisor to double-check this assumption with the local parish priest. The priest offers to visit the family, and together they agree to have a mass of remembrance and prayer for the deceased niece. The ritual provides closure, and the whole family is able to move on with their grieving process. Soon after, the family's depressive symptoms begin to dissipate.

suicide with happier memories of her. Such an approach would have been premature, as it neither identified nor addressed the crux of the family's dilemma. The acknowledgement of key cultural dimensions of family life (unresolved grief) and their connection to other key social systems (church) resulted in positive change.

Families, which are formed by individuals in committed relationships that may not involve biological ties, are one of the strongest institutions in the United States as well as the rest of the globe. However, American society is characterized by a high rate of divorce, out-of-marriage births, and little contact between members of divorced families. Not only does the United States have one of the highest rates of divorce in the world, with about half of all first marriages ending in divorce, but it also has a high rate of remarriage. Over three-fourths of those who divorce eventually remarry. As a result, about one child in five under the age of eighteen is a stepchild (Mechoulan, 2006). Nonetheless, despite dramatic changes in family structures over the last few decades, mainstream American culture tends to attach negative definitions to any form of family that does not conform to the traditional family structure of breadwinner father, homemaker mother, and their biological children.

Such dated beliefs about family are sometimes reflected in U.S. family policies, such as prohibitions and limitations on adoptions of children by gay couples and unmarried individuals. How families are formed is sometimes seen as more important than how well they perform essential functions for their members. Various efforts have aimed at regulating how families form without considering the needs of children first.

Families' different cultural backgrounds provide different cultural environments in which children become socialized. As part of that socialization process, children develop a worldview and a culture and learn how to interact with an outside environment that makes them aware of their race and ethnicity, often through the lens of racism, ethnocentrism, and acculturation. It is within this context that social workers best enact their roles as advocates and cultural mediators.

CULTURALLY GROUNDED SOCIAL WORK WITH GROUPS

Members of oppressed and disadvantaged communities face a host of barriers in their quest to advance socially, economically, and spiritually. Some of these difficulties emerge from misunderstandings concerning their cultural status, racial inequality, lack of support systems, and stereotypical media portrayals. These and other factors reinforce a master narrative of who these groups are, why they experience life as they do, and what change is possible for them. By employing a mutual aid approach, group work provides an effective counterforce to the devaluation of cultural identities that occurs when cultural minorities are cast as the "other." In groups, individuals can deconstruct and challenge stereotypical messages from the majority culture and can become aware of their own internalized oppression. The group helps them normalize their feelings and perceptions. Culturally grounded social work with groups connects individuals with their cultural roots and then explores what the group members have in common in terms of the past, the present, and their dreams for the future. This approach maximizes the potential of the members' narrative legacies and allows their commonalities to emerge. This culturally grounded process follows the identity development approach by helping group members to become aware of their identity in the context of their cultural background and its connection to their experience of oppression. Resources from the culture can be used creatively and respectfully to support this process as group members gain or regain awareness of their norms, values, and traditions. Group members from ethnic minority communities can share and support each other in their own challenges as they navigate between the two worlds represented by minority and majority communities.

Social workers of different identity backgrounds are often challenged to become familiar with the unique cultures that group members represent and the issues their communities are facing. Such knowledge is crucial for the effective facilitation of group activities. Regardless of their background, social workers can educate themselves about a community's historical traditions, cultural beliefs, and norms, and they can learn how to integrate appropriate styles of communication respectfully. They can also work to comprehend the magnitude and implications of the loss of culture and be conscious of the members' level of assimilation into the dominant culture.

Most social work with groups takes place within agency settings, and agencies customarily adopt a traditional "culturally neutral" approach to group facilitation. Group members are generally expected to absorb new knowledge, store it, and use it when needed. Freire (1994) described pedagogy of this type as "the banking approach to teaching," in which it is assumed that the teacher (worker) possesses something the student (client) needs but lacks. This approach is problematic because it pays no attention to the differences between the worker and the group members, relies on and reinforces client passivity, and disregards the complex contextual factors that contribute to the formation of the client's attitudes and behaviors.

Workers and clients perceive and evaluate their worlds differently. Developmental life experiences—as well as gender, sexual orientation, ability status, social class, and ethnicity—all shape an individual's worldview. When there are substantial differences in developmental factors and experiences, there are even greater gaps between what workers and clients perceive as valuable knowledge. Culturally grounded group work attempts to remedy this situation by rescuing and validating community-based narratives.

Clients who find their culture reflected in the substance and format of group interventions are more likely to be motivated to participate and to benefit from the experience. Group interventions that are grounded in the culture of the targeted population reflect and recognize norms of behavior and other cultural products of the group. Therefore, culturally grounded group work uses culture to inspire group members. The objective is to highlight the resiliency factors that are present in the evolving cultural narratives that emerge from the group members' communities.

One way to ground work in the culture of the group members is to utilize practices from ethnographic interviewing (see chapter 14). To develop empathy among all members of a therapeutic group, group sessions can begin with an ethnographic interview, during which group members are invited to identify important parts of their culture (Corey, 1992). The interview may include questions on how individuals think their culture will influence their participation in the group or what things each individual may see differently from the rest of the group because of a unique cultural background. If a taboo topic is identified by a group member, the group facilitator can help the group address the topic and develop a culturally appropriate strategy to know when avoidance of a topic is resistance, and when it is being avoided because the subject is taboo.

Group composition plays an important role in group outcomes. For example, the gender composition of the group has salient implications for group functioning (Martin & Shanahan, 1983). Therefore, it is possible for gender to operate like any other status characteristic during group work. If the practitioner or the other group members bring rigid expectations about appropriate male and female behavior to the group, those expectations may actually affect behaviors and perceptions. Note from the field 11.2 describes a case study where a group with a homogenous gender and cultural composition was used to address the needs of a specific

---

NOTE FROM THE FIELD 11.2
Missing School

Manuel Benitez is a school social worker assigned to the bilingual and multicultural program of a large urban midwestern school district. One of his roles is to monitor the academic achievement of students enrolled in the program who speak different languages. In a quarterly report to his supervisor, he notes an alarming trend among Arabic-speaking female middle school students. Their academic achievement continues to be very high, but they also have very high levels of absenteeism. Manuel interviews the Arabic-speaking teaching aides and learns that most of these girls are Palestinian and they are missing school so that they can visit their families' villages and refugee camps in preparation for prearranged marriages. He suggests the formation of an Arabic girls' group as a means to explore the situation and look for possible alternatives. Because he is male and does not speak Arabic, his first reaction was not to get involved and to find an Arabic-speaking female social worker to facilitate the group. His supervisor did not agree and encouraged Manuel to co-facilitate the group. He recruited an Arabic-speaking female social worker to co-facilitate the group with him. The two of them went together to all of the families' homes and explained the purpose of the group and asked them to sign permission slips allowing their daughters to attend the group. All except one of the mothers agreed to allow their daughters to participate in the group. The group members spoke mostly in Arabic and the co-facilitator summarized the exchanges for Manuel. How can the group leaders facilitate the group without alienating the group members from their families and culture?

cultural group. The homogeneous group composition in this example provided a safe environment where the young Arabic women were able to discuss the situation without being afraid of being judged by others.

Culture must be integrated from the pre-group phase to the formation and termination phases. Different cultures deal with conflict in different ways, and some individuals may not have a great need to express themselves verbally. Thus, culturally grounded group work takes into account not only the content of the group sessions, but the process itself, such that the "how" is as important as the "what."

CULTURALLY GROUNDED SOCIAL WORK WITH COMMUNITIES

Oppressed ethnic communities in the United States often are located in the bottom strata of income and wealth. Sometimes racism and discrimination become additional barriers to community development, and social workers may need to understand that in these ethnic communities, people often find themselves in powerless positions. Social work in such communities is rooted in the settlement house movement, during which social workers not only provided services to the community but also worked to empower marginalized groups. They organized communities, improved services, and administrated health programs. Although settlement houses still exist today (often in the form of community centers), they are under threat (Fabricant & Fisher, 2002b), and social work with communities in general is jeopardized by government downsizing and the abdication of responsibility to meet human needs. As a result, the importance of advocacy and client mobilization has increased. When working with communities, social workers need to remember that they "do not hold the answers to problems, but that in the context of collaboration, community members will develop the insights, skills, and capacity to resolve their own situations" (Gutierrez & Lewis, 1998, p. 8). Social workers build capacity for change by recognizing that members of the community live in oppressive circumstances that inhibit their ability to act effectively. When people begin to exercise control over the direction of their lives and have opportunities to join together to set priorities for their communities, their capacity for meeting personal and community goals is enhanced. The role of the community-building practitioner is to facilitate and strengthen the development of social networks as the means to support the development of strong communities that are able to exercise change and improve their living conditions (Fabricant & Fisher, 2002a).

It has been argued that community organizing has lost its purpose and relevance in post-industrial societies. Social and economic transformations produced by neoliberal policies ended the democratic/redistributive phase of community development and resulted in new forms of purposive social action aimed at achieving social justice (Newman, 2006). These new types of community organizing efforts tend to be at the grassroots level and are playing a significant role in the creation of a more just society for the most oppressed and vulnerable sectors of society (Fisher & Kling, 1994). Many contemporary community-based social movements are being organized by ethnic minority groups, women, youth groups, and other sectors of society that were not well represented in the old social movements that flourished between World War II and the 1970s. These new movements tend to be identity based (e.g., based on ethnicity, gender, sexual orientation). These community efforts toward change and transformation originate in a collective identity, or shared sense of self, and the organizing efforts that are inspired by this collective identity, which in turn reinforce the group's sense of identity. In this way, individuals achieve a collective sense that their shared identity is a source of oppression and at the same time can become a source of power through organizing (Duyvendak & Nederland, 2007).

The challenge for social workers who are practicing from a culturally grounded perspective is to bring together diverse grassroots efforts inspired by collective identities that share a geographic space and have similar social and political goals to form coalitions that can create lasting social change. Coalitions could help identity-centered efforts aim at lasting structural and policy changes beyond their own more limited change agendas.

FORMING COALITIONS WITHIN DIFFERENT ETHNO-CULTURAL COMMUNITIES

In recent years, given the increasing intensity and frequency of interethnic conflicts around the world, numerous forces have demonstrated the need for multiethnic coalitions. The Los Angeles riots in 1992 revived and refocused research on interethnic conflicts in the United States because they revealed the complexity of relationships between different ethnic groups. Political conflict between African American and Latino communities can reflect competition for scarce resources between these ethnic groups, overlaid by conflict between immigrant and resident populations. Nationalistic interests and the interests of different ethnic groups also contribute to inter- and intra-racial and ethnic group tensions. Many grassroots efforts are concerned about the lack of recognition of common interests across communities and a rise in competition among groups on issues like jobs, education, housing, health care, crime control, and the role of government. At the same time, there has been a decline in the role played by mediating institutions like religious organizations, unions, and political parties in addressing these community issues.

The creation of cross-cultural alliances and coalitions may very well be an important step in decreasing the level of cultural and ideological fragmentation that characterizes many urban centers around the globe. When members of communities focus exclusively on their cultural differences, the resulting fragmentation tends to obscure the problems that they have in common, such as power differentials, privilege, access to resources and services, and wealth. Coalitions are a way of organizing across group lines to address these inequalities. While differences in multiethnic and racial communities are important, coalitions can provide a mechanism to take action around common interests on issues such as employment, income, housing, and medical care. Whereas at the macro level, these differences may be very difficult to reconcile, short-term and issue-oriented multiethnic coalitions that develop at the neighborhood level may be able to surmount these differences around more specific issues. One strategy available to less powerful ethnic groups is the formation of partnerships with more established groups. Such coalitions are necessary to enhance the chances that less influential groups will be incorporated in a dominant local coalition.

As coalitions addressing a variety of social and health problems become more common, research has begun to identify the factors associated with effective coalitions. Butterfoss, Goodman, and Wandersman (1996) found the effectiveness of the coalition's leadership, staff-committee relations, organizational climate, the coalition members' influence on decision making, and community linkages to be associated with member participation and satisfaction. Interestingly, these factors did not directly influence the quality of the coalitions' plans or the primary outcomes of coalition activities. A case study of two health promotion coalitions found that their effectiveness was related to a number of diverse factors. Most important were a grassroots rather than bureaucratic source of vision; more staff time devoted to coalition organizing activities than to the daily maintenance of the organization; a backstage role for staff in carrying out coalition activities, which allows coalition leaders to have a more visible role; frequent and productive communication among staff and members; high levels of cohesiveness; a more complex coalition structure during the intervention phase; and intensive and ongoing training and technical assistance (Kumpfer, Turner, Hopkins, & Librett, 1993).

The theoretical and empirical literature on multiethnic coalition building is limited; however, many explanations for why people form coalitions point to the self-interest of individuals and groups and the realization that cooperation can maximize their benefits. Carmichael and Hamilton (1967) presented four requirements for successful multiethnic coalitions: (1) recognition of the interests of each party, (2) a shared belief that each party in the coalition stands to benefit, (3) acceptance that each party has its own base of power and decision making, and (4) agreement that the coalition must deal with specific and identifiable goals and issues. Shared views and ideologies may also be a prerequisite for the development of effective alliances based on a set of common interests.

Before functional coalitions can be developed, divisive issues like nationalism and identity politics may need to be addressed. Multicultural change is a process that recognizes the difference between groups while increasing interaction and cooperation between them, and recognizing differences and building bridges at the community level. Issues that may compromise or limit the effectiveness of a coalition include nationalistic ideologies, intense ethnic solidarity, and cultural and class differences that create barriers between its members. In addition, differences in group size, economic status, and resources can interfere with the coalition-building process.

In sum, a shared minority status does not automatically facilitate the formation of social and political coalitions. Members of ethno-cultural minority communities form coalitions as they recognize their differences and honor their intergroup heterogeneity. Ideally, on the long list of issues that different groups bring to the table, a shared set of concerns can be identified. It is around the short list of shared issues or grievances that the social worker supports the formation of community coalitions and facilitates the identification of the shared power the coalition members have.

FOSTERING CULTURAL COMPETENCE IN AGENCIES AND AMONG STAFF

It is important for agencies to make an effort to become culturally competent and to be welcoming to different ethno-racial communities. The agency space itself—the behavior of the receptionist, the decor of the waiting room, and the way in which the social workers' offices are organized—can determine whether or not clients feel welcome. A very small reception area and clinical offices with one desk and two chairs are often the norm in agencies, even though cultural minority clients tend to seek help as a family or arrive accompanied by members of their extended family, family of choice, or other members of their support network. When there is no physical space for them, the message, whether intentional or unintentional, is that people in the client's support network are not welcome.

There are generally two main avenues to attain cultural competence in work with different ethno-cultural communities: culturally specific agencies and culturally specific outreach programs within existing "culturally neutral" service-delivery systems. Both of these avenues have advantages and shortcomings: unfortunately, culturally specific agencies tend to lack technology and have fewer resources, while larger mainstream agencies with outreach programs run the risk of treating outreach to minority cultures as an add-on to their regular agency services.

Culturally specific social service agencies were developed in response to Native American, immigrant, and religious groups' search for grassroots solutions to their problems. For example, as a response to a lack of bicultural and bilingual social workers, many Latino communities around the nation have started Latino-centered agencies. Social workers in these agencies often play a cultural mediation role as their clients navigate the acculturation process, helping them to access opportunities and advance economically and socially. To mediate effectively between these two worlds, workers need to be familiar with both cultures and ideally in both languages. However, the reality is that the availability of bilingual and bicultural social workers is limited, so social workers who are not bicultural are being trained by ethnic-specific agencies to provide culturally competent diagnostics and develop treatment plans for ethnic minority clients.

Culturally specific outreach programs within existing "culturally neutral" service-delivery systems are also very common among established social service agencies. These agencies recognize the need to serve minority ethno-cultural clients and are aware of their own lack of culturally grounded services and outreach programs. Thus in order to address their lack of cultural specificity, these agencies establish outreach programs staffed by members of the targeted community. These outreach programs are created as appendices to the main organizational and leadership structures, and the minority constituencies are often not well represented in governing board and executive positions. Starting an outreach program is certainly a commendable effort, but representation in the decision-making and supervisory roles is very important in order to ensure a horizontal rather than a subservient relationship with the main agency structure.

Regardless of the organizational pathway that an agency follows, staff must remember to avoid stereotyping the minority client and to keep in mind that every population is heterogeneous and every individual is unique. In order to avoid ethnocentrism, clients should be regarded as experts in the interpretation of their own symptoms, strengths, and treatment preferences.

While working with cultural minority communities, the worker must examine the insider-outsider role as part of any practice effectiveness assessment. Acceptance of the role of the outsider often allows the process of enculturation to begin. Enculturation into a different culture does not mean pretending to be someone else, but rather gaining familiarity and respect for a different cosmology or worldview. It is a long process, and it requires patience, open minds, and open hearts. This process can be monitored in supervision, and contradictory feelings can be identified and sorted out.

Social workers may turn to supervisors for guidance, or they may turn to a colleague in a type of interaction called peer consultation. Peer consultation allows the social worker to receive critical yet supportive feedback within an egalitarian relationship in which neither party has official responsibility for evaluating the other's performance. In work with members of an unfamiliar community, consultation with a cultural expert (such as those discussed in the next chapter) is highly recommended. Note from the field 11.3 illustrates a possible strategy

---

NOTE FROM THE FIELD 11.3
Doña Matilde's Stamp of Approval

During a family violence prevention campaign involving *curanderas* (Latina traditional healers), the social worker coordinating the campaign engages the help of Doña Matilde, a well-respected *curandera* in the community who is originally from the Dominican Republic, as the liaison with the other women. Doña Matilde helps develop the contact list, co-signs the invitations to the planning meeting, and co-facilitates the meeting, which is held in her own home. Her role and respected status in the community give the effort immediate credibility. The social worker also gains credibility because at the meeting, Doña Matilde introduces Ms. Adler as a good person who cares about the community's children and youths.

---

for workers to follow when seeking entry into an unfamiliar community. These consultants should be paid and must adhere to the same professional standards as any other form of consultation, such as confidentiality. Community-based cultural consultants are best identified through referrals.

Either through supervision, consultation, or a combination of the two, practitioners can reach out when confronted by ethical dilemmas connected to cultural differences. Ethical dilemmas with a cultural basis often emerge when cultural practices and norms appear to be in conflict with the standards set by the Code of Ethics of the National Association of Social Workers. For example, clients may express their appreciation for the social worker's assistance in traditional cultural ways that cross professional boundary lines. A family may ask the worker to become their child's godparent. In these cases, a combination of cultural expert and professional consultation may be advisable in order to arrive at the best ethical decision without alienating or offending community members.

The repertoire of social work methods and interventions utilized by a given agency may not meet culturally grounded standards. If a type of intervention does not feel right to a worker, the chances are very high that it will not feel right to her or his clients. Social workers should listen to their "culturally grounded radar" and explore possible reasons why such feelings of discomfort emerge. Social workers may think that they do not know how to work across cultural boundaries and may perceive themselves to be lacking the awareness and knowledge needed for competent practice. Not honoring their own knowledge and experiences makes them vulnerable to adopting simplistic recipes that may result in oppressive approaches to practice. Honoring knowledge and common sense can be a much better starting point for professional growth and effective practice. An important question to ask is "How can I be more in tune with and responsive to the values and norms of my clients?" Social workers need to ask how their practice is consistent with their own norms and values and those of the profession. The practitioner's own background and professional experience, however, may not be sufficient to reconcile contradictions and gaps in her or his practice. If she or he cannot interpret or understand certain value conflicts, the practitioner should probably seek the assistance of a cultural expert from the community. It is not up to the social worker to decide in isolation what is the best culturally grounded practice for her or his clients.

In order to ensure that they are practicing culturally grounded social work, workers must screen evidence-based practices for cultural specificity. Interventions can be culturally biased even after going through the most rigorous effectiveness tests such as randomized trials. Workers must consider sample composition and contextual factors before unconditionally embracing science-based interventions. Issues of fidelity (Was the intervention carried out as designed?) and sustainability (How long lasting are the desired outcomes?) need to be considered as well. Very effective but short-lived interventions may not be the ideal vehicle for sustainable change in resource-poor communities. The blending of traditional helping systems (discussed in the next chapter) and practices with innovative science-based approaches is suggested as the next generation of intervention research.

When the assumptions or ideology behind social work interventions are not questioned, ethnocentric ideas can be perpetuated. Culturally grounded social work practice requires critical thinking and constant assessment of the needs of clients and the assets arising from their cultures, assets that can be tapped to propel transformative change. Identifying those assets and utilizing them effectively are part of an ongoing assessment of what is essential and what is not essential in the client's culture.

Key Concepts

Culturally grounded one-on-one interventions individualized ways of helping that approach culture as a possible source of strength for the individual, starting at the intake and assessment points

Culturally grounded family interventions interventions that emphasize connections between individuals and view interactions systematically and structurally, and in which the nuclear and extended family are approached as support networks

Culturally grounded social work with groups interventions that connect individuals with their cultural roots and explore what the group members have in common in terms of the past, the present, and their dreams for the future

12

Culturally Grounded Community-Based Helping

UNTIL RECENTLY, TRADITIONAL HEALTH SYSTEMS WITH NON-WESTERN worldviews served the therapeutic needs of virtually every human group. Although these are important systems for delivering care, professionals trained in the West generally have little understanding of and tolerance for them. A professional degree is always desirable, but it does not necessarily guarantee culturally appropriate or effective services. There is much knowledge and service effectiveness to be gained through partnerships with paraprofessionals and traditional community-based helpers. Knowledge and experience come in different forms and are passed on in different ways.

Paraprofessionals can play a vital role in supporting the delivery of effective high-quality services. For example, a study comparing the effectiveness of three types of counselors—professional counselors with at least a bachelor's degree and no background of addiction, paraprofessional counselors who are addicts in recovery, and paraprofessional counselors who have no history of drug addiction—found no differences between the professional and paraprofessional counselors in their overall effectiveness (Aiken, LoSciuto, & Ansetto, 1984). Culturally and community-based helpers often bring life experiences and unique skills and knowledge of the community, which compensate for the lack of a higher academic degree, to professional teams. Often, many of the needs of clients can be channeled through traditional practitioners, but other physical and mental health needs require access to mainstream care systems. The two systems can complement each other, and the culturally grounded social worker can play the role of cultural mediator between the two systems. This chapter will review some of the culturally based helpers and paraprofessionals used by social service agencies and different cultural groups, and the important roles they play in the lives of clients. Social workers are encouraged to incorporate these traditional folk healers and other paraprofessionals and to view these individuals as professional colleagues, as they represent a source of therapeutic help and can make valuable contributions to the well-being of clients.

PARAPROFESSIONALS

Paraprofessionals are aides who are often hired by social service agencies because of their cultural familiarity with the community the agency serves. Paraprofessionals receive direct supervision from a professional regarding the planning, delivery, and processing of services.

Social services agencies often employ paraprofessionals who are familiar with the community the agency serves. Paraprofessionals have generally not completed a course of formal training leading to professional credentialing in the field, or if they have completed such a course, it may not be recognized in this country.

One service that paraprofessionals often provide is interpretation. Many clients from cultural minority backgrounds, particularly refugees and other immigrants, may not speak English or may not feel comfortable communicating in English. Paraprofessionals are often used in social service agencies as interpreters of not only the language but also clients' affect and tone, as well as other cultural aspects of communication. They can advise practitioners on whether a client's attitudes and behaviors are considered the norm and are acceptable in the culture of origin. For example, refugees and other immigrants, who have various mental health needs as they adjust to a new life in the United States, are often unfamiliar with Western social services. Their English may be limited, and they may experience cultural prohibitions that act as barriers to their ability to access services. In such cases, agencies may engage paraprofessionals who are bilingual and bicultural to provide interpretation services to bridge the cultural and linguistic gap between services and clients. Thus, paraprofessionals who are indigenous to the community are an ideal source of support and make valuable team members. They are effective at establishing trusting relationships with the people they serve. Nonetheless, because of the close networks in many immigrant and ethnic minority communities, one primary concern is confidentiality. Once hired by a social service agency, a paraprofessional must be trained and oriented to the profession and its code of ethics. Paraprofessionals must practice the same ethical standards as the professionals in the agency in terms of confidentiality. Paraprofessionals may be unfamiliar with such concepts, and it may be inadequate merely to provide them with written material to review. A face-to-face orientation that offers opportunities for exchange and debriefing is needed.

Because most social workers in the United States are English monolingual, interpreters are often a key part of social services delivery teams. There are several guidelines that agencies and workers should observe in working with interpreters. Use only certified interpreters. If they are not available in your community, recruit your own, but provide them with comprehensive training. Ask a native speaker to help you check candidates' fluency and familiarity with social service and mental health vocabulary. When meeting with clients,

1. Introduce yourself and introduce the interpreter. Explain to the client the role each one of you plays and how you work together so that she or he will receive the best services available.
2. Always look at the client when speaking to her or him, and look at the interpreter only when you are talking to her or him. When the client speaks, look at her or him and express empathy. Do not give her or him a blank look.
3. Avoid saying to the interpreter, "Ask him . . ." or "Tell her. . . ." Speak in the first person; the interpreter will do the same.
4. Speak in short units of speech—do not use long, involved sentences. Interpreters often use the consecutive interpreting format. In this system, the worker and client take turns speaking, and the interpreter interprets at the end of each turn. The longer either party talks, the greater is the possibility of error.
5. Be patient. An interpreted interview takes longer. Careful interpretation often requires the interpreter to provide long explanations. Not all words and concepts exist in other languages; therefore, interpreting in another language may require more words to express the same meaning.
6. Expect that the interpreter may occasionally pause to ask you for an explanation or clarification of terms in order to provide an accurate interpretation.
7. Agree on some basic rules when interviewing a family. For example, only one person speaks at a time; otherwise it will be difficult for the interpreter to translate.
8. Avoid colloquialisms, abstractions, idiomatic expressions, slang, similes, and metaphors.
9. The interpreter will relay all that is said in the presence of the client, will not omit anything that is said, and will not make remarks to others in the room that the client does not understand.
10. Listen to the client and watch for nonverbal communication. Often you can learn a lot by observing facial expressions, voice intonations, and body language.
11. Repeat important information more than once. Always give the reason or purpose for an intervention or referral, and engage the client in all decisions.
12. Check the accuracy of the interpretation by asking the client to repeat in her or his own words any important information or instructions that have been communicated, with the interpreter facilitating (University of Michigan Health System Interpreter Services, 2007).

Third-party translation is ideally a temporary stage. The recommended path is for social workers working with a specific language group to learn that language. There is no substitute for direct communication between the worker and the client. Even the most efficient interpreter creates distance in the therapeutic relationship.

CULTURALLY BASED HELPERS AND HEALERS

Whereas a middle-class European American client may believe that she is empowered to address health challenges in a self-reliant manner, a Latina client may be perceived as possessing a fatalistic or passive attitude of *si Dios quiere* (God willing). A Haitian client may subscribe to a belief system in which good health is viewed as the ability to achieve equilibrium between *cho* (hot) and *fret* (cold), and illness is attributed to spiritual imbalances. These beliefs lead to the expectation that illness should be treated through both natural practices (herbs and human touch) and those that address supernatural forces.

Spirituality can be a strong component of the client's cosmology, and social workers are learning more and more about how to explore the spiritual aspects of their clients' lives. Culture shapes spiritual beliefs, especially during a crisis event such as bereavement, and affects how the crisis is processed and resolved. Because spirituality may oppress or liberate the client, spirituality may or may not contribute to the client's empowerment. For example, social workers may need to help a client reflect upon or reframe deeply held religious beliefs if those beliefs are leading the client to blame herself for being a victim of domestic violence. It is through an exploration of the client's narratives and the respectful empathy that the social worker provides in response that the strengths arising from spirituality can be separated from beliefs that may be harmful. As evidence that spiritual practices and beliefs can play a role in a client's recovery mounts, social workers are seeking to improve their understanding of their clients' spiritual resources through the assessment process and one-on-one interventions.

Organized religion is one source through which spirituality is channeled, and it serves to reinforce spiritual and cultural practices, norms, and values. Some religions foster a type of spirituality that provides consolation, inspiration, and guidance and may promote responsibility, identity, and community building. On the other hand, other forms of organized religion may lead followers to resist change, implicitly promote self-blame, or encourage a fatalistic or passive perspective on life problems. In these instances, the social worker can engage with the client in a process of reflection to distinguish between the prescribed norms and behaviors that are helpful and the ones that are harmful. Learning about the basic tenets of the client's religion will assist the social worker to understand the client's behavior better and to identify possible misunderstandings. Having good working relationships with pastors, shamans, priests, rabbis, and other clergy in the community can be beneficial in arranging the consultations that are often needed. Thus understanding clients' spirituality is helpful at least at two levels. First, it provides the social worker with an understanding of the client's perceived purpose in life that may help explain the rationale for many behaviors and family patterns. Second, it helps the social worker understand the subjectively perceived spiritual forces that may serve as cues or motivations for the client's behavioral changes (Pellebon & Anderson, 1999).

Native American Traditions

Social work practitioners may feel challenged when working with clients from cultures in which needs and crises are explained by supernatural factors and addressed by spiritual powers and influences. Practitioners cannot address the needs of traditional Native American clients in isolation, as if the presenting problems were only psychosocial phenomena. Native American medicine men and women (sometimes called shamans) have traditionally performed the Western roles of physician, psychiatrist, and spiritual leader (Lange, 1988). Working in partnership with shamans and other tribal healers is congruent with Saleebey's (2002) strengths perspective, and using traditional healing methods in addition to mainstream interventions may prove very valuable. As note from the field 12.1 demonstrates, social workers can play an important role in assisting clients who use traditional healers and methods of healing in addition to standard social work interventions.

Some Native American communities have medicine men and women who use rituals and herbs to cure ailments. Individuals who practice Native American religions believe that disease as well other forms of mental, spiritual, and physical unbalance are produced by a disruption of intrapersonal and interpersonal connections between the physical self (the body), the mental self (the mind), and the spiritual self (the soul/spirit). The individual aims at nurturing a good relationship with other human beings, the forces of the universe, and divine forces bigger than the individual (Wills, 2007). Therefore, the medicine man or woman's most important task is to maintain and restore harmony and health in the world through magical manipulation of daily life that affects the relationship of the individual with the forces of the cosmos.

Integrating traditional ways of healing with social work interventions may increase success in work with members of traditional Native American communities. For example, the Cheyenne River Indian Reservation in South Dakota approved a delinquency prevention program and an alcohol treatment program using traditional methods such as sweat lodges, the pipe fast, and the Sun Dance (Voss, Douville, Soldier, & Twiss, 1999). Since the 1980s there has been a resurgence of traditional healing methods across the nation's Native American communities, but this often has not been strictly tribal in nature, as many communities have lost their connection with some of their traditional ways of healing. Encultu-

NOTE FROM THE FIELD 12.1

Ho'oponopono

Scott is a social worker in a family social service agency in Kona, Hawaii. The Waipa family is having a difficult time with eighteen-year-old Lana, who has applied and has been accepted to a college on the mainland. Her parents, grandparents, uncles, and aunts are upset, mostly because she did not say anything about it until she received her letter of acceptance from the university congratulating her on her admission. Scott suggests the use of *ho'oponopono*.

Ho'oponopono is a traditional mediation process that Native Hawaiian families use to settle arguments, resolve hurt feelings, and mediate family conflicts. It is rooted in the Hawaiian values of respect for extended families, an emphasis on maintaining harmony in relationships, and the fostering of goodwill. The process is designed to restore harmony in the family. When an important issue arises, a member of the family is chosen as the leader, who mediates the process. The discussion encompasses therapeutic aspects like identification of the problem, consideration of its effects on the family system, possible solutions, and ways to implement the chosen solution (Hurdle, 2002).

The session takes place at home and the grandmother is chosen to lead it. Scott attends to support the family in the process, but he does not speak during the session.

ration efforts have been implemented by tribal government councils and other leaders to balance the erosion of traditional healing practices resulting from acculturation. A study conducted among the Yupik people found that more traditional tribal members as well as those who had gone through a process of enculturation used traditional healing practices more often than other tribal members and were in better health than more acculturated members who used only Western medical services (Wolsko, Lardon, Mohatt, & Orr, 2007). Social workers need to assess the availability and quality of traditional healing services, assess levels of acculturation, and develop connections with medicine men and women and other healers in order to make effective referrals when necessary.

African American–Centered Approaches

There is a long and rich history of African American indigenous healers and folk healing, which blends some aspects of traditional African healing with coping practices that emerged as a response to the experience of slavery. In African

American cultures, representatives of organized religion such as ordained ministers and clerics play a very important role as helpers, especially in matters of mental health or psychological distress (Harley, 2005). Many African American cultures also make use of other healers who are not connected to organized religion, such as hoodoo priests. Hoodoo's magic healing is based on African folk medicine, which evolved in the United States and is sometimes called conjure. The American Southern hoodoo has much in common with Haitian voodoo, and both traditions can be traced to specific regions in Africa such as the Congo and those inhabited by the Igbo, Yoruba, and Bambara (Mitchem, 2007). In some areas of the South, some of these practices are still common among the elderly in general, but more so in rural communities. Many communities in the South have a strong connection to the original African cultures brought to the country by the slaves (Patterson, 2005). The historical unavailability of institutional health care in many of the black communities made the folk healer the preferred, most reliable, and most cost-effective option for many African Americans (Mitchem, 2007).

Folk healing in the African American community is as much about relationships as it is about responding to specific health needs and providing treatments (Fett, 2002). Social work interventions with African Americans are increasingly attempting to connect to traditional and informal helping systems that are present in communities in order to increase their effectiveness. African American–centered family healing, for example, aims at integrating communal knowledge, communal values, and existing mental health constructs as part of mental health treatment interventions (Elijah, 2002). The focus of the intervention and the main change-producing agent are the family and the healing powers connected to African American culture. The family is seen as an interdependent system whose members can all support one another to overcome stressors. A culturally grounded perspective views the family as the main source of healing, while social workers are encouraged to be social healers, meaning that they can work with the family in its effort to heal its relationship to the rest of society and to identify and address sources of oppression such as racism and their effects on the well-being of family members.

Afrocentric approaches rely on strengths from the culture, but those strengths may or may not be present in families and communities. Many of the healing and coping mechanisms that have been used historically by members of different African American communities have been quantified and standardized. For example, the Africultural Coping Systems Inventory is a thirty-item measure consisting of culturally grounded coping strategies based on an African American–centered framework (Utsey, 2000). The strategies are categorized along four dimensions: cognitive/emotional debriefing, spiritual-centered coping, collective coping, and ritual-centered coping. This measurement tool can be useful at the assessment stage and can provide the practitioner with information about the client's level of connection to her or his culture of origin. The absence of any of these dimensions can be explored, and actions can be taken to enhance and strengthen these connections when appropriate.

African American women in many communities around the nation provide informal support to each other through what has been called "kitchen talk," informal gatherings of friends around the kitchen table during which they eat and talk about whatever is in their hearts and on their minds (Robinson & Howard-Hamilton, 2000). In contrast to mainstream support groups, kitchen talk groups integrate individuals' communications with a variety of healing rituals (Harley, 2006).

African American healing practices and beliefs can be integrated into social work through a narrative approach. For example, Parks (2007) suggests several questions regarding coping strategies, spirituality, and the use of ritual that can be used as a point of departure to help the social worker integrate specific coping mechanisms and beliefs into social work practice.

1. Describe your most helpful coping and problem-solving strategies. How do you make sense of your problems and life difficulties?
2. How does spirituality play a role in your life? How do you benefit from spirituality in your life? How do you believe good and evil play a role in your life? What are your beliefs about death?
3. What activities do you feel strengthen your bonds with your family members? How do you honor your ancestors? What activities make you feel a connection to your community?
4. Are there any folk beliefs or healing practices that are important to you? How comfortable do you feel talking about them with relatives and friends?
5. What meaning do you give to your dreams? Describe how your dreams provide insight into your life.
6. Do you have a family or community advisor or a spiritual advisor? If so, describe how she or he has played an important part in your life. What would she or he say about your problem or life's difficulties? Imagine and then describe a positive image that you can use as a resource to draw upon your strengths.

Healers in the Latino Community

The folk healing tradition of the Spanish-speaking Caribbean is the product of a centuries-old process of spiritual and cultural syncretism between the pre-Colombian, African, and Spanish Roman Catholic traditions. This culturally blended form of spirituality is called *espiritismo* (spiritism) and is a valuable resource for assisting clients with their medical needs as well as with their psychosocial and emotional needs (Rivera, 2005). Owing to the underrepresentation of Latinos in higher education in general and in social work in particular, paraprofessionals are commonly found in Latino-centered agencies. In such agencies, paraprofessionals may include *promotoras* (health educators), *curanderos* (healers), *herbolarios* (herbalists), and *parteras* (midwives). *Promotoras* have been employed for many years by agencies to conduct home visits, primarily for carrying out prevention interventions. Home visits by *promotoras* have improved the health outcomes of families (Martin, Camargo, Ramos, Lauderdale, Krueger, & Lantos, 2005). *Promotoras* (this role is generally filled by women; men are called *promotores*) are trained bicultural and bilingual Latina lay community health advisors who can play important roles in increasing the Latino community's awareness of the risks of certain diseases. They distribute information and make appropriate referrals, educate the community, provide emotional support, build the community, and advocate (May, Bowman, Ramos, Rincones, Rebollar, Rosa, et al., 2003). In addition, they provide a link between the community and the health care system. Lack of fluency in English and the lack of education, coupled with low socioeconomic status, act as barriers to health care access for some Latino families. In these cases, *promotoras* are a bridge between the community and needed services.

Curanderism is a form of natural and practical medicine that works well with the Mexican American population, as well as with other Latino subgroups (Trotter & Chavira, 1997). These traditional healers are called upon to perform curative rituals and are often thought to have more authority and power than mental health professionals do (Zea, Quezada, & Belgrave, 1994). Some illnesses, such as *empacho* (upset stomach) and *susto* (fright), are believed to come from supernatural sources and as such are much more effectively treated by *curanderos*. Since different Latino communities use *curanderos* and *curanderas* (female *curanderos*) in different ways, in work with Latinos, it is essential to take into account the folk beliefs of the particular community to which the clients belong, and the community's possibly unique use of *curanderos*. *Curanderos* believe that human beings occupy a natural world that interacts with, and even infuses, various parts of the self. The restoration of good health requires that these parts of the self and their connections to the natural world be brought into harmony. *Curanderos* blend some aspects of the Catholic tradition with indigenous non-Western medicinal beliefs and practices. As note from the field 12.2 illustrates, involving *curanderos* and other community-based paraprofessionals as partners in interventions may require special and creative forms of communication and outreach.

Parteras, or midwives, also play an important role among Latino women. Home visits by lay workers may be more acceptable to pregnant women than a visit to a nurse or a doctor, which may have an impact on health outcomes as well as social and environmental risk factors. It has been demonstrated that home visits increase the use of preventive services by pregnant women and encourage healthier behaviors (Biermann, Dunlop, Brady, Dubin, & Brann, 2006). For

---

NOTE FROM THE FIELD 12.2

More Condoms, Please!

At the beginning of the AIDS pandemic, a group of Latino social workers became involved with an HIV/AIDS service agency to address the prevention needs of the Latino community in a large midwestern city. The agency already had an information hotline, and the committee agreed to staff a Spanish-language hotline. A number was secured, training was conducted, and bilingual volunteers took turns staffing the hotline. Days, weeks, and months went by, but community members were not calling. The committee reassessed their strategy and concluded that a hotline was not a culturally grounded approach to reaching out to the target population. After a long brainstorming session, they decided to try a completely different strategy. They invited all the *curanderas* they knew in the city and offered them training on "HIV/AIDS 101." A dozen *curanderas* accepted the invitation. They were receptive to the information but often had much better insight into the issues than the professional trainers. They agreed to include safer sex as part of their discussions with their visitors. Rosa, one of the trainers, was concerned about distributing condoms at the end of the session, a common practice in all agency-sponsored trainings. She decided to leave a basket full of condoms on the table and say nothing because she did not want to offend the women. At the end of the training, the women in attendance opened their purses and filled them with as many condoms as they were able to carry. Doña Teresa commented that she had grandchildren and many of her neighbors had children and grandchildren and then asked: "Do you have any more condoms?" At the end of the session, the basket was empty.

---

women who have a strong cultural identity, home visits may even affect psychological functioning. Some *parteras* actually assist with the home delivery of babies, a practice that may align with the client's rural traditions and also provides an alternative for undocumented pregnant women who are unwilling or unable to receive care in a health center.

Herbolarios and *herbolarias* (female *herbolarios*) identify and categorize herbs according to their medicinal properties and look at clients' patterns of food intake in order to address ailments. Herbs are used to fight both physical and emotional ailments. One study in Mexico found that 83 percent of family physicians accept the therapeutic use of herbal medicines, while 100 percent of nurses and other non-MD health workers accept them, and 90 percent of patients use herbs (Taddei-Bringas, Santillana-Macedo, Romero-Cancio, & Romero-Tellez,

1999). The help of herbalists is sought not only by Latinos, but by traditional African Americans, Native Americans, and Chinese Americans, among other groups.

Asian Americans and Healing

Asian Americans have one of the highest use rates of complementary and alternative medicine (CAM) of all ethnic minority groups in the United States. A large California-based study found that three out of four Asian American respondents had used at least one type of CAM in the past twelve months, which is significantly higher than the national prevalence rate. Chinese Americans reported the highest prevalence of any CAM use (86%), while South Asians reported the lowest prevalence (67%). In contrast with other ethnic groups, acculturation and access to conventional medical care was unrelated to any CAM use for most Asian American subgroups. The study found that spirituality was the strongest predictor of CAM use for most Asian American subgroups (Hsiao, Wong, Goldstein, Becerra, Cheng, & Wegner, 2006).

Traditional Chinese medicine is a rational healing system developed and perfected over 5,000 years in China and used by the descendants of Chinese immigrants in the United States and all over the world (Ng, 2006). Traditional Chinese medicine is based on the ancient Taoist idea of unity of the opposites of yin and yang. Health is believed to emerge from the balance of the yin and yang of the body, mind, and spirit, while disease emerges when there is no balance. The balance of yin and yang is achieved or restored through a combination of methods such as the use of herbs, acupuncture, corrective posture techniques, and exercise.

Many Asian Americans and clients of other ethnic backgrounds bring with them ideas about healing that can be traced to Buddhism. In many regards, Buddhism and other traditional philosophies such as traditional Chinese medicine are very well aligned with social work approaches to culturally grounded interventions. Buddhism looks for the relationship between the biological, physical, mental, and spiritual dimensions of healing. Social workers interacting with clients whose beliefs are influenced by Buddhism can emphasize their holistic approach and avoid separating the psychosocial aspects of a presenting problem from the overall aim of achieving balance. Buddhists understand good health to be the result of a balanced interaction between mind and body, as well as between life and its environment ("Buddhism and Health," 1996).

Elderly Asian and Asian American clients may have a much deeper connection to traditional beliefs than do their children and grandchildren, as a result of the process of acculturation. However, the whole family system is probably affected by these beliefs, and as such they can be a good entry point for interventions. For example, mindfulness and meditation are often integrated into social work interventions. In Buddhism, mindfulness is a skill that allows the individual to be aware of what is happening in the moment and to be less reactive. *Sati,* the word for "mindfulness" in Pali, the language of the earliest Buddhist canon, connotes awareness, attention, and remembering (Germer, 2005). Mindfulness has been shown to have important clinical value in complementing treatment efforts to address stress, depression, eating disorders, and addictions (Ostafin, Chawla, Bowen, Dillworth, Witkiewitz, & Marlatt, 2006). Chawla and Marlatt (2006) encourage clinicians to incorporate techniques for achieving mindfulness in their practice with Asian Americans and other clients as well as engage in the personal practice of meditation as a means to connect with the client.

ASSESSING CLIENTS' CONNECTIONS TO TRADITIONAL HEALING BELIEFS AND PRACTICES

David Haber (2005) offers a set of open-ended questions to assess the client's level of connection to traditional healing beliefs and practices that can be incorporated into the assessment phase of the culturally grounded approach with clients from different cultures:

1. What do you think causes your specific health problem?
2. What is your favorite home remedy or other treatment that you turn to when you are experiencing this health problem?
3. Do you know others who have had a similar health problem, and what do they do to treat it?
4. Do you think there is a way to prevent this health problem, and, if so, how?
5. How is the tradition of health care in your heritage different from the type of help you receive at the hospitals or clinics in the United States?
6. Do you have problems getting the help you need from doctors and other American health care professionals, and if so, why?
7. Who else besides doctors and other American health care professionals do you rely on for help with health problems?
8. Do you keep your doctors and other American health care professionals informed about other sources of health care that you are receiving?
9. Are you active in a religious institution or religious or spiritual group, and are health services provided there?
10. Is there a religious healer or leader who can help support the management of your health problem?

When assessments reveal that clients have a strong connection with cultural healing beliefs and practices, it is important that social workers, in addition to implementing culturally competent interventions, make use of the expertise of community helpers and healers. The integration of indigenous and innovative approaches not only will advance science but will strengthen culturally grounded social work practice.

Key Concepts

Paraprofessionals aides who assist professionals and are often social service agency employees who are usually hired because of their cultural familiarity with the community the agency serves

Shamans Native American medicine men and women who use spiritual rituals and herbs to cure ailments

Promotores (promotoras) Latino lay health educators (who are usually female) who provide prevention intervention services in the homes of clients

Curanderos (curanderas) Latino traditional healers who use a combination of spiritual rituals and prayers and touch to cure common ailments such as *empacho* (indigestion), *mal de ojo* (evil eye), and *susto* (fright)

Parteras traditional midwives in Latino communities who are often part of the support system of the mother before and after she gives birth

Herbolarios (herbolarias) Latino healers who prescribe herbs to fight both physical and emotional ailments

13

Social Policy and Culturally Grounded Social Work

SOCIAL POLICY AND SOCIAL WORK PRACTICE GO HAND IN HAND. SOCIAL policies often affect funding for various social programs, which in turn affects what social programs individuals can access as well as what types of services social work practitioners can provide. Since social policy is directly connected to the social work profession, social work practitioners have a key role as advocates for social policies that help meet the needs of communities in an effective and culturally grounded manner. This chapter introduces the concept of distributive justice and explains its relevance to culturally grounded social work; describes some of the government policies and programs that have been implemented in an effort to ensure distributive justice, as well as some of the debates surrounding them; and discusses the ways in which policy affects social work practice and the importance of advocacy by practitioners.

Historically, social work in the United States has made an effort to connect clients with social services responding to their needs with social policy development and social policy change. For example, settlement houses and charity organizations emphasized their clients' relationships with larger systems in their social environments such as labor unions and political parties. This focus continues to be of great importance in social work. Social policy is concerned with the decision-making process that takes place in the legislative arena, the implementation of social programs, and the fundamental question of where to allocate resources.

DISTRIBUTIVE JUSTICE

The Aristotelian concept of distributive justice is deeply rooted in policy analysis as it is conducted by social workers. Distributive justice aims at ensuring that members of society have access to reasonable economic resources, education, social services, and other resources based on the ethical principles of equity and solidarity among the least privileged. These principles often must compete with other principles embedded in the national identity of the country. For example, the economic structure of the United States has been strongly influenced by the eighteenth-century writings of Adam Smith, whose thesis of the "invisible hand" of the market proposed that natural market forces should take care of the distribution of resources in the most efficient and effective manner without the intervention of the state. This perspective expects that not everyone will be equally successful and that social class differences are an inevitable, even welcome, condition for the healthy functioning of the overall society and economy.

On the other end of the spectrum from Smith's invisible hand is John Rawls's theory of justice, a perspective used in social work to operationalize the concept of distributive justice. Through the application of the principle of distributive justice, Rawls aims at ensuring that in cases of unequal distribution, the most disadvantaged individuals reap the greatest benefits. Rawls maintained that the redistribution of resources to benefit the disadvantaged should be guided by two main principles: equal liberty (meaning that no person or entity may compromise the freedom of the individual in order to access services or goods) and the fair distribution of social goods.

Distributive justice can also be understood as the fair distribution of benefits and burdens, which is achieved by way of the mechanisms and tools provided by procedural justice (i.e., the fair administration of justice). Thus distributive justice does not refer only to economic goods but also to the fair allocation of socially produced goods like opportunity, power, and self-respect. For individuals to pursue their life plans, each must possess a fair share of the available social resources. For example, although health is not a tangible good, the ability to access the health care system is a social good, as a healthy individual is better equipped to compete for jobs, advance socially, and achieve an optimal quality of life than an individual who does not have access to health care. The concept of distributive justice is relevant to culturally grounded social work because in the United States, individuals are often denied goods, benefits, and access to social resources based on their membership in various groups with whom social workers frequently come in contact. For example, even when agencies are able to offer the best services available to members of different cultural communities, their target populations may not always be able to access them. If only a few people can access the services, then it is not an issue of some individuals being hard to serve, but rather a sign that something is clearly wrong with the service delivery system. What renders a person hard to serve is the person's inability to access services. The social work tenets of self-determination and self-direction are consistent with current economic trends and realities; however, they need to be implemented with justice, empathy, and common sense. When providers design systems of services, they often neglect to focus on how clients will experience a system as they attempt to navigate it. That is, during system design there is a tendency to group services according to their function instead of focusing more on clients and the paths they must follow to receive services and achieve positive outcomes.

Residential segregation—which has been fueled by economic institutions like mortgage lenders, and protected by housing policies that reflect the political influence of the well-off—is the physical separation of ethnic or racial groups in a residential context. As a result, it restricts employment opportunities and leads to a higher concentration of poverty in certain areas. Political leaders are more likely to cut spending in poor neighborhoods than in more affluent areas because many residents of poor neighborhoods are ethnic minorities with less political clout than residents in wealthy neighborhoods.

Transportation enables people to access basic needs such as work, education, and health care. Unfortunately, decision making about public transportation and transportation infrastructure is biased in favor of those with political power and resources and largely ignores accessibility differences by gender, physical ability, and ethnicity. As a result, it rarely brings about necessary changes. Another important aspect of the provision of social services is the societal practices and conditions that make some communities invisible. For example, as whites moved to the suburbs, public policies contributed to the development of suburbs through such measures as massive subsidies to build freeways while federally approved discriminatory practices in lending and sales helped the suburbs remain predominantly white. While some of the more egregious acts of discrimination have since been outlawed, disparities between whites and ethnic minority applicants still exist in their ability to obtain loans and home insurance. Because of such disparities, welfare recipients from many poor neighborhoods who want to move into the labor force face a challenge finding employment since social networks of employers and job seekers are often limited by location. Many welfare recipients are not only at a disadvantage because they are members of an ethnic or racial minority and frequently have low skill levels, but also because they are restricted in where they can live and how easily they can travel to available educational and career opportunities. They often face situations in which the jobs have moved away from them but they cannot afford to move to the jobs.

To correct these inequities and address the lack of distributive justice, the government has intervened over the years in different ways, with varying degrees of success. Such organized efforts usually have both supporters and critics, which generates intense policy debate.

THE WELFARE STATE

Although the tax and regulatory structures of U.S. society create what has been called a corporate welfare system that gives more resources and privileges to corporations than to the most disadvantaged members of society, the word "welfare" is generally associated with the poor. Historically, the idea of promoting social welfare has been embraced by most religions (Hungerman, 2005), and it was common in the past for religious institutions to care for the less fortunate, such as widows and orphans. For example, in Christian societies, it was the church that assigned the roles of providers and recipients within the community. Today a welfare society can be described as one that is devoted to the well-being of its members and that has social welfare institutions operating at the state level. For example, the Scandinavian states have traditionally been described as model welfare societies (Slothuus, 2007). Although the version of the social welfare state implemented in the United States after World War II cannot be considered a classic welfare state in the Scandinavian tradition, it follows what might be called a mixed or hybrid model that combines strong social welfare characteristics with a liberal economic model.

In the United States, the phrase "social welfare" is commonly understood to mean a payment in-kind or in cash to a person who needs support because of age, disability, poverty, or mental illness. The term "entitlement" is frequently used in the social policy literature to describe programs in which these types of transactions between the state and individuals and families take place. For example, Social Security and Medicare are entitlement programs. Workers who contributed to the system during their working years are entitled after retirement to receive a monthly check and health care benefits once they meet the established qualification criteria. Those qualifications may change over time. For instance, the minimum age for drawing full Social Security retirement benefits will increase gradually from sixty-five to sixty-seven, and the amount that seniors pay as co-payments for Medicare can be increased every year through congressional action.

When social welfare and labor policies are in development, conflicts often arise among different groups. Sometimes the state tries to support a group that has been underprivileged for a long time, which often fosters resentment among the dominant group. One view is that the welfare state perpetuates unemployment by allowing workers to live in comfort while unemployed, which inhibits their motivation to look for work or accept work that is demanding. People who have not paid into the welfare system, such as children, some disabled people, and people with other disadvantages who have never been in the labor force, are often made to feel that they are not entitled to the benefits provided by the welfare state. For example, retirees on Social Security are not generally stigmatized in the way that single mothers on TANF (Temporary Assistance to Needy Families) are.

Public opposition to social welfare is caused in part by the misconception that recipients would rather sit at home than work, that they are undeserving of these benefits, and that they are predominantly ethnic minorities. The fact is that in order to receive benefits from a social welfare program, a family or individual has to be either below or very close to the poverty line. Still, a large proportion of the U.S. population, about two out of every five Americans, will use a social safety net program for at least five years during their working lives (Rank & Hirschl, 2002).

Societies often use outsider groups like recent immigrants and guest workers as scapegoats and question these groups' rights to receive benefits that are guaranteed to citizens. From a distributive justice perspective, it could be argued that if children born to undocumented immigrants have no right to education or health care, they will grow up to be uneducated (and therefore minimally employable) and in poor health, a hardship not only for them but for society as a whole. As a result, as adults, they will not be able to contribute as much to the system and will depend more on services. Moreover, when they are barred from receiving publicly funded health care, their normal childhood development is threatened and they increase the risk that uncontrolled infectious disease will spread through the general population. This example illustrates the concept of the welfare state as a safety net not only for those in need of services but indirectly for all of society as an interconnected and interdependent living organism. The term "safety net" refers to the strategies society uses to respond to its members' unplanned needs. These individuals often make up a transitional group that people constantly enter and leave. In the United States, the Food Stamps program and WIC (Women, Infants and Children) are examples of safety net strategies used by a very diverse group of recipients.

In 1996, the U.S. Congress, with the support of President Bill Clinton, enacted sweeping welfare reform with strict work requirements for parents receiving TANF and lifetime limits on eligibility. Critics at the time charged that the changes were in large part motivated by the demonization of single mothers, who were often pejoratively called "welfare queens." Overlooked at the time was the inconvenient reality that the vast majority of TANF beneficiaries were dependent children. Unfortunately, these federal and state welfare policies have both directly and indirectly discriminated against racial minorities, in particular African Americans. Many families were forced to rely on inadequate provisions for child care, and some became ineligible for health services provided through Medicaid. A decade after the passage of the welfare reforms, more than one-fifth of all U.S. children are still classified as poor by UNICEF (2005). The United States ranks twenty-seventh among developed countries in terms of the percent of children not living in poverty, just slightly better than Mexico, and twenty-six places away from Denmark, the country with the fewest children living in poverty (UNICEF, 2006).

Antifamily social policies have forced families to depend on overburdened public and private services, as well as their own extended families. A study of ninety nonprofit organizations found that the 1996 welfare reforms had a substantial enough impact on these organizations—particularly on those serving a high proportion of minority clients—that they were unable to keep up with client demands (Reisch & Sommerfeld, 2002). The stated objective of these reforms was for poor parents to achieve full employment rather than continuing to rely on public assistance. Critics have charged that they were implemented in many states without adequate regard to the consequences for vulnerable families and children, and without recognition of the difficulties presented by labor market conditions. The reforms provided minimally for child care, forcing many single mothers to choose between placing their children in inadequate child care facilities, burdening their extended family or friends with child care requests, and leaving children unattended. The job training and employment counseling services that were supposed to create bridges from welfare to work were insufficient for many recipients who lacked educational credentials and job experience, and for those trapped in economically depressed communities, jobs were not waiting on the other side of the bridge.

AFFIRMATIVE ACTION

Affirmative action, discussed briefly in chapter 2, is defined as government policies that attempt to improve the educational and employment opportunities of historically oppressed populations in the United States. In 1961, President Kennedy established the President's Committee on Equal Employment Opportunity to end discrimination in employment and ensure that race, religion, and national origin would not be factors in employers' consideration of job applicants. Later, President Lyndon Johnson transferred the committee's responsibilities to the Department of Labor. Johnson also prohibited discrimination in employment based on sex. In 1971, under President Nixon, all large employers of five hundred or more workers were required to perform an annual analysis of areas in which they were deficient in the hiring of minority groups and women, file a report to the Office of Equal Employment Opportunity, and move to correct such deficiencies. However, the process for making these corrections, known as affirmative action, has been a controversial and contentious area of debate. Over time, affirmative action was extended to mean equal access not only to employment but to government contracts and higher education as well.

One of the arguments against affirmative action rests on the assumption that affirmative action undermines merit-based hiring and promotion practices, and that white men suffer reverse discrimination as a result of affirmative action. The charge that affirmative action undermines merit-based systems of employment misses an important point. As more of the skills needed for jobs are learned through on-the-job training rather than educational credentialing, those who are excluded from the bottom rungs of the job ladder remain at a permanent and ever-growing disadvantage. Rather than undermining merit-based systems for hiring and promotion, affirmative action may actually overcome some of this largely hidden bias by ensuring that recruitment and promotion practices do not exclude women and ethnic minorities. The issue here is not formal qualification, an automatic prerequisite for consideration, but the willingness of employers to train women and ethnic minorities to move up the ladder. There is no law that requires employers to explain why they have trained none when they say they have no qualified female or minority applicants for a job. Affirmative action reporting requirements are an important means of calling attention to these disparities.

Affirmative action programs in employment have been the focus of much controversy, but the thorniest issues concern questions regarding what is fair, and for whom. The charge that affirmative action leads to reverse discrimination against white men seems to strike a chord with many who view it as an unfair practice regardless of the benefits it might offer others. However, instances of proven reverse discrimination are few. In fact, research shows that despite affirmative action regulations, white men, not ethnic minorities, are most likely to receive preferential treatment in employment (Belliveau, 1996; Chao & Willaby, 2007). In truth, affirmative action can serve as a convenient scapegoat. That is, relatively few people are able to rise up the organizational pyramid to the top or choicest positions, but white men can attribute their failure to do so to imagined advantages that women and minorities are presumed to enjoy through affirmative action.

Affirmative action has also been an issue in education. Policies have been designed to provide greater parity in access to higher education, promoting the acquisition of the skills and credentials needed for success in the workplace. In our society, education is the main mechanism for social mobility, and a college degree is frequently a requirement for entering and remaining in the middle class. Schools in the United States are supposed to be environments in which young people of different socioeconomic status can mingle, but in reality, residential segregation by social class means that each school and school district tends to enroll students from a limited socioeconomic range. Even when schools are socioeconomically diverse, children from well-off families, a disproportionate number of whom are from white and Asian backgrounds, are more likely to do well on standardized aptitude tests and are tracked into more advanced courses and college-preparatory programs (McDonough & Fann, 2007).

As residential segregation has increased in our society, economic disparities between school districts are also increasing. While policy makers work to reduce class disparities and address the problems associated with poverty (such as poor health, greater family instability, frequent moves, unsafe communities, environmental pollution, and so on), affirmative action can play a leveling role in ensuring more equitable access to higher education. Affirmative action in college and graduate school admissions helps counterbalance the disadvantages that children from less well-off ethnic minority and white families experience as a result of large disparities in funding for elementary and secondary public education from one locality to another.

Affirmative action programs for college admissions are quite controversial, and the programs have narrowed their focus and reach over the past three decades in the face of a series of legal challenges. As a result, ethnic and racial quota systems are not permitted, and admissions policies permit consideration of an applicant's ethnicity or race as only one factor among many others. Admission of members of ethnic and racial minorities as a way to increase cultural diversity among students is still permissible. However, some states have moved away from affirmative action based on race and ethnicity toward a social class–based system. Some critics contend that all forms of affirmative action in college admissions are misguided or even harmful because they can create institutional mismatches that lead to high failure rates. After World War II there was a similar outcry regarding the benefits that returning soldiers received through the GI Bill, which granted millions of young men and women who otherwise would not have gone to college access to higher education. Such opposition failed to sway public policy in large part because veterans were widely seen as deserving the help they received, a perception that seldom applies to today's beneficiaries of affirmative action. Some critics charge that academic standards are lowered when ethnic minority students are admitted to top schools for which they are unprepared academically (Hoffman & Lewitzki, 2005). However, these critics do not raise the same objections regarding legacy admissions, a widespread form of institutionalized discrimination in college admissions that favors applicants whose parents attended the college; these students generally come from the most privileged groups in society. In addition, such criticism disregards the role of other factors that may lead ethnic minority students to fail, such as tokenism, harassment, and an unsupportive campus climate.

Opposition to policies designed to compensate for unequal beginnings and provide the same opportunities to all individuals often reflects the belief that U.S. society is a meritocracy, and that differences in occupational and educational attainment are simply a result of individual differences in aptitude, motivation, and character. This thinking assumes members of different ethnic groups compete for advancement on a level playing field and downplays the fact that each group's history, circumstances, characteristics, and relative advantages vary at the start of the contest. Some may question the strategies or specific goals of affirmative action efforts. For example, proponents of partial inclusion may dismiss talk of societal parity as an elusive or impossible goal. Rather than setting parity in recruitment, promotion, and representation at the highest organizational levels as the benchmark for full inclusion of women and ethnic minorities, their less ambitious definition of successful inclusion might be to simply increase the visibility of target groups—such as having women achieve 5 percent representation among those in upper management rather than a percentage corresponding to their fraction of the labor pool, or showing evidence of incremental progress in increasing the representation of Latino college students.

SCHOOL RESEGREGATION

There is an important difference between racial desegregation and racial integration. The first refers to the ending of policies and practices that disallow or discourage contact between people of different races, while the second refers to the encouragement of interactions that occur between them. In the 1896 U.S. Supreme Court decision in *Plessy v. Ferguson*, the justices decided that according to the doctrine of "separate but equal," the state-sanctioned segregation of public facilities, including schools, did not violate the U.S. Constitution. This doctrine was challenged in 1954 in *Brown v. Board of Education of Topeka, Kansas*, when the Supreme Court ruled that the "separate but equal" clause was unconstitutional because it separated children based on skin color alone.

Today, more than fifty years after this pivotal Supreme Court decision spurred a decades-long struggle to desegregate public schools in the nation, there is still a wide achievement gap between African American, Latino, and white students, one that begins in elementary school and continues throughout high school (Wiggan, 2007). Although children who attend racially integrated schools perform better than their counterparts in segregated schools, progress toward desegregation has stalled or been reversed in some cases. Some argue that this is a distributive justice issue, not a race issue: all-white schools and schools with substantial white enrollments tend to have more resources and better-trained teachers, and poorly performing schools are often in lower-income African American and Latino neighborhoods. The flight of the wealthy to the more culturally and economically homogenous suburbs and the faltering political will in recent years to address educational inequities make it very difficult to improve the educational attainment of children from ethnic minority communities and to address resegregation.

Harvard University's Civil Rights Project examined the racial and ethnic composition of the nation's school districts between 1986 and 2000 and found that the segregation of white and black students remained the same or grew worse as the twentieth century came to a close. As discussed in chapter 5, starting in the 1960s and 1970s, some districts were ordered to promote desegregation. Because many of the cities were residentially segregated, busing was implemented to transport children across the city from their homes to schools located in different neighborhoods. Some parents were angry that their children had to attend schools outside their neighborhood, and minority students were harassed during bus rides as well as in school, where they were called derogatory names and teased, taunted, and intimidated. Moreover, students reported that many of the teachers lacked an understanding of African American culture and behavior, and their belief that black students had lower capacity for learning resulted in these students' placement in lower-ability groups (Harmon, 2002).

THE ROLE OF SOCIAL WORKERS IN POLICY

Social workers can play important roles as advocates in working to influence policy and change the allocation of resources to improve the quality of life of members of oppressed populations. Through its advocacy role, social work provides a strong voice in often hostile policy environments. Although there has been some progress, advocacy efforts have not yet sufficiently influenced the legal and legislative systems to improve decisions and better serve the needs of cultural minorities.

Advocacy is possible when individuals and groups are empowered, and when community members have a voice in making decisions that affect their lives, successful advocacy leads to higher levels of empowerment among the oppressed. Empowerment can be fostered through a variety of political activities, from individual resistance to oppression to mass political mobilization that challenges basic power relations in society. The empowerment process begins with the awareness that communities and individuals gain when they recognize the impact of inequalities related to religion, nationality, gender, socioeconomic status, age, race, ability status, sexual orientation, and other factors on their lives. The reflection and action that follow lead to policy analysis and policy change.

Social workers are in an ideal position to help individual clients and communities recognize the tools that can help them produce changes in policy. Practitioners hear their clients' complete stories rather than fragmented pieces of their lives, and the most effective advocacy occurs when individuals and communities are able to present themselves as whole people regardless of their circumstances. Society and its institutions tend not to see people with disabilities, poor people, and other oppressed people as whole people. For example, at the beginning of the AIDS epidemic, it was common to refer to a person with AIDS as an "AIDS victim" instead of "a person living with AIDS." Referring to someone as a homeless person has the same essentializing effect that reduces the person to a single defining characteristic drained of her or his full humanity. Society in general and helping professionals in particular can easily fall into this trap of focusing narrowly on the characteristic that is seen as the presenting problem. One of the many ways in which social workers can play a role in culturally grounded policy development is by coaching their clients in how to present themselves as whole people in communicating with policy makers, as well as by educating those policy makers. This type of communication informs a progressive policy agenda that benefits the community, and in turn the larger society.

Policy analysis is an essential step of advocacy that involves defining the problem, obtaining and interpreting the information needed to make sound decisions, developing and judging alternatives and considering ethical dilemmas, and deciding what the best choice is. From a culturally grounded perspective, clients' voices and narratives are a vital source of information for any policy analysis. Clients can inform policy makers not only about the problem but also about the strengths and resources communities have to overcome the challenges they face, as well as their policy recommendations. Social workers in partnership with their clients often have opportunities to transform the policy-making process from one that rewards power and privilege to one that ensures distributive justice for all.

Culturally grounded policy development is a form of policy work that is informed by consumers. It bridges the gap that often exists between policy makers and the needs of cultural minority individuals and communities and the effects that policy decisions have on them. Policy initiatives should be examined through the lenses of culture and social justice. For example, since the abolishment of apartheid, the South African government has led a process of participatory policy development that includes blacks and other people of color who were excluded from any policy development during the whites-only rule. During apartheid, social policy development was a top-down process that did not take into consideration any of the needs and assets of the black township residents. For ten years representatives of the excluded communities engaged in active policy development and planning activities, which led to the development of the idea of local economic development and institutionalized local participation in policy and decision making as a key aspect of democratic South Africa.

Public policies at the local, state, and federal levels affect millions of people in significant and lasting ways. It is vital that policy decisions be made based on accurate information, informed analysis, and comprehensive interpretations, not on assumptions or half-truths. Uninformed policy makers run the risk of misinterpreting or manipulating the findings of research in social work and other social sciences, and relying on simplistic constructs or overgeneralizations about minority communities and oppressed groups. Overgeneralizations and stereotypes can misguide social policy formulation and social work practice, which can have the intended or unintended result of impeding the promotion of social justice. Note from the field 13.1 provides an example of such risks.

Social justice was the impetus for the development of social work and has grown into the central mission of the profession. Social workers are not only prac-

---

NOTE FROM THE FIELD 13.1
Saturday Night's Not All Right for Fighting

The Los Alamos City Council passes a resolution to forbid the Saturday evening lowriders *paseo* (drive) in order to increase the safety of the central city and enforce its gang prevention policy. Very few of the mostly Mexican American youths who enjoy fixing up their lowriders and driving them through the downtown area are gang members. Moreover, fixing their cars has become a very positive and creative leisure activity in the neighborhood, as well as a means of expressing ethnic pride. The report provided to the city council was clearly developed from an outsider's perspective and reflects stigma and prejudice about lowriders and their owners. There is no Mexican American representation on the city council.

titioners but also data gatherers and analysts who have direct access to clients and view them as expert informants. As experts, clients identify what system reforms are necessary. Historically, partnerships between oppressed groups and social workers have played important roles in policy reform. For example, in the early 1990s, low-income residents in Illinois successfully took part in the development and implementation of a welfare-to-work policy (O'Donnell, 1993). The professional social worker plays an important role as the facilitator of clients' examination of their own interests and in planning appropriate courses of action. Unfortunately, recipients of benefits are rarely engaged in the policy-making process.

Eradicating social inequalities and working with the oppressed to help them reach optimal functioning is part of the call of social work. Not only do social workers need to work to ensure that the voices of oppressed populations are heard, but they must also promote the development of policies that establish a pathway toward change and provide the needed resources that will bring more members of oppressed populations onto college campuses as students and into social service agencies in order to develop a new workforce that is representative of the diverse demographics of U.S. society.

Key Concepts

Empowerment the ability to feel and act in control of one's destiny despite social and economic adversity

Distributive justice a philosophy that aims at ensuring that all members of society have access to reasonable economic resources, education, social services, and other resources, based on the ethical principles of equity and solidarity

Social welfare in the United States, a payment in-kind or in cash to a person who needs support because of age, disability, poverty, unemployment, or mental illness; also a society that is devoted to the well-being of its members and that has social welfare institutions operating at the state level

Entitlement programs programs that provide payments to individuals who have paid into the program and have met other eligibility requirements, such as years of employment or age, and are therefore entitled to benefits

TANF (Temporary Aid to Needy Families) the major welfare program in the United States, which enforces strict work requirements and limits on lifetime eligibility

Safety net the strategies a society uses to respond to its members' unplanned needs

Plessy v. Ferguson 1896 Supreme Court decision that sanctioned the segregation of public facilities, including schools, by establishing the "separate but equal" doctrine

Brown v. Board of Education of Topeka, Kansas 1954 Supreme Court decision that ruled that the "separate but equal" clause allowing racially segregated schools was unconstitutional

14

Culturally Grounded Evaluation and Research

RESEARCH IS A VITAL AND INTEGRAL PART OF SOCIAL WORK, EVEN FOR social workers who do not conduct research themselves. Effective social work requires social workers to be effective consumers of research. Research helps us understand the scope and severity of a problem, its trends over time, and its cost to individuals and communities. Research is concerned with building knowledge about the root causes of social problems and effective ways to address them. Social work informs many types of clinical, experimental, and survey research that develop from theory. Rigorous research either confirms or disconfirms theory, leading to improvements in concepts and how they are measured. Social workers engage in naturalistic research conducted in the field in order to observe behavior in its natural social and physical context. This more qualitative research also builds theory. Unfortunately, too often practice and research are not well connected in social work, and researchers in universities and practitioners in the community are not always linked effectively through their professional organizations. However, culturally grounded social work practice cannot assume its proper place within the profession without culturally grounded research and evaluation to inform that practice.

Engagement in research is natural because social work as a profession studies the interrelationships of individuals, communities, families, and social institutions and provides the empirical evidence that is needed to formulate effective social policies and improve service delivery. Because practitioners, unlike many researchers, work directly with members of the cultural groups they are studying, they have a critical role in identifying gaps in knowledge and in generating research ideas. The researcher, the outsider looking in through the lens of difference and privilege, often arrives at conclusions that do not reflect the experience of the group being studied. In contrast, social work practitioner-researchers are in a unique position that allows them to partner effectively with oppressed minority groups in generating knowledge.

Practitioners often are more closely involved with evaluation than with research. They may engage in evaluation to document the effectiveness of a program or amass evaluation results when seeking to defend or increase funding for that program. In today's increasingly multicultural society, evaluators are expected to be culturally competent and capable of adapting evaluation processes in a systematic way so that they are appropriate for the setting. The challenge for evaluators is to work effectively in different cultural settings in such a way that trust is maintained and partnerships are long lasting. Practitioners have an ethical responsibility to select interventions that can be evaluated for their effectiveness, and this requires them to be involved in conducting or making appropriate use of research. Unfortunately, clinicians are sometimes reluctant to assume the role of researcher because the time they can dedicate to research is limited, they often lack funds and training, and/or they do not have support from their agencies and their organizations do not offer incentives to conduct research. In addition, when consumed by the daily pressures of providing direct services, practitioners may see research as abstract, irrelevant, and disconnected from the needs of their clients. These views may foster the negative attitudes toward research held by many social workers. Practitioners sometimes believe research findings to be of limited clinical relevance because they regard their practice as rooted in the here and now, or the specific needs of their clients. Research findings are sometimes viewed with suspicion by those who live in, work with, and advocate for communities. They may be considered irrelevant abstractions that do not apply to a particular case or community.

Although research and evaluation findings can have significant impacts on jobs, programs, and community investments, studies that have clear policy implications are often ignored. This occurs for many reasons. The findings and their policy implications may not be presented clearly for use by non-researchers, or they may not be implemented because they run counter to deeply held values and beliefs or challenge entrenched interests. Sometimes practitioners are not reading the current research literature and lack the appropriate methodological background to interpret research results and apply the findings. However, increasing demands for accountability from governmental and private funders require social workers to demonstrate the efficacy of what they do, which provides new impetus to engage in research. A good way for practitioners to start contributing is by assessing the outcomes of their own practice.

OUTCOME ASSESSMENT AND ACCOUNTABILITY

The pressure for practitioners to engage in evaluation and research in general has significantly increased over the past two decades. Phrases such as "outcome based," "evidence based," and "best practices" have become part of the social work lexicon in the same way that they have been integrated into the professional jargon of other applied research fields. Social work, like these other fields, has been heavily influenced by what is commonly called the accountability movement.

Professional practitioners are being called upon by government funding agencies, social service administrators, private foundations, and consumers to demonstrate that methods, practices, and interventions are achieving the desired outcomes and are being implemented in a cost-effective manner. Some believe that this movement has called into question the identity of social work as a profession because the only social service delivery systems that will survive are those that can demonstrate that they provide needed, useful, competent, and cost-effective services. Critics of the drive toward accountability propose an alternative benchmark for evaluating social work practice that emphasizes the inherent value of serving vulnerable communities even when results are difficult to document. There is also a risk that, taken to an extreme, outcome-based evaluation can hinder social work practice by prematurely concluding that an intervention should be stopped because of its lack of results. This risk is magnified in culturally grounded practice because it is essential that not just outcomes but also the appropriateness of the methods and practices being utilized be evaluated. Although evaluation and research are not neutral tools and can be manipulated to serve different ideologies, they are much needed. They are the best available means to ensure that innovation occurs, that the best existing science is used to design interventions, and that services achieve the intended outcomes in a culturally relevant manner.

Outcome assessment is a kind of evaluation that is used to decide whether a program is meeting its objectives—in other words, whether it is effective. In social work practice, there are two main outcomes: the results of the practice, treatment, or intervention, or how the client's presenting problem was addressed, and the outcome of the professional behavior, or what was done to change the nature of the problem. The first outcome has to do with the client's well-being, and the second with the quality of the treatment protocols (Hudson & McMurtry, 1997). Outcome assessments help determine whether practice innovations and interventions are useful.

The concept of accountability is not new to the profession. For example, the Code of Ethics of the National Association of Social Workers (1999) stresses the importance of engaging in systematic evaluation of the outcomes of practice in order to guarantee that clients receive the best services possible. Practice evaluation provides a means to monitor the effectiveness of efforts to reach out to those in need. This type of evaluation is important because social workers work with clients who have serious real-life problems, and ineffectiveness can have serious implications for those we serve.

Effectiveness can be an elusive concept in work with cultural minority clients because interventions and practices often are not culturally grounded or appropriate. What does one do when an evaluation concludes that a standard intervention is not effectively reaching cultural minority clients? Rather than taking steps to terminate the intervention, it is important to bring innovation into play. Practitioners can design new interventions by involving community members, and the designs can be tested through rigorous research. Thus, research and evaluation are key tools for ensuring that cultural minority clients are able to access effective services.

EVALUATION AND RESEARCH

Evaluation and research are related but are not the same. Evaluation identifies gaps in the applicability of existing models and methods of social work practice, and through research and innovation, those gaps are addressed. Once new treatments and interventions have been tested and the results carefully analyzed through research involving randomized trials or quasi-experimental methods, they can be implemented and evaluated in real-life settings. In social work, the word "evaluation" is typically used to mean program evaluation. In contrast, research addresses a wider range of questions about the behavior of clients, their families and communities, the actions of social work practitioners and agencies, and the connections among helping professions, organizations, and larger societal institutions. The evaluation process helps social workers determine whether programs and interventions are effective and make the appropriate changes. Evaluations are not free of bias because they are conducted by evaluators who bring their own cultural biases to their work. In addition, even when an evaluator has good intentions and very good methodological tools at her or his disposal, those evaluation tools or methodologies may be culturally biased.

Well-designed evaluation is client centered and confidential and targets specific issues and questions. As note from the field 14.1 demonstrates, when evaluation is not culturally grounded and the cultural characteristics of providers and clients are disregarded, inaccurate assessments can lead to the wrong practice or policy recommendations. Because the findings of evaluations can be manipulated by a program's supporters as well as its opponents, the program evaluation process often involves intense political pressure. Politics may influence the way a research study is designed or how the findings are interpreted. Because their survival depends on their ability to demonstrate accountability through program evaluations based on concrete, measurable outcomes, it is not unusual for agencies to put technocrats in charge of program evaluation and to focus the evaluation on the most readily available numerical measures. Without a background in social science or social services, they may be directed to rely on selective data and narrow methods that are most likely to generate the desired conclusions. Such pressures may distort the process of evaluating whether the program adequately serves the target population's needs, and the distortion may be particularly acute when it involves cultural minority populations because their perspective may not be taken into account in the evaluation process.

Because members of oppressed communities tend to have less power and lack

---

NOTE FROM THE FIELD 14.1
Remembering Clients' Needs

An evaluator is ordered to assess the rates of utilization of a newly established county health clinic located in a largely traditional Muslim community. He evaluates the clinic's utilization rate by reviewing intake records. He concludes that the services of the doctor assigned to the clinic are not needed because he has the lowest patient-physician ratio in the county. The patient-to-practitioner ratio for the nurse practitioner and social worker, however, fall within the county's recommended range. He concludes that the clinic is underutilized and recommends its closure. His rationale is that it is not cost effective to maintain its expensive medical services with such low patient utilization. Fortunately, the chair of the clinic's community advisory board reviews the report before it is sent to the county health authorities. She is perplexed by the fact that the report leaves out the gender of the three key professionals who form the interdisciplinary team. She insists that the evaluation fully consider the cultural implications of the gender of the clinic's clients and practitioners. While most of the clients are female, as are the nurse practitioner and the social worker, the physician is male. The report is modified to recommend that the clinic engage the services of a female physician to serve the needs of the clientele, for whom any intimate cross-gender physical contact is problematic.

---

representation, evaluations affecting their lives often do not take into account their voices and perceptions. Evaluation reports often make recommendations regarding the provision or interruption of services without consulting those who are most affected by them. Due to the serious quality-of-life implications of such decisions, program evaluations need to be guided by the best empirical methods at the disposal of the evaluator. However, these tools are only effective from a culturally grounded perspective when they are embedded within the social and cultural contexts in which the phenomenon being studied takes place. Thus culturally grounded evaluation is a participatory and reciprocal process where the professional evaluator contributes her or his technical expertise and the community contributes its knowledge of the services or programs being evaluated.

CULTURALLY GROUNDED RESEARCH QUESTIONS, MEASURES, AND DESIGNS

Gaps in research on cultural minorities limit our understanding of how to engage these populations and how to tailor interventions for them. Critical social work focuses on challenging the oppression of marginalized groups by taking their voices and perspectives into consideration. To advance this key imperative of critical social work, new forms of research methods have been developed and other methods have been adapted from other fields as a means of taking into account the voices of oppressed populations and more accurately interpreting their perspectives regarding key social phenomena.

Much progress has been made, yet much remains to be done, especially regarding issues of cultural bias and non-generalizability in the way that behaviors and attitudes are measured in research with cultural minority populations. There are potential problems with validity (i.e., whether or not measures gauge what they are intended to measure), and with reliability (i.e., measures' internal consistency and stability). Researchers and practitioners alike cannot assume that an instrument measuring behavioral tendencies, attitudes, or mental health states that appears to be reliable and valid when tested with people from one culture will be reliable and valid when used with members of other cultural groups. However, the construction of culturally competent measures involves complex issues that go beyond resolving language difficulties to achieve linguistic or semantic equivalence. Effective intercultural communication requires knowledge of the other culture and its communication symbols. The process starts with immersion in the literature and the development of theory-based research questions or hypotheses and corresponding research designs with appropriate measures and analysis strategies.

Culturally grounded research requires not only a serious critique of measurement tools, but fundamental reflection on how researchers frame their research questions and design studies. Asking the right question in research is very important, perhaps more important than the methods used to find an answer to the question. For example, studies of substance abuse etiology and treatment that compare different cultural groups may overlook important factors if they ask questions limited to whether there are differences in rates of use or different treatment outcomes among various groups. An approach more likely to generate culturally relevant findings might start by asking how substance use is defined in the culture and what social meaning it has to users and non-users.

Because cultural specificity is a key concern of the culturally grounded approach, practitioners may wonder whether any form of cross-cultural generalizability is possible in measurement. This question requires consideration of the technical problems associated with cultural bias known as metric and structural equivalence (Burnette, 1998). To achieve metric equivalence, the items comprising a scale should work together in the exact same way across cultures and reflect the same underlying construct. In designing a scale to measure quality of life, or life satisfaction, for example, researchers have to make choices about the various arenas of life that might be represented (self, spouse, children, friends, school, work, home, income, etc.) and the weight given in the scale to each one. It would be a mistake to assume that all cultures have the same priorities regarding different life arenas, or that the relative weight given to each one is culturally universal.

Instruments are structurally equivalent across cultures when they have the same relationships with other key measures and outcomes. For example, an adolescent risk behavior scale that is used to screen youths for targeted prevention programs in schools might count the number of risky behaviors in which respondents have engaged in the last six months and develop cutoff scores to designate thresholds indicating high, moderate, low, and no risk. Questions of cultural bias can arise concerning whether the cutoffs should be the same for youths from all cultures, and whether engagement in different kinds of risk behaviors may be used to identify those in most need of targeted prevention from different ethnic and racial groups.

In addition to the problems that may be inherent to the assessment tools themselves, assessments are complicated by the fact that cultural minorities may understand, interpret, and express answers to survey questions differently from members of the dominant culture. These potential problems regarding culturally biased assessment pose challenges for researchers and practitioners. How is it possible to have confidence in the reliability and validity of any of our assessment tools when we are working with members of cultural minorities? Until proved otherwise, shouldn't it be assumed that instruments are somehow culturally biased? There is no simple answer and no easy solution to these problems. The key issue is ensuring that social workers are educated and critical consumers of assessment tools. Even when practitioners lack the training, resources, or support necessary to engage in the work of developing and testing culturally unbiased assessment tools, they can still become educated and critically aware consumers of assessment tools.

A major challenge facing social work researchers is the need to generate knowledge that will enhance the relevance, effectiveness, and quality of social work practice for cultural minority groups. In order to do so, measures that capture the essence of culturally relevant and culturally sensitive variables must be developed. This is a very important task for researchers, just as the development of culturally competent interventions is important for practitioners. To make assessment tools culturally responsive, researchers need to become immersed in the culture before constructing the measures and must use community-based informants to identify and resolve any problems related to the cultural competence of the measures.

Single Case Designs

Evaluation methods and research methods in social work often use methods that examine an individual or small group of individuals; these are called single case designs or case studies. In fact, most social workers are required to engage in ongoing evaluation of their practice by using single case designs. Progress notes and standardized assessment scales form the core of the data used in this type of evaluation. The problem with these data sources is that they are very vulnerable to cultural bias. Progress notes mostly reflect the client's spoken words and the worker's interpretation of them. Assessment tools that are normed on samples that do not take into consideration a minority client's culture can generate a distorted and misleading client profile. Even if the assessment tools are culturally appropriate, the power differential between practitioners and their clients and a shortage of culturally competent supervision can undermine the effectiveness of the practice. The practitioner may then misinterpret the unsuccessful practice as a lack of engagement by the client, or she or he may exaggerate the client's deficiency or pathology.

In single subject evaluation, the risk of bias is heightened because it is only human to want to obtain findings that support the effectiveness of the intervention and indicate that the client's problems and suffering are being ameliorated. In single subject designs there is only one chance to demonstrate success, and success reflects positively on both the practitioner and the client. Clients may want to believe that practice interventions have yielded positive results for various reasons: to justify their decision to seek help, to have a sense of positive closure, to be assured that they have responded in a way that is considered normal or expected, or simply to please the practitioner (Rubin & Babbie, 2002). The use of self-reporting and satisfaction surveys as the sole source of data is often not enough to arrive at any solid conclusions about the effectiveness of an intervention. Effectiveness needs to be assessed based on outcomes and outcomes need to reflect the unique cultural characteristics of clients.

Another problem with single subject designs for evaluation and research in social work is that they often rely on client assessment instruments and methods that have been developed for the cultural majority. Even instruments that use the best methods to ensure reliability and validity can be inappropriate when used with populations for whom they were not intended. Biased assessment tools are of special concern in work with cultural minorities; for example, the instrument may take for granted certain assumptions related to mainstream culture that do not apply to minority culture groups. For many members of cultural minorities who are immigrants, the language of the assessment instrument, and how it is translated and interpreted, may require close attention. Assessment scales may use words to describe moods and emotional states that do not translate exactly into other languages or mean the same thing in other cultures. Even when these ways of describing feelings can be translated accurately into other languages, cultural differences in emotional expression may affect one's willingness to express these feelings.

Research on the generalizability of a widely used screening instrument for depression, the Center for Epidemiologic Studies Depression scale (CES-D), illustrates several ways that assessment tools may be culturally biased. Among U.S. populations, scores on the CES-D vary according to nativity (U.S. born or not), country of origin, and level of acculturation. Latino immigrants to the United States, for example, are less willing to express positive emotional states than Latinos born in the United States (Iwata, Turner, & Lloyd, 2002). There are also substantial variations on the CES-D among Latinos from different generations, and these differences show that perceptions of depressive mood are tied to the current level and nature of social support among Latinos (Liang, Van Tran, Krause, & Markeides, 1989). Not just overall scores but also the underlying structure of the CES-D have been shown to vary by culture. Research with different ethnic minority groups shows that their responses to the CES-D do not always cluster into distinctive subscales as they do for samples representing the cultural majority (Posner, Stewart, Marín, & Pérez-Stable, 2001). For example, for Chinese Americans and Native Americans, the items reflecting somatic complaints (depressive effects on energy level, appetite, and sleep) are inseparable from items measuring general depressive affect (Dick, Beals, Keane, & Manson, 1994; Kuo, 1984; Ying, 1988). It is as if the physical and mental repercussions of depression are expressed inseparably for these groups but are separate realms for other ethnic groups.

A similar example of cultural issues in assessment comes from a study of Chinese American families that showed that a widely used general assessment of family functioning—the Self-Report Family Inventory (C-SFI)—required modification when used with this population. The scale was designed to assess several distinct areas of family life, such as competence, conflict, cohesion, expressiveness, and leadership. Only two stable factors out of the original six emerged from a factor analysis of responses from families of Chinese heritage. One general area concerned positive family behaviors and the absence of family problems, and the other focused on unhealthy family problems (Shek, 1998). The clustering of responses from the Chinese American families along fewer dimensions than those for the general population suggests that they have relatively undifferentiated attitudes toward their families, possibly because their culture does not encourage them to reveal their emotions in public. These findings suggest that the original C-SFI scale may be inappropriate for use with Chinese American populations, and that the revised subscales should be used instead.

Some of the problems relating to culturally biased assessment tools can be resolved through a back-translation process in which different groups of bilingual experts translate the instrument from English into another language and then another group translates the tool back to English. A comparison between the original and the translation reveals discrepancies in meaning, and those discrepancies can then be corrected (Rogler, Malgady, & Rodriguez, 1989). Back-translation is an etic approach to research and assessment; etic approaches use comparative tools to assess cultural appropriateness and cultural bias, often working backwards to adapt mainstream tools for different cultural groups. Although back-translation ensures a high degree of linguistic or semantic equivalence in translated instruments, it does not eliminate the potential for serious problems of equivalence in content. Even when perfectly translated, phrases can resonate differently across cultures, and responses to them are influenced by cultural norms. For example, a scale developed for non-Latino whites to measure caregiver burden may pose questions that seem inappropriate to clients from communities that value filial obligations to elderly parents, because the questions assume that assistance to parents entails personal sacrifices, an assumption that may not be accurate in some cultures. Cultural norms that stress personal modesty (for example, some Asian cultural norms) can influence one's willingness to acknowledge personal achievement. Clients from these cultures may hesitate to suggest that they have "much to be proud of," as they are asked to do on the most widely used self-esteem scale in the social sciences (Rosenberg, 1989).

Qualitative and Mixed Methods

For many decades, quantitative research based on experimental or quasi-experimental methods, large probability samples, structured interviews or close-ended survey questions, hypothesis testing, and inferential statistics has been the accepted prototype for rigorous research. These quantitative research methods help us advance knowledge regarding the "what": what is happening, and who are the key players in the social phenomenon? Qualitative research is regaining legitimacy in social work research because it is more suitable for dealing with issues of social meaning and narratives, or the "how" and "why," issues that are especially important to consider in research with cultural minorities. To pursue the different kinds of questions that emerge in work with different cultural communities, researchers may need to use qualitative and mixed methods designs (combinations of qualitative and quantitative methods) rather than close-ended interviews, survey methods, or experimental approaches.

Qualitative methods encompass an array of research methodologies, including content analysis of documents and scripts, participant observation, open-ended and semi-structured interviews, focus groups, and ethnography. Like more quantitative survey and experimental methods, qualitative research can be employed effectively in research with cultural minorities and can be utilized to address different questions than those that are typically addressed in quantitative research. In studies of cultural minority populations, a key advantage of most qualitative research tools is that the methods are emic in nature, meaning that they require the researcher to become intimately familiar with the culture from the perspective of its members, rather than using preconceived terms, typologies, or concepts to study and describe the group. The emic perspective is incorporated into several research methods, such as focus groups, intensive open-ended interviews, and systematic observation in natural settings. Each of these methods utilizes key informants from the community and allows them to characterize and assign meaning to their lives in their own terms (Rogler, 1989). The ethnographic method exemplifies the types of cultural processes and issues that qualitative research can address well. Ethnography is also an example of an approach that typically employs different research methodologies in combination.

Ethnography is the study of a particular culture or group, and an approach to studying ways of life that are different from our own. The ethnographer's approach is emic. Ethnographers usually incorporate interviews with open-ended questions as part of the research to allow the interview subject's cultural ideas, categories, and themes to emerge, from which the ethnographer builds subsequent questions, analyses, and, in some cases, refined concepts and theories. Ethnographic research may draw on a selection of different qualitative and quantitative methodologies, including historical, demographic, economic, and geographic profiles of the group being studied; participant observation, where the researcher participates directly in the group's activities; intensive interviewing; and the use of key informants. It is distinctive in that it focuses on understanding cultural beliefs and culturally influenced behaviors not from preexisting theory but from the perspective of members of the community. Ethnographers spend time in the field to become familiar with the language, norms, values, and experiences of those who are being studied and to acquire insight into their experiential world.

The broad applicability of ethnography for culturally grounded social work research is clear. Ethnography is an excellent tool for revealing similarities and differences in the way that people from different cultures view issues in their lives. For example, a study designed to improve the effectiveness of a peer education model for preventing HIV transmission among adolescents used one-on-one ethnographic interviews with adult staff, peer educators, and student participants (Ott, Evans, Halpern-Felshr, & Eyre, 2003). A form of content analysis was then used to transcribe and analyze the interviews in order to identify beliefs and ideas that were shared among, as well as unique to, each group of informants. The study found that although the three groups possessed similar beliefs and knowledge about HIV transmission and prevention, there were important differences in how they described their perceptions of HIV risk. While staff tended to describe HIV risks within a larger social developmental context, emphasizing the need to learn how to make healthy decisions about intimate relationships and sexual health, the student participants focused on HIV risks in sexual behaviors and demonstrated a good deal of anxiety about them. The peer educators held a variety of views similar to those of both the staff and student participants. The study showed that a focus on the content of the prevention message was not enough to address the program's effectiveness, and that evaluations needed to consider the different perceptions of HIV risk among adults, students, and peer educators.

In social work, ethnography can fill important gaps in knowledge about a community, such as information on their beliefs regarding risk behaviors, resiliencies for coping with adversity, and the operation of social services. The exploratory nature of ethnography allows the researcher to study issues and problems that are not easy to learn about through traditional quantitative or experimental methods alone, such as how people learn about and access services, and how they behave as program participants. Ethnography is particularly valuable for gaining insight into people's perspectives. Federal agencies such as the National Park Service and the U.S. Census Bureau have used ethnographic studies to improve their understanding of the sociocultural life of groups whose beliefs and behavior are important to the missions of these programs. Even in clinical settings where there is an emphasis on the client's unique perspective and challenges, an ethnographic approach that considers the communities in which clients reside can help practitioners understand the cultural worlds that shape individual psychological and social lives, fill in the environmental context contributing to social and psychological disorder, and suggest culturally appropriate treatments.

While there is a century-old tradition in ethnography of combining different methods of data collection—such as observation, interviews, and documentary evidence—it is only in the last decade that researchers have begun to systemize the use of mixed method designs that employ both qualitative and quantitative approaches in a single study (see Tashakkori & Teddlie, 1998, 2003). Several types of mixed methods designs have emerged; these differ in whether qualitative and quantitative methods are employed in tandem or in sequence, whether precedence is given to qualitative or quantitative approaches or they are given equal weight, and how data from the different methods are integrated in analysis. Regardless of the way that these approaches are combined, mixed methods designs have been shown to be powerful techniques for addressing issues in research with cultural minorities. The initial qualitative phase of a mixed methods study of an African American community affected by HIV/AIDS used open-ended ethnographic interviewing techniques to find recurrent themes in the participants' language as they described living with the epidemic, such as struggles over blame and acceptance of both oneself and others (Hopson, Lucas, & Peterson, 2000). Analysis of the language used within the community to interpret the meaning and consequences of HIV/AIDS revealed the role of culture in risk behaviors and their prevention. Along with semi-structured interviews that assessed community members' backgrounds and risk and protective behaviors, the researchers were able to design a subsequent quantitative instrument for a post-intervention evaluation that contained questions that were phrased in ways that resonated with participants' understanding of their relationship to the epidemic.

The development of a culturally grounded assessment tool for Native American adolescents at risk of drug use provides an example of how culturally sensitive research can make effective use of mixed methods (Okamoto, LeCroy, Tann, Rayle, Kulis, Dustman, & Berceli, 2006). The researchers combined qualitative focus group and quantitative survey methods to identify the most common and difficult situations in which Native youths were offered drugs. The focus groups were structured to allow small groups of youths to relate narratives of their daily lives and place their encounters with drugs within the social contexts that were meaningful to them. Qualitative analysis of the transcripts from the focus groups identified sixty-two distinctive situations of encounters with drugs, defined by the type of drug, the youth's relationship to the person offering the drug, the physical setting, and the presence of others from the youth's social network (Okamoto, LeCroy, Dustman, Hohmann-Marriott, & Kulis, 2004).

In the subsequent quantitative survey phase, another group of Native youths indicated how often they had encountered each of the situations and how difficult they were to navigate; demographic and risk behavior information was also gathered. Researchers then analyzed the data from those self-administered questionnaires to identify the most common sources of drugs used by each youth and placed their risk of and resiliency against drug use within its social context (Kulis, Okamoto, Rayle, & Sen, 2006; Rayle, Kulis, Okamoto, Tann, LeCroy, Dustman, & Burke, 2006).

While these examples of mixed methods involve a sequence where a qualitative approach preceded the quantitative phase, sometimes that order may be reversed with productive results. An example is the use of GIS analysis. A geographic information system is a computer-based system that collects, stores, analyzes, and graphically displays data that can be mapped by geographic coordinates. Although this system is relatively new to the social sciences, GIS has quickly become a powerful tool for analyzing the physical, health, and social circumstances of geographically defined communities such as neighborhoods and schools, as well as any group that can be demarcated according to zip code, school district boundaries, census tracts, political boundaries, and any other geographic subdivision.

The mapping capabilities of GIS are frequently combined with information from the U.S. Census Bureau and government or industry reports. The merged information can be used to detail the demographic characteristics of geographical communities (e.g., population changes, ethnic and immigrant composition, and family structures), their health and behavioral risks (e.g., disease rates, exposure to environmental hazards, and crime and drug use rates), and their level of access to economic opportunities and needed services (e.g., location and density of employers, hospitals, clinics, and social service agencies). Using GIS, a researcher can compare the geographic concentrations of people at risk and in need of social services to the locations of the service providers and then visualize transportation-related obstacles to service access. With GIS, variations in poverty levels can be assessed not at the neighborhood level, but block by block. In a study of elderly people living in South Carolina, GIS techniques provided information regarding elderly population characteristics for a particular county, located government and private sector resources, and identified gaps between the concentrations of elderly residents and the available resources, helping to target potentially unmet needs (Hirshorn & Stewart, 2003).

GIS can help identify social welfare issues that might go unnoticed when needs assessments rely primarily on those who come forward for services, as these individuals' needs may not represent the needs of cultural minorities. It can help social workers and service planners conceptualize and address issues at the community level and lead them to investigate distinctive cultural forces at work in these communities. GIS can be a springboard for effective mixed methods designs. It helps researchers formulate questions about the reasons for variations across geographic communities in health and welfare. These questions are best answered through subsequent qualitative methods such as focus groups, intensive interviews, and observational studies. GIS analysis is an important tool for administrators, as it allows them to visualize supply and demand and expand services where they are most needed; for community development plans that attempt to address a community's embedded political, social, and economic assets and liabilities; and social service providers and agencies that want to compile and disseminate information about a community's service options to current and potential clients. It is also useful for gaining an understanding of community trends and changes.

BRIDGING THE GAP BETWEEN RESEARCH AND PRACTICE

There is a need for research with cultural minorities that can be translated into practical applications for policy and practice, a task that typically requires collaboration among practitioners, researchers, and policy makers. Advances in mixed methods hold great promise for improving the quality and relevance of research for social work practice, but it is more likely that practitioners will be educated consumers applying the published results of these methods than active participants in conducting the research. Social work practitioners seldom have the time or the support to conduct research and may see themselves as operating in a here-and-now world that is set apart from that of researchers. Researchers may appear to be concerned with the pursuit of abstract truths, while practitioners are accustomed to relying on their own practice experience to help their clients. To make research more relevant to practice, academics, practitioners, universities, and social service agencies have to collaborate to develop approaches for integrating practice and research integration that empower practitioners with useful information rather than scientific demonstrations of hypothetically effective but impractical practices. Two methods that have been proposed as means to bridge the gap between research and practice are participatory action research and translational research.

Participatory Action Research

Epstein (1995) advocates practice-based research rather than research-based practice, that is, research that is designed to be relevant to practice rather than to establish effectiveness in the abstract. When social workers let research ideas develop from their clinical observations rather than basing them exclusively on past theories and findings, the chances that findings that are relevant to practice will emerge are enhanced. As long as social workers define themselves exclusively as either practitioners or researchers, there is little hope for meaningful advances in practice knowledge development. If social workers were to define themselves as both practitioners and researchers, creative and productive knowledge-building efforts could occur.

The participatory action research (PAR) model allows the necessary role integration between the practitioner and the researcher, but with a more manageable level of practitioner involvement than is often required by other methods. PAR follows the key principles of Paulo Freire's work on effective pedagogy, which showed how researchers benefit from the experience and knowledge of local people. The difference between Freire's action research and participatory action research in that action research is focused on stimulating a fundamental change process that empowers the community being studied, while PAR is focused more narrowly on finding solutions to concrete problems. PAR is used to consider the perspectives of all parties in the examination of problems with the goal of solving them. In traditional research settings, the researcher is thought to be the expert, the repository of knowledge who enlightens others; in contrast, PAR gives communities the task of locating the needed knowledge. In participatory action research, those who are affected are the ones who select the problem to be studied and collect the data used to address it. PAR is similar to other participatory models such as action inquiry, action science, community-based research, and cooperative inquiry, all of which view the individuals under study as active participants in generating information.

PAR advocates a more egalitarian relationship between the researcher and the participants, and equal distribution of tasks. The democratic philosophy of participatory action research requires participants to be involved in all stages of the study and to be treated as equals by the researchers. In PAR, community members are treated as full stakeholders. This means that the research methods are developed and applied in community settings and are based on collective community action, not on a design conceived in advance by university researchers. PAR seeks to raise the consciousness of the oppressed and to encourage a collective response to social disadvantages. In PAR, participants help develop research questions, design measures and instruments, collect information, and reflect on the results. This engagement and reflection not only give the researcher a more valid and reliable interpretation of the data but also transform the community's understanding of the nature of their problem. In terms of PAR's applicability to culturally grounded social work, while traditional research may be conducted *on* cultural minorities, PAR is research *with* and *by* minority group or community members. In traditional research, the project ends when the data is analyzed, but in PAR, action is the next logical stage once the analysis has been completed. PAR may contribute to social progress for communities. Its main outcomes are not only findings, conclusions, and policy recommendations, but also increased social inclusion, participation by community members, and improved service user participation.

PAR operates from an ecological perspective and consists of four processes—planning, action, observation, and reflection—all of which interact in a cycle until the research objectives are attained. The objective of PAR is to promote health and social justice within the community and to help community members identify solutions to their problems. PAR involves practitioners, community members, and researchers in a melding of research with education and action that takes advantage of the strengths, competencies, and potential promises in the research setting. Collaborations among researchers, community members, government agencies, and nonprofit organizations—all focused on collective action to address identified issues—are essential to both the PAR process and its outcome.

Participatory action research, which emphasizes deliberate and concerted efforts to work with members of traditionally oppressed communities, is thus well aligned with social work's commitment to social justice. PAR often takes place in communities that have been exploited or oppressed and addresses their concerns with the goal of achieving positive social change. The guiding principles of PAR approach oppression as a problem rooted in macro social systems that require fundamental transformation of the social order, principles that are consistent with social work's progressive outlook.

For example, researchers used PAR in a multi-phase study of cultural and institutional obstacles that contribute to the reluctance of African Americans to use hospice services (Reese, Ahern, Nair, O'Faire, & Warren, 1999). The study used intensive open-ended interviews with African American pastors as well as questionnaires completed by hospice patients, churchgoers, and others from the community. The interviews helped the researchers identify a number of cultural beliefs and practices that were inconsistent with the hospice philosophy—such as opposition to accepting terminal disease, planning for death, and receiving care from strangers—sometimes for spiritual reasons. Pastors said that African American members of their congregations preferred to pursue vigorous medical treatment and rely on home remedies or prayer rather than accept palliative care from hospice, with its implicit acknowledgment of impending death. The wide-ranging research identified institutional barriers, such as the paucity of African American hospice staff and general distrust of the health care system, and demonstrated that African Americans were more reluctant to consider hospice than European

Americans. The study's foundation in PAR guided its conclusions and recommendations; for example, the study called for culturally sensitive social work practice with African Americans that honors their spiritual beliefs and the adaptation of hospice services to the needs of African Americans and recommended that African American community and religious leaders be trained to present hospice options to their congregations in a realistic and sensitive way that recognizes culturally based concerns.

Translational Research

Translational research was used first in the medical field, where it provided a model for addressing the gap between research and practice. The translational process involves overcoming all the obstacles that prevent the dissemination of research findings beyond academic circles and professional journals, and identifying the best systems and incentives for rapidly incorporating proven findings into real-life practice. It is a form of technology transfer. In social work, practitioners can play a key role as partners in translational research and the testing of promising emerging practices.

Several practical strategies have been suggested to promote translational research in social work. A first step is for researchers to make their findings more accessible by providing clear summaries and explicating practice implications. A more difficult task is the creation of viable opportunities for researchers, academics, service providers, clients, and policy makers to come together and focus their attention on a given issue. Collaboratories have been suggested as one means to link these different groups technologically over distance (Finholt & Olson, 1997). Collaboratories use the Internet to allow individuals to share information, enlarge their understanding of an issue, and identify solutions in a collaborative way. The objective of translational research is not only to design or recraft research findings so that they are more accessible to practitioners, but also to make it possible for social work researchers, practitioners, and policy makers to work together on issues of common concern.

DEVELOPING KNOWLEDGE ON DIFFERENT CULTURES

Both evaluation and research can be designed to enhance knowledge of cultural diversity through the recognition and incorporation of the different ways that knowledge can be generated. Research and evaluation that follow the principles and logic of the scientific method and that are empirically supported through careful observation are one of many ways of gaining knowledge. Although they may not receive the blessing of the scientific establishment, other forms of knowledge can also be of great use in the study of different cultural groups. This knowledge can be based on the personal experiences of members of the cultural groups, or it may be based on what people assume to be true because of what they have learned about the world through their families and communities.

Because of our society's preference for scientific knowledge, our knowledge of cultural groups tends to be generated not by them or with them, but rather for them by others. Historically, oppressed groups such as women and cultural minorities have not played an equal role in the development of knowledge about themselves because they have had problems gaining entry into and acceptance as students and professors within the university circles where researchers are trained and where much research is conducted. In her or his position as outsider, the researcher may arrive at conclusions that do not reflect the experience of the group being studied. Much progress has been made in transforming academia into a more inclusive system where nontraditional perspectives are welcome. The ways that knowledge can be developed in partnership with members of oppressed communities discussed in this chapter need to be utilized more widely, and practitioners and researchers must continue to perfect them.

Key Concepts

Etic a type of research approach that analyzes cultural phenomena from the perspective of one who is not a member of the culture being studied

Emic a type of research approach that analyzes cultural phenomena from the perspective of a member of the culture being studied

Quantitative research typically an experimental or survey research method in social work that employs hypothesis testing and inferential statistics to study a group and is used to study the "what"

Qualitative research research methodologies that study the "why" and the "how," such as content analysis of documents and scripts, participant observation, open-ended and semi-structured interviews, focus groups, and ethnography

Ethnography a way of studying and describing a culture and an approach to gaining an understanding of a way of life different from one's own in which the researcher immerses her- or himself in the field to acquire insight into the experiential world of people; usually employs a variety of methods, such as intensive interviews and participant observation

Mixed methods research the use of both qualitative and quantitative approaches in a single study

Participatory action research a research method that uses representatives of the community being studied to help frame the research questions and methods and analyze and interpret findings

15

Culturally Grounded Social Work and Globalization

AS INFORMATION, GOODS, AND PEOPLE CROSS NATIONAL BORDERS IN unprecedented numbers, globalization is affecting all aspects of society, including social work practice. The globalization process brings new opportunities and unfamiliar challenges to the profession. Globalization can be defined as the process by which the geographical, political, and cultural boundaries that separate individuals and societies weaken or dissipate. Globalization produces transculturation, which changes the way individuals perceive their world (Mastrogianni & Bhugra, 2003). Transculturalism may be experienced, for example, by a teenager residing in the Mexican city of Monterrey who sings along to American rap music without fully comprehending the lyrics. Transculturation allows him to experience an array of social processes simultaneously without leaving Mexico (Wagner, Diaz, Lopez, Collado, & Aldaz, 2002). The first is an acculturation process into American culture that occurs as he integrates and adopts aspects of American culture such as its music and dress code but does not require him to cross the Mexican-U.S. border. The second is a deculturalization process, which takes place as he lets go of aspects of his native Mexican culture, such as its traditional music. The third is the process of neoculturation, or the creation of new cultural artifacts incorporating elements of both the traditional and the new cultures, such as rap music with Spanish lyrics and Mexican cultural themes. Transculturation creates a mosaic of all these cultural contributions. Those who live on the figurative and literal borders of countries and cultures may more easily embrace transculturalism because they exist in a bicultural or multicultural space, occupying two or more worlds simultaneously.

Although globalization is often seen as the opposite of nationalism or regionalism (Powell, 2007), societies that are very much involved in the globalization process have shown a parallel tendency to grow more regional and sectarian in outlook. In some ways, the stronger regional identity becomes possible as a result of the weakening of national governments, an outcome of globalization. As Spain, for example, has become increasingly integrated into the European Union, expressions of long-suppressed regional identities have become stronger. Spain's numerous autonomous regions have increased their demands for more social, cultural, and political autonomy, as well as recognition of regional languages and different political discourses in different regions. As communities become more global in their economic outlook and their national and regional identities are strengthened, the traditional concept of cultural identity is challenged. Globalization is connecting the economies and the cultures of the world in ways that make countries more dependent on each other.

Technology and transportation advances have compressed time and distance. The Internet places people around the globe in instant contact with the "other," but it is not clear if this type of contact encourages understanding. Immigrant families may still arrive in the United States with an idealized and unrealistic view of what life in the United States is like, and migrants often develop a positive or idealized narrative of their experience in order to cope with the dislocation of being separated from their homeland. Technology allows for constant information flow for the narratives of recently arrived immigrants to the United States to be ever present in the lives of those who remain behind.

Globalization is transforming the collective lives of societies through the accelerated movement of money, technology, goods, and people. People in the wealthy societies of the Northern Hemisphere and other developed nations enjoy comfortable incomes and shelter and marketable skills. They are in a position to choose where to live and where to work. On the other hand, in the Southern Hemisphere and developing nations, the marginalized, the poor, and the disabled; refugees from war-ravaged areas; and immigrants escaping economic crises must rely on their blood ties, kin groups, and other support systems connected to their ethnic or religious affiliations to survive because the governments of their countries of origin have withdrawn much of their support under pressure from global forces. From a social justice and distributive justice perspective, globalization appears to distribute benefits to some people, but not others. When a job is outsourced to a developing country, the impact of globalization is experienced very differently by the now-unemployed worker, the CEO of the outsourcing corporation, its profit-earning shareholders, and the newly hired worker who receives low wages and no fringe benefits.

One consequence of globalization is that many problems that certain societies experience can become globalized. Social and economic vulnerabilities and the problems they generate tend to merge and amplify across affected countries within the same region. The exportation of youth gangs from Los Angeles to cities in Central America—often spurred by U.S. deportation policies—has generated distressing social and legal challenges for communities in Tegucigalpa, Honduras, and Guatemala City, Guatemala (Arana, 2005). Globalization is not unidirectional and works at many different levels. The AIDS pandemic, which affects communities and social work practice around the world, is perhaps the most widely publicized example of this. The social work profession is being increasingly challenged to think globally as policy makers and service providers are no longer able to think about the psychosocial needs of their constituencies in isolation.

GLOBALIZATION AND SOCIAL WORK

Some may argue that globalization is producing a homogeneous culture based on consumerism at the expense of local cultures and other contextual differences, as well as the environment. This text adopts the viewpoint that social work practice promoting social justice needs to be grounded in the cultures of the communities being served. Perhaps recognizing and celebrating the centrality of culture is a means of resisting the homogeneity and oppression that people experience as part of consumer society, and a way of increasing participation and action in the pursuit of social justice. By strengthening their connections to their cultural identities, communities can begin to share and expand their collective power for social action, which in turn stimulates more social participation.

There are some concerns that globalization will lead to passivity and disengagement as groups outside the mainstream lose their cultural moorings. Although this is a valid concern, this does not have to be the case. However, communities cannot maintain their unique social identities and worldviews if their younger members are not aware of them. This is the reason why interventions promoting social justice need to start at the cultural awareness level, or with Freire's conscientization efforts. It is from this perspective that a culturally grounded approach to social work practice is applicable in a globalizing world.

A global social work perspective has the potential to produce the desired outcomes at a global level if practitioners use their understanding of the differences and similarities between countries to engage in international problem-solving activities. For example, human trafficking has become a global issue that affects members of many oppressed communities. The social work profession is well qualified to deal with these issues and their consequences.

The following steps have been proposed as a way to foster a proactive response to globalization among social workers.

1. Embrace a global social and political justice agenda.
2. Develop a more direct role in solving issues of poverty at a global level within schools of social work.
3. Support the meaningful interaction of social workers with international bodies such as the World Bank and the United Nations as well as international social work organizations.
4. Facilitate the building of political solidarity among the poor (Seipel, 2003).

The same forces that allow businesses to operate as if national borders are irrelevant also allow social activists, labor organizers, journalists, academics, and many others to work on a global stage. Globalization can have a positive effect on the lives of individuals and communities if there is some mechanism in place to fairly distribute the economic benefits that come from it, as well as the means to prevent or manage the negative consequences that globalization may produce, such as ecological degradation and violations of human and civil rights.

The Code of Ethics of the National Association of Social Workers (1999) states that "social workers should promote the general welfare of society, from local to global justice" (p. 24). Social workers tend to focus on local needs, and programs and services are designed to respond to those needs, but there is a need for social workers to become more active globally. In order to do so, social workers must be knowledgeable about the global environment because international economic and political forces have a direct impact on the well-being of local communities.

Social workers increasingly confront international problems directly, for example, through their work with refugees and vulnerable workers whose livelihoods are disrupted by the global economy. Lasting solutions will emerge as professionals increase their awareness and advocate for the creation of international institutional frameworks for problem solving across borders.

The profession of social work is going through its own process of globalization in order to respond to the needs of a transcultural client base. For example, a transnational and transcultural social work practice has been proposed as a means to intervene with the social and economic needs of immigrant communities (Lyons, 2006). Having a global perspective helps the practitioner understand the origin of problems as well as the complex relationships between the culture of origin and the emergence of transcultural identities within communities.

The globalization of social work can only happen if social work education is globalized. There is a need to broaden students' and faculty members' perspectives regarding their professional role at the international level. There is no substitute for international educational experiences. Traveling to the country of origin of an immigrant community would greatly benefit the social worker in her or his understanding of the traditional culture as well as the possible tensions and contradictions that clients may be experiencing as they navigate the host culture.

The International Federation of Social Workers, for example, is an organization whose mission is to advance social justice and development through cooperation between social workers. Other social work organizations have an international focus; for example, the International Association for the Advancement of Social Work with Groups has chapters in several countries, and their members share their research and practice experiences at annual conferences. NASW and CSWE have their own international offices and programs, which offer useful information and international exchange opportunities. Many schools of social work offer international summer immersion (language and culture) programs. Through these efforts and many others, the profession continues to become more international and globalized.

Another way the profession may address these issues is by recruiting social work students from within the communities being served. Globalization has made it increasingly important for practitioners, service providers, and even researchers to be truly bilingual and bicultural in order to reach members of many Latino and immigrant communities. A study of Head Start families found that mastery of the English language is the key that unlocks the door to the community for immigrant families, and bilingual social workers help overcome the barriers that prevent community members from accessing services and achieving their goals (Wall, Timberlake, Farber, Sabatino, Liebow, Smith, & Taylor, 2000). In such situations, social workers often play a cultural mediation role as their clients navigate through the acculturation process, allowing them to access opportunities and advance economically and socially. To mediate effectively between these two worlds, workers need to be competent in both cultures. However, the reality is that the availability of bilingual and bicultural social workers is limited. Recruiting future social workers from these communities would allow the profession to address not only the growing need for bilingual practitioners and researchers but the them-versus-us mentality that is common among immigrants and other minority clients and often presents barriers to effective social work practice.

Globalization is challenging the one-on-one approach commonly used by practitioners and is making social workers recognize the importance of communities and groups as sources of transformation. Social workers from around the world are working together to design and test innovative interventions to ensure that oppressed communities benefit from globalization and address the challenges of globalization. Many aspects of their research and practice innovation are applicable to communities in the United States, and through professional exchange and collaboration, the interventions can be shared and jointly researched and evaluated.

THE RESEARCHER-PRACTITIONER AS THE INSIDER AND THE OUTSIDER

The culturally grounded approach to social work puts forward a horizontal relationship based on honest exchanges that positions both the practitioner-researcher and the community as the experts. The ever-changing nature of culture and the rapid process of globalization make the development of a social work practitioner-researcher role imperative. The practitioner-researcher is always willing to ask another question and is ready to think outside the comfortable box of the familiar. Polarized conceptions of culture (i.e., old culture versus new culture, culture of origin versus host culture) are being questioned by transculturalism. The resurgence of qualitative methods in research involving cultural minorities, such as the use of ethnography and participatory action research, helps practitioner-researchers understand how communities understand themselves and their own changing cultures (Somerville, 2006). A common question in research with groups demarcated by race, ethnicity, gender, and sexual orientation is the extent to which one needs to be a member of the group to conduct meaningful research about it. As Robert Merton (1972) asked over three decades ago in an article on the benefits and limitations of being an insider or an outsider, "Do you have to be one to understand one?" It is important to consider the practitioner-researcher's stance as an insider or outsider. Is it possible to speak of insiders and outsiders in a global and transcultural world? Do outsiders lack the insider's special insights into the group because they have not had the socialization and group experiences that are crucial for understanding the community's ever-changing culture, language, and behavior? Is awareness of the process of transculturation becoming more relevant to social workers than an awareness of the values and norms of the community's culture of origin? It appears that social workers need to do both: continue to be aware of and comfortable with the culture of origin while becoming familiar with the processes of cultural transformation (transculturation) and its impact on individuals, families, and communities.

The challenges faced by practitioner-researchers who are outsiders looking in seem more evident than the possible advantages. While insiders, by virtue of their social position, tend to share central interests with their communities, outsiders may intervene as a result of reflecting the conflicting interests of their communities. Insiders and outsiders may frame assessment and research questions differently. For outsiders, especially those who occupy privileged positions in the cultural and economic mainstream, the main challenge is being aware of how their positions may shape their conceptions of cultural minority communities and the kinds of questions and the frames of reference they bring to their practice with and research on these communities. They need to be conscious of their lack of understanding of the communities and find ways to incorporate the community members' perspectives in the research.

Practitioners also need to be aware of how privilege affects their access to the community. Inquiries into issues of cultural difference posed by outsiders may emphasize how the "other" is different, implicitly assuming and reinforcing the idea that the mainstream represents what is normal. This is the basis for the criticism that much practice and research conducted by outsiders presumes that only nonwhites have racial and ethnic identities, that gender is significant only in the lives of women, and that sexual orientation is only of interest to homosexuals. White researchers run the risk of carrying what Peggy McIntosh (1990) calls the "knapsack of invisible privilege" into the practice and research processes. Outsiders' social awkwardness and psychological discomfort—in addition to the potential for them to misunderstand or misrepresent cultural minorities—may compromise the effectiveness of the intervention; they may attempt to compensate with overzealousness but fail to devote sufficient attention to building trusting relationships within the community over time. Exploitation is also an issue, especially for practitioner-researchers whose approach is to drop into a vulnerable community briefly to try to fix the problem or extract data for their own research agenda and then disappear.

Despite the difficult issues faced by those who are not members of the community under study, there are potential advantages to being an outsider. Outsiders may not be expected to screen their language and behavior in the same way as insiders and are less likely to face appeals to or questions about their loyalties to the group. Outsiders may elicit fuller and richer responses to certain questions than insiders because respondents may assume that insiders already know the answers. This may be one reason that some practitioner-researchers find that working with clients of a different ethnicity or gender sometimes is easier than working with those who are similar (Cannon, Higginbotham, & Leung, 1988). In addition, as the problems of cultural outsider status become more widely recognized, outsiders may develop a heightened awareness of the need to be clear and self-conscious about the methodological choices they make.

Insiders also face significant (though often more subtle) challenges in practicing and conducting research within their own communities. One challenge for insiders is avoiding equating their familiarity with their communities with effective practice. As a result of acculturation and transculturation, the ideas that practitioners have about culture may be outdated. Whereas outsiders run the risk of imposing their own cultural assumptions, categories and meanings on the group being studied, insiders may struggle to gain some distance from their personal experience as a member of the community under study and avoid judging culture as good or bad, correct or incorrect, or authentic or inauthentic. As members of the cultural minority group under study, insiders may have a history of deeply personal and emotional experiences of marginalization, experiences that, though similar, need to be kept distinct from those of the clients or research subjects (Kanuha, 2000).

Insiders have a special authenticity that is very useful in gaining access and the trust of the community but may compromise their objectivity. Insider status can also pose a problem by leading to the presumption of insider knowledge. Respondents may confide to insider practitioners through cultural code words and phrases and through nonverbal behaviors and gestures that reflect tacit understandings in the community. Respondents may feel comfortable making vague references or failing to clarify their ideas and expect the researcher to intuitively understand what they mean. Often these ideas may be communicated in a way that reinforces their common membership—"*You* would know what I mean" or "You know how *they* are." The problem here is twofold. The practitioner-researcher may not have knowledge of the person's experience of culture or of her or his local community, or of the effects of transculturation in the original culture, and may not understand various aspects of the culture in the same way as the respondent. In addition, any implicit cultural understandings have to be made explicit before they can be addressed or analyzed. Another set of problems for insiders is that the boundaries between practitioner and client or researcher and subject can easily blur.

Despite these different challenges, in a globalized world insiders and outsiders confront similar issues. Both groups need to reflect on their social position within a given community, the power differential between practitioners and their clients, and how they represent their own perspectives and those of their clients. Consciousness of social positions requires recognition of the tremendous variability that exists within cultural communities. Practitioners and researchers can be similar or different from those they work with in terms of education and social class background as well as in race, ethnicity, gender, sexual orientation, and age. The multiple ways that these social statuses may intersect and the effects of globalization and transculturation suggest that practitioners can only be partial insiders and seldom are complete outsiders. Those who grew up in the culture may change, such that even though they continue to be able to gain the trust of community members and understand their ways and values, they may or may not endorse all those practices and values.

Differences in power—across lines of ethnicity, class, gender, age, and sexual orientation—shape relationships between the researcher and the community under study regardless of whether the researcher is a relative insider or outsider. Social workers emphasize the importance of empowering the clients by both developing culturally appropriate interventions that take their perspective into consideration and negotiating with them their involvement and stake in the helping process. All practitioner-researchers face the difficult question of how they can represent the voices and perspectives of their clients while also presenting assessments as reflections of truth. Most choose a course between two extremes. Logical positivism, at one end, maintains that through careful observation, rigorous methods, and detached objectivity, practitioners can uncover facts and dynamics that exist in a social world independently of their perspectives. Postmodernism, on the other hand, maintains that all knowledge is socially constructed by individuals and by communities, such that any needs assessment reveals a multiplicity of perspectives rather than a single truth. Some postmodernists view attempts to seek truth not only as futile but as political acts that are designed to strengthen the powerful and privileged and silence the powerless. Regardless of where practitioners fall between these extremes, and whether they are relative insiders or outsiders to the cultural communities they are working with, they should consider how to represent the needs and desires of their clients and research subjects accurately and authentically. Eliot Liebow (1967), a sociologist who documented his groundbreaking qualitative research with African American men in *Talley's Corner*, described the challenge as always being aware of the distance between the perspectives of the researcher and the researched, but "walking the margins."

What separated him from his research subjects was less a wall than a "chain-link fence, since despite the barriers we were able to look at each other, walk alongside each other, talk and occasionally touch fingers. When two people stand up close to the fence on either side, without touching it, they can look through the interstices and forget that they are looking through a fence" (pp. 250–251).

A culturally grounded perspective challenges the researcher-practitioner to be aware of the fence and at the same time to reach through it to hear the voices and capture the stories from the other side.

Key Concepts

Globalization the process by which the geographical, political, and cultural boundaries that separate individuals and societies weaken or dissipate into a more universal set of norms and behaviors

Transculturation an identity status produced by globalization that is not connected to one nation or one culture but instead is a blend of multiple cultural sources from across the globe

Neoculturation the creation of new cultural artifacts through the incorporation of elements of both the traditional and the new cultures that does not require the individual to leave her or his country of origin

References

Abalos, D. T. (2002). *The Latino male: A radical redefinition.* Boulder, CO: Lynne Rienner.

Abed, M. (2006). Clarifying the concept of genocide. *Metaphilosophy, 37*(3–4), 308–330.

Abram, F. Y., Slosar, J. A., & Walls, R. (2005). Reverse mission: A model for international social work education and transformative intra-national practice. *International Social Work, 48*(2), 161–176.

Abusharaf, R. M. (2007). *Female circumcision: Multicultural perspectives.* Philadelphia: University of Pennsylvania Press.

Adams, C. L., & Kimmel, D. C. (1997). Exploring the lives of older African American gay men. In B. Greene (Ed.), *Ethnic and cultural diversity among lesbian and gay men* (pp. 132–151). Thousand Oaks, CA: Sage.

Aiken, L. S., LoSciuto, L. A., & Ansetto, M. A. (1984). Paraprofessional versus professional drug counselors: The progress of clients in treatment. *International Journal of the Addictions, 19*(4), 383–401.

Akresh, I. R. (2006). Occupational mobility among legal immigrants to the United States. *International Migration Review, 40*(4), 854–884.

Alba, R., & Hee, V. (1997). Rethinking assimilation theory for a new era of immigration. *International Migration Review, 31*(4), 826–874.

Aldrich, R. (2003). *Colonialism and homosexuality.* London: Routledge.

Alexander, G. M., & Hines, M. (1994). Gender labels and play styles: Their relative contribution to children's selection of playmates. *Child Development, 51*, 869–879.

Allport, G. W. (1954). *The nature of prejudice.* Garden City, NY: Anchor Books.

Altman, D. (1996). Rupture or continuity? The internationalization of gay identities. *Social Text, 48*(3), 77–94.

Alvarez, R., & Lutterman, K. (1979). *Discrimination in organizations.* San Francisco: Jossey-Bass.

American Indian Movement. (1972, October 31). *Trail of broken treaties 20-point position paper.* [Press release]. Retrieved October 17, 2007, from http://www.aimovement.org/ggc/trailofbrokentreaties.html

Anbinder, T. (2006). Nativism and prejudice against immigrants. In R. Ueda (Ed.), *A companion to American immigration* (pp. 177–201). Malden, MA: Blackwell.

Andall, J. (2002). Second-generation attitudes? African-Italians in Milan. *Journal of Ethnic and Migration Studies, 28*(3), 389–408.

Anderson, M. L., & Collins, P. H. (2004). *Race, class, and gender* (5th ed.). Belmont, CA: Thomson Wadsworth.

Angle, P. M. (Ed.). (1991). *The complete Lincoln-Douglas debates of 1858.* Chicago: University of Chicago Press.

Anthis, K. (2002). The role of sexist discrimination in adult women's identity development. *Sex Roles, 47*(9/10), 477–484.

Aponte, H. J. (1994). *Bread and spirit: Therapy with the new poor: Diversity of race, culture, and values.* New York: W. W. Norton.

Appleby, G. (2001). Dynamics of oppression and discrimination. In G. Appleby, E. Colon, & J. Hamilton (Eds.), *Diversity, oppression, and social functioning* (pp. 36–52). Boston: Allyn and Bacon.

Arana, A. (2005, May/June). How the street gangs took Central America. *Foreign Affairs, 84*(3), 98–110.

Aron-Dine, A., & Shapiro, I. (2006, October 13). *New data show extraordinary jump in income concentration in 2004.* Washington, DC: Center for Budget and Policy Priorities.

Asante, M. K. (Ed.). (2000). *Socio-cultural conflict between African American and Korean American.* Lanham, MD: University Press of America.

Ashcroft, B., Griffiths, G., & Tiffin, H. (2000). *Post-colonial studies: The key concepts.* London: Routledge.

Ashford, J. B., LeCroy, C. W., & Lortie, K. L. (2001). *Human behavior in the social environment* (2nd ed.). Belmont, CA: Wadsworth.

Aybars, A. I. (2007). Work-life balance in the EU and leave arrangements across welfare regimes. *Industrial Relations Journal, 38*(6), 569–590.

Bacal, A. (1994). *Types of ethnic identity responses to ethnic discrimination: An experiential approach to Mexican American identity.* Göteborg: Göteborgs Universitet.

Baca Zinn, M. (1982). Chicano men and masculinity. *Journal of Ethnic Studies, 10*(2), 29–44.

Baca Zinn, M., & Thornton Dill, B. (1996). Theorizing difference from multiracial feminism. *Feminist Studies, 22*(2), 321–33.

Bailey, J., & Martin, N. (1995). *A twin registry study of sexual orientation.* Paper presented at the annual meeting of the International Academy of Sex Research, Provincetown, MA.

Bailey, J., & Pillard, R. (1991). A genetic study of male sexual orientation. *Archives of General Psychiatry, 48*, 1089–1096.

Bailey, J., Pillard, R., Neale, M., & Agyei, Y. (1993). Heritable factors influence sexual orientation in women. *Archives of General Psychiatry, 50*, 217–223.

Baker, D. K. (2005). Beyond women and economics: Rereading "women's work." *Journal of Women in Culture and Society, 30*(4), 2189–2209.

Bamshad, M. J., & Olson, S. E. (2003). Does race exist? *Scientific American, 289*(6), 78–85.

Bandura, A., & Bussey, K. (2002). On broadening the cognitive, motivational, and sociostructural scope of theorizing about gender development and functioning: Comment on Martin, Ruble, and Szkrybalo (2002). *Psychological Bulletin, 130,* 691–701.

Barbee, A. P., Cunningham, M. R., Winstead, B. A., Derlega, V. J., Grulley, M. R., Yankeelov, P. A., & Druen, P. B. (1993). Effects of gender role expectations on the social support process. *Journal of Social Issues, 49*(3), 175–191.

Barinaga, M. (1991). Is homosexuality biological? *Science, 253*(5023), 956–958.

Barnett, E., Braham, V. E., Casper, M. L., Elmes, G. A., & Halverson, J. A. (2007). *Men and heart disease: An atlas of racial and ethnic disparities in mortality.* CDC and West Virginia University. Retrieved December 11, 2007, from http://hdl.handle.net/123456789/9053

Barrie, T., & Luria, Z. (2004). Sexuality and gender in children's daily worlds. In M. S. Kimmel & R. F. Plante (Eds.), *Sexualities: Identities, behaviors, and society* (pp. 74–85). New York: Oxford University Press.

Barton, K., & Delgado, M. (1998). Murals in Latino communities: Social indicators of community strengths. *Mark Social Work, 43*(4), 346–357.

Baubôck, R. (2002). Political community beyond the sovereign state, supranational federalism, and transnational minorities. In S. Vertovec & R. Cohen (Eds.), *Conceiving cosmopolitanism: Theory, context and practice* (pp. 110–136). London: Oxford University Press.

Baum, S., & Payea, K. (2005). *Education pays 2004: The benefits of higher education for individuals and society.* New York: College Board.

Becker, G. S. (1975). *Human capital.* New York: Columbia University Press.

Becker, T. (1998). *Reflections on traditional American Indian ways report.* Retrieved December 21, 2007, from http://www.americanindianpolicycenter.org/research/reflect.html

Becker, D., McGlashan, T., Vojvoda, D., & Weine, S. (1999). Case series: PTSD symptoms in adolescent survivors of "ethnic cleansing": Results from a 1 year follow up study. *Journal of the American Academy of Child and Adolescent Psychiatry, 38*(6), 775–782.

Behrens, A., Uggen, C., & Manza, J. (2003). Ballot manipulation and the "menace of Negro domination": Racial threat and felon disenfranchisement in the United States, 1850–2002. *American Journal of Sociology, 109*(3), 559–605.

Bejel, E. (2001). *Gay Cuban nation.* Chicago: University of Chicago Press.

Belliveau, M. A. (1996). The paradoxical influence of policy exposure on affirmative action attitudes. *Journal of Social Issues, 52*(4), 99–105.

Benard, B. (1991). *Fostering resiliency in kids: Protective factors in the family, school, and community.* Portland, OR: Northwest Regional Educational Laboratory, U.S. Department of Education.

Benard, B. (2002). Turnaround people and places: Moving from risk to resiliency. In D. Saleebey (Ed.), *The strengths perspective in social work practice* (3rd ed., pp. 213–227). Boston: Allyn and Bacon.

Begard, L. (2007). *The comparative histories of slavery in Brazil, Cuba, and the United States.* London: Cambridge University Press.

Belkin, A., & Bateman, G. (2003). *Don't ask, don't tell: Debating the gay ban in the military.* Boulder, CO: Lynne Rienner.

Berger, P. L., & Luckmann, T. (1966). *The social construction of reality: A treatise in the sociology of knowledge.* New York: Doubleday.

Berkhofer, R. F. (1978). *The white man's Indian images of the American Indian from Columbus to the present.* New York: Random House.

Berliner, D. C. (2006). Our impoverished view of education reform. *College Teacher Record, 108*(6), 949–995.

Berry, J. W. (1997). Immigration, acculturation and adaptation. *Applied Psychology, 46,* 5–34.

Berry, J. W., Kim, U., Power, S., Young, M., & Bujaki, M. (1989). Acculturation attitudes in plural societies. *Applied Psychology, 38,* 185–206.

Bielby, W., & Baron, J. (1984). A woman's place is with other women: Sex segregation within organizations. In B. F. Reskin (Ed.), *Sex segregation in the workplace: Trends, explanations, remedies* (pp. 27–55). Washington, DC: National Academy Press.

Bielby, W., & Baron, J. (1986). Men and women at work: Sex segregation and statistical discrimination. *American Journal of Sociology, 91*(4), 759–799.

Biermann, J., Dunlop, A., Brady, C., Dubin, C., & Brann, A. (2006). Promising practices in preconception care for women at risk for poor health and pregnancy outcomes. *Maternal and Child Health Journal, 10,* S21–S28.

Birzer, M. L., & Birzer, G. H. (2006). Race matters: A critical look at racial profiling, it's a matter of the courts. *Journal of Criminal Justice, 34*(6), 643–651.

Blakey, M. L. (1999). Scientific racism and the biological concept of race. *Literature and Psychology, 1999*(1/2), 29–37.

Blauner, R. (1972). *Racial oppression in America.* New York: Harper and Row.

Blum, L. (2006). Comments on Eamonn Callan. *Symposia on Gender, Race, and Philosophy, 2*(2), 1–4.

Blum, L., & Smith, V. (1988). Women's mobility in the corporation: A critique of the politics of optimism. *Signs, 13,* 528–545.

Blumberg, R. L. (1984). *Civil rights: The 1960s freedom struggle.* Boston: Twayne.

Bly, R. (1990). *Iron John: A book about men.* Cambridge, MA: Da Capo Books.

Bobo, L., & Fox, C. (2003). Race, racism, and discrimination: Bridging problems, methods, and theory in social psychological research. *Social Psychology Quarterly, 66*(4), 319–332.

Boes, M., & Van Wormer, K. (1997). Social work with homeless women in emergency rooms: A strengths-feminist perspective. *Affilia: Journal of Women and Social Work, 12*(4), 408–427.

Bogenschneider, K. (1996). An ecological risk/protective theory for building prevention programs, policies, and community capacity to support youth. *Family Relations, 45,* 127–138.

Bond, S., & Cash, T. F. (1992). Black beauty: Skin color and body images among African-American college women. *Journal of Applied Social Psychology, 22,* 874–888.

Bonilla-Silva, E. (1997). Rethinking racism: Towards a structural interpretation. *American Sociological Review, 62*(3), 465–480.

Bonilla-Silva, E. (2006). *Racism without racists: Color-blind racism and the persistence of racial inequality in the United States.* Lanham, MD: Rowman & Littlefield.

Bonvillain, N. (2001). *Women and men: Cultural constructs of gender* (3rd ed.). Upper Saddle River: Prentice Hall.

Borjas, G. J., & Katz, L. F. (2007). *Mexican immigration to the United States.* Chicago: University of Chicago Press.

Bower, B. (1996). Trauma syndrome transverses generations. *Science News, 149*(20), 310.

Boyd-Franklin, N. (1991). Recurrent themes in the treatment of African-American women in group psychotherapy. *Women & Therapy, 11*(2), 25–40.

Boyd-Franklin, N. (2003). *Black families in therapy: Understanding the African American experience.* New York: Guilford Press.

Boykin, K. (2005). *Beyond the down low: Sex, lies and denial in black America.* New York: Carroll & Graf.

Brammer, R. (2004). *Diversity in counseling.* Belmont, CA: Thomson.

Brannon, R. (1976). The male sex role—and what it's done for us lately. In R. Brannon & D. David (Eds.), *The forty-nine percent majority* (pp. 1–40). Reading, MA: Addison-Wesley.

BraveHeart, M. Y. H. (1995). *The return to the secret path: Healing from historical unresolved grief among the Lakota and Dakota.* PhD dissertation, Smith College.

Bronfenbrenner, U. (1986). Ecology of the family as a context for human development. *Developmental Psychology, 22,* 723–742.

Brookey, R. A. (2002). *Reinventing the male homosexual: The rhetoric and power of the gay gene.* Bloomington: Indiana University Press.

Brooks, W., & Hampton, G. (2005). Safe discussions rather than first hand encounters:

Adolescents examine racism through one historical fiction text. *Children's Literature in Education, 36*(1), 1573–1693.

Brown, K. T., Ward. G. K., Lightbourn, T., & Jackson, J. S. (1999). Skin tone and racial identity among African Americans: A theoretical and research framework. In R. L. Jones (Ed.), *Advances in African American psychology: Theory, paradigms, and research* (pp. 191–215). Hampton, VA: Cobb & Henry.

Brown, R. H. (1993). Cultural representation and ideological domination. *Social Forces, 71*(3), 657–677.

Brown-Dean, K. L. (2007). Permanent outsiders: Felon disenfranchisement and the breakdown of black politics. In G. A. Persons (Ed.), *The expanding boundaries of black politics* (pp. 103–120). Edison, NJ: Transaction Publishers.

Browne, C., & Broderick, A. (1994). Asian and Pacific Island elders: Issues for social work practice and education. *Social Work, 39*(3), 252–259.

Buddhism and health: Healing the ills of body and spirit. (1996). *Soka Gakkai International Quarterly.* Retrieved January 24, 2008 from http://www.purifymind.com/Buddhism Health.htm

Buekens, P., Notzon, F., Kotelchuck, M., & Wilcox, A. (2000). Why do Mexican Americans give birth to few low–birth weight infants? *American Journal of Epidemiology, 152*(4), 347–351.

Bureau of Justice Statistics. (2007). *Patterns of victimization and offending vary by age, gender, and racial group.* Washington, DC: U.S. Department of Justice.

Burnette, D. (1998). Conceptual and methodological considerations in research with non-white ethnic elders. *Journal of Social Service Research, 23,* 71–91.

Burr, C. (1996). *A separate creation: The search for the biological origins of sexual orientation.* New York: Hyperion.

Burstein, P. (1994). *Equal employment opportunity: Labor market discrimination and public policy.* Edison, NJ: Aldine Transaction.

Butterfoss, F. D., Goodman, R. M., & Wandersman, A. (1996). Community coalitions for prevention and health promotion: Factors predicting satisfaction, participation, and planning. *Health Education Quarterly, 23*(1), 65–79.

Caldas, S. J., Bankston, C. L., & Cain, J. S. (2007). A case study of teachers' perceptions of school desegregation and the distribution of social and academic capital. *Education and Urban Society, 39*(2), 194–222.

Campbell, C., & Jovchelovitch, S. (2000). Health, community and development: Towards a social psychology of participation. *Journal of Community & Applied Social Psychology, 10*(4), 255–270.

Campbell, G., Miers, S., & Miller, J. C. (2006). Children of European systems of slavery: Introduction. *Slavery & Abolition, 27*(2), 163–182.

Cannon, L. W., Higginbotham, E., & Leung, M. L. A. (1988). Race and class bias in qualitative research on women. *Gender and Society, 2*(4), 449–462.

Carmichael, S., & Hamilton, C. V. (1967). *Black power: The politics of liberation in America.* New York: Vintage.

Carver, P. R., Yunger, J. L., & Perry, D. G. (2003). Gender identity and adjustment in middle childhood. *Sex Roles, 49*(3/4), 95–109.

Casas, B. de las. (1992). *A short account of the destruction of the Indies.* New York: Penguin.

Cassin, S. E., & von Ranson, K. A. (2005). Personality and eating disorders: A decade in review. *Clinical Psychology Review, 25*(7), 895–916.

Catterall, H. T. (Ed.). (1968). *Judicial cases concerning American slavery and the Negro* (Vol. 1). New York: Octagon Books. (Originally published 1926)

Centers for Disease Control and Prevention. (1999, November 18). *HIV prevention within faith communities and communities of color* [Satellite broadcast]. Atlanta, GA: Author.

Centers for Disease Control and Prevention. (2003). HIV/STD risk in young men who have sex with men who do not disclose their sexual orientation—six U.S. cities, 1994–2000. *Morbidity and Mortality Weekly Report, 52,* 82–86.

Centers for Disease Control and Prevention. (2006). Racial/ethnic disparities in diagnoses of HIV/AIDS—33 states, 2001–2004. *Morbidity and Mortality Weekly Report, 55,*121–125.

Centers for Disease Control. (2007). *National health interview survey on disability.* Retrieved July 31, 2007, from http://0-www.cdc.gov.mill1.sjlibrary.org/nchs/about/major/nhis_dis/nhis_dis.htm

Chao, G. T., & Willaby, H. W. (2007). International employment discrimination and implicit social cognition: New directions for theory and research. *Applied Psychology, 56*(4), 678–688.

Chatterjee, P. (1998). The gold rush legacy: Greed, pollution, and genocide. *Earth Island Journal, 3*(2), 26–27.

Chávez, E. (2002). *My people first! "Mi raza primero!" Nationalism, identity, and insurgency in the Chicano movement in Los Angeles, 1966–1978.* Berkeley and Los Angeles: University of California Press.

Chawla, N., & Marlatt, G. (2006). The varieties of Buddhism. In E. T. Dowd & S. L. Nielsen (Eds.), *The psychologies of religion* (pp. 271–286). New York: Springer.

Cheung, Y. W. (1993). Approaches to ethnicity: Clearing roadblocks in the study of ethnicity and substance use. *International Journal of the Addictions, 28,* 1209–1226.

Chodorow, N. (1978). *The reproduction of mothering.* Berkeley and Los Angeles: University of California Press.

Choi, Y., & Lahey, B. B. (2006). Testing the model minority stereotype: Youth behaviors across racial and ethnic groups. *Social Service Review, 80*(3), 419–452.

Clair, J. A., Beatty, J. E., & MacLean, T. L. (2005). Out of sight but not out of mind: Managing invisible social identities in the workplace. *Academy of Management Review, 30*(1), 78–95.

Clark, N. (2004). Mirror, mirror on the wall . . . are muscular men the best of all? The hidden turmoil of muscle dysmorphia. *American Fitness, 22*(1), 52–55.

Clarke, J. H. (1976). African cultural continuity and slave revolts in the New World, part one. *Black Scholar, 8*(1), 41–49.

Clarkson, J. (2005). Contesting masculinity's makeover: Queer eye, consumer masculinity, and "straight-acting" gays. *Journal of Communication Inquiry, 29*(3), 235–255.

Clement, R. W., & Krueger, J. (2002). Social categorization moderates social projection. *Journal of Experimental Social Psychology, 38*(3), 219–231.

Cohen, M. B. (1998). Perceptions of power in client/worker relationships. *Families in Society: Journal of Contemporary Human Services, 79*(4), 433–443.

Cohn, S. (1985). *The process of occupational sex-typing: The feminization of clerical labor in Great Britain.* Philadelphia: Temple University Press.

Collins, P. H. (1998). *Fighting words: Black women and the search for justice.* Minneapolis: University of Minnesota Press.

Comas-Diaz, L. (1997). Mental health needs of Latinos with professional status. In J. G. Garcia &

M. C. Zea (Eds.), *Psychological interventions and research with Latino populations* (pp. 142–165). Needham Heights, MA: Allyn and Bacon.

Committee on Lesbian, Gay, & Bisexual Concerns. (1999). *Just the facts about sexual orientation & youth: A primer for principals, educators and school personnel.* Retrieved October 12, 2007, from http://www.apa.org/pi/lgbc/publications/justthefacts.html

Community Policing Consortium. (2004). *To protect and serve: An overview of community policing on Indian reservation.* Retrieved December 10, 2007 from http://www.communitypolicing.org/pf/am_ind/ch2.html

Connell, R. W. (1987). *Gender and power.* Stanford, CA: Stanford University Press.

Connell, R. W. (1990). An iron man: The body and some contradictions of hegemonic masculinity. In M. A. Messner & D. F. Sabo (Eds.), *Sport, men and the gender order: Critical feminist perspectives* (pp. 83–95). Champaign, IL: Human Kinetics Books.

Constantinople, A. (2005). Masculinity-femininity: An exception to a famous dictum? *Feminism & Psychology, 15*(4), 385–407.

Cook, S. W. (1988). The 1954 social science statement and school desegregation: A reply to Gerard. In R. A. Katzan & D. A. Taylor (Eds.), *Eliminating racism: Profiles and controversy* (pp. 237–256). New York: Plenum.

Cooley, C. H. (1918). *Social process.* New York: Scriber's Sons.

Corey, G. (1992). *Group techniques.* Pacific Grove, CA: Brooks/Cole.

Crawford, I., Allison, K. W., Zamboni, B. D., & Soto, T. (2002). The influence of duel-identity development on the psychosocial functioning of African American gay and bisexual men. *Journal of Sex Research, 39*(3), 179–189.

Creedon, P. J., & Cramer, J. (2006). *Women in mass communication.* Thousand Oaks, CA: Sage.

Crenshaw, K. (1991). Mapping the margins: Intersectionality, identity politics, and violence against women of color. *Stanford Law Review, 43*(6), 1241–1299.

Crichlow, W. (2004). *Buller men and batty boys: Hidden men in Toronto and Halifax black communities.* Toronto: University of Toronto Press.

Crocker, J., & Knight, K. M. (2005). Contingencies of self-worth. *Current Directions in Psychological Science, 14*(4), 200–203.

Crocker, J., & Major, B. (1989). Social stigma and self-esteem: The self-protective properties of stigma. *Psychological Review, 96,* 608–630.

Cross, T. A., Earle, K. A., & Simmons, D. (2000). Child abuse and neglect in Indian county: Policy issues. *Families in Society: The Journal of Contemporary Human Services, 81*(1), 49–65.

Dancey, C. P. (1990). Sexual orientation in women: An investigation of hormonal and personality variables. *Biological Psychology, 30*(3), 251–264.

Davis, J. R. (2007). Making a difference: How teachers can positively affect racial identity and acceptance in America. *Social Studies, 95*(5), 209–216.

Dean, R. G. (2001). The myth of cross-cultural competence. *Families in Society: The Journal of Contemporary Human Services, 82*(6), 623–631.

Derrida, J. (1982). *Margins of philosophy.* Chicago: University of Chicago Press.

Dhooper, S. S. (1991). Toward an effective response to the needs of Asian-Americans. *Journal of Multicultural Social Work, 1*(2), 65–81.

Dhooper, S. S. (2003). Health care needs of foreign-born Asian Americans: An overview. *Health and Social Work, 28*(1), 63–74.

Dhooper, S. S., & Tran, T. V. (1998). Understanding and responding to the health and mental health needs of Asian Americans. *Social Work in Health Care, 27*(4), 65–82.

Diamond, L., & Savin-Williams, R. (2000). Explaining diversity in the development of same-sex sexuality among young women. *Journal of Social Issues, 56*(2), 297–313.

Diaz, R. F. (1997). Macho, Latino, HIV+ (AIDS prevention among Latinos). *Advocate, 747,* 9–10.

Dick, R. W., Beals, J., Keane, E. M., & Manson, S. M. (1994). Factoral structure of the CES-D among American Indian adolescents. *Journal of Adolescence, 17,* 73–79.

Dickinson, J., & Young, B. (2003). *A short history of Quebec.* Montreal: McGill-Queen's University Press.

Di Palma, S. L., & Topper, G. G. (2001). Social work academia: Is the glass ceiling beginning to crack? *Affilia: Journal of Women and Social Work, 16*(1), 31–45.

DiPiero, T. (2002). *White men aren't.* Durham, NC: Duke University Press.

Dixon, J., & Seron, C. (1995). Stratification in the legal profession: Sex, sector, and salary. *Law & Society Review, 29,* 381–412.

Dode, L. (2004). *A history of homosexuality.* Victoria, BC: Trafford.

Dominguez, V. R. (1986). *White by definition: Social classification in Creole Louisiana.* New Brunswick, NJ: Rutgers University Press.

Downey, J., Ehrhardt, A. A., Schiffman, M., Dyrenfurth, I., & Becker, J. (1987). Sex hormones in lesbian and heterosexual women. *Hormones and Behavior, 21*(3), 347–357.

Droogsma, R. A. (2007). Redefining hijab: American Muslim women's standpoints on veiling. *Journal of Applied Communication Research, 35*(3), 294–319.

DuBois, E. C. (1999). *Feminism and suffrage: The emergence of an independent women's movement in America, 1848–1869.* Ithaca, NY: Cornell University Press.

Du Bois, W. E. B. (1969). *The souls of black folk.* New York: Signet. (Originally published 1903)

Dugger, W. (1996). *Inequality: Radical institutionalist views on race, gender, class, and nation.* Westport, CT: Greenwood Press.

Duran, B. M. (2005). American Indian/Alaska Native health policy. *American Journal of Public Health, 95*(5), 758.

Durkheim, E. (1965). *The elementary forms of religious life.* Glencoe, IL: Free Press. (Originally published 1912)

Durkheim, E. (2004). *The division of labor.* New York: Free Press. (Originally published 1933)

Duyvendak, J. W., & Nederland, T. (2007). New frontiers for identity politics? The potential pitfalls of patient and civic identity in the Dutch patient's health movement. In P. G. Coy (Ed.), *Research in social movements, conflict and change* (pp. 261–282). St. Louis, MO: Elsevier.

Dwairy, M. A. (2006). *Counseling and psychotherapy with Arabs and Muslims: A culturally sensitive approach.* New York: Teachers College Press.

Edelsky, C. (1981). Who's got the floor? *Language in Society, 10,* 383–421.

Elijah, M. (2002). African centered family healing: An alternative paradigm. *Journal of Health & Social Policy, 16*(1–2), 185–193.

Eltis, D. (2000). *The rise of African slavery in the Americas.* London: Cambridge University Press.

Emerson, S., & Rosenfeld, C. (1996). Stages of adjustment in family members of transgender individuals. *Journal of Family Psychotherapy, 7*(3), 1–12.

England, P. (1992). *Comparable worth: Theories and evidence.* New York: Aldine de Gruyter.

England, P., Herbert, M. S., Kilbourne, B. S., Reid, L. L., & Megdal, L. M. (1994). The gendered valuation of occupations and skills: Earnings in 1980 census occupations. *Social Forces, 73*(1), 65–99.

England, P., Kilbourne, B. S., Farkas, G., & Dou, T. (1988). Explaining occupational sex segregation and wages: Findings from a model with fixed effects. *American Sociological Review, 53*(4), 544–558.

Epstein, I. (1995). Promoting reflective social work practice. In P. McCartt Hess & E. Mullen (Eds.), *Practitioner researcher partnerships* (pp. 83–102). Washington, DC: NASW Press.

Espiritu, Y. L. (1996). *Asian American women and men: Labor, laws and love*. Thousand Oaks, CA: Sage.

Esposito, L., & Murphy, J. (2000). Another step in the study of race relations. *Sociological Quarterly, 41*(2), 171–187.

Exner, T. M., Meyer-Bahlburg, H. F., & Ehrhardt, A. A. (1992). Sexual self-control as a mediator of high risk sexual behavior in a New York City cohort of HIV + and HIV– gay men. *Journal of Sex Research, 29*, 389–406

Eyerman, R. (2002). *Cultural trauma: Slavery and the formation of African-American identity*. New York: Cambridge University Press.

Fabricant, M., & Fisher, R. (2002a). Agency based community building in low income neighborhoods: A praxis framework. *Journal of Community Practice, 10*(2), 1–22.

Fabricant, M., & Fisher, R. (2002b). *Settlement houses under siege: The struggle to sustain community*. New York: Columbia University Press.

Farley, J. E. (2000). *Majority-minority relations* (4th ed.). Upper Saddle River, NJ: Prentice Hall.

Farrell, W. (2005). *Why men earn more: The startling truth behind the pay gap—and what women can do about it*. New York: American Management Association.

Fasching, D. J. (1992). *Narrative theology after Auschwitz: From alienation to ethics*. Minneapolis, MN: Augsburg Fortress Press.

Fausto-Sterling, A. (1993). The five sexes: Why male and female are not enough. *Sciences, 33*, 20–25.

Fay, R. E., Turner, C. F., Klassen, A. D., & Gagnon, J. H. (1989). Prevalence and patterns of same-gender sexual contact among men. *Science, 243*, 338–348.

Feagin, J. (2000). *Racist America: Roots, current realities, and future reparations*. New York: Routledge.

Feagin, J., & Eckberg, D. (1980). Discrimination: Motivation, action, effects and context. *Annual Review of Sociology, 6*, 1–20.

Feagin, J., Johnson, J., & Rush, S. (2000). Doing anti-racism toward an egalitarian American society. *Contemporary Sociology, 29*(1), 95–110.

Feher, M. (1994). The schism of '67: On certain restructurings of the American Left from the civil rights movement to the multicultural constellation. In P. Berman (Ed.), *Blacks and Jews: Alliances and agreements* (pp. 263–285). New York: Delacorte Press.

Fein, H. (1979). *Accounting for genocide: National responses and Jewish victimization during the Holocaust*. New York: Free Press.

Feinberg, M. E., Rindenour, T. A., & Greenberg, M. T. (2007). Aggregating indices of risk and protection for adolescent behavior problems: The community that cares youth survey. *Journal of Adolescent Health, 40*(6), 506–513.

Feinstein, J. S. (1993). The relationship between socioeconomic status and health: A review of the literature. *Milbank Quarterly, 71*(2), 279–322.

Fenzsch, N. (2005). "It is scarcely possible to conceive that human beings could be so hideous and loathsome": Discourses of genocide in eighteen- and nineteenth-century America and Australia. *Patterns of Prejudice, 39*(2), 97–115.

Ferguson, I., Lavalette, M., & Whitmore, E. (2005). *Globalization, global justice and social work.* London: Routledge.

Ferraro, K., & Koch, J. (1994). Religion and health among black and white adults: examining social support and consolation. *Journal of Scientific Study of Religion, 4,* 362–375.

Fett, S. M. (2002). *Working cure: Healing, health, and power on southern slave plantations.* Chapel Hill: University of North Carolina Press.

Field, C. A., & Caetano, R. (2005). Intimate partner violence in the U.S. general population: progress and future directions. *Journal of Interpersonal Violence, 20*(4), 463–469.

Finholt, T. A., & Olson, G. M. (1997). From laboratories to collaboratories: A new organizational form for scientific collaboration. *Psychological Science, 8*(1), 28.

Finnigan, D. (1995). Our cheap clothes and their horror stories: Thais, other minorities abused in sweatshops that keep prices down. *National Catholic Reporter, 32*(6), 10–11.

Fisher, R., & Kling, J. (1994). Community organization and new social movement's theory. *Journal of Progressive Human Services, 5*(2), 5–23.

Fisher, A., & Sonn, C. (2003). Identity and oppression: Differential responses to an in-between status. *American Journal of Community Psychology, 31*(1–2), 117–129.

Foucault, M. (1978). *The history of sexuality.* New York: Pantheon Books.

Foucault, M. (1980). *Power/knowledge: Selected interviews and other writings.* New York: Pantheon Books.

Franklin, J. H., & Moss, A. A. (1994). *From slavery to freedom: A history of African Americans* (7th ed.). New York: Knopf.

Frauenglass, S., Routh, D. K., Pantin, H. M., & Mason, C. A. (1997). Family support decreases influence of deviant peers in Hispanic adolescent's substance use. *Journal of Clinical Child Psychology, 26,* 15–23.

Freire, P. (1970). *Pedagogy of the oppressed.* New York: Seabury Press.

Freire, P. (1994). *Pedagogy of hope: Reliving pedagogy of the oppressed.* New York: Continuum.

Friedan, B. (2001). *The feminine mystique.* New York: W. W. Norton. (Originally published 1963)

Friedberg, L. (2000). Dare to compare. *American Indian Quarterly, 24*(3), 353.

Frith-Smith, H., & Singleton, H. (2000). *Urban American Indian children in Los Angeles County: An investigation of available data.* Prepared for the Los Angeles County American Indian Children's Council, UCLA, American Indian Studies Center.

Frye, M. (2003). Oppression. In M. L. Andersen & P. H. Collins (Eds.), *Race, class, and gender* (5th ed., pp. 49–51). Belmont, CA: Wadsworth Press.

Galotti, A. E. (2007). Relativism, universalism, and applied ethics: The case of female circumcision. *Constellations, 14*(1), 91–111.

Garnets, L., & Kimmel, D. C. (2003). *Psychological perspectives on lesbian, gay, and bisexual experiences.* New York: Columbia University Press.

Germer, C. K. (2005). Mindfulness and psychotherapy. New York: Guilford Press.

Gibelman, M., & Schervish, P. H. (1995). Pay equity in social work: Not! *Social Work, 40*(5), 622–633.

Giddens, A. (2006). *Sociology* (5th ed.). Malden, MA: Polity Press.

Girves, J. E., Zepeda, Y., & Gwathmey, J. K. (2005). Mentoring in a post-affirmative action world. *Journal of Social Issues, 61*(3), 449–479.

Givens, S. M. B., & Monahan, J. L. (2005). Priming mammies, Jezebels, and other controlling images: An examination of the influence of mediated stereotypes on perceptions of an African American woman. *Media Psychology, 7*(1), 87–106.

Goffman, E. (1963). *Stigma*. Englewood Cliffs, NJ: Prentice Hall.

Golash-Boza, T. (2006). Dropping the hyphen? Becoming Latino(a)-American through racialized assimilation. *Social Forces, 85*(1), 27–55.

Gordon, C. (1996). Adolescent decision making: A broadly based theory and its application to the prevention of early pregnancy. *Adolescence, 31*(123), 561–584.

Gordon, M. (1964). *Assimilation in American life*. New York: Oxford University Press.

Gray, J. A., Stone, J. A., & Stockard, J. (2006). *Childbearing, marriage and human capital investment*. Retrieved October 29, 2007, from http://hdl.handle.net/1794/2463

Gregg, G. S. (1991). *Self-representation: Life narrative studies in identity and ideology*. New York: Greenwood Press.

Greer, K. (2002). Walking an emotional tightrope: Managing emotions in a women's prison. *Symbolic Interaction, 25*(1), 117–139.

Griffin, H. (2000). Their own received them not: African American lesbians and gays in black churches. In D. Constantine-Simms (Ed.), *The greatest taboo: Homosexuality in black communities* (pp. 110–121). Los Angeles: Alyson Books.

Griffith, R. M., & Savage, B. D. (2006). *Women and religion in the African diaspora: Knowledge, power and performance*. Baltimore: Johns Hopkins University Press.

Guillemin, J. (1975). *Urban renegades: The cultural strategy of American Indians*. New York: Columbia University Press.

Gurman, A., & Fraenkel, P. (2002). The history of couple therapy: A millennial review. *Family Process, 41*(2), 199–260.

Gutierrez, L., & Lewis, E. A. (1998). Strengthening communities through groups: A multicultural perspective. In H. Bertcher, I. F. Kurtz, & A. Lamont (Eds.), *Rebuilding communities: Challenges for group work* (pp. 5–16). New York: Haworth Press.

Gutierrez, L., Ortega, R., & Yeakley, A. (2000). Educating students for social work with Latinos: Issues for the new millennium. *Journal of Social Work Education, 36*(3), 541.

Haber, D. (2005). Cultural diversity among older adults: Addressing health education. *Educational Gerontology, 31*(9), 683–697.

Haj-Yahia, M. M. (1995). Toward culturally sensitive intervention with Arab families in Israel. *Contemporary Family Therapy, 17*(4), 429–447.

Halberstam, J. (2005). *In a queer time and place: Transgender bodies, subcultural lives*. New York: New York University Press.

Hancock, A.-M. (2005). W. E. B. Du Bois: Intellectual forefather of intersectionality? *Souls, 7*(3–4), 74–84.

Hancock, A.-M. (2007a). Intersectionality as a normative and empirical paradigm. *Politics & Gender, 3*(2), 248–254.

Hancock, A.-M. (2007b). When multiplication doesn't equal quick addition: Examining intersectionality as a research paradigm. *Perspectives on Politics, 5*(1), 63–79.

Hand, C. A. (2006). An Ojibwe perspective on the welfare of children: Lessons and visions for the future. *Children and Youth Services Review, 28*(1), 20–46.

Hanley, J. A., Turner, E., Bellera, C., & Telsch, D. (2003). How long did their hearts go on? A *Titanic* study. *British Medical Journal, 327*, 1457–1458.

Hanson, T. L., McLanahan, S. S., & Thompson, E. (1998). Windows on divorce: Before and after. *Social Science Research, 27*(3), 329–349.

Hao, L., & Bonstead-Bruns, M. (1998). Parent-child differences in educational expectations and the academic achievement of immigrant and native students. *Sociology of Education, 71*(3), 175–198.

Harkness, S., & Super, C. (Eds.). (1996). *Parents' cultural belief systems: Their origins, expressions, and consequences.* New York: Guilford Press.

Harley, D. A. (2005). The black church: A strength-based approach in mental health. In D. A. Harley & K. J. M. Dillard (Eds.), *Contemporary mental health issues among African Americans* (pp. 293–306). Alexandria, VA: American Counseling Association.

Harley, D. A. (2006). Indigenous healing practices among rural elderly African Americans. *International Journal of Disability, Development and Education, 53*(4), 433–452.

Harmon, D. (2002). They won't teach me: The voices of gifted African American inner-city students. *Roeper Review, 24*(2), 68–75.

Hassan, I. (2003). Beyond postmodernism: Toward an aesthetic of trust. *Journal of Theoretical Humanities, 8*(1), 3–11.

Hayek, F. A. (1963). *The sensory order: An inquiry into the foundations of theoretical psychology.* Chicago: University of Chicago Press.

Hepworth, D. H., Rooney, R. H., & Larsen, J. A. (2002). *Direct social work practice* (6th ed.). Pacific Grove, CA: Brooks/Cole.

Herek, G. (2002). Gender gaps in public opinion about lesbians and gay men. *Public Opinion Quarterly, 66*(1), 40–66.

Herek, G., Cogan, J., & Gillis, R. (2002). Victims experiences in hate crimes based on sexual orientation. *Journal of Social Issues, 58*(2), 319–339.

Herek, G., & Glunt, E. K. (1993). Interpersonal contact and heterosexuals' attitudes toward gay men: Results from a national survey. *Journal of Sex Research, 30*, 239–244.

Heron, M. (2007). Deaths: Leading causes for 2004. *Centers for Disease Control, National Vital Statistics Reports, 56*(5), 1–96.

Herring, C., Keith, V. M., & Horton, H. D. (2004). *Skin deep: How race and complexion matter in the "color blind" era.* Urbana: University of Illinois Press.

Hill, D. B., & Willoughby, B. L. B. (2005). The development and validation of the genderism and transphobia scale. *Sex Roles, 53*, 531

Hilton, J. L., & von Hippel, W. (1996). Stereotypes. *Annual Review of Psychology, 47*, 237–272.

Hirshorn, B., & Stewart, J. (2003). Geographic information systems in community-based gerontological research and practice. *Journal of Applied Gerontology, 22*(1), 134–151.

Hobfoll, S. E., Jackson, A., Hobfoll, I., Pierce, C., & Young, S. (2002). The impact of communal-mastery versus self-mastery on emotional outcomes during stressful conditions: a prospective study of Native American women (1). *American Journal of Community Psychology, 30*(6), 853–872.

Hobfoll, S. E., Schröder, K. E. E., Wells, M., & Malek, M. (2002). Communal versus individualistic construction of sense of mastery in facing life changes. *Journal of Social and Clinical Psychology, 21*(4), 362–399.

Hochschild, A. (1998). *King Leopold's ghost: A story of greed, terror, and heroism in colonial Africa.* Boston: Houghton Mifflin.

Hochschild, A., & Machung, A. (1989). *The second shift: Working parents and the revolution at home.* New York: Viking.

Hoffman, J. L., & Lewitzki, K. E. (2005). Predicting college success with high school grades and test scores: Limitations for minority students. *Review of Higher Education, 28*(4), 455–474.

Hondagneu-Sotelo, P. (2001). *Domestica: Immigrant workers caring and cleaning in America.* Berkeley and Los Angeles: University of California Press.

hooks, b. (1981). *Ain't I a woman? Black women and feminism.* Boston: South End Press.

hooks, b. (1984). *Feminist theory from the margin to the center.* Boston: South End Press.

hooks, b. (1990). *Yearning: Race, gender, and cultural politics.* Boston: South End Press.

Hopson, R. K., Lucas, K. J., & Peterson, J. A. (2000). HIV/AIDS talk: Implications for prevention intervention and evaluation. *New Directions for Evaluation, 86,* 29–42.

Howe, D. (2005). Modernity, postmodernity and social work. *British Journal of Social Work, 24*(5), 513–532.

Hsiao, A., Wong, M. D., Goldstein, M. S., Becerra, L. S., Cheng, E. M., & Wegner, N. S. (2006). Complementary and alternative medicine among Asian American subgroups: Prevalence, predictors, and lack of relationship with acculturation and access to conventional health care. *Journal of Alternative and Complementary Medicine, 12*(10), 1003–1010.

Hudson, A. (2006). Feminism and social work: Resistance or dialogue? *British Journal of Social Work, 15*(6), 635–655.

Hudson, W. W., & McMurtry, S. L. (1997). Comprehensive assessment in social work practice. *Research on Social Work Practice, 7*(1), 79–98.

Hudson, W. W., & Ricketts, W. A. (1980). A strategy for the measurement of homophobia. *Journal of Homosexuality, 5,* 357–372.

Huffman, M. L., & Cohen, P. N. (2004). Occupational segregation and the gender gap in workplace authority: National vs. local labor markets. *Sociological Forum, 19,* 121–147.

Hungerman, D. M. (2005). Are church and state substitutes? Evidence from the 1996 welfare reform. *Journal of Public Economics, 89*(11/12), 2245–2267.

Hurdle, D. (2002). Native Hawaiian traditional healing: Culturally based interventions for social work practice. *Social Work, 47*(2), 183–193.

Hyde, J. S. (2005). The genetics of sexual orientation. In J. S. Hyde (Ed.), *Biological substrates of human sexuality* (pp. 9–20). Washington, DC: American Psychological Association.

Ignatiev, Noel. (1995). *How the Irish became white.* New York: Routledge.

International Forum on Globalization. (2002, Spring). *Report summary: A better world is possible: Alternatives to economic globalization.* San Francisco: Author.

Iwata, N., Turner, R. J., & Lloyd, D. A. (2002). Race/ethnicity and depressive symptoms in community-dwelling adults: A differential item functioning analysis. *Psychiatry Research, 110*(3), 281–289.

James, J. (2001). Radicalizing feminism. In J. James & T. D. Sharpley-Whiting (Eds.), *The black feminist reader* (pp. 239–258). Malden, MA: Basil Blackwell.

Jandt, F., & Hundley, H. (2007). Intercultural dimensions of communicating masculinities. *Journal of Men's Studies, 15*(2), 216–231.

Jennings, M. K. (2006). The gender gap in attitudes and beliefs about the place of women in American political life: A longitudinal, cross-generational analysis. *Politics & Gender, 2*(2), 193–219.

Jepson, E. S., Thomas, J., Markward, A., Kelly, J. A., Koser, G., & Diehl, D. (1997). *Making room at the table: Fostering involvement in the planning and governance of formal support systems.* Chicago: Family Resource Coalition of America.

Johnson, K. (1997). Melting pot or ring of fire? Assimilation and the Mexican American experience. *California Law Review, 85*(5), 1259–1313.

Johnson, R. M. (1974). Schooling the savage: Andrew S. Draper and Indian education. *Phylon, 35*(1), 74–82.

Jojola, T. S. (1999). *Urban Indians in Albuquerque, New Mexico: A study for the Department of Family and Human Services.* Albuquerque: Community and Regional Planning Program, University of New Mexico.

Jones, D. S. (2006). The persistence of American Indian health disparities. *American Journal of Public Health, 96*(12), 2122–2134.

Josephson, J. (2005). Citizenship, same-sex marriage, and feminist critiques of marriage. *Perspectives on Politics, 3*(2), 269–284.

Kammeyer, K., Ritzer, G., & Yetman, N. (1990). *Sociology: Experiencing changing societies.* Boston: Allyn and Bacon.

Kanter, R. M. (1977). *Men and women of the corporation.* New York: Basic Books.

Kanuha, V. K. (2000). "Being" native versus "going" native: Conducting social work research as an insider. *Social Work, 45*(5), 439–447.

Karp, A. J. (1976). *Golden door to America: The Jewish immigrant experience.* New York: Viking Press.

Kawai, T. (2006). Postmodern consciousness in psychotherapy. *Journal of Analytical Psychology, 51*(3), 437–450.

Keleher, T., & Johnson, T. (2001). Confronting institutional racism. *Leadership, 30*(4), 24–30.

Kenney, K. (2002). Counseling interracial couples and multiracial individuals: Applying a multicultural counseling competency framework. *Counseling and Human Development, 35*(4), 1–13.

Kessler, S. (1997). Creating good-looking genitals in the service of gender. In M. Duberman (Ed.), *A queer world: The Center for Lesbian and Gay Studies reader* (Vol. 1, pp. 153–173). New York: New York University Press.

Kidder, D. L. (2002). The influence of gender on the performance of organizational citizenship behaviors. *Journal of Management, 28,* 629–648.

Kim, B. S. K., Atkinson, D. R., & Yang, P. H. (1999). The Asian values scale: Development, factor analysis, validation, and reliability. *Journal of Counseling Psychology, 46*(3), 342–352.

Kim, B. S. K., Yang, P. H., Atkinson, D. R., Wolfe, M. M., & Hong, S. (2001). Cultural value similarities and differences among Asian American ethnic groups. *Cultural Diversity and Ethnic Minority Psychology, 7*(4), 343–361.

Kimmel, M. (1996). *Manhood in America: A cultural history.* New York: Free Press.

Kimmel, M. S. (2000). *The gendered society.* New York: Oxford University Press.

Kinsey, A. C., Pomeroy, W. B., & Martin, C. E. (1949). *Sexual behavior in the human male.* Philadelphia: W. B. Saunders.

Kisthardt, W. E. (2002). The strengths perspective in interpersonal helping: Purpose, principles, and functions. In D. Saleebey (Ed.), *The strengths perspective in social work practice* (3rd ed., pp. 163–185). Boston: Allyn and Bacon.

Koeske, G. F., & Krowinski, W. J. (2004). Gender-based salary inequality in social work: Mediators of gender's effect on salary. *Social Work, 49,* 309–317.

Koh, C. (2006). Reviewing the link between creativity and madness: A postmodern perspective. *Educational Research and Reviews, 1*(7), 213–221.

Kosberg, J. (2002). Heterosexual male: A group forgotten by the profession of social work. *Journal of Sociology and Social Welfare, 29*(3), 51–71.

Kowalski, K. (2003). The emergence of ethnic and racial attitudes in preschool-aged children. *Journal of Social Psychology, 143*(6), 677–691.

Krause, I., Rosser, R. M., Khiani, M. L., & Lotay, N. S. (1990). Psychiatric morbidity among Punjab medical patients in England measured by general health questionnaire. *Psychological Medicine, 20*(3), 711–719.

Krishnan, H. A., & Park, D. (2005). A few good women—on top management teams. *Journal of Business Research, 58*(12), 1712–1720.

Krovetz, M. (1999). *Fostering resiliency: Expecting all students to use their minds and hearts well.* Thousand Oaks, CA: Corwin Press.

Kulis, S., Okamoto, S. K., Rayle, A. D., & Sen, S. (2006). Social contexts of drug offers among American Indian youth and their relationship to substance use: An exploratory study. *Journal of Cultural Diversity and Ethnic Minority Psychology, 12*(1), 30–44.

Kulwicki, A. D., & Miller, J. (1999). Domestic violence in the Arab American population: Transforming environmental conditions through community education. *Issues in Mental Health Nursing, 20*, 199–215.

Kumpfer, K., Turner, C., Hopkins, R., & Librett, J. (1993). Leadership and team effectiveness in community coalitions for the prevention of alcohol and other drug abuse. *Health Education Research, 8*(3), 359–374.

Kuo, W. (1984). Prevalence of depression among Asian Americans. *Journal of Nervous and Mental Disease, 172*, 449–457.

Kurdek, L. A. (2005). What do we know about gay and lesbian couples? *Current Directions in Psychological Science, 14*(5), 251–254.

Kurland, R., & Salmon, R. (1999). When worker and member expectations collide: The dilemma of establishing group norms in conflictual situations. In A. Alissi & C. Corto Mergins (Eds.), *Voices from the field: Group work responds* (pp. 43–53). New York: Haworth Press.

Landers, S. (1992). Survey eyes therapy fees. *NASW News*, pp. 1–8.

Lange, B. K. (1988). Ethnographic interview: An occupational therapy needs assessment tool for American Indian and Alaskan Native alcoholics. *Occupational Therapy in Mental Health, 8*(20), 61–80.

Larsen, B. W., & Jesch, G. W. (1980). Students training in an American Indian setting. *Social Casework, 61*(8), 512–518.

Laumann, E. O., Gagnon, J. H., Michael, J. T., & Michaels, S. (1994). *The social organization of sexuality: Sexual practices in the United States.* Chicago: University of Chicago Press.

Lawson, J. (2003). The wounds we hide: The silent scars of racism are not limited to communities of color. Until we confront how racism shapes the lives of whites, we will not be healed. *Other Side, 39*(9), 10–17.

Lazarsfeld, P., & Merton, R. K. (1954). Friendship as a social process: A substantive and methodological analysis. In M. Berger, T. Abel, & C. H. Page (Eds.), *Freedom and control in modern society* (pp. 18–66). New York: Van Nostrand.

Leavelle, T. N. (1998). "We will make it our own place." *American Indian Quarterly, 22*(4), 435–457.

Lee, J. A. B. (2001). *The empowerment approach to social work practice* (2nd ed.). New York: Columbia University Press.

Lee, S., & Fernandez, M. (1998). Trends in Asian American racial/ethnic intermarriage: A comparison of 1980 and 1990 census data. *Sociological Perspectives, 41*(2), 323–343.

Lemelle, A. J., & Battle, J. (2004). Black masculinity matters in attitudes toward gay males. *Journal of Homosexuality, 47,* 39–41.

Leppel, K. (2007). Home-ownership among opposite and same sex couples in the US. *Feminist Economics, 13*(1), 1–30.

Lev, A. I., & Moore, B. (2000). Social work embraces transgender. *American Psychological Association, division 44 newsletter.*

LeVay, S. (1996). *Queer science.* Cambridge, MA: MIT Press.

Levin, J., & Levin, W. (1982). *The functions of discrimination and prejudice* (2nd ed.). New York: Harper and Row.

Lewis, G., & Rogers, M. (1999). Does the public support equal employment rights for gays and lesbians? In D. B. Riggle & B. Tadlock (Eds.), *Gays and lesbians in the democratic process* (pp. 118–145). New York: Columbia University Press.

Lewis, O. (1966). The culture of poverty. *Scientific American, 215*(4), 19–25.

Liang, J., Van Tran, T., Krause, N., & Markeides, K. S. (1989). Generational differences in the structure of the CES-D scale in Mexican Americans. *Journal of Gerontology, 44,* 110–120.

Liebow, E. (1967). *Tally's corner.* Boston: Little, Brown.

Link, B., & Phelan, J. (2000). Evaluating the fundamental cause explanation for social disparities in health. In C. E. Bird, P. Conrad, & A. M. Fremont (Eds.), *Handbook of medical sociology* (5th ed., pp. 33–46). Upper Saddle River, NJ: Prentice-Hall.

Link, B., Phelan, J., Bresnaham, M., Stueve, A., Pescosolido, B. A. (1999). Public conceptions of mental illness: Labels, causes, dangerousness and social distance. *American Journal of Public Health, 89*(9), 1328–1333.

Lippa, R. A. (2005). Subdomains of gender-related occupational interests: Do they form a cohesive bipolar M-F dimension? *Journal of Personality, 73*(3), 693–730.

Lobo, S. (1998). Is urban a person or a place? Characteristics of urban Indian country. *American Indian Culture and Research Journal, 22,* 89–102.

Loftus, J. (2001). America's liberalization in attitudes toward homosexuality, 1973 to 1998. *American Sociological Review, 66*(5), 762–782.

Lone-Knapp, F. (2000). Rez talk. *American Indian Quarterly, 24*(4), 635–641.

Longres, J. F. (2000). *Human behavior in the social environment* (3rd ed.). Itasca, IL: F. E. Peacock.

Lopez, I. H. (2005). Race on the 2010 census: Hispanics and the shrinking white majority. *Daedalus, 134*(1), 42–52.

Louw, P. E. (2004). *The rise, fall and legacy of apartheid.* New York: Praeger.

Lyons, K. (2006). Globalization and social work: International and local implications. *British Journal of Social Work, 36*(1), 365–380.

Magana, L., & Short, R. (2002). Political rhetoric, immigration attitudes, and contemporary prejudice: A Mexican American dilemma. *Journal of Social Psychology, 142*(6), 701–713.

Marin, G., & Marin, B. V. (1991). *Research with Hispanic populations.* Newbury Park, CA: Sage.

Marino, R., Minas, H., & Stuart, G. (2000). Acculturation of values and behavior: A study of Vietnamese immigrants. *Measurement and Evaluation in Counseling and Development, 33*(1), 21–41.

Marmot, M. (2003). Understanding social inequalities in health. *Perspectives in Biology and Medicine, 46*(3), S9–S23.

Marsiglia, F. F., Kulis, S., Wagstaff, D., Elek, E., Dran, D. (2005). Acculturation status and substance use prevention with Mexican and Mexican-American youth. *Journal of Social Work Practice in the Addictions, 5*(1/2), 85–111.

Martin, M., Camargo, M., Ramos, L., Lauderdale, D., Krueger, K., & Lantos, J. (2005). The evaluation of a Latino community health worker HIV prevention program. *Hispanic Journal of Behavioral Sciences, 27*(3), 371–384.

Martin, P. Y., & Shanahan, K. A. (1983). Transcending the effects of sex composition in small groups. *Social Work with Groups, 6,* 19–32.

Marx, K. (1970). *Critique of Hegel's philosophy of right.* Cambridge: Cambridge University Press. (Originally published 1843)

Mastrogianni, A., & Bhugra, D. (2003). Globalization, cultural psychiatry and mental distress. *International Journal of Social Psychology, 49*(3), 163–165.

May, M. L., Bowman, G. J., Ramos, K. S., Rincones, L., Rebollar, M. G., Rosa, M. L., et al. (2003). Embracing the local: Enriching scientific research, education, and outreach on the Texas-Mexico border through a participatory action research partnership. *Environmental Health Perspectives, 111*(13), 1571–1577.

McCall, L. (2005). The complexity of intersectionality. *Signs, 30*(3), 1771–1800.

McCollom, S. (1996). *Hispanic immigrant attitude towards African Americans: A study of intergroup contact.* Paper presented at the Annual Meeting of the American Sociological Association, New York City.

McCreary, D. R., Saucier, D. M., & Courtenay, W. H. (2005). The drive for muscularity and masculinity: Testing the associations among gender-role traits, behaviors, attitudes, and conflict. *Psychology of Men & Masculinity, 6,* 83–94.

McDonough, P., & Fann, A. J. (2007). The study of inequality. In P. J. Gumport (Ed.), *Sociology of higher education: Contributions and their contexts* (pp. 53–92). Baltimore, MD: Johns Hopkins University Press.

McGlone, M. S., Aronson, J., & Kobrynowicz, D. (2006). Stereotype threat and the gender gap in political knowledge. *Psychology of Women Quarterly, 30,* 362–398.

McIntosh, P. (1990). White privilege: Unpacking the invisible knapsack. *Independent School, 49*(2), 31–36.

McKeever, M., & Wolfinger, N. H. (2006). Shifting fortunes in a changing economy: Trends in the economic well-being of divorced women. In L. Kowaleski-Jones & N. H. Wolfinger (Eds.), *Fragile families and the marriage agenda* (pp. 127–157). New York: Springer.

McKenna, M. T., Michaud, C. M., Murray, C. J. L., & Marks, J. S. (2005). Assessing the burden of disease in the United States using disability-adjusted life years. *American Journal of Preventive Medicine, 28*(5), 415–423.

McKeown, A. (1999). Transnational Chinese families and Chinese exclusion, 1875–1943. *Journal of American Ethnic History, 18*(2), 73–110.

McKerl, M. (2007). Multiculturalism, gender and violence: Multiculturalism—is it bad for women? *Culture and Religion, 8*(2), 187–217.

McKernan, S.-M., & Ratcliffe, C. (2005). Events that trigger poverty entries and exit. *Social Science Quarterly, 86*(1), 1146–1169.

McManus, P., & DiPrete, T. (2001). Losers and winners: The financial consequences of separation and divorce for men. *American Sociological Review, 66,* 246–268.

McPhail, B. A. (2004). Setting the record straight: Social work is not a female-dominated profession. *Social Work, 49,* 323–326.

McPherson, M., Smith-Lovin, L., & Cook, J. (2001). Birds of a feather: Homophily in social networks. *Annual Review of Sociology, 27,* 415–444.

Mead, G. H. (1934). *Mind, self and society.* Chicago: University of Chicago Press.

Mechoulan, S. (2006). Divorce laws and the structure of the American family. *Journal of Legal Studies, 35,* 143–174.

Melson, R. (1992). *Revolution and genocide: On the origins of the Armenian genocide and the Holocaust.* Chicago: University of Chicago Press.

Menéndez, M., Benach, J., Muntaner, C., Amable, M., & O'Campo, P. (2007). Is precarious employment more demanding to women's health than men's? *Social Science & Medicine, 64*(4), 776–781.

Menjivar, C. (2000). *Fragmented ties: Salvadoran immigrant networks in America.* Berkeley and Los Angeles: University of California Press.

Merton, R. K. (1972). Insiders and outsiders: A chapter in the sociology of knowledge. *American Journal of Sociology, 78*(1), 9–47.

Michael, R., Gagnon, J., Laumann, E., & Kolata, G. (1994). *Sex in America: A definitive survey.* New York: Warner Books.

Mihesuah, D. (1996). *American Indians: Stereotypes and realities.* Atlanta, GA: Clarity Press.

Mitchem, S. (2007). *African American folk healing.* New York: New York University Press.

Moane, G. (1999). *Gender and colonialism: A psychological analysis of oppression and liberation.* New York: St. Martin's Press.

Montagu, A. (1957). *Anthropology and human nature.* Boston: P. Sargent.

Moraga, C. (2004). P. 33. La Guera. In M. L. Andersen & P. H. Collins (Eds.), *Race, class, and gender* (5th ed., pp. 28–35). Belmont, CA: Wadsworth Press.

Morash, M., Bui, M., & Santiago, A. (2000). Gender specific ideology of domestic violence in Mexican origin families. *International Review of Victimology, 1,* 67–91.

Morrissette, P. J. (1994). The holocaust of First Nation people: Residual effects on parenting and treatment implications. *Contemporary Family Therapy, 16*(5), 381–392.

Mosher, W. D., Chandra, A., & Jones, J. (2005). *Sexual behavior and selected health measures: Men and women 15–44 years of age, United States, 2002.* Advance Data 362. Hyattsville, MD: National Center for Health Statistics.

Murguia, E., & Telles, E. E. (1996). Phenotype and schooling among Mexican Americans. *Sociology of Education, 69*(4), 276–289.

National Association of Social Workers. (1999). *Code of ethics of the National Association of Social Workers.* Washington, DC: Author.

Naphy, W. (2006). *Born to be gay: A history of homosexuality.* Gloucestershire, UK: Tempus.

National Center for Health Statistics. (2006). *National hospital ambulatory medical care survey: 2004 emergency department summary.* Hyattsville, MD: Author.

National Institutes of Health. (2006). *National Kidney Disease Education Program fact sheet: African Americans & kidney disease.* National Institutes of Health Publication No. 04–5577 (Rev. April 2006).

Naylor, L. L. (Ed.). (1997). *Cultural diversity in the United States.* Westport, CT: Bergin & Garvey.

Newman, K. (2006). Democracy, bureaucracy and difference in US development politics since 1968. *Progress in Human Geography, 30*(1), 44–61.

Newman, W. M. (1973). *American pluralism: A study of minority groups and social theory.* New York: Harper and Row.

Ng, R. (2006). Exploring healing and the body through indigenous Chinese medicine. In J. F. Kunnie & N. I. Goduka (Eds.), *Indigenous people's wisdom and power* (pp. 95–116). London: Ashgate.

O'Brien, M., Peyton, V., Mistry, R., Hruda, L., Jacobs, A., Caldera, Y., et al. (2000). Gender-role cognition in three-year-old boys and girls. *Sex Roles, 42*(11/12), 1007–1025.

O'Donnell, S. (1993). Involving clients in welfare policy-making. *Social Work, 38*(5), 629–635.

Ogbu, J. U. (1992). Understanding cultural diversity and learning. *Educational Researcher, 21*, 5–14.

Okamoto, S. K., LeCroy, C. W., Dustman, P., Hohmann-Marriott, B., & Kulis, S. (2004). An ecological assessment of drug related problem situations for American Indian adolescents of the Southwest. *Journal of Social Work Practice in the Addictions, 4*(3), 47–63.

Okamoto, S. K., LeCroy, C. W., Tann, S. S., Rayle, A. D., Kulis, S., Dustman, P., & Berceli, D. (2006). The implications of ecologically based assessment for primary prevention with indigenous youth populations. *Journal of Primary Prevention, 27*(2), 155–170.

Omi, M., & Winant, H. (1998). Racial formations. In P. S. Rothenberg (Ed.), *The social construction of race, class, gender, and sexuality* (4th ed.; pp. 13–22). New York: St. Martin's Press.

Ortíz Hendricks, C. (2005). The multicultural triangle of the child, the family and the school: Culturally competent approaches. In E. P. Congress & M. J. Gonzalez (Eds.), *Multicultural perspectives in working with families* (pp. 71–92). New York: Springer.

Ostafin, B. D., Chawla, N., Bowen, S., Dillworth, T. M., Witkiewitz, K., & Marlatt, G. A. (2006). Intensive mindfulness training and the reduction of psychological distress: A preliminary study. *Cognitive and Behavioral Practice, 13*(3), 191–197.

Ostrow, D. G., DiFranceisco, W., & Kalichman, S. (1997). Sexual adventurism, substance use, and high-risk sexual behavior: A structural modeling analysis of the Chicago MACS/coping and change cohort. *AIDS and Behavior, 1*, 191–202.

Ott, M. A., Evans, N. L., Halpern-Felshr, B. L., & Eyre, S. L. (2003). Differences in altruistic roles and HIV risk perception among staff, peer educators, and students in an adolescent peer education program. *AIDS Education and Prevention, 15*(2), 159–171.

Outwin, C. P. M. (1996). Securing the leg irons: Restriction of legal rights for slaves in Virginia and Maryland, 1625–1791. *Early America Review, 1*(3). Retrieved May 31, 2005, from http://earlyamerica.com/review/winter96/slavery.html

Owens, L. H. (1976). *This species of property: Slave life and culture in the Old South.* Oxford: Oxford University Press.

Oyserman, D., Coon, H., & Kemmelmeier, M. (2002). Rethinking individualism and collectivism: Evaluation of theoretical assumptions and meta-analyses. *Psychological Bulletin, 128*, 3–73.

Pagden, A. R. (1975). *The Maya: Diego de Landa's account of the affairs of Yucatán.* Chicago: J. Philip O'Hara.

Paradies, Y. (2006). A systematic review of empirical research on self-reported racism and health. *International Journal of Epidemiology, 35*(4), 888–901.

Paris, M., Añez, L. M., Bedregal, L. E., Andrés-Hyman, R. C., & Davidson, L. (2005). Help seeking and satisfaction among Latinas: The roles of setting, ethnic identity, and therapeutic alliance. *Journal of Community Psychology, 33*(3), 299–312.

Park, R. E. (1930). Assimilation, social. In E. Seligman & A. Johnson (Eds.), *Encyclopedia of the social sciences* (pp. 281–283). New York: Macmillan.

Parks, F. M. (2007). Working with narratives: Coping strategies in African American folk beliefs and traditional healing practices. *Journal of Human Behavior in the Social Environment, 15*(1), 135–147.

Parsons, T. (1961). *Theories of society.* Glencoe, IL: Free Press.

Patterson, J. M. (2002). Integrating family resiliency and family stress theory. *Journal of Marriage and Family, 64*(2), 349–360.

Patterson, O. (2003, June 22). Affirmative action: The sequel. *New York Times,* sec. 4, p. 11.

Patterson, T. R. (2005). *Zora Neale Hurston and a history of southern life.* Philadelphia: Temple University Press.

Patterson, C. J., & Redding, R. (1996). Lesbian and gay families with children: Implications of social science research for policy. *Journal of Social Issues, 52*(3), 29–50.

Pauly, I. B. (1990). Gender identity disorders: Evaluation and treatment. *Journal of Sex Education & Therapy, 16,* 2–24.

Paxton, P., & Mughan, A. (2006). What's to fear from immigrants? Creating an assimilationist threat scale. *Political Psychology, 27*(4), 549–568.

Pellebon, D. A., & Anderson, S. C. (1999). Understanding the life issues of spiritually-based clients. *Families in Society: The Journal of Contemporary Human Services, 80*(3), 229–238.

Peters, A. J. (2003). Isolation or inclusion: Creating safe spaces for lesbian and gay youth. *Families in Society: The Journal of Contemporary Human Services, 84*(3), 331–340.

Phinney, J. S. (1996). When we talk about American ethnic groups, what do we mean? *American Psychologist, 51*(9), 918–927.

Piketty, T., & Saez, E. (2003). Income inequality in the United States: 1913–1998. *Quarterly Journal of Economics, 118*(1), 1–39.

Pope, M. (1995). The "salad bowl" is big enough for us all: An argument for the inclusion of lesbians and gay men in any definition of multiculturalism. *Journal of Counseling and Development, 73,* 301–304.

Porter, C. P. (1991). Social reasons for skin tone preferences of black school-age children. *American Journal of Orthopsychiatry, 61,* 149–154.

Portes, A., & McLeod, D. (1996). What shall I call myself? Hispanic identity formation in a second generation. *Ethnic and Racial Studies, 19,* 523–547.

Posner, S. F., Stewart, A. L., Marín, G., & Pérez-Stable, E. J. (2001). Factor variability of the Center for Epidemiological Studies Depression scale (CES-D) among urban Latinos. *Ethnicity and Health, 6*(2), 137–144.

Powell, D. R. (2007). *Critical regionalism: Connecting politics and culture in the American landscape.* Chapel Hill: University of North Carolina Press.

Powers, K. M. (2006). An exploratory study of cultural identity and culture-based education programs for urban American Indian students. *Urban Education, 41*(1), 20–49.

Preece, J. J. (2006). *Minority rights.* London: Polity.

Pressman, D. L., & Bonanno, G. (2007). With whom do we grieve? Social and cultural determinants of grief processing in the United States and China. *Journal of Social and Personal Relations, 24*(5), 729–746.

Price, D. V. (2004). *Borrowing inequality: Race, class, and student loans.* Boulder, CO: Lynne Rienner.

Probert, B. (2005). "I just couldn't fit it in": Gender and unequal outcomes in academic careers. *Gender, Work and Organization, 12*(1), 50–72.

Raj, A., & Silverman, J. (2002). Violence against immigrant women: The roles of culture, context, and legal immigrant status on intimate partner violence. *Violence Against Women, 8*(3), 367–398.

Ramirez-Valles, J., Fergus, S., Reisen, C. A., Poppen, P. J., & Zea, M. C. (2005). Confronting stigma: Community involvement and psychological well-being among Latino lesbians and gay men. *Hispanic Journal of Behavioral Sciences, 27,* 101–119.

Rank, M. R., & Hirschl, T. A. (2002). Welfare use as a life course event: Toward a new understanding of the U.S. safety net. *Social Work, 47*(3), 237–249.

Rawley, J. A., & Behrendt, S. D. (2005). *The transatlantic slave trade: A history.* Lincoln: University of Nebraska Press.

Rayle, A. D., Kulis, S., Okamoto, S. K., Tann, S. S., LeCroy, C. W., Dustman, P. A., & Burke, A. (2006). Who is offering and how often? Gender differences in drug offers among American Indian adolescents of the Southwest. *Journal of Early Adolescence, 26*(3), 1–22.

Reamer, F. G. (2006). *Ethical standards in social work: A critical review of the NASW Code of Ethics.* Washington, DC: NASW Press.

Reese, D. J., Ahern, R. E., Nair, S., O'Faire, J. D., & Warren, C. (1999). Hospice access and use by African Americans: Addressing cultural and institutional barriers through participatory action research. *Social Work, 44*(6), 549–559.

Reisch, M., & Sommerfeld, D. (2002). Race, welfare reform, and nonprofit organizations. *Journal of Sociology and Social Welfare, 29*(1), 155–177.

Renzetti, C. (1998). Violence and abuse in lesbian relationships: Theoretical and empirical issues. In R. K. Bergen (Ed.), *Issues in intimate violence* (pp. 117–128). London: Sage.

Reskin, B. F., & Hartmann, H. (1985). *Women's work, men's work: Sex segregation on the job.* Washington, DC: National Academy of Sciences.

Reynolds, T. (1997). (Mis)representing the black (super)woman. In H. S. Mirza (Ed.), *Black British feminism: A reader* (pp. 97–112). London: Routledge.

Rice, J. (2001). Poverty, welfare, and patriarchy: How macro-level changes in social policy can help low-income women. *Journal of Social Issues, 57*(2), 355–374.

Richie, B. (2000). A black feminist reflection on the antiviolence movement. *Signs, 25,* 1133–1137.

Ridley, C. R., & Lingle, D. W. (1996). Cultural empathy in multicultural counseling: A multidimensional process model. In P. B. Pedersen, J. G. Draguns, W. J. Lonner, & J. E. Trimble (Eds.), *Counseling across cultures* (4th ed., pp. 21–46). Thousand Oaks, CA: Sage.

Riggs, C. (2000). American Indians, economic development, and self-determination in the 1960s. *Pacific Historical Review, 69*(3), 431.

Rinderle, S. (2005). The Mexican diaspora: A critical examination of signifiers. *Journal of Communication Inquiry, 29*(4), 294–316.

Ring, P. E. (2001). Invisible no more—Native Americans of the Northeast have eluded extinction. *W and I, 16*(10), 179–184.

Ritter, G. (1997). Silver slippers and a golden cap: L. Frank Baum's *The Wonderful Wizard of Oz* and historical memory in American politics. *Journal of American Studies, 31*(2), 171–202.

Rivera, E. T. (2005). Espiritismo: The flywheel of the Puerto Rican spiritual traditions. *Revista Interamericana de Psicología/Interamerican Journal of Psychology, 39*(2), 295–300.

Robinson, T. L., & Howard-Hamilton, M. F. (2000). *The convergence of race, ethnicity, and gender: Multiple identities in counseling.* Upper Saddle River, NJ: Prentice Hall.

Rodriguez, M. S. (2005). Labor rights are civil rights: Mexican American workers in twentieth-century America. *Labor, 2*(4), 106–108.

Rogler, L. H. (1989). The meaning of culturally sensitive research in mental health. *American Journal of Psychiatry, 146*(3), 296–303.

Rogler, L. H., Malgady, R. G., & Rodriguez, O. (1989). *Hispanics and mental health: A framework for research.* Malabrar, FL: Robert E. Kriger.

Rosales, F. A. (1996). *Chicano! The history of the Mexican American civil rights movement.* Houston, TX: Arte Publico Press.

Rosales, F. A. (2000). *Testimonio: A documentary history of the Mexican American struggle for civil rights.* Houston, TX: Arte Publico Press.

Rosas, G. (2006). The thickening borderlands. *Cultural Dynamics, 18*(3), 335–349.

Rosenberg, M. (1989). *Society and the adolescent self-image* (Rev. ed.). Middletown, CT: Wesleyan University Press.

Roth, L. M. (2006). *Selling women short: Gender and money on Wall Street.* Princeton, NJ: Princeton University Press.

Roughgarden, J. (2004). *Evolution's rainbow: Diversity, gender, and sexuality in nature and people.* Berkeley and Los Angeles: University of California Press.

Rubin, A., & Babbie, E. (2002). *Research methods for social work* (4th ed.). Belmont, CA: Wadsworth Thomson Learning.

Rumbaut, R., & Portes, A. (2001). *Ethnicities: Children of immigrants in America.* Berkeley and Los Angeles: University of California Press.

Sakamoto, A., & Woo, H. (2007). The socioeconomic attainments of second-generation Cambodian, Hmong, Laotian, and Vietnamese Americans. *Sociological Inquiry, 77*(1), 44–75.

Saleebey, D. (Ed.). (2002). *The strengths perspective in social work practice* (3rd ed.). Boston: Allyn and Bacon.

Sandstrom, K. L., Martin, D. D., & Fine, G. A. (2001). Symbolic interactionism at the end of the century. In G. Ritz, B. Smart, & S. A. Hucheson (Eds.), *Handbook of social theory* (pp. 271–231). London: Sage.

Sarbin, T. R. (1986). The narrative as a root metaphor for psychology. In T. R. Sarbin (Ed.), *Narrative psychology: The storied nature of human conduct* (pp. 3–21). New York: Praeger.

Savin-Williams, R. C. (2005). *The new gay teenager.* Cambridge, MA: Harvard University Press.

Savin-Williams, R. C., & Ream, G. L. (2003). Suicide attempts among sexual-minority male youth. *Journal of Clinical Child & Adolescent Psychology, 32*(4), 509–522.

Schiele, J. H. (1997). The contour and meaning of Afrocentric social work. *Journal of Black Studies, 27*(6), 800–826.

Schultz, J. (1995). Getting off on feminism. In R. Walker (Ed.), *To be real: Telling the truth and changing the face of feminism* (pp. 107–126). New York: Anchor Books.

Schuman, H., Steeh, C., Bobo, L., & Krysan, M. (1997). *Racial attitudes in America: Trends and interpretations.* Cambridge, MA: Harvard University Press.

Schwalbe, M. (1998). Mythopoetic men's work as a search for communitas. In M. S. Kimmel & M. A. Messner (Eds.), *Men's lives* (4th ed., pp. 565–577). Boston: Allyn and Bacon.

Schwalbe, M., Godwin, S., Holden, D., Schrock, D., Thompson, S., & Wolkomir, M. (2000). Generic processes in the reproduction of inequality: An interactionist analysis. *Social Forces, 79*(2), 419–453.

Schwartz, S. J., Pantin, H., Coatsworth, D., & Szapocznik, J. (2007). Addressing the challenges and opportunities for today's youth: Toward an integrative model and its implications for research and intervention. *Journal of Primary Prevention, 28*(2), 117–144.

Sears, J. T. (2005). *Gay, lesbian, and transgender issues in education: Programs, policies, and practice.* Binghamton, NY: Harrington Park Press.

Seipel, M. M. O. (2003). Global poverty: No longer an untouchable problem. *International Social Work, 46,* 191–207.

Sharlin, S. A., & Moin, V. (2001). New immigrant's perceptions of family life in origin and host cultures: In-group and out-group favoritism effect. *Journal of Comparative Family Studies, 32*(3), 405–420.

Shaw, I., & Shaw, A. (1997). Keeping social work honest: Evaluating as profession and practice. *British Journal of Social Work, 27*(6), 847–869.

Shaw, L. A., & Wainryb, C. (1999). The outsider's perspective: Young adults' judgments of social practices of other cultures. *British Journal of Developmental Psychology, 17,* 451–471.

Shek, D. T. L. (1998). The Chinese version of the self-report family inventory: Does culture make a difference? *Research on Social Work Practice, 8*(3), 315–329.

Sherr, M. E. (2006). The Afrocentric paradigm: A programmatic discourse about social work practice with African Americans. *Journal of Human Behavior in the Social Environment, 13*(3), 1–17.

Sidanius, J., & Pratto, F. (1999). *Social dominance: An intergroup theory of social hierarchy and oppression.* London: Cambridge University Press.

Simmons, T., & O'Connell, M. (2003). *Married-couple and unmarried partner households: 2000.* Washington, DC: U.S. Census Bureau. Retrieved November 14, 2004, from http://www.census.gov/prod/2003pubs/censr-5.pdf

Simons, L. G., Chen, Y., Simons, R. L., Brody, G., & Cutrona, C. (2006). Parenting practices and child adjustment in different types of households: A study of African American families. *Journal of Family Issues, 27*(6), 803–825.

Skrbis, Z., Kendall, G., & Woodward, I. (2004). Locating cosmopolitanism: Between humanist ideal and grounded social category. *Theory, Culture & Society, 21*(6), 115–136.

Slattery, J. (2004). *Counseling diverse clients: Bringing context into therapy.* Pacific Grove: CA: Thomson Brooks/Cole.

Slothuus, R. (2007). Framing deservingness to win support for welfare state retrenchment. *Scandinavian Political Studies, 30*(3), 323–344.

Smedley, A., & Smedley, B. D. (2005). Race as biology is fiction, racism as a social problem is real. *American Psychologist, 60*(1), 16–26.

Smith, D. E. (1988). *The everyday world as problematic: A feminist sociology.* Toronto: University of Toronto Press.

Smith, D. M., & Gates, G. J. (2001). *Gay and lesbian families in the United States: Same-sex unmarried partner households. A preliminary analysis of 2000 United States census data.* Washington, DC: Human Rights Campaign. Retrieved December 17, 2007, from http://www.hrc.org/documents/gayandlesbianfamilies.pdf

Sokoloff, N. J., & Dupont, I. (2005). Domestic violence at the intersections of race, class, and gender. *Violence Against Women, 11*(1), 38–64.

Soltero, C. R. (2006). *Latinos and American law: Landmark Supreme Court cases.* Austin: University of Texas Press.

Somerville, M. (2006). Postmodern emergence. *International Journal of Qualitative Studies in Education, 20*(2), 225–243.

Sowers-Hoag, K. M., & Harrison, D. F. (1991). Women in social work education: Progress or promise? *Journal of Social Work Education, 27,* 320–328.

Stannard, D. E. (1993). *The American holocaust: The conquest of the New World.* New York: Oxford University Press.

Staples, R. (1995). Health among African American males. In D. Sabo & D. F. Gordon (Eds.), *Men's health and illness: Gender, power and the body* (pp. 121–138). Thousand Oaks, CA: Sage.

Steidlmeier, P. (1993). The business community and the poor: Rethinking business strategies and social policy. *American Journal of Economics and Sociology, 52,* 209–221.

Steinberg, S. (1981). *The ethnic myth: Race, ethnicity, and class in America.* Boston: Beacon Press.

Steinbugler, A. C., Press, J. E., & Johnson Dias, J. (2006). Gender, race, and affirmative action: Operationalizing intersectionality in survey research. *Gender & Society, 20*(6), 805–825.

Stewart, A. (2005). Choosing care: Dilemmas of a social market. *Journal of Social Welfare and Family Law, 27*(3), 299–314.

Stewart, A. L., Dean, M. L., & Gregorich, S. E. (2007). Race/ethnicity, socioeconomic status and the health of pregnant women. *Journal of Health Psychology, 12,* 285–300.

Straus, T. (1998). Retribalization in urban Indian communities. *American Indian Culture and Research Journal, 22,* 103–116.

Stryker, S., & Whittle, S. (2006). *The transgender studies reader.* New York: Routledge.

Sue, S. (1998). In search of cultural competence in psychotherapy and counseling. *American Psychologist, 53,* 440–448.

Sundquist, E. (2005). *Strangers in the land: Blacks, Jews, post-Holocaust America.* Cambridge, MA: Harvard University Press.

Suter, E. A., & Toller, P. W. (2006). Gender role and feminism revisited: A follow-up study. *Sex Roles, 55,* 135–146.

Swan, V. (1999). Narrative, Foucault and feminism: Implications for therapeutic practice. In I. Parker (Ed.), *Deconstructing psychotherapy* (pp. 103–114). Thousand Oaks, CA: Sage.

Sweeney, F. (2006). The black Atlantic American studies and the politics of the postcolonial. *Comparative American Studies, 4*(2), 115–133.

Swim, J. K., Aikin, K. J., Hall, W. S., & Hunter, B. A. (1995). Sexism and racism: Old-fashioned and modern prejudices. *Journal of Personality and Social Psychology, 68*(2), 199–214.

Szasz, T. S. (1970). *The manufacture of madness: A comparative study of the Inquisition and the mental health movement.* New York: Harper and Row.

Taddei-Bringas, G. A., Santillana-Macedo, M. A., Romero-Cancio, J. A., & Romero-Tellez, M. B. (1999). Aceptación y uso de herbolería en medicina familiar. *Salud Publica Mexicana, 41,* 216–220.

Takaki, R. (1993). *A different mirror.* Boston: Little, Brown.

Takaki, R. (1998). *Strangers from a different shore.* Boston: Back Bay Books.

Tashakkori, A., & Teddlie, C. (1998). *Mixed methodology: Combining qualitative and quantitative approaches.* Thousand Oaks, CA: Sage.

Tashakkori, A., & Teddlie, C. (Eds.). (2003). *Handbook of mixed methods in social and behavioral research.* Thousand Oaks, CA: Sage.

Taylor, P. S. (1972). *An American-Mexican frontier.* Chapel Hill: University of North Carolina Press.

Taylor, R. J., Chatters, L. M., Jayakody, R. T., & Levin, J. S. (1996). Black and white differences in religious participation: A multisample comparison. *Journal for the Scientific Study of Religion, 35,* 403–410.

Taylor-Brown, S., Garcia, A., & Kingson, E. (2001). Cultural competence versus cultural chauvinism: Implications for social work. *Health and Social Work, 26*(3), 185–188.

Tazi, N. (2007). Is it possible to be both a cosmopolitan and a Muslim? In S. Ossman (Ed.), *The places we share* (pp. 65–76). Lanham, MD: Lexington Books.

Telles, E. E., & Murguia, E. (1990). Phenotypic discrimination and income differences among Mexican Americans. *Social Science Quarterly, 73*(1), 114–119.

Thomas, N. M. (2005). On headscarves and heterogeneity: Reflections on the French Foulard affair. *Dialectical Anthropology, 29*(3/4), 373–386.

Thomason, T. C. (2000). Issues in the treatment of Native Americans with alcohol problems. *Journal of Multicultural Counseling and Development, 78,* 243–252.

Thompson, M., & Sekaquaptewa, D. (2002). When being different is detrimental: Solo status and the performance of women and racial minorities. *Analyses of Social Issues and Public Policy, 2,* 183–203.

Thorton, R. (2000). Population history of Native North Americans. In M. R. Haines & R. H. Steckel (Eds.), *A population history of North America* (pp. 9–59). London: Cambridge University Press.

Thrupkaew, N. (2002). The myth of the model minority. *American Prospect, 13*(7), 38–44.

Tomaskovic-Devey, D. (1993). *Gender and racial inequality at work: The sources and consequences of job segregation.* Ithaca, NY: ILR Press.

Torres-Saillant, S. (2006). Political roots of Chicano discourse. *Latino Studies, 4*(4), 452–464.

Torres Stone, R. A., & Meyler, D. (2007). Identifying potential risk and protective factors among non-metropolitan Latino youth: Cultural implications for substance use research. *Journal of Immigrant and Minority Health, 9*(2), 95–107.

Tran, C. G., & Des Jardins, K. (2000). Domestic violence in Vietnamese refugee and Korean immigrant communities. In J. L. Chin (Ed.), *Relationships among Asian American women* (pp. 71–96). Washington, DC: American Psychological Association.

Trotter, R. T., & Chavira, J. A. (1997). *Curanderismo: Mexican American folk healing.* Athens: University of Georgia Press.

Truett, S. (2006). *Fugitive landscapes: The forgotten history of the U.S.-Mexico borderlands.* New Haven, CT: Yale University Press.

Tsang, A. K. T. (2001). Representation of ethnic identity in North American social work literature: A dossier of the Chinese people. *Social Work, 46*(3), 229–254.

Tse, L. (1999). Finding a place to be: Ethnic identity exploration of Asian Americans. *Adolescence, 34*(133), 121–130.

Tyler, J., & Lichtenstein, C. (1997). Risk, protective, AOD knowledge, attitude and AOD behavior. Factors associated with characteristics of high-risk youth. *Evaluation and Program Planning, 20*(1), 27–45.

UNICEF. (2005). *Innocenti Research Center report card no 6: Child poverty in rich countries.* Rio de Janeiro, Brazil: Author.

UNICEF. (2006). *The state of the world's children 2007: Executive summary.* New York: Author.

United Nations. (1951). *Convention on the prevention and punishment of the crime of genocide.* Geneva, Switzerland: Author.

United Nations. (1991). *Universal declaration of human rights and the international covenant on civil and political rights.* New York: Author.

University of Michigan Health System Interpreter Services. (2007). *Provider guidelines: Tips for working with an interpreter.* Retrieved December 20, 2007, from http://www.med.umich.edu/interpreter/guidelines.htm

U.S. Census Bureau. (2002, July 12). *12th anniversary of the Americans with Disability Act.* Retrieved January 21, 2008, from http://www.census.gov/Press-Release/www/2002/cb02ff11.html

U.S. Census Bureau. (2006). *Nation's population one-third minority.* Washington, DC: U.S. Department of Commerce.

Utsey, S. O. (2000). Development and initial validation of the Africultural Coping Systems Inventory. *Journal of Black Psychology, 26*(2), 194–215.

Valencia, R. R. (2005). The Mexican American struggle for equal educational opportunities in *Mendez v. Westminster*: Helping to pave the way for *Brown v. Board of Education. Teachers College Record, 107*(3), 389–423.

Van Ecke, Y. (2005). Immigration from an attachment perspective. *Social Behavior and Personality, 33*(5), 467–476.

Van Wormer, K. (1984). Becoming homosexual in prison: A socialization process. *Criminal Justice Review, 9,* 22–27.

Verloo, M. (2006). Multiple inequalities, intersectionality and the European Union. *European Journal of Women's Studies, 13*(3), 211–228.

Vertovec, S., & Cohen, R. (Eds.). (2002). *Conceiving cosmopolitanism: Theory, context and practice.* London: Oxford University Press.

Victoroff, M. S. (2006). When should bad behavior become a covered disease? *Managed Care, 15*(3), 24–26.

Vodde, R., & Gallant, J. P. (2002). Bridging the gap between micro and macro practice: Large scale change and a unified model of narrative-deconstructive practice. *Journal of Social Work Education, 38*(3), 439–459.

Voss, R. W., Douville, V., Soldier, A. L., & Twiss, G. (1999). Tribal and shamanic-based social work practice: A Lakota perspective. *Social Work, 44*(3), 228–241.

Vygotsky, L. (1979). *Mind in society: The development of higher psychological processes.* Cambridge, MA: Harvard University Press.

Wagner, F., Diaz, D. B., Lopez, A. L., Collado, M. E., & Aldaz, E. (2002). Social cohesion, cultural identity, and drug use in Mexican rural communities. *Substance Use and Misuse, 37*(5–7), 715–747.

Wainright, J. L., & Patterson, C. J. (2006). Delinquency, victimization, and substance use among adolescents with female same-sex parents. *Journal of Family Psychology, 20,* 526–530.

Wainright, J. L., Russell, S. T., & Patterson, C. J. (2004). Psychosocial adjustment and school outcomes of adolescents with same-sex parents. *Child Development, 75,* 1886–1898.

Wald, K. D., & Calhoun-Brown, A. (2006). *Religion and politics in the United States* (5th ed.). Lanham, MD: Rowman & Littlefield.

Walker, S. (2001). Tracing the contours of postmodern social work. *British Journal of Social Work, 31*(1), 29–39.

Wall, S. M., Timberlake, E. M., Farber, M. Z., Sabatino, C. A., Liebow, H., Smith, N. M., & Taylor, N. E. (2000). Needs and aspirations of the working poor: Early Head Start program applicants. *Families in Society: The Journal of Contemporary Human Services, 81*(4), 412–422.

Wallerstein, I. (1974). *The modern world system.* New York: Academic Press.

Ward, E. G. (2005). Homophobia, hypermasculinity and the US black church. *Culture, Health & Sexuality, 7*(5), 493–504.

Waters, M. (1994). Ethnic and racial identities of second generation black immigrants in New York City. *International Migration Review, 28*(4), 795–826.

Watson, R. L. (2006). Abolition, violence and rape: Thoughts on the post-emancipation experiences of the United Sates and the Cape colony. *Safundi, 7*(2), 1–14.

Weaver, H. (1998). Indigenous people in a multicultural society: Unique issues for human services. *Social Work, 43*(3), 203–211.

Weaver, H. (1999). Indigenous people and the social work profession: Defining culturally competent services. *Social Work, 4*(3), 217–225.

Weber, M. (1968). *Economy and society: An outline of interpretive sociology.* New York: Bedminster Press. (Originally published 1928)

Weber, D. (1973). *Foreigners in their native land.* Albuquerque: New Mexico Press.

Weibel-Orlando, J. (1991). *Indian country, L.A.: Maintaining ethnic community in complex society.* Urbana: University of Illinois Press.

Welch, D., Welch, L., & Piekkari, R. (2005). Speaking in tongues: The importance of language in international management processes. *International Studies of Management and Organization, 35*(1), 10–27.

Werbner, P. (2005). The translocation of culture: "Community cohesion" and the force of multiculturalism in history. *Sociological Review, 53*(4), 754–768.

Werner, E. E., & Smith, R. S. (1992). *Overcoming the odds: High risk children from birth to adulthood.* Ithaca, NY: Cornell University Press.

West, C., & Zimmerman, D. H. (1983). Small insults: A study of interruptions in cross-sex conversations between unacquainted persons. In B. Thorne, C. Kramarae, & N. Henley (Eds.), *Language, gender, and society* (pp. 103–117). Rowley, MA: Newbury.

Whitam, F., Diamond, M., & Martin J. (1993). Homosexual orientation in twins: A report on sixty-one pairs and three triplet sets. *Archives of Sexual Behavior, 22,* 187–206.

White, A. M. (2006). "You've got a friend": African American men's cross-sex feminist friendships and their influence on perceptions of masculinity and women. *Journal of Social and Personal Relationships, 23*(4), 523–542.

White, L., & Parham, T. (1990). *Psychology of blacks: An African American perspective.* Englewood Cliffs, NJ: Prentice-Hall.

Wiggan, G. (2007). Race, school achievement, and educational inequality: Toward a student-based inquiry perspective. *Review of Educational Research, 77*(93), 310–333.

Wilchins, R. (2004). *Queer theory, gender theory.* Los Angeles: Alyson Books.

Wilkins, D. E. (2006). *American Indian politics and the American political system.* Lanham, MD: Rowman & Littlefield.

Williams, R. M., & Peterson, C. L. (1998). The color of memory: Interpreting twentieth-century U.S. social policy from a nineteenth-century perspective. *Feminist Studies, 24,* 7–25.

Wills, M. (2007). Connection, action, and hope: An invitation to reclaim the "spiritual" in health care. *Journal of Religion and Health, 46*(3), 423–436.

Winter, E. (2007). Neither "America" nor "Quebec": Constructing the Canadian multicultural nation. *Nations and Nationalism, 13*(3), 481–503.

Winters, K. (2005). Gender dissonance: Diagnostic reform of gender identity disorder for adults. *Journal of Psychology & Human Sexuality, 17,* 71–89.

Wissler, C. (2005). *The American Indian: An introduction to the anthropology of the New World* (2nd ed.). London: Oxford University Press.

Wolsko, C., Lardon, C., Mohatt, G. V., & Orr, E. (2007). Stress coping and well-being among the Yup'ik of the Yukon-Kuskokwim delta: The role of enculturation and acculturation. *International Journal of Circumpolar Health, 66*(1), 51–61.

Wood, J. (1994). *Gender lives: Communication, gender, and culture.* Belmont, CA: Wadsworth.

Wright, G. (2006). *Slavery and American economic development.* Baton Rouge: Louisiana State University Press.

Ying, Y. (1988). Depressive symptomatology among Chinese-Americans as measured by the CES-D. *Journal of Clinical Psychology, 44,* 739–746.

Zea, M. C., Quezada, T., & Belgrave, F. Z. (1994). Latino cultural values: Their role in adjustment to disability. In D. S. Dunn (Ed.), Psychosocial perspectives on disability [Special issue]. *Journal of Social Behavior and Personality, 9,* 185–200.

Zhou, M. (2004). Are Asian Americans becoming white? *Context, 3*(1), 29–37.

Zimbardo, P. G. (1971). *Politics of persuasion.* Unpublished manuscript, Stanford University, CA.

Zimmerman, M. A., Ramirez-Valles, J., Washienko, K. M., Walter, B., & Dyer, S. (1996). The development of a measure of enculturation for Native American youth. *American Journal of Community Psychology, 24*(2), 295–310.

Index